OPERA

The Extravagant Art

OPERA
The Extravagant Art

HERBERT LINDENBERGER

Cornell University Press

ITHACA AND LONDON

First published 1984 by Cornell University Press.
Second printing, 1985.
First printing, Cornell Paperbacks, 1986.

International Standard Book Number 0-8014-1698-1 (cloth)
International Standard Book Number 0-8014-9425-7 (paper)
Library of Congress Catalog Card Number 84-7092
Printed in the United States of America
*Librarians: Library of Congress cataloging information
appears on the last page of this book.*

*The paper in this book is acid-free and meets the guidelines
for permanence and durability of the Committee on Production
Guidelines for Book Longevity of the Council on Library Resources.*

Contents

[7]

CONTENTS

Preface

This book attempts to continue and renew that significant line of operatic criticism extending from Wagner and Hanslick through Nietzsche and Shaw to such recent commentators as Theodor Adorno, Joseph Kerman, and Carl Dahlhaus. Like its forebears, it works towards a theory of opera—in the present case, as the subtitle implies, towards a notion of opera as a lofty and extravagant form essentially distinct from other modes of artistic communication. I hope to account for the power that opera has exercised on its audiences over the centuries and to provide a historical framework within which operagoers today can reflect on their own experience. I also reconsider such traditional problems within operatic criticism as the relation of words and music; the question of what precisely opera represents; the peculiar status of opera as at once a popular and a high-minded medium; and the disparagement of opera in favor of "purer" forms such as spoken drama and instrumental music.

My approach is that of someone trained in the study of literature, and I make use of techniques developed in contemporary literary theory to look at opera as a phenomenon unique among the various arts and within the history of culture. Indeed, by examining a form that is not ordinarily treated from this angle, I hope to contribute something new to present-day theoretical discussion, above all to our understanding of how genres develop in the course of time and how they establish and transgress the boundaries that mark them off from one another. Like any serious theoretical project, this one strives not merely to illuminate its overt subject but also to provide a model for the exploration of comparable subjects; thus the study of opera can suggest ways in which aesthetic forms interact both with one another and with their social contexts at particular historical moments.

Two audiences, I hope, will find this book useful. The first consists of scholars and students of the humanities—those interested in the theoretical perspectives I have mentioned as well as musicologists concerned with interdisciplinary questions. The second audience consists of operagoers who would like to find an approach to opera more rigorous and also, I hope, more stimulating than what is available in popular guidebooks. In view of the fascination that opera holds for an increasing number of people, I am confident that this is the time for a serious book on the subject. I am also confident that complex arguments can be communicated in clear language, and I have therefore sought to avoid the specialized terminology often employed in my own field. Like those distinguished earlier operatic commentaries in whose line it attempts to situate itself, this book is addressed to all who seek to understand opera's strangeness and potency of effect.

No list of acknowledgments can fully express my gratitude to those colleagues and former colleagues willing to read a long manuscript and tell me where I was unclear, imprecise, incomplete, or on the wrong path. My thanks go to John B. Bender, Edward J. Brown, Joaquim-Francisco Coelho, Guelfo Frulla, Charles R. Lyons, Anne and Ronald Mellor, Robert Polhemus, Egon Schwarz, William Mills Todd III, and Caroline and David Wellbery. In addition, I thank the following colleagues and former colleagues for advising me on matters relating to their own specialties: V. Kofi Agawu and Ann Mueller on musicological details; Jean-Pierre Barricelli on Balzac's use of music; Terry J. Castle on opera in eighteenth-century novels; Gordon A. Craig on Hitler's use of Wagner; Alban K. Forcione on Cervantes; the late Branwen Pratt on opera in Victorian novels; Lucio Ruotolo on Virginia Woolf's relationship to opera; Pierre Saint-Amand on attitudes to opera among French writers; Kendall L. Walton on representation as a category in aesthetics. Gary Schmidgall exchanged ideas with me during the writing of his own book, *Literature as Opera*. Donald R. Howard and David Wellbery helped me to discover the title lurking within my manuscript.

As with all my previous books, my wife, Claire F. Lindenberger, read what I wrote at every stage. Her participation in this project has special relevance, for during our well over twenty years of going to the opera together our intermission conversations suggested many of the ideas I have developed here. It is difficult to reconstruct which one of us came up with a particular notion— though I know for sure that she often challenged me to develop these notions towards the sustained arguments necessary within a scholarly book. I might add that having a major opera company, the San Francisco Opera, nearby helped considerably in stimulating and testing the ideas that later made their way into the book.

I thank the National Endowment for the Humanities and the Stanford Humanities Center for fellowships that have given me the leisure to think out and write this book without the pressure of teaching and administrative duties. Special thanks are due to Ian P. Watt, director of the Center, for the warm and stimulating atmosphere he helped to create. I also thank those institutions and people who have allowed me to try out my ideas at various stages: Stanford's program in Florence, where the undergraduate seminar on Italian opera that I gave in 1974 suggested the idea of doing this study; Paul Hernadi, whose invitation to lecture on opera at the University of Iowa in 1978 forced me to start setting down my notions in writing; the members of the Comparative Literature program at Indiana University, above all Ulrich Weisstein, whose invaluable anthology of operatic criticism, *The Essence of Opera*, long ago had suggested some of the theoretical questions I take up and who invited me to develop my lecture in a new direction at Indiana in 1980; Jackson Cope, who allowed me to try out some connections between Shakespeare and opera at a conference on Renaissance drama at the University of Southern California in 1981.

Segments of the first and second chapters have appeared in the *Yearbook of Comparative and General Literature* ("Towards a Theory of Musical Drama," 29 [1980]) and in the *Stanford Literature Review* ("On the Multiplicity of Operatic Discourse," 1 [1984]). Hank Dobin deserves special thanks for helping me through the complexities of Stanford's former word-processing system. Erica Zweig, aspiring soprano and relative of a famous librettist, also deserves special thanks for helping me with the manuscript in her capacity as secretary to the Fellows at the Stanford Humanities Center. My student Nancy Ruttenburg was kind enough to translate some Russian material that I quote and paraphrase in the second chapter. All other translations, unless otherwise indicated, are my own.

My fundamental debt is to my parents, to whose memory this book is dedicated. They were old enough to be my grandparents, and the so-called "golden age" of opera at the start of our century remained firmly implanted in their memories while I was growing up in the 1930s and 1940s. My father, who preferred the Italian and the French repertory, spoke familiarly of singers such as Patti, Sembrich, Tetrazzini, and Caruso; he liked to recall attending the celebrated debut of Geraldine Farrar as Marguerite in *Faust* in Berlin (she sang in Italian to the other performers' German) when she was nineteen. My mother, who preferred German opera, liked to remember pointing out Wagner's house at Tribschen to a group of children on an excursion from a summer camp she was directing. She took special pride in having journeyed from a job in Breslau to Dresden in early 1911 to attend one of the first performances of *Der Rosenkavalier;* by the time she died sixty-six years later *Der Rosenkavalier* was still (with the exception of *Turandot*) the most recent opera that could be called "popular" in the manner of the great nineteenth-century operas. Well before I knew how to read, my parents had taught me how to hand wind an old Victrola so that I could hear the voices they had admired. Bedtime stories sometimes came from a children's book retelling stories of the Wagner operas. I am certain that many of my parents' attitudes, including their now archaic, nineteenth-century notions of what constitutes the cultural life, have found their way into this book.

HERBERT LINDENBERGER

Stanford, California

OPERA
The Extravagant Art

Introduction

This book starts from the notion that opera is the last remaining refuge of the high style. The time has long passed since people in the Western world listened with pleasure to bards reciting heroic deeds or, to cite a cultural phenomenon less distant from us, since theater audiences were eager to participate in courtly entertainments composed of formal set speeches and extravagant gestures. Even the great literary epics that were once deemed essential to the cultivation of an educated person can be absorbed by readers today only by dint of painstaking academic reconstruction. In view of the suspicion of formal structures and lofty modes of expression that characterizes the consumers of art in a democratic age, it seems genuinely surprising that a form such as opera, with its penchant for exaggeration and its overt artifice, should still play to enthusiastic audiences willing to support it with an extravagance commensurate with the extravagance of deed and expression they witness on stage.

Although the survival of opera, indeed its continuing popularity, may seem strange in an age that cultivates the more understated forms of art, the attitude of audiences towards the creation of new operas has changed radically during the last century. Throughout most of operatic history, and certainly through the heyday of Massenet, *verismo* opera, and the operas that Richard Strauss completed before World War I, audiences eagerly awaited the first production—most often, as it turned out, the last—of new works. With the triumph of modernism as an international style in a number of arts, the new aesthetic of difficulty worked to stabilize the operatic repertory, for audiences felt so discouraged trying to absorb what they witnessed at first hearing that few companies dared risk the expense of mounting productions certain to incur public disapproval. Throughout most of our century the opera house could be called a museum exhibiting what its audiences accepted as the great monuments of the operatic past. The classical age was over, and the creative activity of opera had shifted from the composition of the new to the reinterpretation and rediscovery of the old. Vital though opera still seems as a performing art, our view of the form remains primarily retrospective. To imagine the situation of opera at an earlier time, we have only to glance at cinema, whose audiences expect constantly new products—and quickly discard most of the old ones. Even ballet, which rivals opera in the artifice of its set forms (though not in extravagance of expression) has continued to renew itself while retaining continuity with its nineteenth-century traditions; through its relative abstractness, ballet, unlike opera, could accommodate itself to modernism (in fact, even help promote the movement) without posing the difficulties that might alienate audiences from its new creations.

Opera thus occupies a unique position in our culture: a form of high art distinctly more lofty in its modes of expression than the other forms that attract serious attention; a form whose adherents, though often willing to grant it an uncommon degree of commitment, insist on treating it as a historically closed book, with no new chapters to be added. The operas we have canonized enjoy the status of hallowed texts, unbending in the demands they make upon the uninitiated yet enticing for the exotic distance in time and style they offer their prospective beholders. It is no wonder that they constantly demand mediation in the form of guidebooks, program and record-album notes, and introductory lectures. It may well be that more verbiage is expended on certain famed operas these days than on great literary texts such as *Hamlet* and *Don Quijote* that have less need for mediation.

Despite the vast amount of writing on opera, only a small proportion aspires to the serious level we expect of scholarly and critical writing on the various arts. Since it is ordinarily directed to helping audiences overcome the distance they feel (or at least fear they may feel) between their own world and that of opera, it must concern itself with practical matters—plot explanations, anecdotes about the work's composer or its performance history, indeed, whatever may ease access to an otherwise remote and inaccessible medium. Serious writing about opera is often constrained by the fact that the form does not easily fit into a single discipline—at least as disciplines are defined institutionally to-day. The practitioners and theorists of opera have been conscious since its beginnings of its hybrid nature—its dual tie to music and poetry (symbolized by the perennial conflict between composer and librettist), as well as its dependence upon such other arts as dance, scenic design, and the various crafts associated with the theater. Indeed, the traditional notion of opera's hybridness doubtless stands behind the attempts of its more high-minded practitioners, notably Gluck and Wagner, to emphasize the unity of effect they were attempting to create out of its diverse elements.

In view of the variety of talents that have always played a significant role in the making of opera, it is no wonder that its academic study demands knowledge and skills that no single specialist ordinarily possesses. Not only do its component arts belong to several formal disciplines, but a knowledge of the cultural and intellectual contexts within which opera has been embedded from the start may well affect our understanding of the form in a more immediate way than such knowledge does for other arts. For example, since opera is reputedly the most expensive of the performing arts to produce, an awareness of the patronage it has demanded—whether that of the eighteenth-century despots mirrored in the ruling figures of *opera seria* or of the bourgeois audiences who saw their own strivings glorified in the historical extravaganzas of the nineteenth century—must play a crucial role in the way we interpret earlier operas today.

Moreover, certain thinkers whom we have enshrined as central to modern intellectual history have used opera to work out major ideas. Kierkegaard, for instance, defined the "aesthetic" level of the dialectic that shapes *Either/Or* through the example of such Mozart characters as Papageno and Don Giovanni. Nietzsche's concept of the "Dionysian" is inseparable from his experience of Wagner as composer and thinker. Opera is unique not only for the variety of contexts in which it plays a significant role but also for its origins: unlike other arts whose evolution historians like to trace back to some mysterious, often popular origin, opera was in fact invented by a group of learned theorists, the so-called Camerata, who provided it with a program before the first operas were composed around 1600. The overt artifice and the pretension to lofty utterance that opera has displayed throughout its history follow naturally, if often also unknowingly, from the circumstances of its birth.

[17]

Trained musicologists, aware of the technical knowledge of music that one must have in order to speak in detail of any musical form, can present cogent reasons to guard their traditional rights to operatic territory. Yet there is more to be said about opera than one can learn from musical analysis and music history alone. It is no accident that some of the best writing about opera in our time has come from musicologists such as Joseph Kerman and Carl Dahlhaus who also have a strong interest in literary criticism and cultural history. My own approach in this book comes from the opposite direction, for my formal training has been not in music but in literary scholarship and the history of ideas. Like my earlier book, *Historical Drama*, the present study does not attempt any sustained analyses (whether musical or literary) of individual works, nor does it retell the history of the form; yet its method, which I developed in the earlier study, enables me to suggest certain relationships among works, even to develop insights into particular examples, that detailed interpretations and chronological organization would not so easily allow. Again like the earlier book, the present one does not belong exclusively to the realm of either theory or practical criticism, the two dominant modes of American literary criticism during the last generation. Rather, the method I pursue attempts a new kind of history, one that refuses the constraints imposed by a chronological narrative and that insists on its freedom to practice theory and interpretation at once. Readers will note that the theoretical statements I introduce are constantly qualified by historical observations, which in turn generate new theoretical statements that are themselves tested by further observations.

Readers will also observe that I often speak of opera in the singular. Whether one labels it a *medium, genre, art form,* or simply a *phenomenon* (all these terms appear at one time or another in this study), the presence of an operatic repertory, indeed the very physical presence of opera houses throughout the world, attests to the perimeters within which opera can be demarcated and defined. At various points I have occasion to speak of works that stand at the periphery of opera—for example, an unstaged concert for voices, such as Berlioz's *Roméo et Juliette* (officially labeled a "dramatic symphony"), or a brief epic narration with interspersed dramatic voices such as Monteverdi's *Il combattimento di Tancredi e Clorinda*, or sometimes even "nonoperas" such as Verdi's never-composed *Re Lear* or the puppet show in Cervantes's *Don Quijote*: in each instance the problems confronting an anomalous or even nonexistent work help foreground the problems in works central to the tradition. Since I am concerned throughout the book with the ways that opera has affected the literary and theatrical imagination, I often employ the category *operatic* to refer to characteristics that we have come (rightly or wrongly) to associate with the form—for example, its penchant for exaggeration and its tendency to seek out those higher regions of style that narrative and nonmusical drama have abandoned during the centuries since opera was invented. Although many individual operas will be introduced into my discussion, this study will focus above all on those characteristics that make opera a phenomenon and an ongoing tradition unique among the arts and within the history of culture.

Certain traits that we can ascribe to opera have marked the form since its beginnings and remain discernible despite the changing styles in which individual operas have been created at different times and in different places. For example, as I shall show in detail later, the loftiness and intensity of style that opera pursues can help explain, and in fact has sometimes even helped determine, its relationship to other forms and to the various contexts in which it has played a role in the course of its history. Whenever a play is transformed into an opera, we note at once that the characters assume a more formal, often a more heroic stance than they did when they simply spoke their lines; the dramatic action, moreover, generally assumes a degree of compression and inevitability it did not possess in its earlier form. Similarly, when the description of a scene or passage from an opera appears in a novel— as we in fact find within the work of most of the great novelists— we are ordinarily made aware of the gap that separates the world of opera (associated as it becomes with matters such as passion and artifice) from the more prosaic and lowly world of fiction. In addition, the large range of expressive forms that can shape a single opera—for example, the diverse recitative, aria, and choral forms in a mid–nineteenth-century Italian opera or the daring mixture of chanted speech and florid song in Schönberg's *Moses und Aron*— demonstrates, as I shall show, how a genre in the high style must exploit varying intensities of style in order to articulate its meanings and sustain itself convincingly.

The attitudes voiced towards opera over the centuries, as well as the cultural uses to which it has been subjected, are also linked to the stylistic norm it has sought out. For instance, throughout the history of opera one notes a continuing disparagement of the form on such grounds as the absurdity of its stances or its lack of relevance to anything that people should be taking seriously. At an opposite extreme, the example of Wagnerian music-drama, above all as embodied in the uncompromisingly intense music of *Tristan und Isolde,* served the young Nietzsche as a means for preaching cultural regeneration. The artifice and extravagance of manner so natural to opera have also been central to the celebrated battles that have raged over what should constitute the most appropriate style—for example, the conflict between the ornate manner of *opera seria* and the lofty simplicity that Gluck offered as an alternative.

Although I view this study as an attempt to illuminate a genre, I do not approach genre as a category for which I seek out timeless rules. As in earlier books in which I considered such genres as the history play and the long poem, I treat genre as a term that opens up opportunities for both formal and historical analysis, that in fact allows the analyst to observe the interactions between the aesthetic order and the social order. Each larger section of this book confronts the term *opera* with another term, respectively *drama, representation, novel,* and *society.* Each of these sections constitutes a distinct context shaped by the juxtaposition of these terms. The first chapter, entitled "Opera or Drama" (the *or* plays on the titles of two celebrated earlier studies that linked the two terms with *and* and *as,* respectively), explores the borders and interchanges between opera and drama in order to better define the realms that each characteristically inhabits. Similarly the fourth chapter, on operatic scenes in novels, examines the interplay of the two forms to propose what is at once a theory of opera and a theory of the novel. The second and third chapters, under the umbrella title "Opera as Representation," take up certain formal problems that the creators and theorists of opera have projected about its nature: the pretensions that opera makes to mirroring an actual world; the diversity of expressive forms that it cultivates to articulate meaning; the ways it displays, often even advertises, its links to earlier operatic tradition; its consciousness of an inherent conflict between word and music, a conflict often reflected in real antipathies between librettist and composer. The final two chapters explore some of the social entanglements that have shaped operatic tradition—for example, the various oscillations in the history of opera between its status as a popular and as a high-minded form; the varying political and economic pressures to which it has responded; its ability to reflect, project, and engage with history.

Since each section of the book focuses on a particular configu ration of problems, many of my examples (whether actual oper; or theories of opera) recur from one section to another. In my earlier book on the history play, I called this method a "horizontal approach," by which a work or idea appears at varying points and reveals itself in different lights according to the contexts in which it is taken up. For example, I discuss what Monteverdi called his *concitato* or "agitated" style in several places: in the second chapter to demonstrate the introduction of contrasting forms of discourse early in the history of opera; in the fourth chapter to stress the link that opera has maintained with a language simulating high passion; in the final chapter to point to opera's tie to epic and to opera's appropriateness for the narrating of high deeds from history. Gluck's famous assertion that music should play "servant" to words appears in two contexts, first to examine the recurrent notion that opera must submit itself to what I call the "dramatic principle," second to illustrate the ways that operatic commentary has been trapped into articulating a natural conflict between words and music. Rousseau's attempt, in *Le Devin du village,* to displace the aristocratic style of French opera with the folklike simplicity of Italian comic opera achieves its significance both as a formal innovation and as a political gesture and thus serves to illuminate several sections of this book. Although my first chapter centers on the formal relations between opera and drama, I save my discussion of opera as *historical* drama until the final chapter, which focuses on the social and political meanings latent (often, indeed, manifest) in the form. Certain exemplary works such as *Don Giovanni, Tristan und Isolde,* and *Otello,* all much commented upon since their own time, are significant for so many different reasons that they find their way into virtually every chapter. Whatever cogency my arguments have must ultimately derive from the appropriateness of my examples—both the operas themselves and that distinguished body of operatic commentary that stretches from the Italian theorists who proposed the form through such figures as Rousseau, E. T. A. Hoffmann, Heine, Wagner, Nietzsche, Shaw, Hofmannsthal and Strauss, and Theodor Adorno.

Yet this book is not simply "about" opera, for it also attempts to grapple with certain problems that the example of opera can illuminate perhaps more readily than any other genre—problems about the nature of aesthetic form and representation, about the commerce among genres, about the fortunes of art in society. Indeed, the organization of this study as a series of theoretically focused essays (moving, as I do in some earlier books, from formal to social concerns) allows me to isolate these problems to a degree that a chronological narration or a group of detailed interpretations of works would not allow. Moreover, the particular focus within each chapter (sometimes even within a shorter section) plays on the perspective, to an extent even on the terminology, developed within a particular body of critical theory in our time. For instance, when I speak of the multiple forms of discourse peculiar to opera, I am building on Bakhtin's theory of multiple discourses in the novel, while the chapter on opera scenes in fiction improvises upon certain theories of the novel from Lukács to Barthes. Adorno's extensive body of music criticism helped determine the way I formulate questions on the social and historical contexts of opera.

Despite the diversity of frameworks through which this study approaches opera and the theories that people have held about opera, it also attempts to sustain a recurring theme—the ways in which a genre in the high style has survived and adapted itself to changing aesthetic, institutional, and human pressures. As I look back at three decades of critical writing, I now recognize that, despite the different genres and authors I have treated, this theme constitutes a continuing preoccupation. Similarly, the multiperspectival method I have worked out to develop this and other themes goes back to my first book, a study of Wordsworth's *Prelude*. I by no means wish to claim, as reviewers sometimes thought I claimed, that this method presents a "truer" view of the objects it treats than other, more single-minded approaches. Indeed, terms such as *truth* and *knowledge* in humanistic scholarship still retain much of the meaning they radiated within the positivistic model upon which the academic study of the various arts was founded in the last century and that is still dominant in musicology today.

This model assumed that research in these fields should confine itself to the more publicly verifiable matters surrounding works and their creators—origins, influences, formal details as they were labeled by the author or his or her contemporaries—in short, whatever can hold up as evidence in a courtroom. From this point of view, the main things to be said about opera center on circumstances of composition and performance, changes in musical style and literary theme from period to period, the overt and recorded attitudes of composers, librettists, patrons, and audiences. Within this older model, the differences that one can discern among individual works, composers, or styles take precedence over whatever general statements one might make about opera as a form or about its relationship to other forms. It is likely that music specialists who were trained within this model and who are unfamiliar with developments in literary theory during recent decades will often feel baffled, perhaps even irritated, by the attempt of this study to seek out general principles and to suggest relationships between diverse phenomena such as opera and the novel. Those unfamiliar, for instance, with the analyses of genres and texts by the Russian formalists and their structuralist heirs may well have difficulty understanding the binary opposition I set up in the second chapter between the concepts *operatic* and *verbal*, or the image of operatic evolution as a self-conscious, often parodistic reworking of the past that I present later in this chapter. One of my aims in introducing new critical perspectives into the study of opera is to demonstrate that methods which have proved fruitful in literary study can also yield results for those art forms whose scholarly guilds have stuck to more conservative models; and have sometimes, in fact, so taken their methods for granted as "common sense" that they failed to recognize they were even working within a model. At the same time I acknowledge my gratitude for the factual materials that the positivistic model has unearthed over the years. As the notes to this book show, I have profited greatly from the considerable and distinguished body of work that this model has generated to illuminate the history of opera; indeed, without this scholarship I could not have enjoyed the luxury of generalization and theoretical speculation.

Yet whatever truth or knowledge this book uncovers belongs to a different model of scholarship. For one thing, having worked in literature, a field that has developed a number of diverse methods, I recognize that it is possible to draw upon more than a single such method to illuminate an art form. The multiperspectival approach that I have chosen attempts to use and adapt theoretical instruments developed within several of these methods—for example, in structuralist narrative analysis, in Bakhtin's theory of generic interchange, in that discipline which Adorno called *Musiksoziologie*. I do not claim any special commitment to these instruments or to the particular systems for which they were created; rather, I am concerned with their usefulness and suggestive power in helping me to redefine old problems (for example, the conflict between words and music, or the differences between musical and spoken drama) and to articulate relationships be-

tween phenomena (for example, between opera and society, or between the differing levels of intensity in operatic discourse) that
might otherwise seem farfetched or irrelevant. The fact that these
perspectives occasionally intersect with, even seem to contradict
one another should be taken as a sign that they are not so much
substantive structures in their own right as they are tools to uncover and interpret relationships among objects and ideas that
achieve new appearances in different contexts. Within the interpretive model that guides this study, the process by which ideas
come into play takes precedence over the results and conclusions
towards which they lead. According to this model the goals of
critical inquiry become embodied in its very acts of performance—surely an appropriate designation for a book aspiring to speak
of opera.

[1]

Opera or Drama

Drama into Opera

While reviewing the London musical scene around 1890, George Bernard Shaw made two observations that suggest some central issues underlying the relationship between opera and nonmusical drama. Shaw's first observation compares the actress Eleonora Duse as Santuzza in Verga's play *Cavalleria rusticana* with the singer Emma Calvé in Mascagni's operatic version of the play. "Duse makes the play more credible," Shaw writes, "not because an opera is less credible than a spoken play—for though that can be proved logically, the facts are just the other way, the superior intensity of musical expression making the opera far more real than the play."[1] Though Shaw opts for the reality of opera over spoken drama, Duse's apparent superiority over Calvé turns out to stem from the great verisimilitude of her interpretation: since Duse made herself unattractive and Calvé exhibited her fine looks, Shaw pronounced the latter's abandonment by her lover totally implausible.

The apparent paradox that Shaw notes in comparing the credibility of the two performers and the two media is symptomatic of the confusions that have plagued, though also enriched, discussions of art since at least the time of Plato. Yet one can distinguish two quite diverse ways of applying terms such as *credible* and *real* to the phenomena Shaw is comparing. From a mimetic point of view, Verga's play, regardless of the accidents of interpretation, is doubtless more credible than Mascagni's opera, for a Si-

---

[1] Review of May 30, 1894, in *Shaw's Music*, ed. Dan H. Laurence (New York: Dodd, Mead, 1981), III, 227.

cilian peasant girl betrayed by her fiancé is far more likely to express her sorrow in speech than in song. Yet if one shifts from a mimetic to a rhetorical criterion to determine the relative reality of these two modes of performance, the operatic version clearly can establish an immediacy of communication between performer and audience that the play, especially with its terse, rigorously naturalistic language, is unable to achieve. Note that Shaw resorts to the word *intensity* to describe what he sees as the superiority inherent in musical expression, for this term, like the word *immediacy* that I employed earlier, is characteristic of those forms of critical discourse that stress the rhetorical rather than the mimetic functions of art.

Shaw's second observation has nothing to do with the correspondence of art to the real world but rather with the ability of musical drama to achieve a sublimity that, for Shaw at least, was no longer possible (if it ever was) in spoken drama. Comparing a performance of Victor Hugo's *Hernani* with Verdi's operatic version, Shaw writes, "In the play Charles is sublime in feeling, but somewhat tedious in expression. In the opera he is equally sublime in feeling, but concise, grand and touching in expression, thereby proving that the chief glory of Victor Hugo as a stage poet was to have provided libretti for Verdi." For Shaw, Hugo had written what, after Verdi's transformation of his play, was essentially an opera manqué. Shaw goes on to describe Verdi's opera as "the grandiose Italian opera in which the executive art consists in a splendid display of personal heroics, and the drama arises out of the simplest and most universal stimulants to them."[2] Shaw employs the vocabulary traditionally associated with the sublime—*grand, grandiose, heroics, splendid*, not to speak of the term *sublime* itself—to characterize the musical version of Hugo's drama. And as so often in characterizations of sublimity ever since Longinus's own treatise, the emphasis falls not on a work's relation to whatever reality it is imitating but on its ability to communicate its sublimity to its audience. Note the contrast Shaw makes between the Charles of the play, whom he finds "tedious in expression," and the operatic Charles, who is "touching in expression," and note as well the word *stimulants*, which he employs to indicate the musical means Verdi is using to create his dramatic effects.

I have cited these statements of Shaw's to illustrate certain ways

[2] Review of November 2, 1892, ibid., II, 724–25.

in which we customarily distinguish between the purposes and methods of drama and music. Critics who write about drama tend to stress its affinities with other forms of literature and to underplay its more overtly theatrical aspects. It is therefore not surprising that the imitative functions of drama, as of the other literary genres, have traditionally been granted more importance than its rhetorical effects. Even today, despite strong antimimetic elements in literary criticism, that ancient tradition of measuring a literary work against some external reality it purports to imitate has proved difficult to shake off.[3] By contrast, critics do not customarily stress the mimetic propensities of music but rather its ability to rouse the passions of its listeners; whether they take the Platonic view of the dangers it poses to the republic or hail its power to convey a sense of possible sublimity to a degree to which other artistic "lies" can scarcely aspire, their emphasis rests on the relation a work can establish with its audience.

Whenever we examine the transformations that a literary work, whether narrative or drama, has undergone in the course of becoming an opera, we are aware that despite the wide variety of operatic styles that has prevailed in different times and places since the time of Monteverdi, opera characteristically seeks its own forms. These forms, moreover, are of a distinctly ceremonial, highly formalized nature—prayers, demands for vengeance, expressions of thanksgiving, not to speak of the mimesis of traditional musical forms such as dances, marches, hymns, as well as songs for special occasions such as hunting and drinking. To develop one of Shaw's examples, the transformation of Verga's short play *Cavalleria rusticana* into Mascagni's opera illustrates these differences in an extreme degree. The theatrical version, with its quick verbal exchanges and its dialect-flavored speech, attempts to provide the illusion of Sicilian peasant life "as it really is." If Verga intended to demonstrate primitive passions to his audience, his method, compared with that of earlier Italian tragic drama, was emphatically one of understatement. (One might note that Verga's earlier narrative version was considerably more understated

---

[3]It is significant that the antimimetic bias in contemporary literary criticism has been exercised to a greater degree on narrative than on dramatic literature, which has received relatively little treatment from poststructuralist critics. Can it be that the visual dimension of drama—the scenery, the pantomime, the very physical presence of actors—has inhibited these critics from focusing on works designed for the theater? It scarcely seems accidental that among modern writers for the theater a so overtly antimimetic (indeed operatic) figure such as Artaud should attract the interest of critics like Gilles Deleuze and Jacques Derrida.

than the play, which, despite its attempt to avoid an older form of theatricality, still had to project in the theater.) Mascagni's setting, despite the term *verismo* with which we normally label it, consists of the set pieces we associate with operatic form—such examples of musical mimesis as a serenade, an Easter hymn, a teamster's and a drinking song, as well as lyrical outbursts that manifest themselves variously as lament, plea, cry for vengeance, and valediction. If Shaw believed that an opera should by logical definition be more credible than a play, this is because, with rhetorical effect as the central criterion, the operatic Santuzza conveys her feelings to the audience with characteristically operatic passion, while the theatrical heroine must express herself with the indirectness and verbal limitations one would expect of low-life dialogue conceived within the ambiance of European naturalism.

Similar transformations take place in operas such as *Le nozze di Figaro* and *Otello*, which modern critics automatically cite as perfect musical realizations of major dramatic works.[4] In *Figaro*, for instance, the martial music with which Cherubino is sent off to army service receives only the slightest suggestion in the play, while the deeply moving music for the reconciliation of the Count and Countess at the end could never have been predicted from Beaumarchais's jovial dialogue at this point; even the words that Mozart's librettist, Da Ponte, wrote for this passage supply only the barest hint for the musical setting. Anybody fresh from a performance of Shakespeare's *Othello* would not be surprised to hear Iago's drinking song or Desdemona's "Willow Song" utilized by Verdi; yet despite the reputation *Otello* enjoys for abandoning earlier operatic conventions in the interest of dramatic "integrity," one can point to certain traditional operatic situations that have no equivalent in the original play—for example, the choral serenade addressed to Desdemona, the elaborate concerted ensemble in the third act, and the prayer to the Virgin into which the heroine launches directly after her "Willow Song."

The gap separating verbal and musical drama is evident in a special way in such twentieth-century works as *The Rake's Progress* and in those Strauss-Hofmannsthal operas that self-consciously

---

[4]For an interesting study of how a number of great literary works were transformed into major operas, see Gary Schmidgall, *Literature as Opera* (New York: Oxford University Press, 1977). It is evident from Schmidgall's selection that the number of works one can call "major" within *both* the literary and operatic canons is quite small—at best a dozen or so.

imitate earlier operatic situations and conventions. Zerbinetta's virtuoso piece in Strauss's *Ariadne auf Naxos* and the various arias and ensembles of Stravinsky's opera imitate eighteenth- and nineteenth-century operatic styles with such extravagance that the self-conscious listener is as much concerned with identifying these styles as with following the dramatic situations taking place on the stage. As the Strauss-Hofmannsthal correspondence makes amply clear, composer and librettist often have strikingly different notions of the type of composition they are creating. Hofmannsthal, for example, occasionally expressed regrets about the structural flaws he discerned in his libretto for *Der Rosenkavalier*—for instance, the disappearance of his most engaging character, the Marschallin, from the end of the first act to the middle of the third.[5] In all likelihood the flaws he saw would show up if his text were performed without music. But the composition that Strauss created, with its cunningly contrived succession of ceremonial scenes, conversational patter, lyrical outbursts, and broadly farcical interludes, turned out to be a most appropriate structure in its own right—far different in its effects from a staging of the libretto alone.

Whatever Hofmannsthal's literary qualms about *Der Rosenkavalier*, it is significant that many years later, during their collaboration on *Arabella*, Strauss cited such scenes from the earlier opera as the first-act levee, the silver-rose ceremony, Baron Ochs's waltz scene, and the final trio as examples of the materials out of which he hoped to build their new opera: "In short," as Strauss puts it, "that which is pure image, comprehensible in a pantomimic way—which is what a good opera libretto needs, for wholly a third of the words nearly always get lost, and the best dialogue remains more or less uninteresting to the larger public."[6] Even if one discounts the studied role playing that went on in the Strauss-Hofmannsthal correspondence between the provocatively Philistine stance of the composer and the equally provocative overrefinement of the poet, a passage such as this suggests an essential difference in emphasis and direction that can be found throughout the history of opera.

---

[5] "Quite in contrast to *Der Rosenkavalier*, in which Act I is actually a play in itself, in Act II the actual main character, the Marschallin, does not appear at all (what a defect, theoretically speaking!), and Act III seemed to many people 'patched together'!" Letter of June 27, 1928, in Strauss-Hofmannsthal, *Briefwechsel*, 3d ed., ed. Willi Schuh (Zurich: Atlantis Verlag, 1964), p. 634.

[6] Letter of June 24, 1928, ibid., pp. 632–33.

If Strauss and Stravinsky self-consciously imitate earlier operatic moments—and in Strauss's case, even his own—it is not surprising that what we know of Verdi's plans for his setting of *King
Lear* would doubtless ruffle the sensibilities of literary intellectuals. Verdi's *Lear* is probably the most prestigious opera among
those operas that were proposed but never written. The reasons
are obvious: in *Otello* and *Falstaff*, both composed long after the
Lear plans had fallen through, Verdi achieved a subtlety that has
made these operas palatable to audiences who ordinarily scoff at
nineteenth-century Italian opera, including Verdi's own earlier
setting of *Macbeth*. Moreover, Shakespeare's *Lear* today enjoys a
status as a cultural monument that puts it in a different category
from *Othello* and *Macbeth*, not to speak of *The Merry Wives of
Windsor*. A recent study of Verdi even devotes an entire chapter,
entitled "The Opera That Never Was," to Verdi's *Lear* in order to
speculate on what it might have turned out to be.[7]

Yet the plans for *Lear* that Verdi sent his librettist Cammarano
demonstrate much the same concern for operatic values that
Strauss showed in his demands to Hofmannsthal. "Magnificent
quartet," Verdi writes as he describes the storm scene on the heath.
Throughout the sketches one notes a stress on scenes of rage and
vengeance, emotions that accord both with Shakespeare's play and
the style of Italian opera around 1850, the year in which Verdi
sent out his instructions. It seems natural enough to see such
statements as the following: "The king erupts with anger and re-
alizing his daughter's ingratitude fears going mad," or "He swears
vengeance, exclaiming that he will do terrible things." Yet the
literary mind, which has enshrined Cordelia's terse phrases, "No
cause, no cause" as the ultimate in generosity of spirit, would
probably resist Verdi's plans for the scene in which Cordelia returns from France: "Cordelia has heard of her father's misfor-
tune," Verdi writes. "Great sorrow on Cordelia's part. The doctor
announces that the King has been found and that he hopes to cure
him of his madness. Cordelia, intoxicated with joy, thanks heaven
and longs for the moment of vengeance."[8] Verdi's vengeful Cor-

---

[7] Vincent Godefroy, *The Dramatic Genius of Verdi*, II (New York: St. Martin's
Press, 1977), pp. 327–48. Similarly, Franz Werfel, in his novel on the crisis that the
later Verdi experienced upon witnessing the triumph of Wagnerism in Italy, imagines a last, failed attempt near the end of his hero's life to put Shakespeare's play
into operatic form. See Werfel, *Verdi: Roman der Oper* (Berlin: Paul Zsolnay, 1928),
pp. 116–29, 191–93, 421–27.

[8] Letter of February 28, 1850, in Verdi, *I copialettere*, ed. Gaetano Cesare and
Alessandro Luzio (Milan: Commissione Esecutiva per le Onoranze a Giuseppe
Verdi, 1913), pp. 479–81.

delia has emerged not out of any dramatic necessity but in accord with operatic convention of the time: since an aria ordinarily consisted of an andante section followed by a florid *cabaletta*, the first part would doubtless have been her prayer of thanksgiving, while Verdi must have foreseen a longing for vengeance as the ideal text for the fast-tempoed, furious ending that would bring the aria, and the scene as well, to a suitably rousing conclusion. Verdi's plans for transforming the Shakespearean play he revered above all others thus demonstrates that opera establishes its own territory regardless of, often even transgressing upon, those literary texts it claims to re-present.

Musical versus Nonmusical Drama

Operatic Scenes and Situations

Certain characteristically operatic means of expression have persisted through a multitude of periods and national styles. In the following section I shall distinguish between operatic and nonmusical drama by cataloging the ways that opera treats a variety of dramatic scenes and situations—from small units such as rhetorical set pieces and type scenes to larger issues such as characterization and narrative organization. I start with that simple but pervasive set piece, the prayer. Whether as formal arias or brief, passionate pleas embedded within recitatives and arias, prayers are central to the history of opera. Between the piercing cry to the gods, "Rendetemi il mio ben," with which Monteverdi's Orfeo pleads for the return of Euridice, to Marie's indirect, fragmented prayer ("Herr-Gott! Sieh' mich nicht an!") of the Bible-reading scene in *Wozzeck*, one can point to pleadings with the gods (be they pagan or Christian) in characters as diverse as Handel's Cleopatra, Gluck's Alceste, Mozart's Idomeneo, Weber's Agathe, Bellini's Norma, Wagner's Elisabeth, Berlioz's chorus of Trojan women, and a succession of Verdi heroines from Giselda in *I lombardi* to Desdemona, whose prayer, though not corresponding to anything in Shakespeare, was at least anticipated by her earlier operatic embodiment in Rossini. Within any particular musical style one might not, without close attention to the words or the staging, be able to distinguish a prayer to the gods from a plea to another character: unless we understand the words, our only clue to the difference, say, between Aida's plea to the gods and Amelia's plea to Renato in *Un ballo in maschera* lies in the fact that whereas the latter addresses her husband directly, the former stands alone onstage and, in all but the more iconoclastic productions, looks upward at crucial moments. All operatic pleas and prayers, whoever their literal object of address may be, are ultimately addressed to the audience: thus, the desire expressed in the libretto becomes a pretext for music to exercise its traditional and much-vaunted ability to sway the hearts of its listeners.

Prayers and pleas merge sometimes imperceptibly with laments (by the chorus of Hebrews in *Nabucco*, the Orfeos of Monteverdi and Gluck, and the abandoned Didos of Purcell and Berlioz); expressions of gratitude (La Cieca's aria in *La Gioconda*, the *Fidelio* trio after the starving Florestan has been given bread and water); even of rapture (Agathe's *cavatina* in *Der Freischütz*, the Leonore-Florestan duet after the apocalyptic trumpet call). The other side of the coin from these operatic situations consists of moments of rage (the *furibondo* arias of *opera seria*, Isolde's narrative, Ford's aria in *Falstaff*), or of cursing (Alberich in *Das Rheingold*, Monterone in *Rigoletto*, Berlioz's Dido as well as the Metastasian Dido whom countless eighteenth-century composers had set to music). One can imagine an encyclopedic rhetoric of standard operatic situations, with the proper distinctions articulated as to which musical style fits which situation at any particular moment in history.[9]

Even within the variety of styles that make up nineteenth-century opera, one can distinguish certain components that appear repeatedly. For instance, the conspiratorial oath is often recognizable through a group of male voices brought together with whatever effects the listener can perceive as sinister or threatening (within the context of a particular composer's style). The oath on the Rütli in *Guillaume Tell*, the benediction of the swords in

---

[9]One can also imagine a similar rhetoric for spoken drama, especially the verse drama that prevailed in England, Spain, and France during the earliest stages of opera. A rhetoric of this sort would include set "numbers" such as funeral orations, wooing speeches, and a father's counsel to his son. The difference in effect between the formal elements in spoken drama—the verse, the rhetorical figures, the accompanying gestures—and those in opera are perhaps differences in degree more than in kind. One might speculate that as spoken drama became less overtly formal and more "realistic," the formal elements that had shaped sixteenth- and seventeenth-century spoken drama were taken over by the music of opera. Since music does not have as explicitly referential a function as words, opera could "mark" its numbers in a more overtly formal way than nonmusical drama could do. For example, mid–seventeenth-century Italian composers marked their laments with a quite predictable musical form, the descending tetrachord (see Ellen Rosand, "The Descending Tetrachord: An Emblem of Lament," *Musical Quarterly*, 65 [1979], 346–59).

Les Huguenots, the drawing of the lots in *Un ballo in maschera,* the duet between Siegfried and Gunther or between Otello and Iago—however different in musical style, these scenes make a characteristically ceremonial point for which there is no real equivalent in nonmusical drama except through the use of special theatrical (often, in fact, musical) effects. As one compares Rossini's setting of the oath in *Tell* with Schiller's original, one is tempted to make the same distinction Shaw made between Charles's aria in Verdi and his speech in Victor Hugo. It is significant that Schiller, as though aware of the limitations of verbal drama, resorts to both musical and visual means to make his point: as the characters move offstage after the oath, he brings the scene to an end with a stage direction asking that "the orchestra enter suddenly with splendid verve; the empty stage remains visible for a while and portrays the drama of the rising sun over the snowy peaks."[10] As this example demonstrates, verbal drama can easily, if also temporarily, slip into opera whenever it seeks to represent those ceremonial scenes that opera has made its own.

In his role as critic, Schiller was quite conscious of the differences in means and effect between musical and verbal drama. Long before writing *Wilhelm Tell* he described the ending of Goethe's play *Egmont* as essentially "operatic," by which he meant that Egmont's final speech before his execution could not depend on verbal means alone but on the ceremoniousness indicated by the detailed stage directions, which include not only music and repeated drumbeats but an allegorical representation of the play's heroine, who crowns the doomed hero with a laurel wreath.[11] It seems appropriate that this play, whose final scene advertises its need to move beyond verbal expression, should have inspired Beethoven to compose one of the most distinguished examples of what we have come to call "incidental" music. Indeed, if one looks at the history of incidental music that famous composers prepared for otherwise nonmusical dramas, one notes that the plays for which this music was written are generally what we would term "operatic" in nature—for example, *A Midsummer Night's Dream* (Purcell and Mendelssohn), *The Tempest* (Purcell),[12]

---

[10] *Wilhelm Tell,* end of Act II, in Schiller, *Werke,* Nationalausgabe, X, ed. Siegfried Seidel (Weimar: Hermann Böhlaus Nachfolger, 1980), p. 192.

[11] See "Ueber 'Egmont,' Trauerspiel von Goethe," in ibid., XXII, ed. Herbert Meyer (1958), p. 208.

[12] Whether Purcell's music for plays is "incidental" in nature or whether the mixture of music and play constitutes an opera makes for an interesting generic

Manfred (Schumann), *Peer Gynt* (Grieg), *Pelléas et Mélisande* (Fauré and Sibelius). Incidental music is thus scarcely incidental in the effects it tends to exert on its audiences, for it advertises the fact that the plays for which it was composed stand close to the generic boundary separating verbal from musical drama. Whenever we hear music in the so-called background or in the interstices between the lines a character speaks, we are made aware that the play is no longer attempting an unselfconscious mimesis of some real world but that it is aiming for the ceremoniousness and formality we associate with operatic representation.

Despite the blurring of generic boundaries in plays with strong operatic elements, a comparison of type scenes and other features common to verbal and musical drama reveals the sharply different effects for which each medium strives. Take for instance the difference between a musical and a purely verbal soliloquy. No dramatic speaker is ever fully alone, of course, for we are always conscious that the speaker is sharing his or her words with the audience. An operatic soliloquy is something else altogether, for with the addition of the orchestra the singer's words are variously stressed, questioned, commented upon; arias with solo instrumental obligatos even create the effect of a duet between singer and instrument. Similarly to the addition of incidental music to a play, the musical accompaniment lends the soliloquy a ceremonial dimension that would otherwise be missing. For example, the terrifying orchestral commentary accompanying Iago's "Credo" soliloquy that Boito concocted for Verdi's *Otello* gives this piece a public and rhetorical quality wholly missing from the intimate, self-conscious soliloquies spoken by this character in Shakespeare's play.

Or take the presence of crowds on the dramatic stage. In postclassical drama, larger groups have traditionally functioned as a negative force; once the Greek chorus was no longer a living presence, a large group of anonymous personages became little more than a mob, as in *Julius Caesar* and *Coriolanus*. To the extent that the Greek chorus had served as an emotional participant in the dramatic action, one can accept Wagner's remark that the chorus's role had transferred its functions to the modern orches-

---

question. In his distinguished book on Purcell's theater music, Robert E. Moore refers to Purcell's characteristic form as "the English compromise." See Moore, *Henry Purcell and the Restoration Theatre* (Cambridge, Mass.: Harvard University Press, 1961), pp. 32–37.

tra.[13] But opera affords opportunities for the use of crowds that are largely lacking in all but the most ceremonial forms of spoken drama. The problem with crowds in nonmusical drama may well be that they cannot be heard as a group and thus have no natural language to speak. If a director arranges for members of the crowd to speak individually, as in many modern productions (or as Goethe attempted to do in *Egmont*), they lose their collective power. For Shakespeare the crowd expresses itself most readily when it is threatened or manipulated by its leaders. (In neoclassical drama the crowd could remain conveniently offstage while its potential threat was discussed by those lofty personages through whose eyes we are expected to view the play.)

Whereas opera obviously thrives on crowd scenes, nonmusical theater treats them as, at best, an embarrassment and a challenge to an inventive stage director. However effective the chorus in Greek tragedies or the crowd in Shakespeare's English and Roman histories may have been when these dramas were originally performed, modern directors are forced to all manner of ingenuity to keep large masses theatrically alive. Only when a crowd is directed in an unashamedly operatic manner, as in *Marat/Sade*, does it "work" easily within the contemporary theater. In musical drama the crowd once again becomes a chorus, and music provides it with a wide variety of ways in which to express itself dramatically. Through contrasting voice lines and sharply different timbres, two or more parts of the chorus can enter into conflict with one another or, for that matter, work towards concord. By evoking the audience's associations with popular musical forms such as marches, dirges, hunting songs, and various types of dance, the chorus can express a wide range of attitudes even when—as is usually the case—the audience cannot understand their actual words. During the last century, choruses have sometimes served as a central dramatic force within many operas, notably in *La forza del destino, Boris Godunov,* and *Moses und Aron*—to the extent, in fact, that the chorus achieves a status comparable to that of the main characters.

Many nineteenth-century operas create a diversity of crowds with distinctly different, even antithetical, functions. *Aida,* for instance, displays a wide variety of choral masses, each with its

---

[13] See *Oper und Drama*, pt. 3, sec. 6, in Wagner, *Gesammelte Schriften*, ed. Julius Kapp (Leipzig: Hesse & Becker, n.d.), XI, 298.

own dramatic function: the Egyptian elite sending Rhadames off to war, the priests and priestesses praying for his victory, the slaves flattering Amneris, the populace welcoming the victorious Rhadames back, the priests condemning him to death. In verbal drama the loss of the crowd as a dramatic force after the Renaissance accompanied a shift of focus in drama from public to private, from the political to the psychological realm. If opera, in the course of its development, did not precisely aim to articulate political truths, the crowd at least served as a magnifying force that could lend the medium an epic quality; perhaps more than any single element, it is the crowd that justified the adjective *grand* with which opera was associated during the nineteenth century.

Verbal and musical drama also differ strikingly in their treatment of taboo. If a play such as *The Comedy of Errors* titillates its audience with the possibility of horrendous happenings, by the end it is clear, as the title in fact tells the audience from the start, that whatever fears the play arouses should be taken as simply errors. Theodor Adorno has observed how nineteenth-century opera displays forbidden sexual mixtures to an uncommon degree, for example the miscegenation in *Aida* and *L'Africaine* and the incest in *Die Walküre*.[14] One might add that the musical dimension sharply diminishes the discomfort an audience feels in witnessing the violation of a taboo. It is significant, for instance, that when incest appears in a verbal drama such as *Oedipus Rex*, it remains strictly retrospective; only in such "decadent" dramatic periods as the Jacobean or the mid–twentieth century could one imagine the depiction of Oedipus's actual courtship of Jocasta. By the same token, middle-class audiences witnessing the romance of brother and sister in the first act of *Die Walküre* have generally allowed themselves to be enraptured by the music; indeed, whatever consciousness they retain of the incest being enacted before their eyes doubtless enhances the rapture they feel. One need only imagine the text being spoken without music to note the difference—indeed, Sieglinde's statement to Siegmund that she sees her own image in his face might well evoke more laughter than horror.[15]

---

[14] See "Bürgerliche Oper" in Theodor W. Adorno, *Gesammelte Schriften*, ed. Rolf Tiedemann, XVI (Frankfurt: Suhrkamp, 1978), p. 32.

[15] Robert Donington argues that we are willing to accept the incest in this scene because of the symbolism within which Wagner has embedded it; I argue in return that only the music alters the way we deal with the taboo. See Donington, *Wagner's "Ring" and Its Symbols*, 3d ed. (London: Faber & Faber, 1974), p. 123.

The difference between musical and spoken drama is evident as well through the fact that at certain moments in the history of opera various type scenes have become prevalent at least as much for musical as for dramatic reasons. Take for instance the storm scene that appears in some of Rossini's comic operas. Although nonmusical comedies have of course developed their own type scenes at particular times, the storm is peculiarly suited to opera, if only because it creates an opportunity for an agitated orchestral display to provide momentary tragic relief and, by implication, to contrast with the eventual comic resolution. In *Il barbiere di Siviglia* and *La Cenerentola*, for example, Rossini introduces his storms shortly before he is ready to clear the air, as it were, for each opera's conclusion. Within tragic contexts storm music can serve as a background for violent events (Gilda's murder in *Rigoletto*), as an analogue to a storm within a character's psyche (the opening of Gluck's *Iphigénie en Tauride*), or as a "premonition" of dire events to come (the storm preceding the heroine's suicide in Janáček's *Katya Kabanova*).

Whenever a storm plays a memorable role in the literary models on which an opera is based, it becomes incumbent on the composer to take full orchestral (and even choral) advantage of the medium and demonstrate to what degree music can outdo words. The agitated style of *Katya Kabanova*, an opera based on a nineteenth-century play that is itself called *The Storm*, achieves its maximum degree of agitation in the storm scene; in his recent opera *Lear* (1978), Aribert Reimann utilizes the most unnerving sounds he can muster up from the techniques available to a late twentieth-century composer in order to compete with the most celebrated storm scene in the history of drama. Verdi's brief mention of the storm scene in his *Lear* scenario leads one to imagine that he too planned to compete seriously with the original; the great storm in *Rigoletto*, composed the year after the *Lear* scenario, gives us some notion of what he might have done. Although nobody setting the brief union of Dido and Aeneas would dare omit Virgil's storm, the limited orchestral resources available to Purcell doubtless hinder ears accustomed to Berlioz's brilliant set piece from appreciating the skill with which a great seventeenth-century composer could translate a literary emblem into music.[16] But one does not always need to read operatic storms

[16] For a discussion of how Purcell integrates the storm into his dramatic context, see Moore, *Henry Purcell*, pp. 54–55.

against their literary origins to note their peculiar power. The movement from storm to bliss that marks the first act of both *Die Walküre* and *Otello* (despite their notoriously divergent styles) demonstrates, as well as any operatic examples, the means by which music can shape and define dramatic structure.

If storm scenes serve to show off the dramatic possibilities of the orchestra, the mad scenes popular during the so-called bel canto period provide an opportunity at once for the most florid vocal technique and for whatever gestural histrionics a particular singer cares to engage in. The two most famous such scenes, in *Lucia di Lammermoor* and *I puritani*, were both suggested by passages in novels (respectively, Walter Scott's *Bride of Lammermoor* and *Old Mortality*) whose narrative mode scarcely gave much prominence to the heroines' mental lapses.[17] Even outside the bel canto style, the mad scenes that occasionally appear—for instance the clock scene in *Boris Godunov* or the sleepwalking scene in Verdi's *Macbeth*—remind us that opera depends on showpieces that vie with their nonmusical originals in the dramatic intensity they can display.

Opera's penchant for ceremony and display is particularly evident in the ballet interludes mandatory within French opera as well as in those non-French operas of the late nineteenth century that emulated French operatic grandeur. Only in rare instances do operatic ballets contain sufficient narrative content in their own right to justify their inclusion in an opera for what they might "add" to the story. The standard justification for an operatic ballet cannot be found in whatever story the ballet purports to tell but rather in the ceremonial occasion that would seem to necessitate some dancing at a certain point in the opera's own narrative. Thus it became customary during the nineteenth century to make provision for such occasions in the libretto. Ballets could most plausibly be introduced if the text justified an entertainment in a noble house (Donizetti's *La Favorite*, Ponchielli's *La Gioconda*), a public festival (Rhadames's return in *Aida*), travel to some nonearthly realm (the *Walpurgisnacht* of Gounod's *Faust*), or exotic rites (the temple scene in *Aida*, the Philistine bacchanale in *Samson et Dalila*). Wagner, who worried about verisimilitude more than his predecessors, justified the ballet music in *Rienzi* not as something for which he had sought a mere "pretext" but as "a festival

---

[17] The libretto of *I puritani* derives directly from a French play that gives the heroine's madness a prominence it lacked in the novel. See Jerome Mitchell, *The Walter Scott Operas* (University: University of Alabama Press, 1977), p. 60.

that Rienzi had to give the people and in which he could represent a drastic scene from their early history."[18] Some pretexts are obviously more plausible than others. If the ballet that Wagner inserted in the Venus scene of *Tannhäuser* for the Paris production has seemed sufficiently convincing to remain in the score, the ballet music that Verdi added for the Paris *Otello*—appropriately enough, in the reception scene for the Venetian ambassador—obviously could not remain in a work that has always been singled out for its dramatic economy. Plausibility, of course, was an issue only for the more serious-minded composer; as Berlioz remarked disdainfully, "At the Opéra they would find a pretext for a ballet even in a representation of the Last Judgment."[19]

If the dramatic function of ballet insertions has always been open to question, the various ensemble combinations—trios, quartets, quintets, plus individual voices against the chorus—that opera has cultivated since the late eighteenth century at least make some pretense to furthering the development of the drama. Yet every operagoer (as well as the record listener with libretto or score in hand) knows better than to try to follow the divergent self-reflections of the personages singing, say, the *Lucia* sextet. In arias and even in duets we are likely (if we know the language) to hear *some* of the words, and, even more important, we can at least entertain the illusion that the monologue or dialogue we hear could occur in spoken drama or, for that matter, in real life. It is significant that, in his attempt to reform opera through a return to verisimilitude, Wagner tended to draw the line between duet and trio; indeed, the relative absence of ensembles larger than duets (themselves quite scarce if we define a duet as two voices singing simultaneously) in his music-dramas is one of the primary means by which Wagner signals his disdain for the artifice of French and Italian opera.[20] Yet the ensembles central to non-Wagnerian nineteenth-century opera have their own way of expressing themselves in dramatic terms: when we listen to these

---

[18] "Eine Mitteilung an meine Freunde" in *Gesammelte Schriften*, I, 87.

[19] "Guillaume-Tell de Rossini," *Gazette musicale de Paris*, 1 (1834), 350.

[20] The obvious exceptions are the quintet in *Die Meistersinger* and the trio that ends the second act of *Götterdämmerung*. The "operatic" elements in *Die Meistersinger* can perhaps be explained through the fact that, as the single comedy among the music-dramas, it stands generically alone. As for *Götterdämmerung*, one may recall Shaw's famous attack on the final member of the tetralogy as Wagner's reversion from music-drama to Italian opera; Shaw even compares the trio to that of the conspirators in *Un ballo in maschera*. See "The Perfect Wagnerite" in Laurence, *Shaw's Music*, III, 468–70, 490.

set pieces we experience the drama primarily by musical means—through the particular vocal coloring, through the harmonic development, above all through the sensuousness and the power achieved by the stimultaneous display of virtuoso voices. Whatever artifice we may attribute to the great ensembles of the period, only Wagner's most literal-minded partisans would begrudge him the ecstatic quintet in *Die Meistersinger* or would begrudge his successor Strauss the trio of women's voices in which *Der Rosenkavalier* culminates.

The overt artifice at the heart of opera becomes even more evident when we note how much more slowly musical narrative must be enacted than spoken narrative. A nonmusical drama, whatever its period style, attempts the illusion that the pacing of its dialogue and events corresponds at least roughly with the rate at which things happen in real life. Opera, whether in the fast-paced mode of Mozart's comedies or the slow time of Wagnerian music-drama, generally creates a slowing down of narrative time—what Kierkegaard, comparing opera with spoken drama, describes as "a certain lingering movement, a certain diffusion of itself in time and space."[21] The ordinary full-length opera could be spoken without music in the time it takes to sing a single act. Whenever a play is turned into an opera libretto, only a portion, sometimes even less than half, can be accommodated within the libretto (the slow pace of opera becomes even more strikingly evident when we look at librettos based on whole novels). Although Büchner's *Woyzeck* fragment can be played in a little more than an hour, Alban Berg had to cut the play radically, wholly omitting a number of scenes, to fashion an opera that takes even more playing time.

Individual narratives embedded within operas are likewise notable for the relatively small amount of story material that can be absorbed in lengthy musical passages. Whether in formal arias (Azucena's story of her mother's death in *Il trovatore*) or in the Wagnerian mode (Wotan's synopsis of *Das Rheingold* in *Die Walküre* or Isolde's story of her earlier relationship with Tristan), operatic narratives are less important for the precise plot details they give the spectator than for the opportunity they provide to express the essence of a narrative situation in musical terms. The

---

[21] Søren Kierkegaard, *Either/Or*, trans. D. F. and L. M. Swenson (1944; rpt. Princeton: Princeton University Press, 1959), I, 117. Although operas generally slow down the narrative in comparison with spoken dramas, one can cite an operatic convention that sometimes works to "save" time, namely those ensembles in which a number of characters speak their diverse thoughts at once.

thousands of sexual events that Leporello packs into his catalogue in *Don Giovanni* achieve part of their comic effect through the surprise we feel that this much action (repetitive though it may be) can be narrated within the confines of a single aria. Given the relative paucity of narrative material an opera libretto can accommodate, it is no wonder that many librettos seem disjunctive—to the point, in fact, that a reader who is not at the same time listening to the music will likely find them quite hard to follow.[22] A spoken version of *Il trovatore*, to cite one of the more disjunctive librettos among those written for major operas, would probably be thoroughly confusing to an audience; only through the music do listeners get the commentary they need to make narrative sense of the text. When drawing upon a literary source, the successful librettist picks those moments within the narrative that consort well with operatic convention. If it is operatically proper to follow an aria with a trio and then a choral procession, the librettist must sacrifice narrative continuity in the hope that the musical embodiment of the text will create this continuity—though the story that this musical version tells will always be different in emphasis, pacing, and intensity from its literary original.

Operatic Transformations

Whenever a canonized literary work—be it a drama, novel, or verse narrative—has been turned into an opera, its admirers note and often deplore what has been "lost" from the original in the course of transformation. The transformation of literature into opera is analogous in the reactions it elicits to that more recent phenomenon, the adaptation of literary works into films. In both instances critics and audiences are more likely to dwell on losses than on gains and to ground their opinion in traditional literary values without fully considering the differences in the media they are examining. And, needless to say, during their most creative periods both opera and film have been relegated to a lower aesthetic status than the various literary genres they have drawn upon.

It is not surprising that so literary a composer as Berlioz would complain of "misshapen, shabby, and sometimes silly" distortions within five recent settings—by the composers Bellini, Da-

---

[22] The current project of the Metropolitan Opera to commission well-known writers to transform librettos into short novels is doubtless a comment on the unreadability of most librettos.

layrac, Steibelt, Vaccai, and Zingarelli—of *Romeo and Juliet*.[23] For Berlioz, adding new characters or failing to include Mercutio or the nurse amounted to ruining a classic. Yet by entitling his own musical version of this play a "dramatic symphony" rather than an opera, Berlioz allowed himself liberties he was unable to give composers who intended their settings for the stage. Thus he could concentrate exclusively on those aspects of the play that we associate with ceremony and romance—for example the ball scene at the Capulets, the Queen Mab narrative (for Berlioz an orchestral scherzo rather than a verbal narrative), the progress of love from yearning to consummation, and, in a section that takes up nearly the final quarter of the score, the obsequies following the death of the lovers.

In his own explicitly operatic works, Berlioz deviates as radically from classical texts as the composers he complained of. *Benvenuto Cellini* and *Les Troyens* each lift a few crucial ceremonial scenes from the autobiography and the epic, respectively, on which these operas are based. In *Béatrice et Bénédict* Berlioz abstracts a few selected aspects of *Much Ado about Nothing* and omits Dogberry and his band, the plot against Hero, and most of what we remember about Shakespeare's play except for the bantering of the two characters he has chosen for the title of his opera. Anybody who compares the opera and the play becomes aware more of the distortions than of the congruences. For example, Berlioz vastly expands the minor part of the musician Balthasar into a satirical new character whom he names Somarone. A relatively inconspicuous passage such as Hero's walk with Ursula in the garden becomes a long, ecstatic duet. As in *Roméo et Juliette*, the displacements between the play and the musical setting serve to remind us that the new work, however eccentric it may seem at first, has sought and found its own generic identity.

For Berlioz, as for other composers smitten by certain towering writers or by literary works that had become legendary, the composition of an opera on a classical text becomes a means of creating a dialogue with this text, of asserting at once the composer's reverence for, and independence from, the earlier author. The audience is, as it were, invited to participate in the composer's contention with the earlier text, indeed, to put its own reverence for the classical past to the test. Through the musical dimension that

---

[23] "*Roméo et Juliette;* opéra en quatre actes de Bellini" in Berlioz, *A Travers chants* (Paris: Michel Lévy, 1862), p. 317.

the composer has added to a familiar drama or story, the audience comes to experience the older work with that intensity of response that we associate with operatic representation. Moreover, the deviations that the audience notes from the original text serve to assert at once the autonomy of the individual composer in his role as textual interpreter and the autonomy of opera as a medium different in kind from those nonmusical genres with which it happens to share common narrative themes.

Berlioz's displacements are simply extreme instances of the transformations that take place whenever literature becomes opera. Like virtually every other component we can isolate when we compare the two media, a character in opera turns out to be something quite different from a character in drama and fiction. Frequently we hear critics praise a composer for his ability to create "complex" characters such as the Contessa, Hans Sachs, Falstaff, or the Marschallin, but such praise is simply a sign that the subtly shaded characters we seek in literary works are not the norm in opera. As these examples suggest, complex characters are most likely to appear in comic opera if they appear at all. Ordinarily, operatic characters are obsessed by a single emotion; as such, their closest literary analogies are the humor characters of Renaissance comedy or those tragic heroes and heroines we sometimes dub "slaves of passion." It may well be that the musical need to define oneself with both vocal volume and vocal virtuosity militates for a self-definition as a passionate and obsessed human being. In major operas as stylistically diverse as *Don Giovanni*, *Fidelio*, *Il trovatore*, *Tristan und Isolde*, and *Elektra*, important characters can be defined by a single (and obsessively passionate) emotion.

Just as characterization in opera eschews the subtle shading we demand in most literary forms, sheer goodness and sheer evil find more convincing embodiment in operatic than in literary contexts. The goodness of Elsa in *Lohengrin* or of Desdemona in Verdi's *Otello* becomes evident to us less from their words or the comments of other characters—as they would in spoken drama—than from musical signals such as the orchestral accompaniment to their words, their vocal phrasing, and the fact that in the mid- and late nineteenth century we are generally expected to associate the lyric soprano voice with moral goodness. The badness of Elsa's antagonist Ortrud and of Desdemona's antagonist Iago is rendered by similar means, including the fact that during this period villains expressed themselves in a relatively lower pitch. If operatic characters evoke a "mixed" response from us, the mixture usually consists of sharply opposed qualities—for instance the combination of sublime and grotesque that Hugo advocated in his dramatic theory and embodied in the central characters of *Lucrèce Borgia* and *Le Roi s'amuse*, both of whom achieved their natural fulfillment in the operas that Donizetti and Verdi, respectively, built around them. The fact that an operatic character sings rather than speaks and that music accompanies virtually every word that the character utters leads us to perceive him or her—at least initially—as a more mythical, more heroic, more sublime being than we would a literary character. As Donington has pointed out, for example, the music surrounding Siegfried's death reminds us of the symbolic meanings of the text in a way that a spoken version could never do.[24]

Although critics praise Wagner and Verdi for the "human" qualities with which they have endowed characters such as Wotan, Brünnhilde, King Philip (in *Don Carlos*), and Amneris, our perception of these characters at the beginning of their respective operas scarcely anticipates the subtle shading that we observe in them in the course of the dramatic action. The shading that critics so much admire in literary characters is the exception rather than the norm in most styles of opera; even the lowly and localized characters who inhabit *verismo* operas achieve a public, sometimes even a heroic dimension absent from their equivalents (and models) in the realist literature of the time. Adorno has pointed out how the cynical attitude that Frank Wedekind took to Lulu in the two plays he built around her is not evident in Alban Berg's operatic treatment.[25] Although one might cite the obvious differences in the two men's artistic and private personalities, one could also propose that opera does not easily lend itself to a cynical or even ironic treatment of the central character. Not only *Lulu* but other works such as *Eugene Onegin, Cavalleria rusticana,* and *Thaïs* do not strive for the ironic distance that characterizes their literary sources; even operas that cultivate parody, as *Don Giovanni, Così fan tutte,* and *Ariadne auf Naxos* do, cause us to take their characters seriously at the same time that the music the characters sing can make fun both of earlier music and of the type of character who would sing this

[24] See Donington, *Wagner's "Ring,"* p. 258.
[25] See *Berg: Der Meister des kleinsten Uebergangs,"* "Erfahrungen an Lulu," sec. 2, in Adorno, *Gesammelte Schriften*, XIII, ed. Gretel Adorno and Rolf Tiedemann (1971), p. 484.

music. If the characters of twentieth-century operas often have a subtlety and many-sidedness rare in earlier operatic periods, the reason may not simply be that the great opera composers of our time have been more self-consciously "literary" than their predecessors. The ability of composers such as Strauss, Janáček, Schönberg, and Berg to create characters with "depth effect" may also lie—perhaps even primarily lies—in the fact that the complex musical language at their disposal allowed them to create the illusion of correspondingly complex characters.

Just as characterization differs sharply in musical and nonmusical drama, so a tragic ending is never the same in an opera as in a play. It is significant, for instance, that one rarely finds tragic endings in opera until well into the nineteenth century. Since opera can display Orpheus's gifts for song with a literalness unattainable in verbal drama or narrative, it is appropriate that in his particular operatic embodiments he end up rewarded rather than torn to pieces. Throughout the eighteenth and early nineteenth centuries, the conciliatory gesture suggested by the title of Mozart's last opera, *La clemenza di Tito*, provides the typical ending for operas on serious themes. The tragic endings one can cite— for instance Metastasio's text *Didone abbandonata* or Rossini's *Otello*, were generally the result of a literary precedent too well established in an audience's mind to be altered. When Metastasio allowed the hero of his much-admired libretto *Attilio Regolo* to die, he excused himself on the basis not only of historical verisimilitude but also of the desirable moral effect that Attilio's death could have on the audience because it "leaves posterity a so weighty example of faithfulness and constancy."[26] Wagner, perhaps unaware of the rare early precedents for death on the operatic stage, traced the tragic ending back to 1828, when Auber's *La Muette de Portici* broke the custom that operas had to end in a "cheerful" and "satisfying" way; before Auber, according to Wagner, no composer would have dared to send his audience home with a sad impression.[27]

Yet the deaths in which most nineteenth-century operas culminate often seem mitigated in a way different from those of nonmusical tragedies. Isolde and Brünnhilde go to their respective deaths singing triumphantly, the former with the world dissolving to create a new unity, the latter with a new and "higher," more

[26] "Argomento" to *Attilio Regolo* in Pietro Metastasio, *Tutte le opere*, 2d ed., ed. Bruno Brunelli, I (Milan: Mondadori, 1953), p. 973.
[27] "Erinnerungen an Auber" in *Gesammelte Schriften*, VIII, 127.

human set of values replacing those associated with the older, more material-minded world of the gods. The high strings that accompany the final scenes in many Verdi operas help invoke an order in which forgiveness and reconciliation replace the violence that has gone on—usually at the most frantic possible pace—up to nearly the end. Can it be that the musical need to effect a tonal resolution suggested a triumphant or conciliatory conclusion? Even when, as in the later nineteenth century, composers came to stress catastrophe over reconciliation, we are meant to hear a triumph of sorts—whether the immolation of the protagonist (Brünn-hilde, Tosca, Elektra) or even the simple triumph of fate we are asked to find inherent in tragic situations (as in countless *verismo* operas such as *Cavalleria rusticana, I pagliacci, Andrea Chenier*).

Death in opera is a consummation that the listener awaits al-most as devoutly as his or her favorite arias. When Thomas Mann describes the effect of the death of Aida and Rhadames on the hero of *Der Zauberberg*, he stresses the "extraordinary feeling of well-being" that emanates from the scene:[28] tragic opera, one might say, pushes the Aristotelian notion of catharsis far beyond what a spectator of earlier forms of tragedy could have imagined. The lengthy interval in many operas between the infliction of a fatal wound and the victim's actual death is less an occasion for agony than for a pleasurable display of musical eloquence; thus, the vio-lent death of the king in *Un ballo in maschera* allows moving expressions of farewell and forgiveness, while the long process of Siegfried's death enables the audience to hear once more, and this time in chronological order, the diverse leitmotifs that define the stages of his life.

To the extent that nineteenth-century opera, whatever its tragic pretentions, culminates in reconciliation or triumph, its endings have more in common with those of romance than with what we ordinarily call tragedy. The affinities between opera and romance are evident in the changes that Verdi's librettists for *Don Carlos* made in the ending of the original Schiller play. The latter ends with a cruelly ironic line addressed by the king to the Grand In-quisitor, "Kardinal! Ich habe / das Meinige gethan. Thun Sie das Ihre,"[29] after which Carlos is presumably put into the hands of the Inquisitor, who, together with the king, has suddenly in-

---

[28] Thomas Mann, *Der Zauberberg* (Frankfurt: Fischer, 1960), p. 897 (chap. 7).
[29] "Cardinal! I've done my part. Now do yours!" *Don Carlos* (ll. 5369–70) in Schiller, *Werke*, Nationalausgabe, VI, ed. Paul Böckmann and Gerhard Kluge (1973), p. 339.

truded upon a farewell scene between the queen and her stepson. In the play, Carlos had made his way into the queen's chambers by means of a Gothic ruse, namely by masquerading as the ghost of his grandfather Charles V: the palace guard, we are told, was superstitious enough to believe that the ghost roamed through the halls at night. The opera substitutes magic for what in the play was simply a convenient theatrical device subject to rational explanation; the ghost is no longer the disguised young hero but the "real" ghost of the dead emperor, who, in the monk's costume he wore after his abdication, emerges from his tomb at the end to rescue Carlos from the tyrannical force that is meant to spell his doom in the play. Despite the qualms of literary intellectuals, the grand gestures of romance provide endings for nineteenth-century operas in a way that nonmusical tragedy can scarcely be expected to do.

Verdi's overt use of romance to end *Don Carlos* is a sign of that affinity with romance that has characterized opera since its beginnings. Certain forms of opera—for instance seventeenth-century Venetian and nineteenth-century German opera—consciously cultivated magical transformations and characters with supernatural attributes. In his dialogue "The Poet and the Composer," E. T. A. Hoffmann (now better known to the non-German public as a character in an operatic romance, Offenbach's *Les Contes d'Hoffmann* than as the operatic composer, conductor, and great writer that he was in real life) says through a surrogate speaker, "I regard the romantic opera as the only genuine one, for only in the realm of romance is music at home." The statement is made in response to another speaker, who had asked, "You would thus privilege only romantic opera with its fairies, spirits, marvels, and transformations?"[30]

Yet among the operas we recognize as classic today, those that cultivate the characteristic actions and dramatis personae of the more fantastic forms of literary romance are the exception rather

[30] "Der Dichter und der Komponist" in *Werke*, ed. Georg Ellinger (Berlin: Deutsches Verlagshaus Bong, n.d.), V, 120. I shall often have occasion to cite this celebrated dialogue in the course of this study. One reason for its importance is Hoffmann's affirmation of those features of opera—its penchant for romance and for the fantastic—that separate it from drama. By contrast, the mainstream of operatic theory has stressed the affinities of opera to nonmusical drama. For a detailed discussion of the dialogue's significance within operatic theory and within Hoffmann's own career as writer and composer, see Aubrey S. Garlington, Jr., "E. T. A. Hoffmann's 'Der Dichter und der Komponist' and the Creation of the German Romantic Opera," *Musical Quarterly*, 65 (1979), 22–47.

than the rule. *Die Zauberflöte* and *Die Frau ohne Schatten*, the latter of which consciously evokes the former, are in no sense typical of the present-day repertory. Unlike ballet, which naturally absorbs its sylphs, swans, lemures, and the like, opera, doubtless because it must make its supernatural beings audible as well as visible, cannot easily accommodate the continuous marvels typical of the literary romances from which it often borrows its themes. The talking animals of Janáček's *Cunning Little Vixen* have probably delayed a favorable reception of this opera at the same time that this composer's exercises in *verismo* (*Jenufa* and *Katya Kabanova*) and even science fiction (*The Makropoulos Case*) were establishing themselves on the world's opera stages. The singing elves and sea mussel in *Die ägyptische Helena* may well be responsible for the neglect that this opera has suffered in comparison with the five other operas on which Strauss and Hofmannsthal collaborated; indeed, the correspondence between librettist and composer shows considerable anxiety about how the supernatural beings could convincingly be set, sung, and staged.[31]

When supernatural events and characters appear in opera, they are most often reduced to isolated elements—a character who appears only briefly (Charles V in *Don Carlos*, the moving statue in *Don Giovanni*) or a magic prop that extends its influence over the entire opera (the potion in *Tristan und Isolde*, the potions and the *Tarnhelm* in *Götterdämmerung*). It is as though a certain degree of naturalistic illusion is necessary for opera to sustain our attention. Yet one could put the question another way: as soon as a verbal text has been set to music, it automatically assumes the character of romance, even when it does not contain explicitly supernatural elements. Even those *verismo* operas that focus upon the more lowly aspects of life cannot achieve the documentary bite we find in realistic plays of the period. For instance, the charming music that accompanies the early-morning Parisian street criers in Charpentier's *Louise* creates a fairy-tale quality quite remote from the program of literary naturalism. Schönberg, citing the torture scene in *Tosca* as his example, once objected to the use of "realistic, violent incidents" in music;[32] what he failed to

---

[31] See letters of October 16, 1923; January 29, 1924; March 11, 1924; August 9, 1924; and November 29, 1924, in Strauss-Hofmannsthal, *Briefwechsel*, pp. 499–500, 511, 514, 522–23, 531.

[32] "Gustav Mahler" in *Style and Idea*, ed. Leonard Stein (New York: St. Martin's Press, 1975), p. 450.

note was that in watching this scene on the stage we do not interpret it as "realistic" or "violent" in the same way that we would while watching Sardou's original play. If there is any appropriate literary analogy to how we experience Cavaradossi's offstage screams in the opera, it would be in the way we react to the narration of a hero's pain in the sublime style of verse epic.[33]

In view of the different frames of mind with which the audience approaches musical and nonmusical drama, it is not surprising that Northrop Frye, in his conspectus of the various dramatic genres, uses the spectator's relative involvement in the plot as the central criterion for distinguishing opera from what he calls "mimetic drama." As Frye puts it, "The verbal action of *Figaro* is comic and that of *Don Giovanni* tragic; but in both cases the audience is exalted by the music above the reach of tragedy and comedy, and, though as profoundly moved as ever, is not emotionally involved with the discovery of plot or characters. It looks at the downfall of Don Juan as spectacular entertainment, much as the gods are supposed to look at the downfall of Ajax or Darius."[34] Although our emotional involvement in operatic plots is a more complex matter than Frye admits (one need merely cite the emotional effect created by the Contessa's resolution of the plot in *Figaro*), he is correct in pointing to an essential difference in the ways we apprehend verbal and musical drama.

The differences in an audience's response to verbal and musical drama are evident in a particularly striking way when one examines that dramatic subgenre most notable for the immediacy of response it demands—namely, comedy. Nonmusical comedy, as we know, often strives for a sense of frenzy as new revelations pile up to complicate what may seem an already overburdened plot. Yet when a farcical situation is organized in musical terms, this frenzy can reach proportions that even the finest comic timing rarely if ever achieves with words alone. The changes in key and rhythm that accompany each twist and turn of plot in the two finales to *Le nozze di Figaro* exert effects on an audience that no production of the equivalent scenes in Beaumarchais's play could

---

[33] The difference is evident as well in an exchange between a contemporary theater director-critic and his son. The son objected that although he was allowed to attend sexually explicit operas, he was denied this privilege with plays. "It's all right as long as they sing," his father replied.

[34] Northrop Frye, *Anatomy of Criticism* (Princeton: Princeton University Press, 1957), p. 289.

hope to do. The crescendos and the rhythmic intensifications in Rossini's *Barbiere* attempt to outdo Mozart (not to speak of the plays on which both operas are based) in the frenzied atmosphere they create. Hoffmann describes the difference between spoken and operatic comedy through the effect of madness that the latter is able to achieve. If spoken comedy for Hoffmann is above all a mimesis of ordinary persons, the musical dimension transforms these characters into something essentially unreal: "And now the fantastic actions that they [the characters] set in motion as though afflicted by a strange illness . . . work wondrously upon us, as though a crazy apparition were to go through life and drive us irresistibly into the circle of his delightful mischief-making."[35]

With the resources of the Wagnerian and post-Wagnerian orchestra, the fantastic effects that Hoffmann had earlier found in operatic comedy could come to overpower an audience to a degree that Hoffmann would not have imagined. The street fight in *Die Meistersinger* or the tricks played on Baron Ochs in the tavern scene in *Der Rosenkavalier* utilize the full force of the orchestra to intensify the already frantic movements of the actors—to the point that audiences have been known to complain of the unnecessarily cruel victimization that the comic characters undergo. What might seem like overkill in a nonmusical comedy is the stock-in-trade of operatic comedy; the punishments of a Malvolio or an Harpagon—if a composer could create successful operatic versions of *Twelfth Night* or *L'Avare*—would doubtless be accompanied with considerably more vehemence than Shakespeare or Molière was willing to expend.

Indeed, such great figures of operatic comedy as Bartolo (in *Il barbiere*), Beckmesser, and Ochs, though not perhaps Falstaff, exercise a "larger-than-life" quality even more potently than their equivalents would in stage comedy. The obstructions they create for their respective plots seem all the more formidable through the musical commentary on their actions, while the falls they experience at the end of each opera seem correspondingly abject in their effect. Through the intensity that music lends to comic action, operatic comedy may well be less "funny" than its verbal counterpart. While planning *Ariadne auf Naxos*, Strauss suggested to Hofmannsthal that perhaps there was no such thing as a "true *comic* opera." "When," he asks, "have people ever been

[35] "Der Dichter und der Komponist," p. 127.

made to laugh by music in the theater? At two or three places in the whole opera repertory; otherwise only at the extemporizing of the actors or *at spoken dialogue*."[36] If, as Strauss observes, musical passages do not easily elicit laughter, they also encourage an audience to interpret as essentially mythical occurrences what in spoken drama would simply be comic antics; a bravura aria such as Bartolo's "A un dottor della mia sorte" in Rossini's *Il barbiere* does not so much invite laughter (though the words and the tempo are obviously comic) as awe at the virtuosity and energy that mark both the process of composition and of performance.

This tendency of opera to raise actions to a mythical level is evident from the fact that operas are usually set in times and places far removed from the worlds of the audiences for whom composers write. The only two Verdi operas with contemporary settings, *Stiffelio* and *La traviata*, were failures when first produced; the latter was subsequently given a costumed eighteenth-century setting, the former a wholly new libretto with a different plot and a medieval setting. The eighteenth-century theorist Algarotti spoke for more than his own time, when, in 1755, he recommended exotic subjects for opera as an opportunity for "splendid banquets, magnificent embassies, embarkations, chorusses, battles, conflagrations, etc. so as to give a farther extension to the sovereignty of the musical drama." He went on to recommend an opera on the subject of Montezuma to provide "a display of the Mexican and Spanish costumes" and "the barbaric magnificence of America."[37] (One might note that Verdi's *Otello*, which is customarily praised for its psychological realism and its dramatic compression, contains four of Algarotti's suggested embellishments—an embassy, choruses, fire, and at least an offstage battle— plus a grand arrival in the place of an embarkation.) In light of Algarotti's recommendation of an opera about Montezuma, it is no surprise that operas on the subject have cropped up in quite diverse styles—Graun's *opera seria*, *Montezuma* (1755), with a libretto by Frederick the Great; Spontini's *Fernand Cortez* (1809), a central link between Gluck and French grand opera; and one of the most ambitious modern American operas, Roger Sessions's *Montezuma* (1964).

[36] Letter of July 24, 1911, in Strauss-Hoffmannsthal, *Briefwechsel*, p. 141. Emphasis in the original.

[37] Count [Francesco] Algarotti, *An Essay on Opera* (London: L. Davis & C. Reymers, 1767), pp. 20, 22.

The distant settings we expect in opera scarcely seem surprising in seventeenth-century opera or in *opera seria*, for the reigning theories of drama contemporaneous with them demanded a similar distancing in noncomic musical forms. If the French and Italian operatic traditions stressed foreign settings throughout their history, German opera in the nineteenth century established its roots firmly in the national past—so much so that, together with the Romantic literature and art with which it shared a common cultural purpose, it made romance synonymous with the German Middle Ages. Tragic opera in all national traditions fiercely resisted the movement towards contemporary middle-class themes and settings that entered European drama and dramatic theory beginning with Diderot. Even *Luisa Miller*, which in Schiller's original proudly advertised its contemporaneity with the subtitle *A Bourgeois Tragedy*, lost its present-day immediacy for Verdi's audience by retaining its eighteenth-century setting. "The dreadful attempt to bring the *larmoyant* play into the opera house can only miscarry," Hoffmann wrote to express his disdain for that dramatic form which, up to his own time, had striven most explicitly to render the contemporary world.[38]

If late nineteenth-century *verismo* opera represents a capitulation of sorts to the contemporaneity that the fiction and drama of the time cultivated, it is also notable for the way it manages to distance its situations from the audience's world. In the preceding section I noted how Mascagni translated the naturalistic speech of Verga's play into traditional operatic terms, and I might add that this opera, together with its traditional companion piece *I pagliacci*, was set in a small-town world far removed from that of the urban audience before which it was first performed. (Once they had become familiar, both operas of course made their way back to the provinces—but doubtless with a certain mythical aura, created by the audience's knowledge of their international success, that worked to maintain their distance from the world they claimed to be depicting.) Though Puccini lavished considerable care to achieve authenticity in the church bells and other local details he employed in *Tosca*, the opera was experienced by its Roman audiences as a period piece set a full century to the year before the date of its premiere. The opera's three settings—a baroque church, a Renaissance palace, and an ancient castle, all of them local landmarks—were at once historically removed from,

---

[38] "Der Dichter und der Komponist," p. 127.

yet also a part of, the backdrop against which the original Roman spectators pursued their daily lives.

Most successful *verismo* operas create distance either through their remoteness in time (*Tosca, Gianni Schicchi, Andrea Chenier, Adriana Lecouvreur*) or through the fact that they are set in some exotic foreign spot (*Madama Butterfly, La fanciulla del West*). A work such as Charpentier's *Louise*, located within its Parisian audience's own contemporary urban setting, is rare among the better *verismo* operas—though the street scene, as I indicated earlier, loses much of its naturalistic impact through the ritualized effect of the orchestral accompaniment. Two major twentieth-century composers, Strauss and Schönberg, made attempts at a special type of operatic realism, namely the presentation of domestic anecdotes from their own lives. Yet *Intermezzo* and *Von Heute auf Morgen* are very much the exception within their composers' total work, in which the mythical and the historical predominate. Theodor Adorno has generalized that "costume is an essential of opera—an opera without costume would, in contrast to a play, seem paradoxical."[39]

The distancing that opera has traditionally sought accompanies a perception on the part of composers that the subjects they set must be capable of a higher and more sustained level of intensity than those of a nonmusical drama. Composers on the lookout for suitable operatic subjects have characteristically sought texts (whether in dramatic or narrative form) that affected them intensely—with the hope that in the process of composition they could achieve even more intense effects. Berg, we know, became obsessed with the idea of making an opera out of *Woyzeck* as a result of a performance of the play that he witnessed in 1914. Puccini became fascinated with the operatic possibilities of the David Belasco thriller *The Girl of the Golden West* by watching the scene in which the hero's blood trickles from his bunk bed. The torture scene in *Tosca* to which Schönberg objected was doubtless a factor in attracting Puccini to this plot as well. However much we have come to defend the "seriousness" of Verdi as dramatist and composer, his correspondence amply illustrates that

---

[39] "Bürgerliche Oper," p. 24. Adorno's point can be demonstrated through the fact that in recent years it has become common to revive forgotten operas by composers such as Rossini and Donizetti in concert form. Although the economics of production make a fully staged version impossible, these operas are often performed in what is called "semistaged" form—without scenery but with costumes and gestures.

we must not underestimate his penchant for seeking out those dramas of his time that offered strikingly melodramatic effects.[40] Strauss constantly reminded Hofmannsthal of his need for situations—especially near the end of acts—that could help him intensify his musical effects.[41]

The intensity that operatic composers seek can be linked to an illusion of inevitability that opera is able to create with greater ease than spoken drama. An opera evokes this sense of inevitability less through the dramatic plot it follows than through its musical development. Thus, at the simplest level one might connect the illusion of inevitability with the fact that a musical score imposes limits on a performer's freedom far beyond that of a verbal text. As Stravinsky put it in *The Poetics of Music*, "The dramatic actor . . . finds he has much more latitude in regard to *chronos* and intonation than does the singer who is tightly bound to *tempo* and *melos*."[42] However much particular singers may attempt to impress their own personalities upon a role, through the inexorable beat of the music we remain aware of the severe constraints—as we do not with a dramatic text even as familiar as *Hamlet*—by which the action must follow its foreordained course. This sense of inevitability is evident even in those operas—for example German *Singspiele* and French *opéras comiques*—that alternate musical and spoken segments. Despite the relative freedom we experience in the passages of dialogue—as in the comic antics of Papageno or the sharp verbal exchanges between Carmen and Don José—each time the music begins we feel the characters moving to another, more predetermined and public level of action; moreover, operatic styles mixing speech and music generally culminate in long finales (frequently at the end of each act) that firmly reassert the primacy of the musical flow.

Opera's ability to impose inevitability on action is most discernible whenever a familiar dramatic text has been set to music.

---

[40] Note, for instance, his first mention of *Rigoletto* in a letter asking that Hugo's play be suggested to the librettist Cammarano: "Suggest *Le Roi s'amuse* of Vict. Hugo to Cammarano. Beautiful drama with stupendous situations." Letter of September 7, 1849 (to V. Flauto), in Verdi, *I copialettere*, p. 85.

[41] See, for instance, his demand that Hofmannsthal rewrite the end of Act I of *Arabella*: "The present ending to the act is quite pretty, but not effective enough for an opera. Cosima Wagner once told me: 'The main thing is the act endings!'" Letter of May 3, 1928, in Strauss-Hofmannsthal, *Briefwechsel*, p. 625. Note his citing Wagnerian precedent in this request. In numerous spots within the correspondence, Strauss uses the term *Steigerung* (intensification) to express his need.

[42] Igor Stravinsky, *The Poetics of Music*, trans. Arthur Knodel and Ingolf Dahl (Cambridge, Mass.: Harvard University Press, 1970), pp. 161, 163.

Even in its nonmusical version, Büchner's *Woyzeck* achieves those uncommonly frenzied and feverish effects that so impressed Alban Berg when he attended the play. Yet in its larger organization (the play remained a fragment) *Woyzeck* plays like a loosely, even casually organized collection of short scenes that Büchner structured in conscious revolt against the German classical tradition and that we now see as a direct ancestor of the anti-Aristotelian theater of Bertolt Brecht.[43] As Kurt Oppens compares the play with the opera, "The opera reproduces the drama in a sphere of augmented—if you will, hysterically augmented—intensity. It must achieve this above all in order to justify itself as 'music.'"[44] What Oppens implies is that transforming a work into musical terms automatically intensifies what might have seemed an already tensely dramatic play. But with the forcefulness of his post-Wagnerian orchestra and his imposition of traditional musical forms such as variations, sonata, and a suite of dances, Berg created a rigidly organized structure that contrasts markedly with the apparent disparateness of Büchner's play.

Wagner points out a similar contrast between the play *Romeo and Juliet* and Berlioz's musical realization (which Berlioz, of course, did not intend as an opera in the usual sense). Generalizing on the differences between dramatist and composer, Wagner claims that whereas the former immerses himself in the realities of everyday life, the latter "looks wholly away from the process of ordinary life, completely lifts up [or cancels (*hebt auf*)] its accidents and particularities and sublimates [*sublimiert*] everything situated in it according to its concrete emotional content, which, singularly determined, manifests itself only in music."[45] Despite the unmistakable Hegelian coloring, Wagner's distinction between musical and nonmusical drama is close to Aristotle's distinction between history and poetry: but whereas Aristotle associates history with everyday particularities and poetry with universals, Wagner's dichotomy raises the scale one step upward, with musical drama taking the role that Aristotle had assigned to poetry. Aristotle, one recalls, found poetry "more philosophical"

---

[43] For a more detailed comparison of play and opera, see my book *Georg Büchner* (Carbondale: Southern Illinois University Press, 1964), pp. 126–29. For a far more extended study, by a distinguished musicologist, of Berg's transformation of Büchner's play, see George Perle, *The Operas of Alban Berg*, I (*Wozzeck*) (Berkeley: University of California Press, 1980), pp. 22–92.

[44] Kurt Oppens, "Alban Bergs 'Wozzeck,'" *Merkur*, 21 (1967), 1155.

[45] "Ueber Franz Liszts symphonische Dichtungen" in *Gesammelte Schriften*, VIII, 114.

than history because, "speaking" as it does of universals rather than of the particularities with which history is engaged, poetry moves on a higher level of abstraction.[46] To underline my contention throughout this section that opera inhabits a realm distinct from that of nonmusical drama, I shall give this Aristotelian formulation a further twist: to the extent that the composer subjects human actions to the tight logic of musical form and seems to raise these actions to a mythical, more universal level than they achieve through purely verbal expression, opera impresses its audiences as ultimately more philosophical than spoken drama.

Music, Literature, and the Boundaries of Genre

Music and the Dramatic Principle

The fundamental gap I have proposed between opera and spoken drama suggests an uneasy relationship that has nourished and affected opera since its Florentine origins. Even the sketchiest history of opera generally depicts the form as moving back and forth between two extremes—on the one hand, a dramatic emphasis in which musical values serve the interests of the text; on the other, an emphasis on performative features such as vocal virtuosity and sumptuousness of spectacle. A typical historical narrative takes the following lines: although at its beginnings opera sought to emulate and restore the conditions of Greek tragedy, and although its first great composer, Monteverdi, respected the primacy of drama in opera, Monteverdi's followers lost sight of the dramatic ideal and allowed the medium to become dominated by the needs of singers and the desire of audiences for spectacle; not until Gluck's "reform" of the 1760s was the dramatic model restored—but only temporarily, for the performative and purely musical values once again dominated until the next great "reform," that of Wagner, returned the dramatic element to the foreground, where, despite many changes in operatic style, it has remained to this day.

This sketch, as well as most of those one is likely to see in print, favors the dramatic side of the antithesis—as one might well expect, for those who are verbal enough to theorize on such

---

[46] See Aristotle, *Poetics*, trans. Gerald F. Else (Ann Arbor: University of Michigan Press, 1967), p. 33 (sec. 9).

matters will not ordinarily take the view of a performer who seeks adulation or of an audience avid for "mere" entertainment. Composers who embrace the notion of opera as drama generally express their bias by asserting the primacy of words over music and, as often as not, by attacking performative or purely musical elements as nonfunctional, sometimes even as frivolous. Note, for instance, Gluck's famous formulation of this principle: "I have tried to restrict music to its true office of serving poetry by means of expression and through the situations of the story, without interrupting the action or stifling it with useless, superfluous ornaments."[47] The reference to "restricting music to its true office" is an attempt to legitimate a principle by invoking its origins— though Gluck doubtless had little concrete information about what the earliest opera composers were doing. It is significant that Charles Burney, the product and historian of a musical culture dedicated to the performative side of the antithesis, reported Gluck as calling his *Orfeo* "the first of his operas that was truly dramatic."[48] Perhaps the most extreme statement of the dramatic principle comes not from a composer but from a musicologist, Joseph Kerman, who announced his bias in the very title of his influential book, *Opera as Drama*. Writing in the mode of Anglo-American literary critics such as T. S. Eliot and F. R. Leavis, Kerman was primarily concerned with reforming opera audiences whose taste had been blunted by dramatically unmotivated vocal display and melodramatic effects. Kerman often made his points through such memorable phrases as "stop-and-go" to describe the aria–recitative alternations of eighteenth-century opera, or "shabby little shocker" to label *Tosca*.[49] In his eagerness to educate the unthinking listener, he reduced the canon of fully realized operatic masterpieces that adequately embodied the dramatic principle to less than a dozen: the two *Orfeo*s, *Figaro*, *Fidelio*, *Tristan und Isolde*, *Otello* and *Falstaff*, *Pelléas et Mélisande*, *Wozzeck*, and *The Rake's Progress*. The high seriousness that

[47] Dedication of *Alceste* in Alfred Einstein, *Gluck: Sein Leben, Seine Werke* (Zurich: Pan-Verlag, n.d.), p. 142.
[48] Charles Burney, *An Eighteenth-Century Musical Tour in Central Europe and the Netherlands*, ed. Percy A. Scholes (London: Oxford University Press, 1959), II, 99. Lawrence Lipking's study of eighteenth-century ideas on the relationship of the arts stresses Burney's inability to appreciate the dramatic element in opera: "Seldom if ever does he [Burney] talk of dramatic form, or the relationship of scenes to each other, or the suitability of the musical style to the action." See Lipking, *The Ordering of the Arts* (Princeton: Princeton University Press, 1970), p. 314. It is evident that Lipking takes for granted the superiority of the dramatic principle.
[49] Kerman, *Opera as Drama* (New York: Knopf, 1956), pp. 134, 254.

Kerman's Arnoldian bias demanded invariably took the form of dramatic seriousness.

The nearly three decades since the appearance of Kerman's book have seen a large-scale renewal of interest in that whole performative tradition he had so resolutely condemned. Through the restoration of vocal techniques abandoned by the operatic practice of the later nineteenth century and through the revival of works—*opera seria*, early nineteenth-century bel canto opera—that could display these techniques, audiences have been exposed to a set of values different from those espoused by Kerman and the whole drama-oriented tradition from Gluck through Wagner and the later Verdi.[50] Yet the dramatic principle has maintained its dominance just the same. Maria Callas, who in the 1950s introduced operagoers and record collectors to the older vocal technique, always made this technique subservient to what she interpreted as dramatic values—so much so that she often sacrificed musical precision to histrionic effect. Although Callas's major successors, Joan Sutherland and Montserrat Caballé, can scarcely be lauded for their skills as tragedians, the dramatic principle has remained so firmly entrenched that the productions in which Sutherland and Caballé appear in major opera houses are carefully designed—as productions with comparable singers were not in earlier eras—to create as much of a dramatic effect as these singers' histrionic abilities will permit. However controversial the increasingly powerful role of stage directors has become in recent decades, it is the natural outgrowth of those many discussions since the Renaissance that opera must justify itself, above all, as drama.

The dominance of the dramatic principle by the late nineteenth century is of course due to the prestige and influence of Wagner and the later Verdi. For long it was assumed that Wagner (whether or not one actually espoused his music) had single-handedly restored the primacy of text over music. It is certainly true that whereas Verdi never issued manifestos or even discussed his theories in print, Wagner produced a provocative group of writings, the most important of which, *Oper und Drama* (1851), was finished before he had even put his ideas into practice in that succession of works that his advocates labeled music-dramas. Yet Verdi, as is

---

[50] The scholarly investigations that Kerman, in subsequent years, has undertaken into Verdi's pre-*Otello* operas suggests that his interests, if not necessarily his preferences, are more catholic than his early book implies.

evident to anybody who reads through his correspondence, was equally committed to the dramatic principle, though he found his way to it more gradually, less. stridently, and with considerably less verbal fuss than Wagner. Those who discuss the history of his career today typically organize their narratives as a steady movement from the earliest operas, which stress performative values such as vocal display and a rhythmic regularity that an audience can easily assimilate, to the eventual triumph of the dramatic principle.[51] One can, in fact, chart this development through Verdi's changing attitude, both in his practice and in the remarks in his letters, towards the *cabaletta*, that fiery showpiece with which Rossini, Bellini, Donizetti—and Verdi as well until relatively late in his career—brought their arias and duets to an end. If Verdi in 1850 had no scruples about projecting a revenge *cabaletta* for Cordelia in *Lear*, at least a few of the *cabalette* of the succeeding period—most notably the "Sempre libera" of *La traviata*, as Kerman points out[52]—were designed in a dramatically functional manner that one can analyze as a milestone on the road to *Falstaff*. Similarly, in a statement to his librettist for *Aida*, Verdi makes clear that what justifies a *cabaletta* is its function: "I have always believed that *cabalette* are necessary when the situation demands them. Those for the two duets are not demanded by the situation, and especially the duet between father and daughter does not seem to me appropriate. In that state of terror and moral prostration Aida neither can nor should sing a *cabeletta*."[53]

Long before the *cabaletta* had become an issue in Verdi's com-

[51] See, for instance, Kerman's discussion of *Otello* in *Opera as Drama*, pp. 129–67. It has become a critical convention to view Verdi's earlier works in teleological terms as steps towards the realization of opera as drama in the last two operas. See such standard chronologically organized studies of Verdi as those by Francis Toye, *Giuseppe Verdi: His Life and Work* (New York: Knopf, 1931), esp. pp. 244, 264, 281, 347; Vincent Godefroy, *The Dramatic Genius of Verdi*, I (London: Victor Gollancz, 1975), esp. pp. 161, 174, 241; and Julian Budden, *The Operas of Verdi: From "Oberto" to "Rigoletto"* (New York: Praeger, 1973), esp. pp. 29–30, 215.

[52] Kerman, *Opera as Drama*, p. 147. Kerman shows less sympathy for this *cabaletta* in a later essay, "Opera, Novel, Drama: The Case of *La Traviata*," *Yearbook of Comparative and General Literature*, 27 (1978), 50–51. Both discussions actually show a preference for the *cabalette* of Violetta's duets in Acts II and III. For a useful survey of *cabalette* before Verdi and within Verdi's work, see Frits Noske's essay "The Notorious Cabaletta," in *The Signifier and the Signified: Studies in the Operas of Mozart and Verdi* (The Hague: Martinus Nijhoff, 1977), pp. 271–93. Although Noske demonstrates the varying quality of *cabalette* within the various Verdi operas, he argues strongly for their retention in modern productions.

[53] Letter of September 28, 1870 (to A. Ghislanzoni), in Verdi, *I copialettere*, p. 645.

mitment to the dramatic principle, his desire for verisimilitude had caused him to rethink another matter that proved crucial in both his and Wagner's development—namely, the difficulty of reconciling beauty and smoothness of vocal production with the achievement of dramatic power. In a revival of *Macbeth* in 1848, Verdi objected that the soprano to whom the role was assigned would sing too *well* to be convincing: "Tadolini is too fine a singer to do that part! . . . Tadolini sings to perfection; and I don't want Lady Macbeth to sing. Tadolini has a stupendous voice, clear, limpid, powerful; and I want Lady Macbeth's voice to be hard, stifled, and somber."[54]

Wagner's willingness to sacrifice vocal facility for dramatic effect is evident from an early experience in the theater that exercised a lasting influence upon his development. Hearing the singer Wilhelmine Schröder-Devrient play Leonore in *Fidelio* served as a kind of revelation, and as a result he attributed to her his whole knowledge of dramatic art.[55] Wagner described this decisive moment in his life with a typically histrionic gesture of his own: "Nein! Sie hatte gar keine 'Stimme'" ("No! She had absolutely no 'voice'"), after which he elaborated the effect of her performance with these words: "But she knew how to use her breath so beautifully and through it to let a truly feminine soul stream out sounding so wonderful that one thought neither of singing nor of voice!"[56] Although Wagner was only sixteen when he first heard Schröder-Devrient, he was able to translate the experience into his own artistic practice not simply through the idea of a music-drama that he was to work out much later but also through the physical presence of this singer in his own early operas, whose roles of Adriano (in *Rienzi*), Senta, and Venus were created for her.

Unlike Verdi, who made no attempt to institutionalize his program beyond the example of his own works, Wagner in his voluminous writings rewrote the history of opera to justify his own theory and practice. For instance, he used the occasion of Spontini's death in 1851 to link this composer with the dramatic tra-

[54] Letter of November 23, 1848 (to S. Cammarano), ibid., p. 61. Just as Verdi objected to a fine voice doing Lady Macbeth, so he went out of his way to recommend three poor singers with theatrical presence for the part (albeit uncomposed) of Cordelia: "All three have weak voices but great talent, spirit, and theatrical feeling." Letter of November 11, 1856 (to V. Torelli), ibid., p. 197.
[55] See "Ueber Schauspieler und Sänger" in *Gesammelte Schriften*, XII, 376. See also Wagner, *Mein Leben*, ed. Martin Gregor-Dellin (Munich: List, 1969), I, 44–45.
[56] "Ueber Schauspieler und Sänger," p. 375.

dition established by Gluck and to condemn Rossini—once the most universally revered opera composer throughout Europe—as the man who betrayed this tradition.[57] In depicting the differences between Italian and French opera, Wagner even had some good words to say about Donizetti's French opera, *La Favorite*, which he found closer to the dramatic principle than this composer's Italian works because of its better delineation of characters and its subordination of the "trivial, monotonous and thousand-times worn-out" conventions associated with the Italians.[58]

Wagner not only rethought the history of opera—and in ways that we have accepted to this day—but his extensive participation in all aspects of the production of his own works, an activity unprecedented among composers, served to destroy the traditional hegemony of the singer in favor of an integrated dramatic whole.[59] To the extent that the dramatic principle still dominates our thinking about opera, the values that Wagner propagated have proved difficult to question or refute. Yet if we take his observations about Schröder-Devrient's vocal deficiencies too literally, the ideal opera would not demand any singing at all but would constitute some form of drama wholly dependent on gesture and expressive breathing. In actuality, of course, performative values play a central role even in those operas that lay claim to the dramatic principle. When we attend *Die Walküre* and *Tristan und Isolde*, we demand the utmost in vocal luster and power, for which we are more than willing to sacrifice dramatic skill and even an "interesting" production. *Otello*, as I pointed out earlier, retains many traditionally operatic elements, even though it seeks to "justify" them dramatically. By the same token, the early nineteenth-century Italian operas on which Verdi ultimately turned his back and that Wagner relegated to the dustheap of operatic history were often dramatic in intent or effect. It is known from contemporary accounts that some of Rossini's and Bellini's early performers such as Giuditta Pasta or Maria Malibran exercised a compelling dra-

---

[57] See "Nachruf an Spontini," in *Gesammelte Schriften*, VIII, 97–99.

[58] The typically French virtues he picks out as opposed to what he saw as the Italian vices are "more refined and noble execution of forms, a surer character delineation, above all the suppression of those trivial, monotonous, and thousand-times-worn-out supplements and conventional expedients." "Halévy und die Königin von Zypern," in *Gesammelte Schriften*, VIII, 85.

[59] See, for instance, his advice to prospective directors and singers of *Tannhäuser* in "Ueber die Aufführung des 'Tannhäuser,'" *Gesammelte Schriften*, IX, 31, 40.

matic power that must have been comparable to the power sought by their successor Maria Callas when she recreated their roles more than a century later.[60]

Those operas that have consciously observed what I call the dramatic principle are not necessarily better, or even more "dramatic," than many operas by Handel and Rossini. By invoking this principle, Wagner and Verdi, as well as Gluck before them, were able to establish a set of conventions different in emphasis from those prevalent in their time and, in fact, in their own early work. When Stravinsky, in *The Poetics of Music*, expressed his preference for the Verdi of *La traviata* over the later, more intellectually fashionable Verdi, he was implying that the conventions associated with the dramatic principle had themselves become worn out.[61] Although his own major opera, *The Rake's Progress*, self-consciously uses the "stop-and-go" conventions of eighteenth- and early nineteenth-century opera, it achieves its own form of dramatic integrity, as its inclusion within Kerman's limited canon attests.

The pervasiveness with which the dramatic principle has colored our conception of how operas should be composed and performed is symptomatic of our tendency to use the terminology of drama to confer respectability on other forms of art, and especially on music. One does not have to search far among discussions of nonoperatic, even nonvocal music to find the dramatic principle invoked. For instance, when the musicologist Edward T. Cone tells us that "a proper musical performance must . . . be a dramatic, even a theatrical event,"[62] most listeners would readily accept the linking of drama with instrumental music as a com-

[60] See, for instance, Stendhal's chapter on Pasta in his *Vie de Rossini* (Paris: Calmann-Lévy, n.d.), pp. 279–90.

[61] Stravinsky, *Poetics of Music*, p. 81. Stravinsky's preference for the early Verdi belongs to his polemic against Wagnerian music-drama. Note the following provocative remark: "There is more substance and true invention in the aria La donna è mobile . . . than in the rhetoric and vociferations of the *Ring*" (p. 81). The disparagement of *Falstaff*, likewise, is connected with Stravinsky's anti-Wagnerian program, as in the following remark: "How can we help regretting that this master [Verdi] of the traditional opera, at the end of a long life studded with so many authentic masterpieces, climaxed his career with *Falstaff*, which, if it is not Wagner's best work, is not Verdi's best opera either" (p. 81). Many years later Stravinsky qualified this remark with special praise for *Falstaff*, which he then paired with *Rigoletto* as the Verdi opera "I love best." See Stravinsky and Robert Craft, *Conversations with Stravinsky* (1959; rpt. Berkeley: University of California Press, 1980), pp. 74–75.

[62] Edward T. Cone, *Musical Form and Musical Performance* (New York: Norton, 1968), p. 13.

monplace. Charles Rosen, in his influential study of Haydn, Mozart, and Beethoven, uses the dramatic principle to distinguish the classical style from the baroque. The peculiarly dramatic innovation that marks this style off from its predecessor is an element that Rosen is able to pinpoint by means of musical analysis, namely the movement towards the dominant: "The difference between the Baroque movement toward the dominant and the classical modulation is not only one of degree: the classical style dramatizes this movement—in other words, it becomes an event as well as a directional force."[63] The term *drama* is flexible enough to be applied with rhetorical effectiveness to a wide variety of musical forms. Thus Jacques Barzun, attempting to extend the notion of program music backward in time from Berlioz, locates drama in the very style in which Rosen was to find it deficient: "Without reading any tale of adventure into Bach's chaconne for violin, we perceive in the succession of sounds an involvement of parts, a plot, akin to that of a drama."[64]

Reading music—or at least the music one means to praise—as drama is not simply a contemporary habit but something rooted in the same mode of thought that linked opera to the dramatic principle. It is not accidental that Wagner characteristically approaches the instrumental writings of earlier composers with a dramatic bias. Wagner's descriptions of the Eroica Symphony and the Coriolan Overture put such stress on the heroic actions he discerns in these works that they read almost like scenarios for an opera.[65] The dramatic analogy dominates his analyses even of pre-Beethoven music such as Gluck and Mozart overtures.[66] Underlying this way of reading music is the assumption that all good music has some sort of narrative program it attempts to express. As Michael Mann has pointed out, from the 1830s onwards such verbally oriented music critics as Hoffmann, Heine, and

[63] Charles Rosen, *The Classical Style: Haydn, Mozart, Beethoven* (1971; rpt. New York: Norton, 1972), p. 70.
[64] Jacques Barzun, *Berlioz and the Romantic Century*, 3d ed. (New York: Columbia University Press, 1969), I, 178. Note how Barzun reaches the term *drama* only gradually, through a series of nouns in apposition with one another. First he mentions "an involvement of parts," a notion we readily accept for describing a musical composition. This is quickly transformed into "plot," which shifts us from musical to literary discourse. Once we have accepted this shift, he can introduce the more encompassing literary term *drama*.
[65] See "Heroische Symphonie" and "Ouvertüre zu 'Coriolan'" in *Gesammelte Schriften*, IX, 110–14, 114–17.
[66] "Ueber die Ouvertüre" and "Glucks Ouvertüre zu 'Iphigenia in Aulis'" in *Gesammelte Schriften*, VII, 124–27, 132–33, and IX, 105.

Schumann described musical works as though they were a type of literature.[67] For example, Hoffmann's lengthy analysis of Beethoven's Fifth Symphony compares the musical organization of the symphony with the structure of a Shakespeare play.[68] Schumann approaches an overt piece of program music such as Berlioz's Fantastic Symphony with the observation that music has its origins in some ideal verbal domain: "It seems that music is returning again to its origins, where it has not yet become oppressed by the weight of the beat, to lift itself to an unrhymed poetry, to a higher poetic punctuation as in Greek choruses, Biblical language, and the prose of Jean Paul."[69] For Schumann, who constantly sought inspiration from the writers of his time for his own compositions, music quite clearly aspires to the condition of literature. It is only natural that composers with a literary bias would turn to great writers for the words to their vocal music or the programs for their instrumental pieces. Liszt expressed the sentiment of his time when he wrote, "Music in its masterpieces tends more and more to appropriate the masterpieces of literature."[70] For composers of the mid- and late nineteenth century the overt presence of great literature in a musical work served to endow the work with a cultural dimension and an intellectual substantiality to which music could not lay claim on its own. Although Schumann appropriated mainly the writers of the preceding generation—Byron, Heine, Hoffmann, Eichendorff, as well as Goethe—Berlioz and Liszt deliberately sought out works that they viewed as monuments of world literature, which for Berlioz included *The Aeneid*, Cellini's *Autobiography*, and *Faust*, while Liszt selected *The Divine Comedy*, *Hamlet*, and *Faust*. (The frequent appearance of *Faust*, whatever the musical genre to which it was accommodated, within the oeuvre of nineteenth-century composers suggests that Goethe's play early attained that aura of monumentality which guarantees a corresponding aura to its musical embodiment.)

If the analogy of music to drama should more properly be labeled an analogy to literature or to "poetry," as the Romantics conceived of the word, one might also note that those who invoke

---

[67] Michael Mann, *Heines Musikkritiken* (Hamburg: Hoffmann & Campe, 1971), pp. 19–21.

[68] See "Sinfonie pour 2 Violons . . . ," in Hoffmann, *Werke*, XIII, 43.

[69] In Georg Eismann, *Robert Schumann: Ein Quellenwerk über sein Leben und Schaffen* (Leipzig: Breitkopf & Härtel, 1956), II, 68.

[70] "Berlioz and His 'Harold' Symphony," quoted in *Source Readings in Music History*, ed. Oliver Strunk (New York: Norton, 1950), p. 868.

the analogy tend to stress the dramatic aspect of literature: music as expressive of strong emotion or as a dramatically conceived sequence of frequently unspecified narrative events. Berlioz himself advertised the Fantastic Symphony in dramatic terms as an opera without voices and described the symphony's "narrative" in the concert program. As he explained in his own program note, "The following program should be taken as the spoken text of an opera, designed to introduce certain pieces of music, of which it motivates the character and expressiveness."[71] By treating the symphony's narrative program as a libretto for an opera, of which the actual music he composed is simply the essence, Berlioz suggests a new genre that combines the mimetic qualities of literature—to which the accompanying program must serve as a guide—with the intensity that critics of his time had come to associate with music.

Literature and the Operatic Principle

The ascendancy of the dramatic principle in the development of nineteenth-century opera has its counterpart in the literature of the century in what one might call a corresponding "operatic principle." For Wagner and Verdi, the analogy to drama helped make operatic form more economical, more functional, more discernibly mimetic than they perceived it to be in earlier composers or in their own early work. By contrast, writers could consciously pursue an analogy to opera as a means of liberating themselves from the constraints they perceived in inherited dramatic forms. The operatic quality that Schiller attributed to the end of *Egmont* and that Goethe cultivated above all in the second part of *Faust* represents an attempt to break through the limitations of the theatrical forms available to him. If the dramatic principle stresses such qualities as spareness, realism, and decorousness, the operatic principle stresses such opposing qualities as verbal extravagance, an indifference or hostility to mimesis of the external world, and a tendency to the histrionic.

Among major writers who have cultivated the operatic principle, Walt Whitman and George Bernard Shaw are preeminent for their overt adaptation of what they saw as operatic techniques to create their own quite extravagant styles. The Italian and French operas that Whitman regularly attended in New York during the

---

[71] Quoted in Barzun, *Berlioz*, I, 197.

1840s and 1850s suggested a mode of discourse through which this poet could display the inner workings of the self more adequately than the poetic forms available to him allowed. "But for the opera I could never have written Leaves of Grass," he told a disciple in later years.[72] The antimimetic impetus that Whitman must have experienced at the opera has recently been interpreted in poststructuralist terms in a study of Nietzsche and Whitman: "For Whitman opera represented that simultaneous 'adequate objectification' and 'highest spiritualization and ideality,' that state of projecting at once the visible presence of self-evidential sign and the immediate intuitive conviction of music, which he wished his poetry to achieve."[73]

Similarly, Shaw, whose exposure to the medium both as a professional critic and as the son of an amateur singer was even more thorough than Whitman's, turned to opera as a means of transcending the limitations of a narrowly representational form, which for Shaw was the late nineteenth-century well-made realist play. The result, as Martin Meisel has shown in detail, was a dramatic style that, despite his overtly "realistic" settings and themes, organized the characters of a play according to an operatic model, conceived of verbal expression in the shape of aria and ensemble, and even lent itself, especially when Shaw directed his own plays, to a distinctly operatic type of acting.[74] As Shaw himself tells it, "Harley Granville-Barker was not far out when, at a

---

[72] Quoted by John Townsend Trowbridge in "Reminiscences of Walt Whitman," *Atlantic Monthly*, 89 (1902), 166. Whitman's relationship to opera has been thoroughly documented in many studies, among them Floyd Stovall, *The Foreground of "Leaves of Grass"* (Charlottesville: University of Virginia Press, 1974), pp. 79–100, and even in a full-length book, Robert D. Faner, *Walt Whitman and Opera* (Philadelphia: University of Pennsylvania Press, 1951). A statement similar to Whitman's about the shaping effect of opera on literary production can be found in Alfieri's autobiography. The great Italian dramatist claimed that he was so overwhelmed by the operas he attended that he conceived nearly all his tragedies either during operatic performances or soon thereafter: "And almost all my tragedies were conceived either in the act of hearing music or a few hours later." Vittorio Alfieri, *Vita*, ed. Giampaolo Dossena (Turin: Einaudi, 1967), p. 40.

[73] John T. Irwin, "Self-Evidence and Self-Reference: Nietzsche and Tragedy, Whitman and Opera," *New Literary History*, 11 (1979), 188.

[74] Martin Meisel, *Shaw and the Nineteenth-Century Theater* (Princeton: Princeton University Press, 1963), pp. 38–61. For Shaw's negative reaction to the more overtly theatrical aspects of nineteenth-century drama, see Jonas Barish, *The Antitheatrical Prejudice* (Berkeley: University of California Press, 1981), pp. 451–52. It seems ironic that Shaw used so theatrical a form as opera to oppose what he saw as the worn-out conventions of his own medium. By borrowing the forms of another medium (including forms that had become stale within the context of opera), he sought to renew those of his own.

rehearsal of one of my plays, he cried out 'Ladies and gentlemen: will you please remember that this is Italian opera.'"[75]

A writer's adherence to the operatic principle can serve his or her interpreters in much the same way as a composer's adherence to the dramatic principle. It can, for instance, help to place the writer within a larger historical context. Thus Shaw's pursuit of operatic style suggests a link with such otherwise alien figures as the Symbolist poets, who, like Shaw, used an analogy to musical discourse as a means of setting themselves apart from the realist ideology that had become dominant in late nineteenth-century culture. Similarly, Gluck's identification of his art with the dramatic principle links him to those late eighteenth-century tendencies that strove for economy, simplicity, and nobility in various forms of art. Just as important, a critic's recognition of the analogies an artist draws from other media can inhibit the futile, if all too frequent judgment that would castigate Goethe's *Faust* for "formlessness" or "Song of Myself" for "self-indulgence" or would find *Otello* and *Parsifal* wanting for their lack of melody and their inability to allow a display of traditional vocal technique.

For the more high-minded critic, though not necessarily for the general public, a composer's advocacy of the dramatic principle has been a cause for praise, while, on the contrary, a writer's use of the operatic principle (whether conscious or not) has often provided an occasion for disparagement. Early in this chapter I quoted Shaw's statement that Victor Hugo's "chief glory . . . as a stage poet was to have provided libretti for Verdi." In the near-century that has passed since Shaw's remark, Hugo's reputation as a dramatist (as well as the reputations of all of his contemporary dramatists except for Musset) has not improved significantly from the disparagement of the Romantic drama that Shaw intended. Indeed, it has become a convention of scholarly studies in this field for critics to point out the specifically operatic elements in the plays and to deprecate these plays in favor of the operas they inspired. Charles Affron, for instance, introduces his study of the theater of Hugo and Musset with the honest admission that "the only form of romantic theatre which has survived on the stage is the opera."[76] W. D. Howarth, in his analysis of *Hernani*, pinpoints the operatic quality of the French Romantic drama by means of a

[75] Preface to *London Music in 1888–89* in Laurence, *Shaw's Music,* I, 57.

[76] Charles Affron, *A Stage for Poets: Studies in the Theatre of Hugo and Musset* (Princeton: Princeton University Press, 1971), p. 8.

contrast with the Classical drama, which he characterizes by its linear development and by the fact that "soliloquies normally fulfilled a dialectical function; in place of this, we have a structure in which 'plot' is a framework for a series of solos and duets, arias and recitatives of a very much more static nature."[77] Writing of the French Romantic melodrama, Peter Brooks points out the insufficiency of the nonmusical monologues: "The monologue, we detect, is on its way to becoming operatic aria—and melodrama finds one possible logical outcome in grand opera (which didn't in fact use many libretti from melodrama), where melody and harmony, as much as the words, are charged with conveying meaning."[78] Hugo himself was certainly aware of the operatic principle underlying the type of drama he advocated when, in his preface to *Cromwell*, he spoke of the dramatist as "employing the fascinations of opera," by which he meant the whole spectacular element that French Classical tragedy had rigorously excluded.[79]

French Romantic drama is not the only body of writing whose limitations have been defined by critics invoking the analogy to opera. The validity of Schiller's comment on the ending of *Egmont* is demonstrated by the incidental music that Beethoven later composed for the play: when we hear Egmont speak his fiery final monologue against the heroic orchestral music in the background, we recognize that Goethe's words alone were insufficient to create the effect towards which the play was moving. Wagner developed Schiller's remark to distinguish between the realm of politics (the usual focus of historical drama) and the musical realm, towards which he saw Goethe's play gravitating.[80] Just as Wagner, as I indicated earlier, sought out the dramatic qualities in instrumental compositions in order to assert the centrality of the dramatic principle to music, so he sought analogies to musical form in certain plays he admired—as though to imply that the achievement of his own new and higher mode of opera was the culmination of what great dramatists had been aiming for all along.

---

[77] W. D. Howarth, *Sublime and Grotesque: A Study of French Romantic Drama* (London: Harrap, 1975), pp. 164–65.

[78] Peter Brooks, *The Melodramatic Imagination: Balzac, Henry James, Melodrama, and the Mode of Excess* (New Haven: Yale University Press, 1976), p. 49.

[79] Hugo's mention of opera is part of his definition and defense of what he calls "le drame romantique." See preface to *Cromwell*, in Hugo, *Théâtre complet*, ed. J.-J. Thierry and J. Mélèze, I (Paris: Gallimard, 1963), p. 450.

[80] See *Oper und Drama*, pt. 2, sec. 4, p. 178n. It is worth noting that Wagner objects to Beethoven's setting music for the political element of the play ("die politisch-prosaische Exposition") rather than simply concentrating on the ending.

Thus Wagner treated Goethe's *Iphigenie auf Tauris* as a musical composition that lends itself to an approach similar to that of a piece by Beethoven;[81] for Wagner, Goethe's achievement, in *Iphigenie* and other plays, lay in creating a mythical structure that could avoid the contingencies we associate with ordinary historical narrative.

The operatic analogy has often served modern critics not merely to point out insufficiencies in literary works but also as a means of helping readers understand and appreciate works that do not consort easily with modern taste. Arthur Kirsch has used it, for instance, to defend Dryden's heroic plays, whose extravagant language and violent twists and turns of plot are the product of a poet who also happened to write texts intended for musical composition.[82] In his recent book *Romantic Opera and Literary Form*, Peter Conrad calls Goethe's *Faust* an "opera without music,"[83] though one might add that this work has doubtless invited many more musical settings (whether in symphonic or operatic form, not to speak of the settings of its individual lyrics) than any French Romantic play. Wilhelm Emrich employs the operatic analogy as a sophisticated critical tool to demonstrate how Goethe characteristically resolves tragic situations and transcends the limitations of the literary genres he was reworking.[84]

Extending and Testing Boundaries

Although opera has been used to illuminate only limited segments of the literary canon, certain musical terms have gained considerable currency as a way of explaining, often even of enhancing the prestige of literary phenomena. The term *counterpoint*, for example, has been much employed in the metrical anal-

---

[81] See ibid., sec. 1, p. 131.

[82] Arthur Kirsch, *Dryden's Heroic Drama* (Princeton: Princeton University Press, 1965), p. 151n. One might note that Dryden himself, in his preface to *The Conquest of Granada*, traced the origin of the mode back to the operas that Davenant wrote during the Cromwell period, "it being forbidden [him] in the Rebellious times to act Tragedies and Comedies." See Dryden, *Works*, XI, ed. John Loftis and David S. Rodes (Berkeley: University of California Press, 1978), pp. 9, 440.

[83] Peter Conrad, *Romantic Opera and Literary Form* (Berkeley: University of California Press, 1977), p. 71.

[84] Wilhelm Emrich, *Die Symbolik von Faust II: Sinn und Vorformen* (Bonn: Athenäum, 1957), see especially pp. 72–75, 79–80, 82–87, 116, 294, and 359–61. For the use of the operatic analogy in both Goethe's and Schiller's criticism as a means of transcending the limitations of earlier mimetic theories, see Gloria Flaherty, *Opera in the Development of German Critical Thought* (Princeton: Princeton University Press, 1978), pp. 296–300.

ysis of English poetry—with varying degrees of relevance and precision—ever since Hopkins used it.[85] Bakhtin's use of the term *polyphony* to describe a multiplicity of voices speaking through Dostoevsky's novels has, in recent years, exercised considerable influence on the theory and analysis of narrative.[86] The effect of such musical analogies is generally to broaden our sense of literary possibility, to suggest a nonverbal dimension beyond what we ordinarily take to be the realm of literature. Even the term *operatic*, despite the disparaging overtones that often accompany its application to literary works, implies an opening outwards, a kind of escape from the boundaries of ordinary literary discourse. Above all, the use of musical terms serves to transfer some of the non-rational qualities traditionally associated with music to the predominantly rational orientation with which critics have tended to define literary discourse.[87]

By the same token, terms drawn from literary criticism lend their own color to discussions of music. During the Renaissance the prestige of classical rhetoric encouraged the use of literary terminology (with its resulting literary bias) in humanist theorizing on music.[88] Stravinsky's use of the title *The Poetics of Music* for his Norton lectures was an ideological gesture intended to stress a theoretical dimension within literature that provides an alternative to the more overtly expressive literary situations exploited by late nineteenth-century composers. As one goes through the major music criticism of the last two centuries, one quickly becomes aware of the large number of literary terms employed. Note, for instance, how thoroughly the statements by Shaw quoted at the start of this chapter are rooted in the traditional discourse of literary criticism: "not because an opera is less *credible* than a spoken play"; "in the opera he is equally *sublime* in feeling"; "the superior *intensity* of musical expression." If music has periodically laid claim to be the language of the passions, its expositors have often had to go to literary discourse, as Shaw does with

---

[85] For some cautions on the use of this and other terms, see John Hollander, *Vision and Resonance* (New York: Oxford University Press, 1975), pp. 21–22.

[86] See Mikhail Bakhtin, *Problems of Dostoevsky's Poetics*, trans. R. W. Rotsel (Ann Arbor, Mich.: Ardis, 1973), esp. pp. 4–8.

[87] For a useful survey of research on the interrelations of musical and literary ways of thinking, see Steven Paul Scher, "Literature and Music," in *Interrelations of Literature*, ed. Jean-Pierre Barricelli and Joseph Gibaldi (New York: Modern Language Association of America, 1982), pp. 225–50.

[88] See James Anderson Winn, *Unsuspected Eloquence* (New Haven: Yale University Press, 1981), pp. 156–79.

the terms *sublime* and *intensity*, to find a vocabulary to substantiate this claim. And they have also drawn on literary discourse to find many of the derogatory terms to explain what they see as the inadequacies of particular musical works. Since the status of opera has hovered uncertainly between the musical and the literary realms, those who have sought to disparage opera in favor of literature have found a ready supply of ammunition among the many negative terms available to literary critics. Even the greatest operas—at least the noncomic ones—have on occasion been labeled "melodramatic," their actions condemned for lack of "verisimilitude," their dramatis personae dismissed for their "black-and-white characterization."

For the composer or poet, the interchange of terms between opera and drama has obviously had a liberating function. Gluck's adoption of the dramatic principle, for instance, provided a means for the composer to liberate himself from the *opera seria* style, which, though he had composed successfully in this mode for years, he could dismiss as "ridiculous and tedious."[89] Although it is usual to describe Gluck's reform through the arguments he himself used—the need for verisimilitude, naturalness, direct imitation of the passions—one can also describe it in terms of the Russian formalist notion that artistic forms evolve through the perception, by audiences and artists alike, that an older form has "worn itself out" once its effects have come to seem "automatic." Gluck's turn to what must have appeared as starkly simple drama in relation to *opera seria* was a way of "deautomatizing" the response of his audience, just as Stravinsky's return to the "stop-and-go" alternation of formal recitatives and arias was a statement that by the mid–twentieth century the convention of *durchkomponierte* opera had come to seem worn out. Similarly, though students of American literature take Whitman at his word when he turns away from writing "poems distilled from other poems" in favor of a "medium that shall well nigh express the inexpressible,"[90] one can also view his formal innovations as an attempt, partly inspired by the grandness of gesture and the extravagance of the operatic model, to transcend the limitations of worn-out metrical conventions.

An artist's use of another medium serves functions similar to his or her use of different genres within the same medium. When

[89] Dedication of *Alceste*, p. 142.
[90] Walt Whitman, *Leaves of Grass*, ed. Sculley Bradley and Harold W. Blodgett (New York: Norton, 1973), p. 730.

we define Wagner's place in the history of opera, we refer not only to the dramatic model so conspicuous in both his theory and practice but also to the symphonic model that he applied to operatic form.[91] Both models served similar purposes, for the instrumental music developed by Beethoven and Berlioz offered a model of dramatic form that Wagner found more usable than the type of dramatic action that characterized Italian and French opera of the 1830s and 1840s. Within literary history it is common to note the transformation of a genre through the infusion of the techniques and even the central underlying assumptions of another, wholly different genre. Thus, we speak of the "lyrical novel" as a phenomenon of early twentieth-century literature;[92] or we classify a poem spoken by a single consciousness as a "dramatic lyric";[93] or we can read the powerful recent slogan "epic theater" as an express challenge to a generic distinction that had reigned in the critical tradition since Aristotle.

It is typical of every genre to test its boundaries by absorbing, even flaunting, those characteristic features of other genres whose distance from it has ordinarily seemed essential to its own generic identity. Pastoral poetry, for example, has been conspicuous for its ability to evoke the world of epic at the same time that it has acknowledged the gap that separates it from that world. When Milton in "Lycidas," announces, "That strain I heard was of a higher mood" (l. 87), he refers to his attempt a few lines before to digress into a language and subject matter "higher" than the poem's pastoral mode would ordinarily allow. When, at the end of the poem, he allows his narrator to bid farewell to his sheep in ottava rima, a form his readers would have associated with Renaissance epic, he provides a generic signal to tell us that his pastoral has come to an end as well as to suggest that his poetic career will take the traditional course from pastoral to heroic poetry. The intrusion of epic into Milton's pastoral poem is a means of testing, even relocating the boundaries of the pastoral mode. Similarly, Mozart and Da Ponte constantly test the boundaries of comic opera in *Don Giovanni*. The three masked figures who appear ominously to interrupt Don Giovanni's ball represent an intrusion of *opera seria*

---

[91] Note the title of the chapter on Wagner, "Opera as Symphonic Poem," in Kerman, *Opera as Drama*, pp. 192–216.

[92] See Ralph Freedman, *The Lyrical Novel* (Princeton: Princeton University Press, 1963).

[93] This was, of course, the title that Robert Browning gave to his 1842 volume of poems.

into a predominantly comic context. The confrontation between comic and *seria* worlds is so potent throughout *Don Giovanni* that later commentators, uncertain of this opera's precise generic identity, plunder it for whatever "tragic" meanings they can locate.[94]

The testing of boundaries separating genres within a particular medium is no different in kind from the testing that goes on between opera and those literary genres against which it has periodically sought to define itself. To cite a pithy remark by a recent theorist of genres, "Transgressions *mark* boundaries."[95] Thus Milton's testing of the boundaries of pastoral or Mozart's of comic opera serves to underscore the generic identity of each form. If the present chapter has stressed the differences between opera and spoken drama, it has also attempted to show that opera has periodically renewed itself by emulating what it took to be the principles underlying spoken drama. Similarly, spoken drama has renewed itself by cultivating features we have come to associate with opera. When Shaw wrote, "*Othello* is a play written by Shakespear in the style of Italian opera,"[96] he did not of course mean that Shakespeare was imitating the new medium that, at the time of the play, had manifested itself only in a few courtly entertainments of a type still unknown outside Italy. Shaw had in mind

[94] The classic "tragic" interpretation is doubtless E. T. A. Hoffmann's brilliant narrative entitled "Don Juan" (in *Werke*, I, 72–83). On a more popular level of interpretation, the "tragic" approach to the opera is evident in the fact that for much of its performance history the opera ended with Don Giovanni's fiery death, with the comic epilogue omitted. As often happens in the history of interpretation, those nineteenth-century critics and impresarios who proposed a tragic view of the work were no longer aware of the conventions that the composer and his librettist followed. Figures from *opera seria* intruded not only into Don Juan operas before Mozart's but also into many comic operas of the eighteenth century. As Stefan Kunze has shown, some of the operas on the Don Juan theme before Mozart's work end with the main character's death and have no epilogue. Neither this ending nor the appearance of *seria* characters, whether in Mozart's or his predecessors' operas, would have altered an eighteenth-century audience's view of these works as essentially comic rather than tragic. After all, as Kunze reminds us, a happy ending was still the norm in *opera seria*. By contrast, the nineteenth century preferred to view *Don Giovanni* as tragic—a fact evident not only in nineteenth-century staging and critical interpretation of this opera but also in new plays on the theme. See Kunze, *Don Giovanni vor Mozart: Die Tradition der Don-Giovanni-Opern im italienischen Buffa-Theater des 18. Jahrhunderts* (Munich: Wilhelm Fink, 1972), pp. 55–58, 120–27.

[95] In Gary Saul Morson, *The Boundaries of Genre: Dostoevsky's "Diary of a Writer" and the Traditions of Literary Utopia* (Austin: University of Texas Press, 1981), p. 52. The chapter entitled "Threshold Art" (pp. 39–68) is especially relevant to my own discussion of boundary testing.

[96] "A Word More about Verdi" in Laurence, *Shaw's Music*, III, 579.

the Italian operas he had himself grown up on and that were later to help him shape his own dramatic style. What his statement tells us about Shakespeare is that *Othello* cultivates a verbal musicality and a flamboyance of characterization that set it apart from, say, *Hamlet* or *King Lear*.

Although Shaw's remarks may help us locate *Othello*'s individuality within the Shakespeare canon, no audience would ever confuse it with Verdi's *Otello*, not to speak of the Rossini version that Verdi's displaced. The operatic quality that Shaw attributes to Shakespeare's play finds its complement in the dramatic qualities we customarily praise in Verdi's operatic embodiment. And since we can isolate these qualities by contrasting the Verdi opera with Rossini's (not to speak of a multitude of other operas on other themes in the early and mid–nineteenth century), it is only natural that what we have come to call "opera as drama" should find itself realized in Verdi's great score.[97] Yet if Verdi in his late style managed to cloak the more overt gestures we customarily label "operatic" under the guise of a dramatic principle, his *Otello*, as I have suggested at several points in this chapter, remains steadfastly rooted in those forms of musical expression that we associate with opera: just as all major artists reconstitute the genres in which they work, Verdi, like Gluck and Wagner, has applied a particular—and also rather austere—idea of drama to rethink the possibilities of opera. In the very act of subordinating its "operatic" nature to spoken drama, opera has not merely borrowed from the prestige that belongs to the literary realm but, as I have argued throughout this section, it has also periodically, and powerfully, succeeded in asserting its own identity.

[97] For a brief comparison of passages in the Rossini and Verdi versions, see Kerman, *Opera as Drama*, pp. 144–45.

[2]

Opera as Representation:
I. Opera as a Mixed Genre

The Multiplicity of Operatic Discourse

Interacting Worlds

Thus far I have stressed the gap that separates musical from spoken drama, even in those instances when one medium seeks to extend itself into the other's acknowledged territory. The present chapter, by contrast, will stress the ways that opera has self-consciously absorbed the representational forms not only of spoken drama but of its own earlier styles and of other arts as well. Indeed, since its beginnings opera has proved shameless in expropriating forms of discourse from virtually all other arts to articulate its meanings. One could speak of opera's penchant for drawing within itself those forms that at any given moment seem alien to its audience's expectations. When Stravinsky set *Oedipus Rex* in Latin, he sought to jar an audience accustomed to hear its ancient myths translated into modern languages; yet the defamiliarization he achieved, though unique through its deliberate use of a dead language, in spirit was thoroughly consonant with other major innovative moments that mark the history of opera.

To cite another example contemporary with *Oedipus Rex*, Arnold Schönberg's major operatic work, *Moses und Aron*, contrasts its two central figures through the strikingly different levels of discourse in which they express themselves. Whereas Moses speaks throughout in *Sprechstimme*, a mode characterized by only minimal changes in voice pitch, Aron displays an ornate tenor coloratura. We recognize Moses as a figure out of spoken drama who pits himself against the operatic values represented by his brother and the crowd whom Aron tempts away from divinely prescribed ways. The awesome, protesting bass speaking voice of Moses comes to stand for uprightness against the florid operatic voice of Aron, whom we associate with the dangers of political manipulation and anarchy. The two opposing levels of discourse, one musical, the other dramatic, articulate the conflicting moral codes of Schönberg's opera.

In the course of this chapter I shall extend this point to suggest a larger framework within which we can speak of musical and dramatic interactions. I shall also explore some of the ways in which musical dramatists have exploited such interactions to absorb a diversity of discourses within individual works. For speculative purposes I shall substitute the word *operatic* for *musical*, and *verbal* for *dramatic*. I can thus suggest two extremes of a spectrum: at one end, let us associate what I call *operatic* with such terms as *histrionic, extravagant, gestural, ceremonial,* and *performative*, and let us view its central intent not so much as the imitation of an external world as the achievement of the maximum possible effect on the audience. At the other end let us link the word *verbal* to such terms as *literary, restrained, referential, mimetic,* and to an intention that subordinates potency of effect to the correspondence we are meant to see between the work and the world it claims to reflect.

If we look at any two works—whether musical or spoken drama—in juxtaposition to each other, one of these is always likely to seem closer to the operatic end of the spectrum than the other. Shaw's comparison, cited in the preceding chapter, between Verdi's settings and the plays by Hugo on which they were based, obviously, if also tautologically, shows the operas to be more operatic than their literary models. Yet Hugo's plays seem thoroughly operatic if we view them in relation to the French classical dramas with which they implicitly invited comparison when they were first produced. Similarly, the term *operatic* is applied, as I indicated earlier, to Dryden's heroic plays, with an implied contrast either to Elizabethan drama or the French classical tragedies contemporary with them. But if we look at a Racine play next to a play from Ibsen's realistic period, Racine, with his duets between hero and confidant and his arialike *tirades*, easily invites the term *operatic*. However much Shaw thought his work to emanate from the quintessence of Ibsenism, he could also assent proudly, as I pointed out in the last chapter, to Granville-Barker's labeling his plays "Italian opera."

Along the scale I have suggested any two dramatists, indeed any two writers, appear relatively more or less "operatic" in relation to one another. I am concerned here primarily with appearances, not with whatever "realities" one can discern behind them, for the traditions that critics and audiences construct and the distinctions they make within the various arts are determined by how works and their creators appear to them at any given moment in history. Thus Dickens looks distinctly operatic to us in comparison, say, with his contemporary George Eliot, and Whitman in comparison with Tennyson. Within the oeuvre of a single writer certain works seem conspicuously operatic in a way that others do not. Goethe's *Faust* invites the operatic analogy as his severely neoclassical *Die natürliche Tochter* emphatically does not; the second part of *Faust*, written in a different literary mode and at a much later date than the first part, appears considerably more operatic in character than this earlier part. Shaw's remark, quoted in the preceding chapter, that Shakespeare's *Othello* was "written . . . in the style of Italian opera" implicitly sets the play at an extreme from *Coriolanus*, a work notable for its lack of those particular qualities that I have associated here with the term *operatic*.

In his preface to *Die ägyptische Helena*, one of the most overtly operatic texts that he prepared for Strauss, Hofmannsthal characterized Shakespeare's plays as "pure operas." "With Shakespeare the word is always expression, never information,"[1] Hofmannsthal writes with the intention of separating Shakespeare's language from what he calls the psychological dialogue of nineteenth-century realist drama. The expressiveness of Shakespeare's language is thus close to those ceremonial and affective qualities that I placed at the operatic extreme of the scale, while the informational quality that Hofmannsthal sees as central to realist drama can be associated with the mimetic orientation at the verbal extreme. It is significant that directly after designating Shakespeare's plays as operas, Hofmannsthal associates Shakespeare with Aeschylus and separates both from Euripides, whom he links with the realistic conveyers of information.[2] In each instance, first with Aeschylus, then with Shakespeare, Hofmannsthal suggests a moment of dramatic expressiveness that he

---

[1] Preface to *Die ägyptische Helena* in Hugo von Hofmannsthal, *Prosa*, ed. Herbert Steiner, IV (Frankfurt: Fischer, 1955), p. 458.

[2] "In this sense Shakespeare wrote genuine operas; he is fully with Aeschylus and miles removed from Euripides." Ibid.

characterizes as operatic and that is followed by a decline in the shape of a more rational yet also more impoverished type of drama.

Hofmannsthal is, of course, playing on the traditional German distinction between Aeschylus and Euripides that goes back at least to the Romantics and that received a powerful new impetus in Nietzsche's *Birth of Tragedy*, which describes the decline in dramatic power after Aeschylus as part of a larger cultural decline associated with Socratic rationalism; as Nietzsche's theory goes, this rationalism put an end to that fragile balance of Dionysian and Apollonian which prevailed for its brief and glorious moment in an earlier Greece. It is often forgotten that the full title of Nietzsche's treatise is *Die Geburt der Tragödie aus dem Geiste der Musik* and that the spirit of music that Nietzsche saw presiding at the birth of tragedy is central to its rebirth, symbolized in the final part of his treatise by the presence of a new mode of art, Wagnerian music-drama, in which, particularly with *Tristan und Isolde*, the Dionysian quality of passionate audience engagement is to offer a model for cultural rebirth after two millenia of rationalistic dominance and emotional deprivation. In terms of the scale that I have suggested, the history of drama thus takes the form of a precipitous decline from an "operatic" fullness present at its birth to a "verbal" emptiness that it remains for the new music-drama to overcome.

I have brought up Nietzsche not to extend my own notions of musical drama towards a theory of culture but to indicate how easily a remark such as Hofmannsthal's on the operatic nature of Shakespeare's and Aeschylus's plays suggests—indeed can be confused with—a larger context of ethical and cultural values. If we ignore these cultural implications, it is possible to look at Shakespeare's plays for the widely varying degree to which they exploit the range between what I call verbal and operatic extremes. One can pinpoint Shakespeare's way of placing operatic elements within an essentially nonoperatic context through noting how Verdi, in his last two works, sought to focus upon the contrast that he (or his librettist Boito) sensed in the original plays. In both *Othello* and *The Merry Wives of Windsor*, Verdi found a potentially operatic central character who is put to the test within a relatively nonoperatic context. The progress of Verdi's character Otello, for instance, can be charted as a movement from his grand-style entrance and the romantic sentiments he expresses in his love duet to the degradation that reduces him to the silence of a dead faint by the end of the third act; only with his final words after Desdemona's death is he able, like his Shakespearean original, retrospectively to capture something of his earlier heroism. The bravura of Falstaff's musical statements, together with the traditional operatic vengefulness with which his "rival" Ford voices his jealousy, becomes a perfect foil for the comic tricks that the wives, who in their mad musical chatter seem at least as cunning as they are merry, keep improvising in the course of the opera.

Throughout his career Shakespeare himself played operatic characters and situations against their opposites. For example, the contrast between Richard II and Bolingbroke, or between the worlds of Egypt and Rome in *Antony and Cleopatra*, allowed him to explore the interaction between those values that I have called operatic and other values that one might variously characterize as prosaic, discursive, political, or worldly. In Antony, Shakespeare created a character who participates in both extremes—on the one hand, the Antony who marries Octavia and makes his temporary peace with Rome; on the other hand, the Antony whom we come to associate with mysterious music emanating from under the stage and who, after his death, assumes divine attributes through the language with which Cleopatra mythologizes him.

Whether in Shakespeare or in Verdi's last operas, this interaction of diverse worlds helps define a certain form of drama which, whether in musical or spoken form, contrasts and examines values that we recognize to be at opposing ends of the scale that I have suggested. The three operas that Mozart wrote to Da Ponte's texts, *Le nozze di Figaro*, *Don Giovanni*, and *Così fan tutte*, exploit a similar interaction of contrasting worlds, an interaction that we discover through the differing musical and dramatic styles of their various characters. Each of these operas introduces characters out of eighteenth-century *opera seria* into a larger context governed by comic conventions. In discussing the crossing of generic boundaries in the preceding chapter, I referred to the powerful scene in which the three masked figures—Donna Anna, Don Ottavio, and Donna Elvira—enter Don Giovanni's ball uninvited and intent on vengeance. Throughout this scene we are made both visually and aurally aware of a clash of conflicting worlds, one of these conventionally operatic, the other resting on a comic, realistic base. The arias sung by the *opera seria* characters in Mozart's later comic operas are based on the standard subjects and musical styles that Mozart had himself used in his earlier works in the *seria* genre: demands for vengeance, boastfulness about one's constancy, longings for the possession of a beloved. Within the comic contexts into which they are introduced, these arias, as well as the characters for whom they become vehicles to express emotion, seem conspicuously operatic.

To varying degrees we are meant to see these arias as parodies— of a musical style or of a character who sings in this style, sometimes of both at once. The florid aria in which Fiordiligi in *Così fan tutte* declares herself constant as a rock is at once a parody of a constancy aria and an ironic examination of a character whose constancy is about to be tested, and, as it turns out, lost. At the same time, I might add that we are meant to enjoy the aria for its sheer virtuosity, since our consciousness of the intended parodistic effect in no way detracts from the sensuous pleasure that a distinguished performance of this most difficult aria offers its listeners. Within the operatic realm, exaggeration and histrionic effect can be fully consonant with aesthetic pleasure. In a shrewd discussion of the centrality of exaggeration within opera, Theodor Adorno has written, "The closer opera gets to a parody of itself, the closer it is to the principle most inherent to it."[3] Mozart's parodies, of course, work in a most intricate way, for they are directed at a style alien to the opera's comic base, while at the same time they work to define the characters' roles within the comic action.

It is surely no accident that those who ordinarily scoff at opera as a vulgar form are often willing to lavish praise on the Mozart– Da Ponte operas, as well as the two Verdi–Boito operas, and also on occasional modern examples of operatic self-consciousness such as the Strauss-Hofmannsthal *Ariadne auf Naxos* and the Stravinsky–Auden/Kallman *Rake's Progress*. In all these examples the juxtaposition of diverse forms of operatic discourse enables the composer to reflect ironically on the particular notions that these forms are meant to embody. If I have made a point of naming the librettist with the composer in each instance, I do so because these operas represent collaborations of a major composer with a dramatist or poet of sufficient cunning to suggest a musical situation with the type of complexity on which literary intellectuals in our time have placed special value. Yet this collision of diverse worlds of musical discourse by no means represents the mainstream of operatic tradition, any more than the analogous colli-

---

[3] "Bürgerliche Oper" in Adorno, *Gesammelte Schriften*, XVI, ed. Rolf Tiedemann (Frankfurt: Suhrkamp, 1978), p. 24.

sion of diverse worlds of verbal discourse in Shakespeare represents any central great tradition in drama.

Still, the interaction of worlds that I have suggested in these examples can be related to an aspect of musical discourse applicable to opera in general. I refer to the fact that every operatic style employs varying forms that are meant to contrast strikingly with one another. Note for instance Monteverdi's famous declaration, in the foreword to his Eighth Book of Madrigals (1638), that he had added a third and more heroic level of discourse, the *concitato* ("agitated"), to supplement the two levels, the *molle* ("soft") and *temperato* ("moderate"), that he had located in earlier composers.[4] For Monteverdi the *concitato* form was necessary to depict warlike situations, for which no composer before him had found an adequate language. Each of these three levels corresponds with what Monteverdi sees as "the principal passion or affection of our mind,"[5] respectively wrath (the *concitato*), temperance (the *temperato*), and humility or prayer (the *molle*). Monteverdi dates the introduction of the *concitato* style to the battle music in his miniopera *Il combattimento di Tancredi e Clorinda*, and he sees his achievement as a way of "putting into music the two contrary passions of war, namely, prayer and death."[6] Within the history of opera, his innovation is comparable to Aeschylus's introduction of a second actor: in the latter case there is a confrontation between opposing actors who represent contrasting points of view, in the former a confrontation between opposing musical styles that correspond to "contrary" passions. If Aeschylus thus made possible the dramatic action out of which our theatrical tradition is built, Monteverdi created a type of musical action that remained within opera even during the nearly three centuries when his own works were not heard.

Gradations of Musical Intensity

Monteverdi's development of a heroic musical style in contrast to the two less elevated styles he lists in his foreword suggests a distinction in his mind between more intense and less intense

---

[4]Monteverdi, *Tutte le opere*, ed. G. Francesco Malipiero, VIII (Asolo: n.p., 1929), unnumbered page before p. 1. An English version appears in *Source Readings in Music History*, ed. Oliver Strunk (New York: Norton, 1950), pp. 413–15.
[5]Monteverdi, *Tutte le opere*, VIII, unnumbered page before p. 1.
[6]Ibid.

forms of discourse. It is as though he recognized that dramatic action could be realized in musical terms only through sharply divergent degrees of intensity. To the degree that his *concitato* manner represents a "high" style, it could be called relatively more "operatic" than the other two styles in which he is writing. It was not of course until after his time that opera developed the sharply alternating degrees of intensity we associate with the division between aria and recitative. By the late seventeenth century it had become natural to view opera as a binary form: thus, the essentially "operatic" aria makes possible the expression of passion, the achievement of musical climaxes, and the opportunity for vocal virtuosity, while the more "verbal" recitative was relegated to plot exposition, to the realization of low points against which subsequent high points could be defined, and to periods of relative rest from vocal exertion. However one might describe each side of the binary pattern, the perception of difference between the two sides remained primary. For instance, Dryden, in his preface to his libretto for a now forgotten opera, *Albion and Albanius* (1685), employed a gender analogy to define the two sides: "To distinguish yet more justly, The recitative part of the *Opera* requires a more masculine Beauty of expression and sound: the other, which (for want of a proper *English* Word) I must call *The Songish Part*, must abound in the softness and variety of Numbers; its principal Intention, being to please the Hearing, rather than to gratify the understanding."[7]

The fact that an eighteenth-century *opera seria* consists largely of the alternation of recitative and aria allows any deviation from the norm to create a potentially powerful effect. Ensembles, including choruses, were rare, and even duets were used sparingly; yet when any of these did occur, the audience, as far as one can speculate on a form alien to modern taste, was likely to greet them with a feeling of relief from the seemingly endless alternation of recitatives and arias. It is not accidental that a duet or brief chorus was often used to end an opera or an act, for only a marked deviation from the norm that an audience has experienced throughout a long act or even a whole work could provide an unmistakable sense of closure.[8] The great quartet that Mozart placed

[7] Dryden, *Works*, XV, ed. Earl Miner (Berkeley: University of California Press, 1976), p. 4.
[8] Although each of the various arias that fill an act ends on a cadence, the many cadences that an audience hears in the course of the act demand a closure different in kind at the conclusion of the act.

in the last act of *Idomeneo* broke the accustomed bounds of the genre as emphatically as any innovation he could have introduced.

Although recitative and aria create the dichotomy out of which an *opera seria* is shaped, most examples of the genre actually have two forms of recitative, each of them defined according to its mode of accompaniment. The more common is, of course, the *secco*, or harpsichord type, while the second, the *accompagnato*, employs the orchestra to support the voice. Wherever we have both types of recitative, we can speak of a threefold gradation in operatic intensities: the orchestrally accompanied recitative represents a heightening of passion over the *secco*, while the arias retain their "operatic" primacy over both forms of recitative. The predominance of the *secco* is so strong that the sudden appearance of the *accompagnato* can sometimes affect an audience almost as powerfully as a chorus or a duet. For example, the great *recitativo accompagnato* in which the hero of Handel's *Giulio Cesare* eulogizes Pompey at his grave achieves a majesty of impact that would have proved difficult to create in an aria, if only because arias appear in this and other *opere serie* with consistent regularity. What would seem a lower level of intensity can thus function more powerfully than a manifestly "higher" level, by virtue of the fact that the former occurs rarely and the latter has become too familiar.

If *opera seria* provides a comparatively simple paradigm for the gradation of levels of discourse, Italian opera of the early nineteenth century, though as rigorous in its conventions as any other operatic form, reveals, when compared to the opera of the preceding century, a distinct pluralization of the levels of operatic discourse. The sharp division of arias into andante and *cabaletta* segments enables the audience to expect sharply divergent types of emotion—like the contrast of Cordelia's love and her desire for vengeance that Verdi envisioned for his *Lear* opera. The verbal extreme of the spectrum remains an orchestrally accompanied recitative, yet the most interesting operas of the period offer quite divergent musical resources to create their more operatically elevated moments. For these moments occur not simply in the arias but in the choruses, the larger ensembles at the end of each act, and the smaller groupings such as duets or sextets. The most inventive operas of the period succeed in finding a variety of heightened situations, each of which, at the time we experience it, is meant to suggest a renewed moment of intensification. The scene in Bellini's *Norma* in which the heroine contemplates killing her children is neither an ordinary recitative nor an aria but a dramatic form of musical expression that stands out sharply from the surrounding musical context like a *recitativo accompagnato* in *opera seria*. The mad scenes that Bellini wrote for the heroine of *I puritani*, and Donizetti soon after for *Lucia di Lammermoor*, build upon the conventional aria of the era, yet at the same time they attempt to outdo the andante/*cabaletta* form in virtuosity and dramatic intensity.

Although we are accustomed to think of Wagnerian music-drama as a monolith whose larger symphonic structure breaks down the distinctions present in earlier forms of operatic discourse, Wagner was able to create his own modes for distinguishing levels of meaning and intensification. Even his arch-enemy Eduard Hanslick, whom Wagner caricatured as Beckmesser in *Die Meistersinger*, pointed to certain relatively conventional set pieces—for instance, the Magic Fire music in *Die Walküre* and the quintet in *Die Meistersinger*—as satisfying Hanslick's canons of beauty.[9]

But Wagner's ways of separating segments within a work customarily took more subtle forms. For example, directly after the *Tristan* prelude, with its chromatic harmony and its expression of unfulfilled longing, we hear the song of the young sailor from offstage and immediately recognize that through its folklike verses and its conspicuously unchromatic melodic line it stands in the starkest possible contrast to the prelude. The song, which through its juxtaposition to the prelude immediately evokes a familiar though also a lost and innocent world, is quickly interrupted by Isolde, who has been silently visible onstage throughout the song and who angrily interprets it as directed ironically at herself. The world of passion suggested by the prelude has reasserted itself in Isolde's anger, and the frenzy that is to dominate the succeeding dramatic action, above all in the surging of the orchestra, has been foregrounded by the brief, relatively unoperatic intrusion of the simple song. Similarly, in the third act the feverish pitch of the music purporting to dramatize Tristan's agony is mitigated to a degree by the presence of the shepherd and his simple tunes.

If I have approached these contrasts within Wagnerian style in a formalist manner, I believe these observations share essentially

9 See "Richard Wagners Bühnenfestspiel in Bayreuth" in Eduard Hanslick, *Musikalische Stationen: Der modernen Oper II. Teil* (Berlin: Allgemeiner Verein für deutsche Literatur, 1885), p. 237, and "Die Meistersinger von Richard Wagner" in *Die moderne Oper: Kritiken und Studien* (Berlin: A. Hofmann, 1875), p. 298.

the spirit of Nietzsche's remarks in *The Birth of Tragedy* that in *Tristan und Isolde* the presence of human actors, and in particular Tristan's moments of self-deception, serve as an Apollonian bulwark to protect the audience against the full fury of the Dionysian experience that is unleashed, in the course of this final act, by the uncompromising statements emanating from the orchestra.[10] For Nietzsche a Dionysian experience that remains unmediated by the Apollonian form-giving element is humanly unbearable. In my own terms, a display of musical passion that remains unmediated by less passionate modes of communication is inarticulate and ultimately dull.

Once the continuing orchestral flow established by Wagnerian music-drama had become the norm, each composer found his own means to vary levels of intensity. In *Pelléas et Mélisande* Debussy cultivated a form of vocal and orchestral understatement that allows isolated intense moments—for example, the scene in which Mélisande sings fragments of an old song while combing her hair from the tower window—to glow with a degree of lyric fervor they could not have exercised in any earlier operatic context. *Der Rosenkavalier* includes not only those operatic set pieces such as the silver-rose ceremony and final trio that Strauss continually sought to emulate and imitate in later operas but also widely varying forms of operatic speech—for instance, the half-spoken conversational style used by the Marschallin and Baron Ochs in the breakfast scene, the parody of an eighteenth-century aria sung by the Italian tenor at the levee, and the *Lieder*-style monologue with which the Marschallin, at the end of the first act, contemplates the passing of youth.

The intrusion of a literal song or of a long instrumental passage in an opera also marks off a musical segment from the other modes of discourse out of which the opera is built. Although the sailor's song at the opening of *Tristan*, as I have indicated, is marked as less intense than Isolde's rabid commentary upon it, songs generally mark those moments of high intensity—for instance, Mélisande's song from the tower or Desdemona's "Willow Song"— in which we are made to feel that the opera is briefly revealing its emotional center to us. Musical intrusions are often marked off from the rest of the opera by the foreignness of their idiom: for example, the eighteenth-century pastiche of the tenor aria in *Der*

---

[10] See *Die Geburt der Tragödie*, sec. 21, in Nietzsche, *Werke*, ed. Karl Schlechta (Darmstadt: Wissenschaftliche Buchgesellschaft, 1964), I, 116–20.

Rosenkavalier (which is marked off additionally by its foreign language), the cantata in *Tosca*, or the choral folk tunes in *Wozzeck*;[11] or they may be marked off simply by a foreign instrument, such as the glockenspiel in *Die Zauberflöte* or the offstage trumpet that in its jarringly foreign key interrupts the onstage singers in *Fidelio*. The song contests in *Tannhäuser* and *Die Meistersinger* provide an opportunity not simply for marking off musical numbers but for creating a gradation of intensities from the less "interesting" to the captivatingly dangerous song (those of the various Minnesingers in relation to Tannhäuser's) or from the bad to the successful song (Beckmesser's in relation to his rival Walther's).

The intrusion of musical styles that the listener can place historically also lends an operatic setting a moment of authenticity before the composer returns to his accustomed idiom. The chorale directly after the prelude to *Die Meistersinger* evokes the Reformation as surely as the examples above from *Tosca* and *Der Rosenkavalier* evoke the eighteenth century. The *secco* recitative of *The Rake's Progress* is only one of innumerable eighteenth-century musical reminiscences that Stravinsky employs to remind us that he is playing ironically with Hogarth's already ironic world. Tchaikovsky evokes the eighteenth-century setting of *The Queen of Spades* with an actual aria by Grétry composed near the end of that century. In *Die schweigsame Frau* Strauss implants quotations from Monteverdi and the Fitzwilliam Book to remind us of the period of the play—Ben Jonson's *Epicoene*—from which the libretto was adapted. Ezra Pound imitates the rhythms and intervals of medieval music in his two short operas, *Le Testament* and *Cavalcanti*, both of which are based on incidents from the lives, indeed on actual texts, of two medieval poets, François Villon and Guido Cavalcanti. Adorno points out a number of musical archaisms in Berg's *Lulu*, for example a gavotte in the letter duet that was meant to evoke the popular music of the 1890s, the decade in which the opera was set and during which Wedekind's Lulu plays were written.[12] Yet the evocation of earlier musical mo-

[11] For the special difficulties of marking off folk material in an atonal context, see George Perle, *The Operas of Alban Berg*, I (*Wozzeck*) (Berkeley: University of California Press, 1980), pp. 98–99.

[12] See *Berg: Der Meister des kleinsten Uebergangs*, "Erfahrungen an Lulu," sec. 2, in Theodor Adorno, *Gesammelte Schriften*, XIII, ed. Gretel Adorno and Rolf Tiedemann (Frankfurt: Suhrkamp, 1971), pp. 481–82.

ments in these passages is something more than an attempt at historical reconstruction, for these snippets (in Pound's case, whole operas) also function as emotional signals to awaken a nostalgia for the period—above all, for its musical idiom—in which each opera is set.

If song and other musical quotations call special attention to themselves, so do such attempts at "nonmusical" mimesis as the gunfire in the last act of *Les Huguenots*, the anvils in *Il trovatore* and *Siegfried*, or the guillotine that systematically reduces the chorus of nuns singing their final hymn in Poulenc's *Les Dialogues des Carmélites*. But the introduction of direct speech against an orchestral background can mark off a passage in an equally conspicuous way. Within the German *Singspiel* tradition, in which spoken dialogue regularly alternates with musical passages, the sudden and unexpected combination of music and plain speech can achieve unforgettable effects: I refer to that mode called "melodrama" which was used to such chilling effect by Beethoven in the dungeon scene in *Fidelio* and later by Weber in the Wolf's Glen scene in *Der Freischütz*. In certain operas of the late nineteenth and early twentieth centuries, climactic moments occur when the orchestra becomes muted or stops altogether to allow a character to enunciate a few words in direct or slightly intoned speech. Thus, Santuzza shouts a curse at her unfaithful lover in *Cavalleria rusticana*, and Tosca, with bitter sarcasm, pronounces the words "E avanti lui tremava tutta Roma!" ("And before him all Rome trembled") over the body of the police commissioner whom she has just knifed to death. One of the most dramatically compelling of such spoken moments comes near the end of the Strauss-Hofmannsthal *Die Frau ohne Schatten*, when the Empress, expressing compassion for the first time, refuses to allow others to sacrifice themselves for her and slowly speaks out the words "Ich will nicht!" ("I will not"). We are meant to recognize these words as the spiritual climax of the opera, yet they are also in a sense the musical climax—despite, perhaps even because of the fact that the music, which has maintained an unrelentingly lofty style throughout, has come to a temporary stop. In a work such as *Die Frau ohne Schatten*, which cultivates a high degree of operatic intensity over a long span, Strauss must resort to the idiom of spoken drama to spotlight his moment of highest intensity. Indeed he is so successful that the music he wrote for the scene of jubilation with which the opera resumes and concludes

[87]

after the Empress's great pronouncement has always seemed to me, as it apparently did to Strauss's plain-speaking wife, not quite up to the rest.[13]

No form of discourse, whether direct speech, *Sprechgesang*, or formal aria, is intrinsically more "intense" or "expressive" than any other; rather, we experience its intensity or expressiveness in relation to the other forms surrounding it or, for that matter, through our perception of what has counted as intense or expressive in recent operas. Once a particular form such as *Sprechgesang* has come to seem tiresome, it can no longer create the same effects for which it was originally devised. Thus, while collaborating on their next opera, *Die ägyptische Helena*, Hofmannsthal begged Strauss to set the second-act dialogue between Helena and Aithra as direct speech rather than *Sprechgesang*, and the reason he gives is the ear's need for "relief": the whole younger generation, he reminds the composer, is reacting fiercely to the post-Wagnerian (and partly even to Wagner's) form of *Sprechgesang*.[14] The discussion on how to set this passage goes on in subsequent letters, with Strauss finally insisting on *Sprechgesang*, though with an un-Wagnerian accompaniment that remains light and intermittent.[15]

The powerful effect of an unexpected shift from song to speech is perhaps best illustrated not by an actual operatic score but by an interpretive gesture that the great singing actress Wilhelmine Schröder-Devrient introduced into the second-act quartet in *Fidelio*. While singing the climactic line before the trumpet call, "Noch einen Schritt, und du bist—tot," the singer suddenly and unexpectedly spoke instead of sang the word *tot*. This juxtaposition of opposing modes of discourses affected Wagner in a manner that he felt compelled to describe in the language of Romantic metaphysics: the intrusion was like "a sudden plunging from one sphere into the other, and its sublimity consisted in this—that, as with a stroke of lightning, we gained a momentary insight into

---

[13] As Strauss reports it to his collaborator, "It [the ending] has verve and considerable intensification—but my wife finds it cold and misses the heart-affecting, igniting, melodic quality of the *Rosenkavalier* trio." Letter of July 28, 1916, in Strauss-Hofmannsthal, *Briefwechsel*, 3d ed., ed. Willi Schuh (Zurich: Atlantis, 1964), p. 354.

[14] Letter of August 9, 1924, ibid., p. 523. What Strauss and Hofmannsthal mean by *Sprechgesang* is of course a different and more lyrical form than the *Sprechstimme* we have come to associate with the operatic styles of Berg and Schönberg.

[15] See letters of February 12, 1925, and January 30, 1926, in Strauss-Hofmannsthal, *Briefwechsel*, pp. 536–37, 550–52.

the nature of both spheres, of which one comprised precisely the ideal, the other the real."[16] From Wagner's point of view the ideal sphere that is music can only achieve sublime effect if it intersects occasionally with the "real" sphere of an alien discourse.

It may seem paradoxical that after suggesting a scale whose extremes I have labeled *verbal* and *operatic*, I cite instances in which an operatic highpoint manifests itself in purely verbal, nonmusical terms. Yet when a style we have come to define as heightened has itself become conventional, it periodically must redefine itself—even resorting to seemingly "lower" modes of discourse to achieve a heightening that is otherwise no longer possible. The problem of achieving both continuity and diversity in musical drama is similar to the problem encountered in those heightened literary forms such as the epic and poetic drama that address their audiences over a considerable time span. In each instance the artist must borrow or define a norm that assures some sort of continuity—whether the high style of Virgilian epic or the collocation of disparate images in twentieth-century long poems; whether the classical alexandrine of French tragedy or the loose, conversational verse of T. S. Eliot's dramas; whether the alternation of recitative and aria in *opera seria* or the symphonic continuity of Wagnerian music-drama.

Yet the norm that assures continuity also demands the cultivation of diversity. Thus, the mixture of different levels of musical speech within *opera seria* or music-drama is necessary for a particular stylistic norm to assert itself. A moment of direct speech that interrupts a thickly orchestrated musical continuum can help confirm an audience's acceptance of the high style with which the drama is trying to work its effect. The alternation of spoken dialogue and song in German *Singspiele* such as *Die Entführung aus dem Serail* or *Der Freischütz* confirms the naturalness of each of these seemingly opposite modes of speech at the same time that, in the course of the opera, we come to accept this alternation as a natural form of continuity.

Yet the need for diversity, as Hofmannsthal suggested when he tried to coax Strauss to use direct speech instead of *Sprechgesang*, also manifests itself in the distinction an audience learns to discern between a new norm and the earlier norms to which it was accustomed. Rossini breathed new life into the recitative/aria form

---

[16] "Ueber die Bestimmung der Oper" in Wagner, *Gesammelte Schriften*, ed. Julius Kapp (Leipzig: Hesse & Becker, n.d.), XII, 308.

that he had inherited from the eighteenth century through a radical intensification of both the dynamics and rhythm of his arias. The deliberate overstatement with which Rossini's operas excited all Europe in his time served as a comment on his predecessors, much as Debussy's understatement in *Pelléas* represents a commentary upon the Wagnerian mode. Stravinsky's return to the recitative/aria form is a kind of double commentary on earlier norms: through its refusal to maintain orchestral continuity it turns its back disdainfully on the whole tradition of music-drama from Wagner to Schönberg, while in its unrelenting use of musical parody and unmistakably non–eighteenth-century harmony, it asserts its own identity as distinct from its historical setting and the earlier mode that it pretends to evoke.

It may well be that musical conventions wear out at a faster rate than literary ones. So, at least, thought Eduard Hanslick, who, writing in the 1850s, even before the radical innovations of his enemy Wagner, contended, "There is no art that consumes forms as rapidly and in such numbers as music. Modulations, cadenzas, progressions of intervals, tonal successions wear out in fifty, even thirty years, with the result that the serious composer can no longer use them and is constantly driven to the invention of new, purely musical strokes."[17] Certainly the notorious *Tristan* chord, which Hanslick could not have known when he wrote these words, became a musical cliché in well less than thirty years after it stunned its first listeners. No major operatic style persisted as long—and with as few changes in the course of its history—as *opera seria* between, say, the 1690s and the 1760s; yet in London it flourished for barely two decades before it was dethroned by *The Beggar's Opera*. It is difficult, of course, to separate purely musical conventions such as those Hanslick discusses from the more theatrical aspects of opera. Hofmannsthal may have had both in mind when, asking Strauss to compose a Mozart-like melody for the final duet of *Der Rosenkavalier*, he castigated "the insufferable Wagnerian love-roaring [*Liebesbrüllerei*], . . . a repulsively barbaric, almost animal-like thing, this roaring [*losbrüllen*] at one another by two creatures engaged in passion."[18] In his position as music critic Shaw often commented on the changes in taste and perception that had taken place during the nineteenth century. "I will hardly be believed now," he wrote, "when I say that Donizetti's Lucrezia

[17] Hanslick, *Vom Musikalisch-Schönen* (Leipzig: Johann Ambrosius Barth, 1896), p. 93.
[18] Letter of June 6, 1910, in Strauss-Hofmannsthal, *Briefwechsel*, p. 91.

was once really tragic and romantic."[19] Attending *Der Freischütz,* Shaw noted that the Wolf's Glen scene, which, with its use of booming, direct speech against the orchestra, had once inspired Gothic chills in its audience, was inciting laughter instead.[20] It may be that the more extreme innovations such as Weber's horror scene or Wagner's "roaring" lovestyle are also those whose intended effects are hardest to sustain over time.

Even if musical conventions achieve obsolescence at an uncommonly rapid pace, the multiplicity of discourses available in opera, in comparison with other musical and dramatic genres, has allowed composers to create new operatic styles through the relatively large number of discursive forms they set into combination with one another. The introduction of *seria* characters into Italian comic opera in the course of the eighteenth century made possible the complex dramatic juxtapositions within the Mozart–Da Ponte operas.[21] Adorno describes the Wagnerian style as a combination of *opera seria* and *opera buffa*: while the earnestness of conception and the motif content represent a continuation of the *seria* tradition, Wagner's use of declamation against a main melody carried by the orchestra comes from comic opera.[22] Hofmannsthal's encouragement of Strauss to provide Mozart-like duets and trios (however unlike Mozart these might sound to us) allowed Strauss to cultivate a range of styles—from the high post-Wagnerian to a pre-Wagnerian comic mode—within a single opera such as *Der Rosenkavalier.*

Opera as "Dialogic"

The multiplicity of discourses characteristic of opera finds a certain parallel in the novel, a genre that Mikhail Bakhtin celebrated throughout his work for its ability, in contrast with such "fixed" genres as epic and lyric, to speak out in the most diverse and often conflicting voices. For Bakhtin the novel at its greatest is "dialogic," by which he means an interaction of utterances or, to cite the term he borrowed from music in his early study of Dostoevsky, a "polyphonic" multiplicity of meanings. Although

[19] Review of November 1, 1893, in *Shaw's Music,* ed. Dan H. Laurence (New York: Dodd, Mead, 1981), III, 20.

[20] Review of July 18, 1894, ibid., pp. 271–72.

[21] See Michael F. Robinson, *Opera before Mozart* (New York: William Morrow, 1967), pp. 135–36.

[22] See *Versuch über Wagner,* chap. 3, in Adorno, *Gesammelte Schriften,* XIII (1971), 55.

Bakhtin did not concern himself specifically with opera, in a passage of this study (*Problems of Dostoevsky's Poetics*) he briefly brings opera and the novel together as multiperspectival genres. Bakhtin refers to a moment in Dostoevsky's *A Raw Youth* in which the character Trishatov describes an operatic scene he could imagine setting:

> If I were to compose an opera, I'd choose a scene from *Faust*. I love *Faust*. I keep composing music for that scene in the cathedral—oh, just in my head, of course. . . . The interior of that Gothic cathedral, the choir, the hymns. . . . In comes Gretchen . . . the choir is medieval—you can hear the fifteenth century at once. Gretchen is in despair. First, a recitative, played very softly, but full of suffering and terror, while the choir thunders grimly, sternly, and impersonally, *"Dies irae, dies illa!"* And then, all of a sudden, the devil's voice sings the devil's song. You can't see him, there's only his song mingling with the hymns, almost blending into them, although it's completely different from them—I must manage to convey that somehow. The devil's song is long, persistent. A tenor—it absolutely must be a tenor. . . . And all this time the devil's song continues and pierces her soul deeper and deeper like a spear.[23]

As Dostoevsky's character conceives his imaginary scene, the most diverse voices mix together: that of the chorus, in all its medieval

[23] "The Word in Dostoevsky" in *Problems of Dostoevsky's Poetics*, trans. R. W. Potsel (Ann Arbor, Mich.: Ardis, 1973), pp. 186–87. I have quoted from the Dostoevsky novel as translated under the title *The Adolescent* by Andrew R. MacAndrew (1971; rpt. New York: Norton, 1981), p. 438. Another brief but suggestive allusion to opera appears in a later essay by Bakhtin, "Discourse in the Novel," which discusses the "re-accentuation of images," namely the transformation a literary image undergoes as it is rewritten either in another literary genre or in another art form such as "drama, opera, painting." The one operatic example of reaccentuation that Bakhtin offers is Tchaikovsky's transformation of *Eugene Onegin*, which, as he puts it, "greatly weakens the quality of parody" in the Pushkin poem from which it is drawn. The difference that Bakhtin points to here accords with my argument, in the preceding chapter, that operas based on famous literary texts tend to assume an identity so different from their originals that critics often speak of the loss that takes place in the transformation. Bakhtin's footnote to the remark on Tchaikovsky (though undeveloped) fits in with the perspective I have been developing in the present chapter: "This problem of double-voiced parodic and ironic discourse (more accurately, its analogues) in opera, in music, in choreography (parodic dances) is extremely interesting." (These remarks can be found in Bakhtin, *The Dialogic Imagination*, trans. Caryl Emerson and Michael Holquist [Austin: University of Texas Press, 1981], p. 421.) Although the present chapter stresses the diversity of discourses in opera, it is also possible to view a major operatic work or style from the composer's vantage point and see the individual voices and discursive forms subsumed by the all-encompassing voice of the composer. For an argument from this point of view, see Edward T. Cone, *The Composer's Voice* (Berkeley: University of California Press, 1974), pp. 26–29.

sternness and impersonality; the personal, suffering voice of Gretchen; the insistent, piercing song of the devil. Dostoevsky does not, at least in the novel's final version, refer to Gounod, whose operatic setting of *Faust* he knew quite well[24] and who had himself exploited what Bakhtin would have called the "polyphonic" possibilities of the scene. Although Gounod made the devil a bass rather than a tenor (Russian operatic convention was not as rigid as French and Italian at the time in assigning lower pitches to villains), and although he introduced the voices in a different order from those in Trishatov's projected opera, he strives for a similarly multiperspectival effect: Gretchen's high, plangent voice contrasts with the low, aggressive tones of Mephistopheles, and both contrast with the medieval pastiche of the chorus singing in Latin. The musical accompaniments with which each voice is associated remain distinct from one another: low strings for Marguerite, brasses for the devil, organ for the chorus.

Yet the multiperspectival mode of Gounod's cathedral scene was ready at hand in Goethe's text, which, in the space of some sixty lines, sets the three voices—the Evil Spirit (whom Goethe does not explicitly identify with his Mephistopheles), Gretchen, and the chorus—sharply against one another. Thus, next to the insidious taunting of the Evil Spirit:

> Wo steht dein Kopf?
> In deinem Herzen
> Welche Missetat? . . .
> Grimm fasst dich!
> Die Posaune tönt!
> Die Gräber beben!

we hear the helpless cries of Gretchen:

> Mir wird so eng!
> Die Mauernpfeiler
> Befangen mich!
> Das Gewölbe
> Drängt mich!—Luft!

[24] An early version of the passage shows Trishatov's disapproval of Gounod's setting, which he does not find medieval enough; instead, he prefers a setting more like that of Meyerbeer's *Robert le Diable*, "where you can hear the tenth century . . . and you feel, really feel the tenth century." See Abram Akimovich Gozenpud, *Dostoevskij i Muzyka* (Leningrad: Music Press, 1971), pp. 124–25.

and next to both the unrelenting medieval choral voice:

Dies irae, dies illa
Solvet saeclum in favilla.[25]

Goethe even punctuates the hymn with a stage direction calling for an organ to play. Doubtless readers have "heard" the scene operatically since its first publication.

In one of his later essays Bakhtin speaks of a "novelization," beginning in the late eighteenth century, of such traditional genres as drama and epic.[26] What he means is that the multivoiced character that prose fiction has shown since its beginnings in antiquity came to invade the other genres and transform them to the point that they lost their traditional identity. As examples of novelization he points to Byron's *Don Juan*, Heine's lyrics, and Ibsen's plays. Although Bakhtin does not specifically mention Goethe's *Faust* here, the cathedral scene, which he had used by way of Dostoevsky in his earlier book, would have made his point admirably. Throughout this section I have suggested that opera characteristically speaks out in a multivoiced manner. If *Faust*, as well as countless other literary works of the last two centuries, makes sense within the context created by Bakhtin's term *novelization*, from the point of view I have argued one may as easily speak of an *operatization* whenever, as in the cathedral scene, we encounter that powerful collision of voices which opera has cultivated since its beginnings.

Yet this collision of voices in opera differs in fundamental ways from the collision that occurs in those fictional models—defined above all in the work of Rabelais and Dostoevsky—from which Bakhtin derived his notion of multidiscursiveness. Whereas opera is characterized by clearly marked off gradations in intensity, the novels at the heart of Bakhtin's theory are notable for the raucousness with which conventional barriers are broken down. Whereas opera rigorously sets up frames to contain the distinctions it generates, the Bakhtinian novel allows its multitudinous voices to blend with or assault one another and often to assert their irreconcilability.

---

[25] *Faust* (ll. 3784—3802), ed. Erich Trunz (Hamburg: Christian Wegner Verlag, 1949), pp. 120–21. The German verses can be translated as follows: Evil Spirit: "What's in your mind? / Within your heart / What crime? . . . / Anger clutches you! / The trumpet sounds! / The graves quake!" Gretchen: "I'm short of breath! / The stone pillars / Close in on me! / The vaulting / Presses on me!—Air!"
[26] *Dialogic Imagination*, pp. 5–8.

One need only try out a multivoiced operatic passage several times on a record player—for example, the street fight in *Die Meistersinger* or the first-act finale of *Il barbiere di Siviglia*, both of which seek to render extreme states of confusion—to recognize that behind the babble of voices there lies a rigidly organized structure capable of exact repetition through the timing, the dynamics, and the other musical cues that the controlling hand of the composer has authorized. By contrast, when we read one of Rabelais's more outrageous passages, we are aware of a deliberate refusal to control, of an explosiveness that threatens all prearranged structures.

The difference between opera and the Bakhtinian novel is at once the difference between a ceremonial, ritualized form and an open-ended one constantly about to disrupt and subvert whatever ceremonies and rituals it has set up. It is also the difference between, on the one hand, a performative mode that seeks to overwhelm its audience with a show of power and, on the other, a freewheeling mode that encourages its readers into active participation in its carnivalesque exuberance. Yet despite their differences, the type of novel Bakhtin has isolated shares with opera a propensity towards extravagant utterance that sets both off from the various literary and musical genres among which we are accustomed to classify them. Indeed, both are so marked by an appetite to absorb and even swallow up other genres that it has often proved difficult to classify them at all. It is no accident that we designate both forms with terms suggesting extremes.

Operatic Self-definition

The Inclusiveness of Opera

The propensity of opera to assimilate a variety of discourses is itself a sign of its desire to achieve an illusion of inclusiveness. In a study that argues for generic mixture rather than generic purity as the characteristic attribute of literary works, Rosalie Colie calls opera "*the* mixed genre in the arts."[27] Whereas the preceding section stressed the diversity of discourse that characterizes operatic

---

[27] In Colie, *The Resources of Kind: Genre-Theory in the Renaissance*, ed. Barbara K. Lewalski (Berkeley: University of California Press, 1973), p. 22 (italics Colie's).

style, the remainder of this chapter will stress two related aspects of this style—first, that desire for inclusiveness which has motivated composers to embrace a multitude of seemingly incompatible elements at once and, second, that self-referentiality by which operas repeatedly invoke the unity and the uniqueness of the tradition to which they view themselves as belonging.

When we speak of operatic inclusiveness, we immediately think of Wagner's concept of the *Gesamtkunstwerk*. Yet this concept is not simply a Wagnerian idea but a model that, in one way or another, has been applied to opera at various times in its history. Those who have tried to pinpoint opera's precise generic nature have usually been so conditioned to think in literary categories that they naturally find analogies to more than a single genre. Beaumarchais, the product of a critical system that cultivated generic purity to a relatively high degree, was forced to give up all generic distinctions when, in his preface to a libretto of his own, he stated that "opera is neither a tragedy nor a comedy but participates in both and can embrace all the genres."[28]

If the inclusiveness of opera has made it difficult to "fit" the medium into the more Procrustean structures, its ability to fit a variety of ordinarily exclusive categories has also proved a cause for celebration. For instance, Dr. Burney meted out special praise to Gluck for his ability to bring together the major arts: "It is in scenes of great distress, in which the human heart is torn by complicated misery . . . that Gluck, transported beyond the bound of ordinary genius, gives such energy and colouring to passion, as to become at once poet, painter, and musician." At this point one might have expected some statement about Gluck's creating a *Gesamtkunstwerk* through the combination of scenery, music, and words, perhaps even dance, but as it turns out the inclusiveness that Burney praises manifests itself strictly in musical terms; as the next sentence makes clear, the literary and visual aspects of Gluck's genius are to be taken as analogies: "He seems to be the Michael Angelo of music, and is as happy painting difficult attitudes, and situations of the mind, as that painter was of the body."[29]

When music is made to compete with poetry, more often than

[28] Preface to *Tarare* in *The Essence of Opera*, ed. Ulrich Weisstein (1964; rpt. New York: Norton, 1969), p. 146.

[29] In Charles Burney, *An Eighteenth-Century Musical Tour in Central Europe and the Netherlands*, ed. Percy A. Scholes (London: Oxford University Press, 1959), II, 100.

not music turns out to do everything poetry can do and its own thing as well. In one of those absolute dichotomies typical of his critical writing, Wagner contrasts the poet ("der Wortdichter"), who can at best "compress moments of action, feeling, and expression perceptible only to the understanding to a single point," with the composer ("der Tondichter"), who, in his expectedly superior way, is able "to expand the compressed, dense point to its highest fullness according to its total emotional content."[30] Note such terms as *fullness* and *expand*, which Wagner employs to indicate the superiority of music to poetry: the composer does not simply include more than the poet but also manages to make it last longer.

The notion behind the *Gesamtkunstwerk* takes for granted that "more" is obviously better. When Wagner comes to define the *Gesamtkunstwerk*, he allows its superiority to lie not simply in the broad array of arts it is able to include but also in the inclusiveness of the communicative process he expects to take place between work and audience: "Genuine drama is conceivable only as resulting from the *collective impulse of all the arts* to communicate in the most immediate way with a *collective public*: each individual form of art can reveal itself as *fully understandable* to this collective public only through collective communication."[31] If this more-is-better mentality reaches its extreme in Wagner's theorizing, it has ample precedent both in earlier theories surrounding opera and, perhaps even more telling, in that passage of the *Poetics* in which Aristotle proclaims the superiority of tragedy to epic. Tragedy can perform the same things epic does, Aristotle says, but with a more concentrated effect, and—at least as important—tragedy has musical effects and can communicate with its audience in two ways—through both reading and representation—as opposed to epic's restriction to reading alone.[32]

The Self-consciousness of Opera

Whatever precedent Aristotle may have set in choosing the criterion of inclusiveness to praise tragedy, Greek tragedy (despite,

[30] *Oper und Drama*, pt. 3, sec. 3, in *Gesammelte Schriften*, XI, 246–47.
[31] *Das Kunstwerk der Zukunft*, pt. 4, *Gesammelte Schriften*, X, 158.
[32] "Furthermore, because it has everything the epic has (it can even employ the epic verse) and, what is no small item, the music besides, that source of the vividest of all our pleasures. Further, it has the dramatic vividness in reading as well as in actual performance." In Aristotle, *Poetics*, trans. Gerald F. Else (Ann Arbor: University of Michigan Press, 1967), p. 74 (sec. 26).

perhaps even because of our ignorance as to what actually happened on the ancient stage) remained an ideal form that opera, at crucial moments throughout its history, has attempted to emulate and restore. Each of the two most famous "reformers," Gluck and Wagner, uses Greek tragedy as a legitimizing precedent, though each stresses those elements that coincide with his own talent and what he perceives as the needs of his time. Gluck, for instance, defends the deliberately harsh sounds sung by his character Armide by citing the suffering that Sophocles allowed Oedipus to express after his blinding, and he warns his French librettist, Bailli du Roullet, not to allow the rules of French tragedy to guide him in adapting Racine's *Iphigénie* but "to laugh at rules and to make one's own rules" just like the ancient Greeks, who "were men like us with a nose and a pair of eyes."[33] Although Gluck was far less explicit than Wagner (not to speak of the Camerata) in citing the Greek precedent, the latter is strikingly evident from his use of Greek themes and dramatic plots in most of his "reform" operas as well as from that notion of Greek "simplicity" and "naturalness" which he shared with his contemporary Winckelmann.

Wagner may well have worked out a theory of the conflict of Apollonian and Dionysian elements in Greek drama before his disciple Nietzsche expanded these notions to celebrate *Tristan und Isolde* as the true rebirth of Greek tragedy.[34] In operatic history the example of Greek tragedy serves the same role for composers and theorists that early Christianity serves for reformers who claim a special relationship with what they take to be their origins; what medieval Christianity was to the Reformation, the

[33] Letters of October, 1777 (to J. F. de Laharpe), and December 2, 1775 (to the Bailli du Roullet), in Gluck, *Collected Correspondence and Papers*, ed. Hedwig Mueller von Asow and E. H. Mueller von Asow, trans. Stewart Thomson (New York: St. Martin's Press, n.d.), pp. 101, 75.

[34] Wagner proposes the theory briefly in "Die Bestimmung der Oper," a lecture given in the spring of 1871, a year before the publication of Nietzsche's first major work. (See *Gesammelte Schriften*, XII, 293–94.) Wagner's best-known recent biographers both argue that Wagner introduced Nietzsche to these ideas. (See Curt von Westernhagen, *Wagner: A Biography*, trans. Mary Whittall [Cambridge, England: Cambridge University Press, 1978], pp. 411–12, and Martin Gregor-Dellin, *Richard Wagner: Sein Leben, Sein Werk, Sein Jahrhundert* [Munich: Piper, 1980], pp. 651–53.) On the other hand, a recent study of the genesis and meaning of *The Birth of Tragedy* denies Wagnerian precedence. (See M. S. Silk and J. P. Stern, *Nietzsche on Tragedy* [Cambridge, England: Cambridge University Press, 1981], pp. 214–16.) The frequent conversations between the two men during the early 1870s make precedence hard to establish with the textual certainty that traditional scholarship demands.

corrupt and inauthentic forms of *opera seria* and early nine-teenth-century opera were, respectively, for Gluck and Wagner. The ancient example was little enough understood that it could be used to defend almost any operatic style. Thus, Voltaire cites Metastasian *opera seria,* the very mode that Gluck later at-tempted to reform, as a restoration of Greek tragedy.[35] Metastasio himself claimed to follow the Greeks in the way he shaped his meters, his arias, and his plots.[36]

The classical analogy appears with striking insistence in the official statements of the Florentine founders of opera. Rinuccini, the librettist of the *Euridice,* dedicates his text to the queen of France with these lines: "It has been the opinion of many, most Christian Queen, that the ancient Greeks and Romans, in repre-senting their tragedies upon the stage, sang them throughout. But until now this noble manner of recitation has been neither re-vived nor (to my knowledge) even attempted."[37] The composers Caccini and Peri, each of whom set Rinuccini's text, both make a point of the Greek precedent in their own dedications.[38] When Algarotti wrote his influential essay on opera a century and a half after the genre's foundation, he could take the precedent for granted: "The intention of the poets was to revive the Greek tragedy in all its luster."[39] Even before the first operas were composed, the writ-ings of members of the Camerata were full of speculations about what Greek music and declamation must have been like.[40]

The rebirth of tragedy claimed by theorists from the Floren-tines to Nietzsche is of course no rebirth at all but a new birth that took place whenever a composer, or his spokesman, sought to justify a radical departure from some prevailing operatic norm. Few genres have as abrupt a beginning as opera. Whereas histori-ans of epic or drama (including Greek drama) can usually work from an evolutionary model, historians of opera are faced with a form that emerged full grown from the head of a learned and aris-

[35] "'What!' I am told, 'an Italian opera should bear any resemblance to the Athe-nian drama?' Yes." "Dissertation sur la tragédie" (1748) in *Oeuvres complètes,* IV (Paris: Garnier, 1877), p. 489.

[36] Letter of January 29, 1760 (to F. G. di Chastellux), in Pietro Metastasio, *Tutte le opere,* ed. Bruno Brunelli, IV (Milan: Mondadori, 1954), pp. 435–40.

[37] Strunk, *Source Readings in Music History,* pp. 367–68.

[38] See Caccini, dedication of *Euridice,* and Peri, foreword to *Euridice,* ibid., pp. 371, 374.

[39] Count [Francesco] Algarotti, *An Essay on Opera* (London: L. Davis & C. Rey-mers, 1767), p. 12.

[40] See the essays by Giovanni de' Bardi and Vincenzo Galilei in Strunk, *Source Readings in Music History,* pp. 290–301, 302–22.

tocratic coterie. In positing a mythical, lost operatic past in Greek tragedy, the earliest opera composers and theorists could claim to be doing something new at the same time that they could share in the aura that adhered to ancient drama. Yet this aura represented something more than the revival of a literary genre or a philosophical or political idea. Through the union of words and music that they assumed in Greek tragedy, the creators of opera could imagine themselves participating in a project that carried distinctly religious (though not specifically Christian) overtones.

John Hollander, writing about metrical theories since the Renaissance, has suggested a context that also helps illuminate the origins to which opera lays claim: "Behind so much Western aesthetics since Classical antiquity lies a nostalgia for what was believed quite naïvely to have been a perfect, mystical marriage, in Attic times, of musical mode and ethos, of form and the effect upon human behavior proper to that form: a nostalgia for what was thought to have been a perfect music-poetry that made of human sense an instrument whose own sound was human feeling."[41] Whether the mystical marriage was Apollonian or Dionysian in character, the nostalgia of which Hollander speaks has provided opera since its sudden beginnings with a common reference point in an idealized cultural moment that, through our inability to recover what Greek music sounded like, can never be known well enough for anybody to disprove the connection. Rousseau, tracing the history of opera in his dictionary of music, viewed whatever elements of opera were new as attempts to compensate for the loss of that ideal form which was Greek tragedy: he asserted that while the Greek language was so musical that recitative alone sufficed in their theater, the moderns have had to compensate by formal arias and, in the century before Rousseau, by magical machine effects.[42] The death of ancient tragedy became, in effect, a fortunate fall that could help motivate operatic composers to resurrect (however imperfectly) that great lost genre.

The persistence with which opera has cultivated a myth of ancient origins has also given a sense of continuity to a form that, in view of the changes in performance techniques and the difficulties in transmitting musical scores, has been subject to severe disruptions over the less than four centuries during which it has

[41] John Hollander, *Vision and Resonance: Two Senses of Poetic Form* (New York: Oxford University Press, 1975), p. 160.

[42] See *Dictionnaire de musique* in Rousseau, *Oeuvres*, XV (Paris: Werdet & Lequien, 1826), pp. 34–37.

flourished. The Greek precedent is at best an ideal, an imagined common origin for a form that cannot display a continuing tradition in the way that, say, literature and painting have been able to do during the same period. However much we may complain of the corruptions in Shakespeare's texts, the fact remains that most, perhaps all of his plays have remained extant and generally available since his time. By contrast, most of Monteverdi's operas have not only been lost, but the instrumentation of the three extant scores has had to be reconstructed through the often controversial guesswork of twentieth-century editors.

Whereas writers such as Petrarch, Shakespeare, Cervantes, and Milton experienced a continuing reception and reinterpretation over the centuries, the major opera composers before Gluck—Monteverdi, Cavalli, Alessandro Scarlatti, even Handel—were at best distant memories until their recent rediscovery. During the seventeenth and early eighteenth centuries, few scores even made their way into print. Thus, when a modern musicologist draws analogies between the declamatory mode that Verdi developed in his last two operas and the mode practiced in seventeenth-century Venetian opera, he cannot speak of direct influence, for Verdi could neither have known the scores or heard the works in the theater.[43] From our present vantage point we can speak of Verdi's achievement in restoring recitative to the primary position it had known during the first half-century of opera, but a statement of this sort has even less historical content than the notion that the earliest opera composers were restoring the fusion of several arts that had once existed in Greek tragedy; however wrong the latter were about the nature of Greek tragedy, unlike Verdi they at least believed they were restoring something that once existed.

Although the transmission of music over the ages has been intermittent at best, the memory of earlier periods of opera was sometimes kept alive through librettos. As literary artifacts, librettos could be recorded and transmitted far more easily than musical scores. When Algarotti, in his essay of 1755, wrote of the early days of opera, he cited Rinuccini's texts for *Dafne, Euridice,* and *Arianna* but failed to mention the particular composers—Peri, Caccini, Monteverdi—who supplied the music.[44] Librettos

---

[43] See Simon Towneley Wortshorne, *Venetian Opera in the Seventeenth Century* (Oxford: Clarendon Press, 1954), pp. 55, 70, 137.

[44] Algarotti, *Essay on Opera*, p. 11. Algarotti's knowledge of seventeenth-century operatic style is based largely on hearsay. Indeed, at one point, while arguing against the excesses of the prevailing style at the time he was writing, he calls upon the

have occasionally outlasted the musical styles for which they were created. Although Handel's operatic style has absolutely nothing in common with Cavalli's, a Handel specialist has accounted for the comic element in *Serse* (1738) through its roots in a libretto written for the Venetian composer in 1654.[45] Each of Metastasio's more famous librettos was set by innumerable composers throughout the eighteenth century; Mozart's last opera, *La clemenza di Tito* (1791), reworks a Metastasian text that Gluck had set in his pre-"reform" period and that was certainly intended for a musical style quite different from Mozart's.

Although operatic history in its first two centuries was notable for its disruptions, later composers have succeeded in embedding a consciousness of operatic tradition within their own work. On its simplest level this consciousness can manifest itself as a musical allusion to an earlier opera that the listener readily identifies. The disparaging allusion to Figaro's "Non più andrai" in the banquet scene of *Don Giovanni* is a private joke between Mozart and his audience that breaks the illusion of the work's autonomy to call attention to the continuity of Mozart's endeavors as a composer of opera. Wagner makes a somewhat more complicated statement in the brief quotation from *Tristan und Isolde* during the scene in *Die Meistersinger* in which Eva feels briefly tempted to fall in love with Hans Sachs. Besides warning of the dangers inherent in a match between youth and age, the allusion provides a generic signal asserting the shift from tragedy to comedy within Wagner's oeuvre.

Whether in literature, art, or music, parody stresses the continuity of a tradition at the same time that it deflates earlier works within the tradition. When we hear the parody of earlier operatic styles in modernist operas such as *Ariadne auf Naxos* and *The Rake's Progress*, we are not so much inclined to laugh as to experience a nostalgia for earlier modes of music that can be recreated only in the most self-conscious and deliberately witty way. While Hofmannsthal was preparing the *Ariadne* libretto, Strauss requested him to seek ideas for Zerbinetta's aria by asking Selma

---

memory of those who can still remember what seventeenth-century recitative sounded like: "Numbers now living must remember how certain passages of simple recitative have affected the minds of an audience, to a degree that no modern air is able to produce" (p. 34).

[45] See Winton Dean, *Handel and the Opera Seria* (Berkeley: University of California Press, 1969), p. 38.

Kurz, the singer who was to create the role in the final version, to sing coloratura arias from *La sonnambula, Lucia di Lammermoor*, Hérold's *Le Pré aux clercs*, and *Rigoletto*, as well as some Mozart rondeaus.[46] Although Hofmannsthal balked at this particular suggestion, Strauss's plan betrays a yearning to make contact with a lost operatic world that could be evoked in his time by parody alone.

Since the Strauss-Hofmannsthal correspondence is unrivaled among documents on opera for its self-conscious attitude towards the operatic tradition, examples of virtually every possible relationship to the tradition can be located here. Allusion and parody provide a less fundamental link with the past than the composer's deliberate attempt to emulate great works or passages (often his own) by means of imitation. For example, while awaiting the text of the last act of *Die Frau ohne Schatten*, Strauss wrote to Hofmannsthal, "I hope the third act will give me ample room for lyrical discharges [*Entladungen*] à la the trio of *Rosenkavalier*."[47] As one listens to the endings of most of his operas after *Der Rosenkavalier*, one senses that, in one way or another, each strives to recapture the ecstatic heights that the great trio had once achieved. Hofmannsthal, on the other hand, took special pride in the fact that each opera on which they collaborated was, as he put it, "a genre in itself," except for *Elektra*, which could be taken as a "variant of *Salome*" (in which Hofmannsthal did not in fact participate); by contrast, Hofmannsthal referred disparagingly to Meyerbeer and Puccini for producing "a series of works in the same genre."[48] However much Hofmannsthal strove to stamp each opera with the generic uniqueness he noted in each of Mozart's and Wagner's works, he could not prevent the composer, as he grew older, from consciously reworking those formulas that had brought him a higher degree of acclaim than that achieved, at a similarly early stage of their careers, by those composers whom Hofmannsthal wanted him to emulate.

In vying with the great librettists and composers of the past,

---

[46] See letter of May 25, 1911, in Strauss-Hofmannsthal, *Briefwechsel*, p. 121. Strauss's request to his collaborator suggests a dimension that the resulting opera shares with the Strauss-Hofmannsthal correspondence as a whole (despite their generic differences): the two texts, opera and correspondence, remain unrivaled for the self-consciousness with which they embrace, absorb, and contain the total history of opera.

[47] Letter of March 30, 1915, ibid., pp. 300–301.

[48] See letter of September 18, 1919, ibid., p. 451.

Hofmannsthal and Strauss cultivated what is perhaps the most sophisticated way of asserting continuity with their predecessors, namely the self-conscious rethinking of a major earlier work in contemporary terms. It is a commonplace of operatic history that *Der Rosenkavalier* deliberately recreates the world of *Le nozze di Figaro*, while *Die Frau ohne Schatten* approaches *Die Zauberflöte* in a similar way. In discussing the relationships between the new works and their eighteenth-century models, Hofmannsthal rejected the term *imitation* and insisted instead on the word *analogy.*[49] The analogy is loose enough so that most operagoers remain unaware of the relationship unless their program notes point it out. Yet once the analogy has been made clear, the memory of the earlier work inextricably enters their experience of the later opera. For instance, the Contessa, unrivalled in the history of opera before Mozart for the subtlety of characterization both in her music and her dramatic action, becomes infinitely more complex in her recreation as the Marschallin—to the point that W. H. Auden, Hofmannsthal's greatest successor as an imitator of earlier operatic situations, complains that her celebrated first-act monologue "is so full of interesting detail that the voice line is hampered in trying to follow everything."[50]

Moreover, Mozart's eighteenth-century setting, which, with its revolutionary rumblings, was all too contemporary for his original audience, in *Der Rosenkavalier* becomes an ideal lost world filtered through an early twentieth-century historical consciousness that has been colored by notions of cultural decline—notions that are themselves embodied both in the imitation of earlier musical forms and in the bittersweet musical commentaries interrupting the comic action. Beyond the specific analogies to the two Mozart operas, Hofmannsthal and Strauss sought to encapsulate the essence of an entire genre in *Der Rosenkavalier* and *Die Frau ohne Schatten*: the former becomes an archetypal operatic comedy, a successor not only of *Figaro* but of *Die Meistersinger* and *Falstaff*; the latter, in turn, becomes an archetypal magic opera that, in addition to its analogy to *Die Zauberflöte*, evokes

[49] Letter of March 20, 1911, ibid., p. 113.

[50] Auden, "Some Reflections on Music and Opera," *Partisan Review*, 19 (1952), 17. The one time I met Auden, soon after the publication of this statement, I objected strenuously to his judgment of the monologue. Evidently others objected as well, for Auden, an inveterate reviser of his earlier texts, removed the statement before the republication of the essay, now called "Notes on Music and Opera," in his volume *The Dyer's Hand and Other Essays* (London: Faber & Faber, 1963). The excised statement would have appeared on p. 473.

Der Freischütz and the magical transformations in Wagner's music-dramas.[51]

The differences that Hofmannsthal and Strauss perceived between their own operas and the models they emulated suggest Schiller's classic distinction between naive and sentimental art: whereas the model seems an unselfconscious creation made directly, and without mediation, out of nature, their own work can achieve success only through the most studious assimilation of the whole operatic past. Mozart and Wagner, when measured against their own predecessors, themselves would, according to Schiller's distinction, seem like sentimental artists sophisticatedly rethinking earlier operatic forms. The true naive in opera, one could argue, flourishes during those periods—for instance the eighteenth century and again the early nineteenth century—when the performer enjoys primacy over the composer, whose creative role, even if he displays the greatness of a Handel or a Rossini, is circumscribed by the availability and the vanity of singers, the force of convention, and the economics of production. Until relatively late in his career, Verdi determined his choice of subjects and the disposition of parts according to external requirements over which he had little or no control.[52] An eighteenth-century letter of advice on the preparation of a libretto indicates how operas are made in a performer-centered economy: "For this year there must be two equal parts for Cuzzoni and Faustina. Senesino takes the principal male characters, and his part must be heroic. The other three male parts should be arranged proportionately song for song in the three acts."[53]

If "naive" opera lacks the self-conscious intertextuality central to the Strauss-Hofmannsthal operas, it practices an intertextuality of its own, for the type of role assigned to each voice range is,

---

[51] For references to *Falstaff*, see letter of August 13, 1909, pp. 78–79 of Strauss-Hofmannsthal, *Briefwechsel;* for *Die Meistersinger*, letters of July 11 and 26, 1909, and September 10, 1910, pp. 71, 77, 103, and during the composition of *Ariadne,* letter of March 20, 1911, p. 113; for *Der Freischütz* and Wagner, see letters of January 8, 1911, and June 6, 1913, pp. 110, 232–33. The analogy to *Der Freischütz* was made in relation to a plan for a magic opera on Wilhelm Hauff's fairy tale "Das steinerne Herz"; the plan soon gave way to *Die Frau ohne Schatten* (see letter of March 20, 1911, pp. 112–13).

[52] For a convincing application of Schiller's concept of the naive artist to Verdi, see Isaiah Berlin, "The 'Naiveté' of Verdi," in *Against the Current: Essays in the History of Ideas* (New York: Viking, 1980), pp. 287–95. Note especially the following statement: "Verdi was the last of the great naive masters of western music, in an age given over to the *Sentimentalisches*" (pp. 291–92).

[53] See Giuseppe Riva's letter (1725) to L. A. Muratori in Weisstein, *Essence of Opera,* p. 64.

according to the conventions of a given time, repeated from opera to opera. Anybody who walks into a middle-period Verdi opera for the first time can assume that the baritone and the mezzo-soprano are likely to be losers (however much sympathy Verdi may lend them) and that the tenor and the soprano will ultimately triumph (though usually in death). A century earlier, the casual operagoer would have identified the castrato as a ruler or a heroic male figure; the uncastrated males in the cast would likely have played socially (and vocally) inferior roles. Within any particular style the relationship of voices to one another, as well as the moral and emotional positions each one assumes within the drama, is part of a system that the listener knows in advance. Eighteenth-century librettists were merciless in forcing history and mythology—the assigned matter of *opera seria*—to accommodate themselves to the system. As with commedia dell'arte, its counterpart in nonmusical drama,[54] performer-centered operas adapt so many components from one another that the individual work remains subordinate to the larger system of which it is a part. (Hofmannsthal's aim to make each opera "a genre in itself" is of course antithetical to such a system.) Sometimes composers do not simply adapt components but repeat them: Rossini was notorious for borrowing overtures and arias from his earlier operas to meet his tight deadlines.

Moreover, the virtuosity that performer-centered operas demand places such emphasis upon the individual singer that the roles within a particular musical style come to merge in the audience's mind: from a vocal point of view the Caballé of *Norma* is almost interchangeable with the Caballé of *Roberto Devereux*, just as Grisi must have been in these roles more than a century before or the great castrato Senesino in the various roles that Handel created for him. When the so-called *Puritani* quartet—consisting of the virtuoso singers Grisi, Rubini, Tamburini, and Lablache—during the 1830s appeared together in one new opera after another, each with a different "historical" setting and plot, their audiences were doubtless more aware of their vocal qualities and their ability to engage musically with one another than of their relationship to the particular historical context they pretended to represent. Shaw, referring to Adelina Patti, who by his own time

<hr>

[54] Commedia dell' arte not only serves as a useful analogy to performance-centered opera but the two forms engaged in considerable mutual interchange during the seventeenth and eighteenth centuries. See Nino Pirrotta, "*Commedia dell' Arte* and Opera," *Musical Quarterly*, 41 (1951), 305–24.

counted as the last great exponent of performer-centered opera, wrote disdainfully, "She seldom even pretends to play any other part than that of Adelina."[55]

A brief moment in Ingmar Bergman's film version of *Die Zauberflöte* illustrates with particular force some of the continuities in operatic tradition I have suggested within this section. Between the opera's two acts Bergman provides a backstage glimpse of the Sarastro figure looking at a score of *Parsifal*. The first conclusion one draws from the shot is that the sort of bass who sings Sarastro is also likely to perform Gurnemanz in Wagner's last music-drama: in the older type of repertory company, Wednesday's Sarastro was quite likely to appear as Gurnemanz on Saturday. The interchangeability of parts that the juxtaposition of these two roles suggests is something more than the interchangeability of voices in *opera seria*, however, for both Sarastro and Gurnemanz serve as the chief moral spokesmen within their respective operas. The one speaks as an Enlightenment Mason, the other as a born-again, post-Enlightenment Christian. Yet however different their particular moral positions, Bergman makes us see these two figures as standing at the beginning and at the end of a century during which opera, at least in Germany, exercised cultural claims to a degree it has never been able to do before or after. Bergman's short, allusive comment, made another century later, also seeks to evoke nostalgia for a tradition that we now see as long since ended.

[55] Review of April 18, 1890, in Laurence, *Shaw's Music*, II, 32.

[3]

Opera as Representation: II. Words against Music, Music against Words

The Question of Primacy

Between Text and Musical Setting

The question of whether words or music are primary has nourished discussions of opera ever since the meetings of the Camerata. If the question was originally bound up with the Camerata's opposition to the hegemony of counterpoint in musical composition, it has reappeared in new guise whenever a composer or critic saw fit to invoke what, in the first chapter, I called the "dramatic principle." My concern throughout the present chapter is to explore the motivations that stand behind the long-persisting critical insistence on a dichotomy between words and music, as well as the effects that this dichotomy has exercised on the creation and transmission of operas. Since composers, librettists, and audiences alike have interchanged such terms as *words*, *text*, *poetry*, and *drama* to designate the verbal side of the dichotomy, I shall also use these terms interchangeably in the course of this chapter: the dichotomy remains primary to any discriminations we may make among the terms used to characterize either of its sides. Whereas the first section of this chapter will treat the dichotomy as a power struggle to assert the primacy of one side or the other, the second section will explore the implications of this struggle for the ways we have come to speak of opera as an imitative and representational art form.

To illustrate the continuing relevance of the word–music dichotomy to the history of opera, note the remarkable similarity between the following statements, each by a major composer and each a century or more removed from the last:

> My brother says that he does not do his work by chance; considering that (in this kind of music) it has been his intention to make the discourse the mistress of the harmony and not the servant. (G. C. Monteverdi's annotation to Claudio Monteverdi's foreword to the Fifth Book of Madrigals, 1605)[1]

> I have tried to restrict music to its true office of serving poetry by means of expression. (Gluck, dedication of *Alceste*, 1769)[2]

> Let us therefore inform the *composer* that every instance of his expression, even the most trivial, *that fails to embody the poetic intention* is superfluous, annoying, bad. (Wagner, *Oper und Drama*, 1851)[3]

> At the moment I decided to write an opera, I thought of nothing—not even matters related to the technique of musical composition—except giving the theater what belongs to the theater, that is, of shaping the music in such a way that at every moment it remain conscious of its duty to serve the drama. (Berg, "Das 'Opernproblem,'" 1928)[4]

Note how these statements, far removed in time though they are, virtually echo one another. For instance, the notion that the music must literally *serve* the text appears in three of them—in the words *serva*, *servire*, and *dienen* respectively (doubtless one could find the word *dienen* in Wagner as well if one looked hard enough).

---

[1] "Dice mio fratello, che non fa le sue cose a caso; atteso che la sua intentione è stata (in questo genere di musica,) di far che l'oratione è sia padrona del armonia è non serva." In Monteverdi, *Tutte le opere*, ed. G. Francesco Malipiero, X (Asolo: n.p., 1929), p. 69.

[2] "Pensai di ristringer la Musica al suo vero ufficio di servire alla Poesia per l'espressione." In Alfred Einstein, *Gluck: Sein Leben, Seine Werke* (Zurich: Pan, n.d.), p. 142.

[3] "Erklären wir dem *Musiker* daher, dass jedes, auch das geringste Moment seines Ausdruckes, *in welchem die dichterische Absicht nicht enthalten* . . . überflüssig, störend, schlecht ist." In Wagner, *Gesammelte Schriften*, ed. Julius Kapp (Leipzig: Hesse & Becker, n.d.), XI, 315. Emphasis in the original.

[4] "[Es] schwebte mir, in dem Moment, wo ich mich entschloss, eine Oper zu schreiben, nichts anderes, auch kompositionstechnisch nichts anderes vor, als dem Theater zu geben, was des Theaters ist, das heisst also, die Musik so zu gestalten, dass sie sich ihrer Verpflichtung, dem Drama zu dienen, in jedem Augenblick bewusst ist." In Willi Reich, *Alban Berg: Leben und Werk* (Zurich: Atlantis, 1963), p. 60.

Although this recurrent sentiment has sometimes passed unreflectingly for common wisdom within operatic criticism, it by no means exhausts serious inquiry into the relationship between words and music. Berg's statement, for instance, echoes the prevailing wisdom only to subvert it a few lines later when he defends his use of traditional musical forms within the opera: "Without prejudicing the otherwise absolute (purely musical) rights of such music; without prejudicing its autonomous life through anything extra-musical."[5] One suspects that Berg needed to invoke the dramatic principle to earn the right to voice a doctrine that, at least on the surface, would seem to be its antithesis.

In a letter written in 1856, as Wagner's ideas were beginning to circulate, Berlioz, while commenting on his difficulties in composing *Les Troyens*, came out resoundingly on the musical side of the word-versus-music conflict (and, interestingly enough, uses the word *slave*, as though echoing the prevailing doctrine only to twist it around):

> The great difficulty throughout is to find the musical form—that form without which music does not exist, or exists only as the abject slave of the word. There lies Wagner's crime; he wants to dethrone music and reduce it to expressive accents. This is to outdo the system of Gluck, who most fortunately did not succeed in following his own impious theory. I am for that kind of music which you yourself call "free"—free, imperious, all-conquering. I want it to seize everything, to assimilate everything, and for it to have no Alps or Pyrenees.[6]

Berlioz's statement is less interesting as a comment on his own compositions—one could argue whether or not his or Wagner's music was more "faithful" to the words that each composer set—than as a symptom of the vehemence with which composers and critics have come out for one side or the other of the word–music dichotomy. Yet in the course of the letter Berlioz undercuts his demand for music to be "free, imperious, all-conquering" just as Berg, in his note on *Wozzeck*, moves away from his earlier acknowledgment of the centrality of the word: "To find the means of being expressive, and truthful, without ceasing to be a musician: rather, to endow music with new means of action—that is

---

[5] Ibid.

[6] Letter of August 12, 1856 (to the Princess Sayn-Wittgenstein), in Berlioz, *A Selection from His Letters*, trans. and ed., Humphrey Searle (New York: Harcourt, Brace, 1966), pp. 149–50.

the problem."[7] The movement from one to the other side of the dichotomy illustrates what Hanslick, in a statement contemporaneous with Berlioz's letter, calls the "unending struggle between the principle of dramatic exactitude and that of musical beauty."[8] And like Berlioz, Hanslick comes out on the side of music in this conflict—not, as with Berlioz, to protect the artistic freedom of the composer but because Hanslick felt himself committed to a principle of "beauty" (Schönheit) that was bound to be compromised by any theory, such as Wagner's, that gave precedence to words over music. (It is ironic, though also appropriate, that the music Wagner later composed for his caricature of Hanslick in Die Meistersinger sounds distinctly ugly within the context of that opera.)

The priority that a composer or theoretician assigns to either words or music can usually be linked to the ideologies or practical motives that govern a particular historical moment. Berlioz's assertion of the autonomy of music is at once an assertion of the Romantic doctrine of artistic genius and an attempt to guard his own identity against the danger of Wagnerian intrusion. Gluck's opting for words over music can be read as a reaction against the hegemony of the performer (to whom he had remained subservient in the many, now forgotten opere serie that marked the first half of his career) and a musical embodiment of that direct and simple expression of the emotions that we see as characteristic of the later eighteenth century.

However closely the bias towards either words or music is embedded in a particular historical context, the conflict between the two—as the verbal similarities in the above quotations from Monteverdi to Berg make clear—has remained a constant and provocative issue throughout the history of opera. The centrality of the issue is evident, for example, in Strauss's decision to build his final opera, Capriccio, around the question of whether words or music have primacy in opera. Strauss at one point considered entitling the opera Prima le parole dopo la musica, an attempt both to echo and twist around the title of a Salieri opera, Prima la musica e poi le parole (1786). Strauss could thus bring his long career to a close by asserting the continuity of operatic history and, by implication, his own central place within the canon. Strauss evokes this continuity in innumerable ways, for example, through

[7] Ibid., p. 150.
[8] Eduard Hanslick, Vom Musikalisch-Schönen (Leipzig: Johann Ambrosius Barth, 1896), p. 61.

his setting the opera in Paris in 1777, the place and time in which Gluck's theory and practice excited public attention to a degree that the word-versus-music controversy never did before or after. In the opera's long, ecstatic finale, the indecision of Strauss's main character, Madeleine, about whether to opt in favor of the words or music tells us that the issue is unresolvable, that it will, in fact, go on as long as operas continue to be written.

The persistence of this issue doubtless can be attributed to the consciousness that opera, like the madrigals and shorter pieces in which its earliest practitioners first tried out their theories, is essentially a hybrid form, an uneasy mixture of elements from two distinct, institutionalized forms of art, each of which retains an identity and a sense of its wholeness that opera can never hope to emulate. Once we think of opera as hybrid, it is easy enough to describe its history as an oscillation between periods in which the music dominates, for example, when the singer or even, as sometimes in the post-Wagnerian period, the orchestra takes over, and those in which, as at the time of Gluck's and Wagner's reforms or that of Verdi and Boito's collaboration, the words reassert their rightful place. If one shifts from historical narrative to formal description, it is equally easy to describe opera as a binary form, as Wagner did, when, employing sexual opposites, he labeled the music as the female or "child-bearing" (*Gebärerin*) element and the text as the male or "procreating" (*Erzeuger*) element.[9] By giving the procreating role to the text, Wagner by implication assigns that priority to words against music which his theory as a whole claims to establish.

If I may refer again to the spectrum between *verbal* and *operatic* that I suggested in the preceding chapter, one could say that discussions of the nature of opera tend to voice particular biases that adhere to the extreme ends of the spectrum. Those who privilege the verbal end of the spectrum expect opera to stress its representational and mimetic elements—indeed, for those who take this attitude too literally, opera is expected to approximate as closely as possible to the conditions of spoken drama. Since words, from this point of view, imitate some sort of external reality, music best realizes its nature when it is "faithful" to the

---

[9] *Oper und Drama*, pt. 1, sec. 7, in *Gesammelte Schriften*, XI, 105. Wagner's sexual analogy, which begins simply enough with a discussion of Beethoven's achievement in setting words to music, quickly turns into a long theoretical discussion that, with his characteristic verbal extravagance, exploits the sexual dichotomy.

words it sets. From the mimetic point of view, opera is at its most authentic when it remains least removed from whatever reality its text purports to imitate. It does not seem accidental that literary intellectuals, who generally also command the verbal power to write the most influential operatic criticism, tend to idealize such moments in operatic history as the "reforms" in which music claimed to make itself subservient to words. Those who invoke the primacy of words are also, in effect, acknowledging the greater prestige that poetry, at least until the Romantic period, enjoyed in relation to music: within the framework of the classical tradition, music, unlike poetry, could not invoke the authority of a Homer or a Virgil, nor could its practices claim the long-standing legitimacy that the treatises of Aristotle and Horace had accorded its sister art.

Those who embrace the opposite end of the spectrum acknowledge a minimum of shame in accepting those elements of opera I have characterized by terms such as *extravagant, histrionic,* and *performative.* From the performative standpoint, vocal brilliance or orchestral sumptuousness must take precedence over a composer's or a performer's fidelity to the text or to the external world that the text claims to represent; the willingness of audiences for centuries to pay higher prices for opera than for other forms of theatrical entertainment testifies to the spell that the performative element has persistently exercised. The physical production of opera, from this point of view, becomes an expression and extension of musical possibilities; thus the financial extravagance of, say, seventeenth-century "machine" opera or present-day productions in which designers exploit the resources of modern technology serves as an outward sign of the spiritual extravagance consonant with a performative bias in opera.

Between Librettist and Composer

The conception of opera as a hybrid form has resulted not only in a bifurcation of values in the direction of either the literary or the performative, but it has also generated an ongoing uneasiness as to who precisely is the creator of an opera. Since the Renaissance, the prevailing conception of authorship in all the arts has been that of a single agent who bears sole responsibility for an art work and who consequently gains whatever glory accrues to his creation. However much a Renaissance or Baroque artist depended on his pupils to "fill in" the details of his painting or sculpture, convention dictated attribution to the master of the workshop, until modern scholarship, committed as it is to a concept of historical veracity, ignored that agreement between artist and public which dictated single authorship, whatever the actual circumstances of composition. If the authorship of English dramas in the Renaissance often was assigned to writing teams (or not specifically assigned at all), this can be attributed to the low prestige that popular drama enjoyed in comparison, say, to poetry, in which single authorship remained unquestioned. Shortly before the advent of opera, Thomas Morley, in his treatise on music (1597), celebrated the autonomy of the composer through praise of the fantasy, a form which, in contrast to the various types of song he had earlier discussed, allows "more art [to] be shown than in any other music, because the composer is tied to nothing but that he may add, diminish, and alter at his pleasure."[10] For later composers who prized their freedom or their autonomy, opera, because of the constant compromises that librettists, impresarios, and performers imposed, would scarcely seem a desirable form.

It is no wonder that the dual authorship intrinsic to operatic composition should work both to lower the status of opera in relation to other forms and to raise continuing questions as to who should be designated the "chief" author of a particular opera. When Gluck, in a famous defense of his style, assigned the "chief merit" of his art to Calzabigi, the librettist of his first three reform operas,[11] he was obviously voicing that bias towards words over music that stands as a central assumption of his reform.[12] In matters of artistic origin, the number *two* is obviously as different in kind as it is in degree from the number *one*. The division of labor that has marked the composition of opera since its beginnings by its

[10] "A Plain and Easy Introduction to Practical Music" in *Source Readings in Music History*, ed. Oliver Strunk (New York: Norton, 1950), p. 276. After the fantasy, Morley takes up various kinds of dance, which he subordinates to the fantasy because of the particular rhythmic formulas that limit the composer's freedom.

[11] "It is to M. de Calzabigi that the chief merit belongs; and if my music has met with some approbation, I feel bound to admit that it is to him I am indebted for this, since it is he who made it possible for me to develop the resources of my art." Letter of February, 1773 (to *Mercure de France*), in Gluck, *Collected Correspondence and Papers*, trans. Stewart Thomson, ed. Hedwig Mueller von Asow and E. H. Mueller von Asow (New York: St. Martin's Press, n.d.), p. 30.

[12] This bias is still evident on the title pages of the Strauss-Hofmannsthal scores, which typically assign authorship as follows: "Comedy in———acts by Hugo von Hofmannsthal, music by Richard Strauss, Op.———." For their long discussion of how to assign the authorship of *Der Rosenkavalier*, see Strauss-Hofmannsthal, *Briefwechsel*, 3d ed., ed. Willi Schuh, (Zurich: Atlantis, 1964), pp. 102–4.

very nature implies the possibility of a unity that we feel realized at those rare moments—as in the Mozart–Da Ponte or the Verdi-Boito operas—when verbal and musical intentions appear to coincide.

This dream of unity was voiced by Metastasio, who, despite his own imperious attitude to the many composers who set his librettos, told Dr. Burney that "no music drama would be perfect or interesting till the poet and musician were one, as in ancient times, and that when Rousseau's *Devin du Village* came out, and so delighted every hearer, the literary patriarch Fontenelle attributed its success to that union of poet and musician."[13] As so often in operatic criticism, Metastasio makes his point by citing opera's ancient origins in that union of the arts which supposedly marked Greek tragedy. If Berlioz, Wagner, and Mussorgsky, a century later, built upon Rousseau's precedent by preparing their own librettos, they have remained exceptions in the history of opera until our own century, when major composers such as Debussy, Janáček, Berg, and Schönberg asserted artistic control through the preparation of their own texts. Yet to the extent that Debussy and Berg attempted to retain as much as possible of the plays they set, their work as librettists assumed more of an editorial than what one might call a "creative" nature. Joseph Kerman's designation, "Opera as Sung Play,"[14] to portray their mode suggests the subservience they exercised towards the original dramas, which in effect retain something of the status that Metastasio's librettos had for eighteenth-century composers. One might note that the twentieth-century composers who prepare their own texts generally write in prose:[15] it is as though doing a libretto in verse would force a composer to pass muster as a poet in an age skeptical about anybody's ability to pursue two distinct vocations successfully.

The dual authorship that marks most of operatic history reveals tensions as well as possibilities foreign to other major forms of art. Among the great collaborations none has been documented as thoroughly as that of Strauss and Hofmannsthal, whose lengthy correspondence, which runs to over seven hundred pages on the six operas they created together, strikes the tone of a dialogue

---

[13]In Charles Burney, *An Eighteenth-Century Musical Tour in Central Europe and the Netherlands*, ed. Percy A. Scholes (London: Oxford University Press, 1959), II, 103.

[14]See the chapter, specifically on Debussy's opera, with that title in Kerman, *Opera as Drama* (New York: Vintage, 1956), pp. 171–91.

[15]On the development of prose librettos in the late nineteenth century as a means of achieving musical "realism," see Carl Dahlhaus, *Musikalischer Realismus* (Munich: Piper, 1982), pp. 95–98, 128–32.

that, from the start, seems to have been intended for eventual public consumption. (Had the collaboration taken place a half-century later, verisimilitude would have dictated that communications between the two men be conducted by telephone—and consequently lost from public view.) The major role that this correspondence plays both in the present chapter and throughout this study is a consequence not so much of its intrinsic interest—though it remains one of the liveliest exchanges of letters to be found among any two artists at any time—but of the fact that through the representativeness of its examples and the range of relevant operatic topics it takes up it is paradigmatic of the dynamics underlying the relationship of librettist and composer and of words and music as an ongoing dialogue over the centuries.

The traditional tension between words and music manifests itself throughout the Strauss-Hofmannsthal correspondence in the contrast between the poet's stance as the verbally sophisticated man of letters and the composer's stance as the naive and sometimes vulgar bourgeois whose talents (already internationally acclaimed at the time the collaboration began in 1906) are of a distinctly nonverbal nature.[16] Hofmannsthal, for instance, enjoyed instructing Strauss on the complexity of meaning to be found in the texts he prepared for him. For instance, during the composition of *Die Frau ohne Schatten* Strauss objected to the line "Ein gepriesener Duft von Fischen und Oel" ("A praiseworthy smell of fish and oil") on grounds that the fish, which Hofmannsthal intended as symbols of the dyer's unborn children, would seem offensive in too explicitly culinary a context. As in most instances, Hofmannsthal prevailed, this time reminding Strauss that in the fairy-tale world of this opera "the little fish do not *exist* also as the children, but are merely the vehicles of a kind of magic."[17]

Hofmannsthal's intellectual overbearingness is especially evident in an exchange set off when Strauss, during the composition of the final duet of *Ariadne auf Naxos*, asked Hofmannsthal for more text in order that he could achieve the "lively intensifica-

---

[16]Hofmannsthal complained privately of his collaborator's lack of sensitivity, commenting in a letter to his friend Count Kessler, for example, that "Strauss is such an incredibly unrefined person." Letter of June 12, 1909, in Hofmannsthal-Strauss, *Der Rosenkavalier: Fassungen, Filmszenarium, Briefe*, ed. Willi Schuh (Frankfurt: Fischer, 1971), p. 244.

[17]Letter of July 8, 1914, in Strauss-Hofmannsthal, *Briefwechsel*, p. 276. Strauss's objection was stated on p. 275. His subsequent letter (July 10, p. 279) renews the objection, but Hofmannsthal continues his defense of the line in his own subsequent letter (July 12, pp. 281–82), which evidently puts the matter to rest.

tion" that he customarily sought at the ends of acts and operas. Hofmannsthal assented to the request with the proviso that Strauss pay attention to the deeper meanings of the libretto, after which the poet (who had himself been formally trained as a literary scholar) launched into a detailed analysis of the "ironic connection" between the two "spiritual worlds," the divine and the human, not only in *Ariadne* but in their earlier opera *Elektra*.[18] But Hofmannsthal was not to have the last word in this exchange, for Strauss, characterizing himself, with polite defiance, as simply a "superficial musician," thanks the librettist for enlightening him on the meaning of the opera and reminds him that if he, Strauss, failed to see the proper meaning, how would the public and the critics ever see it?[19] The conflict between the refined poet and the Philistine composer revealed in these exchanges is not simply a reflection of the two men's personalities (Strauss, in fact, exaggerated the role in which he was cast) but of the social meanings latent—at least in earlier times—within each man's occupation: thus, whereas the poet was seen to bear the weight of a long-standing cultural tradition, the composer was essentially an unreflective craftsman, who, even if assigned the role of genius, was not expected to display much verbal skill.

If Hofmannsthal often played the poet's traditional role in an overbearing way, Strauss could also treat his collaborator's texts in a cavalier way, as when he inadvertently wrote music for a stage direction in *Die ägyptische Helena* and then asked Hofmannsthal for additional words in order that he could retain what he called "a pretty phrase of song."[20] Despite the underlying tensions in the collaboration, one finds many moments in which one partner compliments the other on finding an appropriate meeting of words and music: on receiving the first scenes of the *Rosenkavalier* libretto, for example, Strauss, using a characteristically homely simile, predicts that the text "will compose itself like oil and butterfat."[21]

---

[18] Strauss had asked simply for "a more lively inward intensification" in the duet. Hofmannsthal's lengthy reply is built around the notion that "the two spiritual worlds [the divine and the human] are brought together ironically in the ending." Letters of July 14 and mid-July (exact date uncertain) 1911, ibid., pp. 132, 134.

[19] Letter of July 19, 1911, ibid., pp. 135–36.

[20] Letter of December 31, 1927, ibid., p. 615. Strauss had earlier set a stage direction in the first act of *Der Rosenkavalier*.

[21] Letter of April 21, 1909, ibid., p. 56. Strauss uses the same simile again two weeks later (p. 58).

However much Hofmannsthal and Strauss defended the prerogatives that belonged to their respective domains, neither hesitated unduly to invade the other's territory. While discussing the last act of *Der Rosenkavalier*, the librettist told the composer to come up with "an old-fashioned, partly sweet, partly impudent Viennese waltz that must weave through the whole act."[22] Strauss obviously took him at more than his word, for the opera became suffused (anachronistically, as has often been pointed out) with waltzes throughout. When Strauss attempted to rewrite some lines in *Die Frau ohne Schatten*, Hofmannsthal chided him for "sounding sentimental,"[23] but when Strauss sketched out what he calls "a popular type vaudeville verse" for the final duet of *Der Rosenkavalier*, Hofmannsthal used the rhyme words *Zeit* and *Ewigkeit* (among the most commonplace rhymes in German) but retained nothing more than the metrical framework of Strauss's admittedly banal lines.[24]

Although Hofmannsthal, doubtless because of his literary eminence, succeeded in keeping Strauss from contributing the actual words he was to set, the history of composer–librettist relations reveals some famous instances of composers rewriting crucial passages whose words failed to satisfy them: Bizet redid the text of the "Habanera" in *Carmen*, and Verdi, unhappy with the verses that Ghislanzoni had prepared for the final scene in *Aida*, created his own text, which he set to music before the librettist could

[22] Letter of April 24, 1909, ibid., p. 58.
[23] As Hofmannsthal puts it, "To have him say, 'Work no longer tastes good to me,' sounds sentimental." Letter of July 12, 1914, ibid., p. 281. Hofmannsthal's original text has "food" (*Essen*) in place of Strauss's "work" (*Arbeit*).
[24] The composer's poem reads as follows (the metrical dividers were put in by Strauss):

> Süsse / Eintracht, du / holdes / Band,
> voll treuer / Liebe / Hand in / Hand
> fest ver / eint für / alle / Zeit
> fest ver / eint in / Ewig / keit

In Strauss-Hofmannsthal, *Briefwechsel*, p. 65. Hofmannsthal filled in the metrical scheme with the following far superior lines:

> Ist ein Traum, kann nicht wirklich sein,
> dass wir zwei beieinander sein,
> beieinand für alle Zeit
> und Ewigkeit.

In Hofmannsthal-Strauss, *Der Rosenkavalier*, p. 137. For the placement of lines on the page, see the photofacsimile of Hofmannsthal's manuscript (fig. 7, after p. 304). Note that Hofmannsthal drops a foot in the last line.

send him a new version.[25] Indeed, the conflicts inherent in the relationship between composer and librettist have shown remarkable similarities over the ages, as Hofmannsthal noted when, in leafing through Verdi's correspondence, he commented on the analogies he discovered to his own relation with Strauss.[26] When, at several points in the correspondence, Strauss praises Hofmannsthal as a Scribe or a Da Ponte, he treats the librettist's role as, in effect, an archetypal one.[27]

The mutual compliments exchanged in the composer–librettist relationship are doubtless necessary to create and sustain a bond in which conflict is more often the norm than harmony. At one moment of conflict Hofmannsthal scored a point against Strauss by reminding him that it had been generations since a poet of the first rank, as he specifically called himself, had devoted his talents wholeheartedly to a composer's service.[28] Yet Hofmannsthal was also generous enough to accept the primary responsibility when an essentially literary idea he had initiated went wrong. Thus he apologizes to Strauss for the failure of their adaptation of Molière's *Le Bourgeois Gentilhomme* by pointing to the fact that the music and the drama were kept separate: in this experimental work, music and drama fail to work towards a common goal, and the music ends up, as Hofmannsthal puts it, "retarding" the dramatic action.[29]

The pairing of two equally gifted collaborators that marks the Strauss-Hofmannsthal relationship represents only one of several ways that words and music have been balanced within the history

[25] For a discussion of Bizet's changes, see Winton Dean, *Bizet* (1948; rpt. London: Dent, 1975), pp. 214–15; for Verdi's changes in the final scene, see the undated letters of late 1870 to A. Ghislanzoni in *I copialettere*, ed. Gaetano Cesare and Alessandro Luzio (Milan: Commissione Esecutiva per le Onoranze a Giuseppe Verdi, 1913), pp. 669–71. For a strong argument on the power that Verdi's librettist could exercise despite the composer's attempts to keep him in his place, see Philip Gossett, "Verdi, Ghislanzoni, and *Aida*," *Critical Inquiry*, 1 (1974), 291–334.
[26] Letter of December 12, 1926, in Strauss-Hofmannsthal, *Briefwechsel*, p. 565.
[27] Thus, in complimenting Hofmannsthal on the first scenes of *Der Rosenkavalier*, Strauss writes, "You are Da Ponte and Scribe in a single person." At another point, in complimenting Hofmannsthal on the second act of *Die Frau ohne Schatten*, he addresses him as "My dear Daponte," only to change the name after the first edition of the correspondence—as though the great opera librettists are ultimately interchangeable—to Scribe. Letters of April 21, 1909, and October 8, 1914, ibid., pp. 56, 289.
[28] Letter of December 18, 1911, ibid., p. 151.
[29] Letter of July 8, 1918, ibid., p. 413. Earlier Hofmannsthal had referred to the experiment as "a genre in itself." Letter of July 16, 1917, ibid., p. 375.

of opera. Most famous composers have had a distinct edge in talent over their librettists—as Verdi, for instance, had until his collaboration with Boito. During the late nineteenth and early twentieth centuries, librettists often came in pairs, like the famous teams Barbier and Carré (Gounod's *Faust* and *Roméo et Juliette*), Meilhac and Halévy (*Carmen* and *La Belle Hélène*), and Illica and Giacosa (*La Bohème*, *Tosca*, and *Madama Butterfly*); as Patrick J. Smith cleverly puts it in his history of the opera libretto, "The dual-librettist form . . . was a perfect arrangement for the composer because it effectively divided responsibility for the libretto and thus weakened each librettist's hold on the work."[30] It seems ironic that during the long gestation period of *Capriccio*, a work that thematizes the relation of words and music, Strauss used some half-dozen different librettists—and as a result exercised a dominance that would have been impossible during his collaboration with Hofmannsthal.[31]

In the absence of a working relationship between two parties who can acknowledge one another as more or less equal, the delicate balance between text and music has, more often than not, shifted to one side or the other. As E. T. A. Hoffmann, whose great dialogue on opera bears the title "The Poet and the Composer," complained, words and music all too often fail to make contact, with the composer "working instinctively for himself and the miserable poem running alongside without finding its way into the music."[32] The independence of text and music reached its extreme in the practice of Metastasio, who issued his librettos as "finished" works and whose literary prestige often worked to intimidate the many composers—sometimes a score or more for a single text—who set them in the course of the eighteenth and

[30] Patrick J. Smith, *The Tenth Muse: A Historical Study of the Opera Libretto* (New York: Knopf, 1970), pp. 292. By concentrating on the role of the libretto rather than on the music, Smith can approach the history of opera from an unaccustomed angle of vision. For another history of the libretto that complements Smith's through its greater emphasis on German examples (including a chapter on Goethe as librettist), see Kurt Honolka, *Kulturgeschichte des Librettos: Opern, Dichter, Operndichter*, 2d ed. (Wilhelmshaven: Heinrichshofen's Verlag, 1978).

[31] The official credit for the *Capriccio* libretto was given to Strauss's disciple, the conductor Clemens Krauss, as well as to the composer. For a detailed discussion of the various contributions made to the libretto by diverse hands, including Strauss himself, see William Mann, *Richard Strauss: A Critical Study of the Operas* (New York: Oxford University Press, 1966), pp. 361–68.

[32] Hoffmann, *Werke*, ed. Georg Ellinger (Berlin: Deutsches Verlagshaus Bong, n.d.), V, 125.

early nineteenth centuries.[33] Metastasio's real rival, one might say, was not the composer but the virtuoso singer, who used both text and music for his or her own, quite distinct purposes. Even the union of poet and musician supposedly exemplified by Wagner represents less a "collaboration" than a division of labor, for Wagner wrote his librettos before addressing himself systematically to the music. For example, Wagner published the libretto of *Der Ring des Nibelungen* in 1853, by which time he had made only limited musical sketches for the tetralogy; the composition not only took him the next two decades to complete, but the revisions in the libretto remained minimal. Since Wagner even held public readings of the *Ring* libretto while working on the music, one could say that this libretto achieves something of the literary status of a Metastasian text. Michael Tippett's practice of writing his words *simultaneously* with the music is the exception rather than the rule even among those composers who have served as their own librettists.

Although critics are wont to speak of "good" and "bad" librettos, a study of any libretto without knowledge of the particular music to which it has been set does not allow reliable predictions of how successful an opera might result from it. The librettos that Boito wrote for Ponchielli's *La Gioconda* and for his own *Mefistofele* are probably not intrinsically inferior to those he wrote for Verdi's last two operas, but they were set by lesser composers. Although Metastasio's librettos still occupy an honorable place in Italian literary history, only one of their musical settings, Mozart's *La clemenza di Tito*, whose text had been considerably revised by the time Mozart got to it, comes close to occupying a place in the operatic repertory today. However negatively one may evaluate the play (and the resulting libretto) on which *Fidelio* is based, Beethoven's opera lends the play an aura that its various other musical settings (including even Beethoven's earlier version, entitled *Leonore*) do not. Strauss remarked to Hofmannsthal that if their contemporaries were to read the librettos of *Die Meistersinger* or *Parsifal*, 90 percent would declare them "unspeakably boring" and "uncomposable."[34]

---

[33] See the chapter on Metastasio in Smith, *Tenth Muse*, pp. 74–100, as well as the librettist's letter to the then famous composer Johann Adolf Hasse conveying the most detailed musical instructions on setting his text *Attilio Regolo* (included as an appendix to Smith's book, pp. 403–8).

[34] Letter of December 15, 1913, in Strauss-Hofmannsthal, *Briefwechsel*, p. 250.

Every operagoer who has seriously followed the librettos of the major operas in the original language is aware how few read "well" as literature. Most, in fact, read very badly indeed.[35] Nineteenth-century Italian librettos were generally written in a literary language that already sounded archaic and that bore little relation to the various dialects spoken in Italy at the time. Our ability to tolerate indifferent and even poor writing in most operas is at least partly due to the fact that even in one's native language we miss a good bit, often even most of the text. Strauss's comment on this fact—"It is unbelievable, very sad, but true, how little of the text one understands in opera despite every precaution on the composer's part"—was, ironically enough, addressed to Hofmannsthal, one of the few librettists whose words everybody would want to hear in their entirety.[36]

Making a point typical of those who compare the text and the music of most of the great operas, E. T. A. Hoffmann stressed the discrepancy between the bad poetry and the beautiful music of *Die Zauberflöte*. Yet Hoffmann noted as well that despite the poetry the work's subject matter was "genuinely operatic" and "ro-

[35] Even the most respected librettos sometimes fail to stand up under scrutiny, especially if one is translating them. In an essay about his own experience translating Da Ponte's *Don Giovanni*, Auden describes the words of Donna Anna's "Non mi dir" as "of an appalling banality." See "Translating Opera Libretti" in *The Dyer's Hand and Other Essays* (London: Faber & Faber, 1963), p. 497.

[36] Letter of April 20, 1914, Strauss-Hofmannsthal, *Briefwechsel*, p. 265. The opera audience's difficulty in understanding the words has been mentioned periodically over the centuries. Note, for instance, Beaumarchais's comment, "To our cooperative actor I gave but one advice: ENUNCIATE CLEARLY! To the best orchestra in the world I addressed only the words: PLAY MORE SOFTLY!" Preface to *Tarare* in *The Essence of Opera*, ed. Ulrich Weisstein (1964; rpt. New York: Norton, 1969), pp. 150–51. It goes without saying that Strauss's orchestra, despite his attempts to utilize only individual sections for crucial vocal passages, proved a more challenging instrument to control than the orchestra for which eighteenth-century composers wrote. Whether or not Strauss, during the rehearsals for *Elektra*, really told the musicians to play louder, since he could still hear the words, his compositional practice (which included experimenting with a chamber-size orchestra in *Ariadne auf Naxos*) shows that he went to considerable effort to allow the words to come through. Weisstein, not only through the quotation from Beaumarchais that he included in his anthology of opera criticism but also in a recent article on the word–music dichotomy, has ascribed the age-old difficulty of understanding the words "to the extreme verbal economy which librettists are forced to practice in order to accommodate the music which, slow to gather momentum, needs ample room for expansion." In this article Weisstein suggests that the stage spectacle has traditionally given the audience the signals that the musically muffled words have often been unable to provide. In Weisstein, "Librettology: The Fine Art of Coping with a Chinese Twin," *Literatur und die anderen Künste*, Komparatistische Hefte, nos. 5–6 (1982), p. 29.

mantic."[37] It is as though the larger theme or the dramatic action as a whole plays a more important role for the composer than the individual words. In the same passage Hoffmann also put his finger on a principle central to the relationship of a text to its musical realization, namely its ability to "stimulate the composer's imagination."[38] The quality of a libretto is thus definable not so much through its words or its organization but through the motivating force it can exercise on a particular composer at a particular time. Wagner, forced to account for the uncommon musical power of the fourth-act love duet in *Les Huguenots*, whose composer ordinarily served as his whipping boy, credited the dramatic situation that Meyerbeer's librettist had prepared for him; Wagner even spoke of this librettist—the boulevard dramatist Scribe, whom he chose to leave unnamed—as "breathing life" into the composer by analogy to divine creation.[39] Even with as stimulating a librettist as Hofmannsthal, Strauss, in the course of demanding a more climactic arrangement for the second act of *Der Rosenkavalier*, complained, "I need a great dramatic buildup if I'm to maintain interest in a world for such a long period."[40]

Whether through some private human situation or a particular type of dramatic structure, a librettist can tap a composer's best musical resources in ways peculiar to that composer. However "perfect" we label everything in the major Mozart operas, one can also cite his special genius for the swiftly changing dramatic situations that Da Ponte provided in his finales and in the second-act sextet in *Don Giovanni*. Puccini's imagination was stimulated by the plight of acutely suffering women (Mimi, Tosca, Butterfly, Liu). Every operagoer is aware how powerfully Verdi's talents responded to plangent father–daughter confrontations, for example, in *Rigoletto*, *Simon Boccanegra*, and *Aida*, among many other operas; indeed, his attraction to *King Lear* (which was left uncomposed not through any lack of motivation) doubtless owed a goodly amount to the possibilities for musical stimulation he discerned in the overwhelming father-daughter entanglements in Shakespeare's play.

Long before much evidence had accumulated about an operatic composer's need for motivation, Monteverdi told Alessandro

[37] "Der Dichter und der Komponist" in Hoffmann, *Werke*, V, 130.
[38] Ibid.
[39] *Oper und Drama*, pt. 1, sec. 6, p. 96.
[40] Letter of July 9, 1909, in Strauss-Hofmannsthal, *Briefwechsel*, p. 69.

Striggio, the distinguished librettist of *Orfeo* and *Arianna*, why he objected to a subject, *Le nozze di Tetide*, for which Striggio was preparing a libretto: "And as to the story as a whole—as far as my no little ignorance is concerned—I do not feel that it moves me at all (moreover I find it hard to understand), nor do I feel that it carries me in a natural manner to an end that moves me. *Arianna* led me to a just lament, and *Orfeo* to a righteous prayer, but this fable leads me I don't know to what end. So what does Your Lordship want the music to be able to do?"[41] *Le nozze di Tetide* is only an early example of countless librettos or proposed subjects at which major composers have balked—whether through fear that they would not be motivated to write good music or simply that the project would not work well in the theater.[42] A sampling of rejected operas (some of these considered over a long period of time) by Verdi, Wagner, and Strauss alone would comprise an illustrious *répertoire des refusés* covering a broad spectrum of world history and literature. Verdi at one time or another was offered texts on Judith, Cleopatra, Francesca da Rimini, and Hamlet;[43] Wagner prepared scenarios or partial librettos for prospective operas on Achilles, Buddha, Jesus, and Wieland the Smith;[44] Strauss considered a Saul and David as well as a Semiramide with Hofmannsthal, and an Amphitrion and a Celestina, respectively, with his later librettists Stefan Zweig and Josef Gregor.[45]

Although a dramatic situation and even a setting (the Middle Ages or Reformation for Wagner, the eighteenth century or mythical Greece for Strauss) work in special and powerful ways on a particular composer, the actual verbal texture of a libretto can exercise a suggestiveness that allows the music to take off on its own in a manner that would be unpredictable for anybody reading

---

[41] Letter of December 9, 1616, in Monteverdi, *Letters*, trans. Denis Stevens (Cambridge, England: Cambridge University Press, 1980), p. 117.

[42] As it turned out, Monteverdi did set a good bit of the music to *Le nozze di Tetide*. In a subsequent letter (January 6, 1617) he tells Striggio that once he saw that the subject was intended for an intermezzo rather than an opera he felt content enough to start setting it (p. 125). Like most of his longer scores, *Le nozze di Tetide* is no longer extant, nor is there a record of any performance.

[43] See letters of September 22, 1847 (to G. Appiani); April 14, 1849 (from Cammarano to Verdi); February 5, 1856 (from T. Ricordi to Verdi); and June 17, 1850 (to G. Carcano), in Verdi, *I copialettere*, pp. 461, 71, 185n., 482–83.

[44] These librettos and scenarios are reprinted in *Gesammelte Schriften*, VI, 249, 278–79, 194–247, 249–77.

[45] See letters of June 5, 1906, and December 22, 1907, in Strauss-Hofmannsthal, *Briefwechsel*, pp. 22, 30–31, and Mann, *Richard Strauss*, pp. 301–2, 333.

the words alone. Adorno, building upon a remark by Hofmannsthal but writing specifically about *Wozzeck*, describes opera as "an interlinear version of its libretto,"[46] that is, a musical commentary on what goes on between the interstices of dialogue, on what the actual text has not in itself realized. To put it another way, the composer fills in what stage directors call the "subtext" of a play. For Berg, at the time of *Wozzeck*, the text also served as a kind of crutch: during the so-called atonal period, from the breakdown of tonality in 1908 until the adoption of the twelve-tone scale in the early 1920s, Schönberg and his disciples depended on the verbal texts they used for songs, cantatas, and operas (*Erwartung, Die glückliche Hand, Wozzeck*) as a stabilizing force and a means of continuity that musical form alone could not provide.[47]

Yet one could say that a verbal text serves a composer as a crutch in *any* musical style, for it gives music a prop by means of which the composer can assert a measure of freedom and autonomy while at the same time displaying the composer's dependence on the words and situations that the librettist has devised. To the extent that music and words belong to a different order of expression, music can use its interactions with words as a way of declaring at once its limitations and its ability to transcend, magnify, embellish, comment, or improvise upon (or whatever else composers conceive themselves to be doing) the texts that give it its starting point and even its authority. In *Dr. Faustus*, Thomas Mann's description of an imagined music, namely, his character Adrian Leverkühn's setting of two odes by Keats, suggests more eloquently than expository prose could how a text motivates its composer to go beyond itself: "I can well understand the challenge emanating from the urnlike beauty of these odes, that the music crown them: not to make them more perfect—for they are already perfect—but to articulate their proud, melancholy grace more forcefully and set it in relief, to lend a fuller duration to the priceless mo-

[46] Berg: *Der Meister des kleinsten Uebergangs*, "Zur Charakteristik des Wozzeck" in Adorno, *Gesammelte Schriften*, ed. Gretel Adorno and Rolf Tiedemann, XIII (Frankfurt: Suhrkamp, 1971), p. 429.

[47] See Anton von Webern's statement about the need for texts to "carry" a composer through during those years: "The longer works written at the time were linked with a text which 'carried' them . . . that's to say, with something extra-musical. With the abandoning of tonality the most important means of building up longer pieces was lost." In *The Path to the New Music*, trans. Leo Black (Bryn Mawr: Theodore Presser, 1963), pp. 53–54.

ment of their every detail than is [ordinarily] granted to the breathed-out word."[48] The ability of a "perfect" poetic text (as Mann describes the odes that his hero was setting) to achieve even greater perfection in musical form doubtless can happen only in the unheard music of fiction. Wagner commented on the reluctance of composers to set certain poems of Goethe that strike them as "too beautiful, too perfect for musical composition";[49] in actuality, Wagner explains, a musical setting "dissolves" such poetry into prose and thence creates an "autonomous" music wholly different from the essentially illusory music we claim to hear in poetry.[50] Too great a reverence for a text may thus inhibit a composer—unless the latter realizes, like Wagner, that the act of musical composition automatically transforms, in fact lowers the status of the text.

Despite the unending debate about the primacy of words or music, the attitude emerging from most composers' accounts of their activities is that the text never really loses its subservience to the music. Rather than the collaboration of equals that Gluck and Strauss sometimes pretended to engage in with their librettists, the relation of text to music is more like that of scenario to film; or, to cite the modest stance that Auden voiced towards Stravinsky soon after they had completed one of the most successful collaborations of our century, "The verses which the librettist writes . . . are really a private letter to the composer. . . . They must efface themselves and cease to care what happens to them."[51] However much the great opera composers have felt the need (at crucial occasions) to declare themselves servants to the word, most operagoers, even if they dutifully read their librettos before a performance, are likely to applaud Auden's self-effacing attitude. As should be evident by now from the range of attitudes I have cited in this section from many times and places, the stance that a

---

[48] Mann, *Doktor Faustus* (Frankfurt: Fischer, 1971), pp. 264–65 (chap. 27). The Keats poems that Leverkühn "set" are "Ode to a Nightingale" and "Ode on Melancholy."

[49] *Oper und Drama*, pt. 3, sec. 1, p. 224.

[50] Ibid. For a recent argument that "great poetry does not lend itself to the making of great libretti," see Irving Singer, *Mozart and Beethoven: The Concept of Love in Their Operas* (Baltimore: Johns Hopkins University Press, 1977), pp. 8–11.

[51] "Notes on Music and Opera" in Auden, *Dyer's Hand*, p. 473. As Ulrich Weisstein points out, Auden's whole approach to opera—whether in his role as librettist, as translator of librettos, or as operagoer—emphasizes the primacy of music over words. See Weisstein, "Reflections on a Golden Style: W. H. Auden's Theory of Opera," *Comparative Literature*, 22 (1970), 108–24.

person (whether composer, librettist, critic, or simply the member of an audience) takes in the words-versus-music debate and the reasons given for this stance are less indicators of any final truth in the matter than signs of the social and psychological role that this individual finds it convenient or necessary to assume at a particular historical moment.

Opera and Mimesis

The Persistent Notion That Music "Imitates"

Critics who wish to stress the mimetic qualities of music can easily point to the inspirational and shaping force that a poetic text exercises on a composer. On the other hand, those committed to the notion of music as an autonomous art can point to the powerful transformation a text undergoes in the process of musical composition. The question whether music, and opera in particular, imitates some world beyond itself is a special instance within that larger debate over the primacy of words and music that I discussed in the preceding section. Among those who have opted for the nonreferentiality of music, Hanslick, in his treatise on musical aesthetics, recalled the controversy during Gluck's time as to whether Orpheus's famous lament could not as easily have been sung with happy words, for instance "J'ai trouvé mon Euridice."[52] Hanslick, of course, represents an antimimetic extreme in operatic criticism. He distinguishes sharply, for example, between the representational and nonrepresentational elements in opera. Referring specifically to Orestes in Gluck's *Iphigénie en Tauride*, he limits the represenional element to the librettist's words, the actor's gestures, the costume, and the designer's set. "What the composer adds is perhaps the most beautiful of all," Hanslick writes, "but it is precisely the one thing that has nothing to do with the real Orestes: song."[53] Hanslick has cunningly

[52] Eduard Hanslick, *Vom Musikalisch-Schönen*, pp. 46–48. Gluck himself did not maintain that a melody in itself implied any particular meaning, but he recognized that an audience's interpretation of its meaning could be manipulated by a performer: "Little or nothing, apart from a slight alteration in the mode of expression, would be needed to turn my aria in *Orfeo*, 'Che faro senze Euridice?' into a puppet-dance. One note more or less sustained, failure to increase the tempo or make the voice louder, one appoggiatura out of place, a frill, a passage or roulade, can ruin a whole scene in such an opera." Letter of October 30, 1770 (to the duke of Braganza), in Gluck, *Collected Correspondence and Papers*, pp. 27–28.

[53] *Vom Musikalisch-Schönen*, p. 210.

chosen his examples from a composer who was committed to ridding operatic music of its nonrepresentational elements and who could proclaim that "to imitate nature is the acknowledged aim which [all artistic productions] must set themselves."[54]

Hanslick's attempt to break opera into two components, one representational, the other abstract, is not likely to satisfy anybody today as an approach to the medium. Yet through its commitment to *both* words and music (despite the prevalence of one or the other element at different times), opera has proved an ambivalent example for those theorists who, ever since Romanticism, have celebrated music for its freedom from the mimetic concerns characteristic of other arts such as literature and painting. When Northrop Frye claims, "I am by no means the first critic to regard music as the typical art, the one where the impact of structure is not weakened, as it has been in painting and still is in literature, by false issues derived from representation,"[55] he uses the old notion of music as nonrepresentational to voice an antimimetic bias typical of literary criticism during recent decades. If even literature has lost its mimetic power, the arguments of those composers, from Monteverdi to Berg, who believed that music could represent human situations are rendered meaningless. Frye himself, in a passage cited in the first chapter, distinguished opera from verbal drama through the observation that in *Le nozze di Figaro* and *Don Giovanni* the spectator, "though as profoundly moved as ever, is not emotionally involved with the discovery of plot or characters."[56] By shifting the experience of opera to some lofty plane above and beyond the human realm, Frye can preserve the affective element (for example, in his notion of the spectator

---

[54] Letter of February, 1773 (to *Mercure de France*), in Gluck, *Collected Correspondence and Papers*, p. 30.

[55] Northrop Frye, "Expanding Eyes," *Critical Inquiry*, 2 (1975), 213.

[56] Frye, *Anatomy of Criticism* (Princeton: Princeton University Press, 1957), p. 289. Peter Brook's recent production of *Carmen*, which tampers with the plot, cuts the score, and even eliminates the chorus and most of the characters of this opera, represents a radical attempt (on the part of a theater director rather than a composer) to endow opera with the mimetic qualities that we have traditionally associated with verbal drama. As Brook himself puts it in an interview, "For over a hundred years, opera has been largely considered an art form in which one accepts and cultivates artificiality for its own sake." His own production, by eliminating most of the work's operatic qualities, attempts to restore "such intimacy that form vanishes and you actually believe in the reality of what you see." ("Peter Brook," *New Yorker*, November 14, 1983, p. 42.) To restore the mimetic element in opera, Brook is assuming a role similar to that of the "reform" composers and librettists who invoked the dramatic principle to justify their practices.

being "as profoundly moved as ever") present in most theories of opera-as-drama without having to commit himself as well to a notion of music as representational.

Certainly those who wish to stress the nonmimetic aspects of opera can find ample argument in the actual practice of composers (however they may have stated their intentions). For the sake of achieving the type of musical effect congenial to their own talents, great composers have tinkered with finished librettos or cajoled their librettists into bending to their will. For example, Bellini in *I puritani* shifted a hymn to liberty that his librettist had planned as an opening chorus of Puritans to the end of the second act, where it no longer made dramatic sense but provided words for the *cabaletta* of a duet between two Cavaliers.[57] Moreover, until late in the nineteenth century composers routinely designed arias for particular performers—with the result that the expressiveness of the aria was often suggested more by a performer's vocal style than by the libretto the composer was setting. Even so sacred a classic as *Le nozze di Figaro* has no secure text, for Mozart—as was customary in his day—added arias, some no longer extant, for specific performers whenever the casting changed. As I indicated in the first chapter, the vengefulness so conspicuously missing in Shakespeare's portrayal of Cordelia crept into Verdi's scenario for his *Lear*, doubtless because at the time when he was writing the scenario (1850) he still assumed that an aria should end with a *cabaletta*. The intensifications ("Steigerungen") that Strauss constantly asked Hofmannsthal to supply were necessary to support his particular musical style. The editing to which Berg subjected Büchner's *Woyzeck* by his own account placed musical above dramatic considerations; moreover, although Berg claimed that the audience was not expected to be aware of the traditional musical forms—suite, symphony, variations—that he used to lend structure to *Wozzeck*,[58] once we *are* aware of them we may also choose to hear them as an assertion of musical autonomy against the realistic narrative enacted before us. In listening to Verdi's *Aroldo*, we may well find our faith in the work's dramatic integrity shaken if we remember that the composer transferred the music to an entirely new libretto, with different setting and characters,

---

[57] See Andrew Porter, "Exhumations," *New Yorker*, April 5, 1976, pp. 124–26, and Herbert Weinstock, *Vincenzo Bellini: His Life and His Operas* (New York: Knopf, 1971), p. 535.

[58] See "Das 'Opernproblem'" in Reich, *Alban Berg*, p. 61.

from his opera *Stiffelio*, which had failed on the stage seven years before.[59]

Whereas spoken drama and film encourage us, at least much of the time, to suspend our disbelief, an opera, even with the most "realistic" costumes, scenery, and acting, does not allow us to forget that people do not actually converse with one another (or to themselves) in song. Compared to spoken drama, opera does not easily allow us to suspend disbelief in the illusion we are witnessing.[60] Jurij Lotman has written of the "duality of perception" with which we experience a work of art: on the one hand we believe in the illusion, and on the other we retain an awareness of the artifice. As Lotman puts it, "*Almost* forgetting that he is experiencing a work of art, the viewer or reader must never forget it *completely*."[61] If I may improvise on Lotman here, in cinema and in realistic fiction, and certainly in most forms of spoken drama, we come considerably closer to "forgetting" the artifice than in, say, verse epic or opera. Certainly there are times in opera when the forgetting occurs in a particularly powerful way, for instance in the Marschallin's monologue in the first act of *Der Rosenkavalier* or in the final moments of *Le nozze di Figaro*. One could also say that poor or even dull singing reminds the listener of the artifice. What separates opera from the more overtly realistic forms of art is the fact that the forgetting that Lotman talks about is not as frequent in opera nor does it last as long.

Whenever we hear an unfamiliar opera after reading the synopsis that appears in guidebooks and program notes, we ordinarily experience difficulties in integrating what we see and hear with what we have read. Narrative intricacies that take several sentences to tell may well be disposed of in a few measures of music, while a simple emotional response that demands only the barest mention in the prose summary may find a lengthy musical development in an aria and a subsequent ensemble. However misleading opera synopses may be, the mimetic bias of the ordinary au-

---

[59] For a study of how Verdi accomplished his musical transfer, see Julian Budden, *The Operas of Verdi: From "Il Trovatore" to "La Forza del destino"* (New York: Oxford University Press, 1979), pp. 337–58.

[60] With certain high-style spoken dramas, for example Marlowe's *Tamburlaine* or Hugo's *Hernani*, we are doubtless more conscious that we are witnessing an illusion than we are with certain operas such as *Pelléas et Mélisande* and *Wozzeck*. It is no accident that critics attach terms such as *rhetorical* and *operatic* to these plays.

[61] Lotman, *Semiotics of Cinema*, trans. Mark E. Suino, Michigan Slavic Contributions, no. 5 (Ann Arbor: University of Michigan, 1976), p. 18.

dience is powerful enough to necessitate a ready-at-hand document connecting the performance to the story it supposedly tells. Even a reading of the complete libretto shows comparable difficulties in integration; indeed, many operatic ensembles are impossible to follow in a libretto even while one is listening to the music. Until technology made the full dimming of houselights possible during the nineteenth century, audiences customarily followed the libretto in the theater much as today's operagoers prepare themselves in advance by listening to records with libretto in hand. Yet one wonders if the synopses and librettos do not accentuate the representational power of opera in a misleading way. Stendhal, while writing of *L'italiana in Algeri* in his book on Rossini, expressed his skepticism towards a reliance on librettos by telling of a Venetian lady who refused to allow anyone to bring a libretto into her box. Although she allowed a very brief synopsis of the plot, she relied mainly on a guide that linked the plot to the musical organization at every point: "She was told, in four or five words, the subject of each aria, duet or ensemble, which had been numbered 1, 2, 3, 4, etc.: for instance, Sir Taddeo's jealousy, Lindoro's impassioned love, Isabella's coquettry towards the Bey."[62] Although the lady's method of instruction would seem to lend itself best to pre-Wagnerian opera, one suspects that the following tags for the opening of Act II of *Die Walküre*—(1) monologue—Brünnhilde's exultation; (2) duologue—Fricka's anger at incest; Wotan's defensiveness; Fricka's victory—would provide a more precise guide than the usual synopsis alone.

Despite the arguments one can muster up for the autonomy that music enjoys over what it purportedly imitates, the dependence that audiences over the centuries have felt on librettos and synopses points to their need to believe that what is being sung on the stage enacts a series of events that are in one way or another retellable. As long as these events form what seems a coherent narrative, operatic audiences will put up with a high degree of improbability. Complain as they may of the absurdity of opera plots, they are more concerned that the musical action be

---

[62] Stendhal, *Vie de Rossini* (Paris: Calmann-Lévy, n.d.), pp. 56–57 (chap. 3). The New York City Opera's policy, announced in 1983, of projecting English translations (or paraphrases) of the libretto on a screen above the stage during a performance restores the audience's privilege, still prevalent in Stendhal's time, of following the words at the same time that they experience the dramatic action. Just as nineteenth-century technology forced operagoers to study their texts *before* the lights went out, so late twentieth-century technology once again gives them the option of figuring out from moment to moment what the singers are "saying."

rooted in a series of connected events than that the latter establish plausible links to the external world. The verisimilitude we ordinarily demand in the novels we read is held in abeyance in the operas we attend. Even the great *verismo* operas manifest their verisimilitude less in their plots, which allow black-and-white characters to bring about the most improbable concatenation of events, than in their settings.

To the extent that opera, in contrast with the novel, has traditionally cultivated the extraordinary and the extravagant, explaining in what way opera is mimetic has generally demanded ingenious arguments. One such argument treats music, in contrast to painting and literature, as an essentially affective form that performs its mimetic functions in an indirect way. Thus, Rousseau, in his essay on opera in his dictionary of music, is able to retain the idea of music as a mimetic art: "The composer's art consists in substituting for the insensible image of the object that of motions which stimulate its presence in the spectator's mind; he does not represent the thing directly, but he awakens in our soul the same feeling we experience in seeing it."[63] For Rousseau music does not imitate the external world directly, as painting, for instance, can; rather, the composer awakens a "substitute" in the listeners for some presence they have experienced or observed in the real world. An argument of this sort would allow for all manner of absurdity to take place on the operatic stage as long as we believe that the events we witness are a translation into musical terms of something that once incited the composer to imitation. Music thus retains its mimetic hold on the external world, no matter how far it may seem removed from this world.

The illusion that we experience some form of mimesis in opera has remained sufficiently strong that Hanslick's skepticism as to whether Gluck's music for Orpheus's lament actually fits the words makes sense only within the context of philosophical inquiry. In the opera house we know we must take the aria as a lament as soon as we hear the words, and even if (in case we don't know French or Italian, or if the accompaniment is too loud) we fail to understand them, we get our cues from a variety of sources such as the libretto, the synopsis, the singer's gestures, our knowledge of the myth that Gluck was using, and the sight of Euridice fall-

[63] *Dictionnaire de musique*, in Rousseau, *Oeuvres*, XV (Paris: Werdet & Lequien, 1826), p. 48.

ing dead a moment before. The various flowing tunes with which Bellini's character Norma moves through a succession of stances ranging from rage to forgiveness could not easily be linked to any specific referents if, after hearing them hummed or played on the piano, we were asked which stance any single one of them claimed to imitate; yet in the opera house, despite the Wagnerian dogma that music must accommodate itself to the text from one word to the next, we are able to follow Norma's emotional shifts with relative ease.[64]

Once we elect to attend an opera, we become predisposed to making narrative sense of what we see and hear. To put it more precisely, we allow the singer and the director to give us clues by means of which we are to interpret the dramatic action. In view of the essential arbitrariness with which music can be assigned narrative meaning, it is not surprising that operatic audiences are willing to accept a range of possible interpretations for a particular passage and even a whole work. In recent years audiences (if not necessarily critics) have even gone along with radical reinterpretations of operatic texts such as Jean-Pierre Ponnelle's *Der fliegende Holländer* (San Francisco, 1975) and Patrice Chéreau's *Der Ring des Nibelungen* (Bayreuth, 1976). Unlike plays, which usually demand the pruning of passages difficult to reconcile with a striking new interpretation, operas can undergo reinterpretation without any change in either the libretto or the music, for the director can give us what signals we need through the scenery, costumes, acting, and sometimes, as well, through the synopsis that is handed out as we enter the opera house. Ponnelle's version of *Der fliegende Holländer*, which fuses the roles of Erik and the Steersman and interprets the entire action of the opera as the latter character's dream, utilizes the purely orchestral passages as a means by which the singers mime the director's new interpretation. Overtures and long orchestral interludes prove particularly inviting to directors seeking opportunities to fill out the narrative they are creating; Ponnelle, for example, uses the *Cavalleria rusticana* intermezzo (San Francisco, 1976), which throughout most

---

[64] For a brief but incisive distinction between the different word–music relationships in Bellini, Wagner, and Verdi, see Smith, *Tenth Muse*, p. 205n. Despite their fundamental differences, Wagner never wholly lost his early enthusiasm for Bellini. Moreover, his 1837 article on Bellini had praised the fusion of music and drama in *Norma* and compared the opera in this respect to the works of Gluck and Spontini. See "Bellini: Ein Wort zu seiner Zeit" in *Gesammelte Schriften*, VII, 29.

of the opera's history allowed the audience to relax, as it were, from the work's dramatic tensions, as a chance for the heroine to enact her sufferings in pantomime.

This desire to narratize nonvocal music goes beyond operatic performance. One remembers, for example, the bumptious cartoons that affix textual meanings to orchestral pieces like Mussorgsky's "Night on Bare Mountain" and Ponchielli's "Dance of the Hours" in Walt Disney's *Fantasia*. A television production of the late 1970s presented an interpretation of the prelude and *Liebestod* (the latter in its orchestral version) from *Tristan und Isolde* by means of animated abstract designs, which, despite the absence of easily identifiable objects and events, came to occupy the status of a narrative quite separate from the story of the opera. Choreographers in our time have often turned to instrumental works that were never intended for ballet—for instance, the Chopin piano pieces used for *Les Sylphides* or Bizet's Symphony in C—to build a narrative of sorts through dance movements. The impulse behind these various endeavors is similar to that guiding literary-minded composers from Berlioz to Mahler and Strauss to accompany their orchestral pieces with programs (sometimes even written after the music) that read much like opera synopses and, in fact, serve an analogous function for listeners. The tendency of even such abstract art forms as music and ballet to organize themselves into narrative sequences may well be common to all media: witness how a nontemporal medium such as painting has sometimes narratized its images in cycles such as the biblical stories "told" by Giotto and Michelangelo, or how the sonnet, with its brief and fragmentary narrative elements, could be multiplied into an extended narrative cycle by Renaissance poets.

The translation of music into textual equivalents on the part of directors, choreographers, and instrumental composers is not perhaps different in kind from the attempts of vocal composers to find musical equivalents for the words they are setting. Since the beginnings of opera, composers have shown an awareness of the need to utilize whatever technical resources were available to them to establish these equivalents for their listeners. Peri, in his foreword to *Euridice* in 1601, showed how, by rhythmic and harmonic means, he could accommodate music to words: "Having in mind those inflections and accents that serve us in our grief, in our joy, and in similar states, I caused the bass to move in time to these, either more or less, following the passions, and I held it firm throughout the false and true proportions [nonharmonic and harmonic tones respectively] until, running through various notes, the voice of the speaker came to a word that, being intoned in familiar speech, opened the way to a fresh harmony."[65] Peri does not need to raise the type of question that Hanslick raised about Gluck's aria—namely, whether music can generate meaning independent of the words to which it is attached; for Peri, words simply suggest their musical equivalents, for which he makes no claim to independent meaning.

Wagner's famous discussion about how tonal modulation can be used to express a shift in verbal meaning is a natural and powerful extension of the argument that Peri and the Camerata initiated. In a detailed demonstration of how words and music are to be accommodated to one another in the music-drama of the future, Wagner points out how a composer would set the line "Die Liebe bringt Lust und Leid." By the time the composer receives the line, it has already moved a step towards its musical realization through the poet's use of alliteration to reconcile the two contrary emotions "Lust" ("pleasure") and "Leid" ("sorrow"); the alliteration represents these emotions to the listener, according to Wagner, "as related in kind."[66] For Wagner the "music" of poetry suggests meanings separate from, but complementary to, the music to which the poetry will be set. The composer's job, once the poet has made the connections by means of alliteration, is to find the appropriate musical technique to signal the inherent opposition between the two emotions. This technique, according to Wagner, is tonal modulation, which the composer introduces in the transition from one word to the next.[67]

For Wagner, words have primacy over music only in a temporal sense; although they provide the composer with the necessary direction he is to take, only the composer has the technical means at his disposal to bring them to their full realization in creating the desired effects upon an audience.[68] Wagner does not claim that a change of key or any other purely musical device expresses a particular meaning independent of the words it is setting; rather, musical meaning is inseparable from the dramatic context in which it is articulated. Long before Wagner's treatise *Oper und Drama*,

[65] Strunk, *Source Readings in Music History*, p. 374.
[66] *Oper und Drama*, pt. 3, sec. 3, p. 260.
[67] Ibid.
[68] Wagner uses the word *Verwirklichung* ("realization") several times to indicate the composer's role in relation to the liberettist's. For a fuller discussion of the relationship, see ibid., pp. 261–62.

in which this discussion takes place, Hoffmann had demonstrated that in the hands of a major theatrical composer such as Mozart a modulation can express its dramatic meaning even for listeners without any technical knowledge of music; Hoffmann's example is the sudden shift of key, from E to C, at the moment the Commendatore accepts Don Giovanni's invitation to dinner.[69] Since the libretto has temporal primacy over its musical realization, a wise librettist can guide the composer towards effects for which he can then find the musical means. While working on the libretto of *The Rake's Progress*, Auden, whose ear for English meters was unsurpassed among poets of our century, wrote Stravinsky that "to distinguish Baba in character and emotion from the two lovers . . . I have given any line of Baba's twice the number of accents as compared with the equivalent line of Anne's or Tom's."[70] Since Auden was collaborating with a composer equally gifted in rhythmic matters, it seems no wonder that the sharp character distinctions that the listener hears in the music—even without the full context that an actual production offers—could be effected by Stravinsky's transformation of verbal into musical rhythms.

The attempts of composers throughout the history of opera to find musical "equivalents" for particular verbal situations in the texts they were setting by no means exhaust the ways that composers, whether in opera or in other forms, have sought to make music refer to something beyond itself. For example, the tone painting of natural phenomena can be found in a wide variety of musical styles. One thinks, for example, of the sea waves for which Bach employed an undulating bass and for which Debussy, in the section of *La Mer* explicitly labeled "Jeux de vagues," created a far more complex mode of description; or of the music meant to suggest the moving fish that accompanies the mention of fish in Haydn's *Die Jahreszeiten*, and of the jumping fish that Schönberg identified privately in the third of his "Five Pieces for Orchestra."

---

[69] *Kreisleriana*, chap. 6, in Hoffmann, *Werke*, I, 299. Charles Rosen cites this passage in his discussion of the ways Mozart uses modulation to create specific dramatic effects. See Rosen, *The Classical Style: Haydn, Mozart, Beethoven* (1971; rpt. New York: Norton, 1972), pp. 309–12. See also the discussion of Mozart's coordination of shifts of key with shifts in the dramatic action in the recognition scene of *Le nozze di Figaro*, pp. 290–95, and in the second-act sextet of *Don Giovanni*, pp. 296–302. Rosen's analysis is a brilliant expansion of the idea latent in Hoffmann's brief comment.

[70] Igor Stravinsky and Robert Craft, *Memories and Commentaries* (1959; rpt. Berkeley: University of California Press, 1981), p. 163.

The essentially arbitrary nature of this type of mimesis makes it possible for listeners to identify or to understand the reference only if they have been initiated into the convention. Each period—sometimes, in fact, each composer—sends signals to the listener in a distinct way: if tone painting was an assumed but not explicitly identified convention in baroque music, during the nineteenth century listeners expected to have their referents labeled in the title or in the accompanying program.[71]

Just as arbitrary is the use of thematic repetition, whether it takes the psychologically complex form of the leitmotif or simply repeats a conspicuous theme a few times in the course of an opera.[72] Yet the link between music and words is arbitrary only at

---

[71] Manfred Bukofzer, in a classic study of referentiality in baroque music, sharply contrasts the "intellectual, non-psychological" and "non-expressive" purposes of baroque referential devices with the psychological purposes of nineteenth-century program music. See "Allegory in Baroque Music," *Journal of the Warburg and Courtauld Institutes*, 3 (1939), 20. Although I agree that tone painting had radically different purposes at different times, what concerns me here are the different ways in which signals are transmitted and, above all, the arbitrary nature of tone painting, a principle that Bukofzer, writing specifically of baroque vocal music, recognizes when he states, "The unambiguous interpretation of the allegory is only possible with the text before us" (p. 20). Bach's sharpening a note at the mention of the cross is a local phenomenon in German, in which *Kreuz* happens to mean both cross and sharp (Bukofzer, p. 14); the meaning is obviously lost to those belonging to another linguistic domain. Although Haydn's musical fish can be identified by the words "Seht die Fische, welch Gewimmel!" ("See the fishes, what a multitude!") and by the audience's expectation that Haydn will seek as many equivalents as possible for the natural phenomena around which his text centers, Schönberg's listeners are dependent on the revelation that he made to his disciples. See Robert Craft, notes to *The Music of Arnold Schoenberg*, III, Columbia Records, M2S 709 (1965), p. 15. For an example of an anapestic rhythm that has been used repeatedly in opera during many periods to symbolize death, see Frits Noske's essay, "The Musical Figure of Death," in *The Signifier and the Signified: Studies in the Operas of Mozart and Verdi* (The Hague: Martinus Nijhoff, 1977), pp. 171–214. Noske traces the figure back to seventeenth-century French opera and shows in detail how Verdi made powerful use of it in a number of works. Like the other musical devices I have discussed, this figure depends on an audience's knowledge that the composer is establishing a connection—arbitrary though it must perforce remain—between this rhythm and death. For some fine discussions of how ideas of musical mimesis have changed from one period to another, see James Anderson Winn's comprehensive history of the relation of music and poetry since antiquity, *Unsuspected Eloquence: A History of the Relation of Poetry and Music* (New Haven: Yale University Press, 1981).

[72] Although the Wagnerian leitmotif has generally commanded critical attention in a way that less complex forms of recurrence have not, simple recurrence is a central mode of referentiality in nineteenth-century opera. See Joseph Kerman, "Verdi's Use of Recurring Themes," *Studies in Music History: Essays for Oliver Strunk*, ed. Harold Powers (Princeton University Press, 1968), pp. 495–510. Kerman points out Verdi's use of recurrent themes throughout his career, as well as the roots of Verdi's practice in Donizetti and Meyerbeer.

the theme's first appearance, for once the link has been established in our minds we come to associate the musical theme with its verbal referent at each recurrence (and in much the same way that we learn to associate a word and the object to which it refers). To cite a simple, non-Wagnerian example, early in *Don Carlos* the title character and Rodrigue vow friendship and invoke liberty in a *cabaletta* whose theme is repeated at crucial moments in the opera. At each repetition the audience not only remembers the original context, but it also *reinterprets* the motif against the developing dramatic action. Thus the theme gains additional significance for us when it is played after Rodrigue uses Carlos's friendship and his dedication to Flemish liberty as a means of obtaining state documents from him; still other meanings accumulate when the theme recurs at the time of Rodrigue's assassination. If thematic repetition provides interpretive cues, it also works to guarantee the narrative cohesiveness and temporality of a musical work, as well as to remind us that music can make dramatic statements and that these statements gain new significance in the course of the work. (By an interesting irony, Thomas Mann's use of the leitmotif in fiction asserts not merely the narrativity and temporality we find in its use in opera but also asserts the fact that a novel can display the complexity of organization we associate with music and can aspire to that condition of pure, wordless communication which was attributed to music in Mann's youth.)

Any attempt to find what would seem nondebatable forms of musical referentiality must be limited to the direct imitation of auditory phenomena within the external world. "Music can produce imperfect imitations only of those aspects of reality which generate sounds," Rossini was recorded as saying, and he proceeded to list examples drawn, as it turned out, from the sounds for which he had sought musical equivalents in his own operas: "rain, thunder, storms, lamentable chatter, and fictive noise."[73] Yet one wonders if Rossini's settings of these commonplace sounds would be readily identifiable without our hearing them in the context of their operas or at least having a previous knowledge of the musical style that Rossini employed for each type of sound; as though needing to underscore the referent of a Rossini *temporale* both audibly and visually, the Jean-Pierre Ponnelle production of *La Cenerentola* (San Francisco, 1969) allowed vast amounts

[73] Excerpt from conversations quoted in Weisstein, *Essence of Opera*, pp. 188–89.

of water to pour onto the stage as an accompaniment to the music. The clock chiming to twelve during the Marschallin's disquisition on time in *Der Rosenkavalier* would probably not even be recognized as a clock unless we are aware, as she tells us, that she defies temporality by turning the clocks off. Although sound imitations are part of the charm we attribute to Renaissance madrigals, listeners today need to be taught to look out for the bird calls and zephyrous breezes to identify them readily. To create the *concitato* style depicted in the battle in *Il combattimento di Tancredi e Clorinda*, Monteverdi tells us he employed a fast measure, the repeated semiquaver, which he assumed corresponded to the Pyrrhic measure that ancient philosophers had stipulated for "warlike dances."[74] Whether or not Monteverdi's early listeners recognized a connection between the semiquavers and whatever warlike dances they were familiar with, we accept the relation between this rhythm and its referent as strictly conventional. Yet once we are familiar with Monteverdi's late style, we know he is depicting battle (often only figuratively, for instance when he is setting a Petrarchan simile about war) as soon as we hear the semiquavers.[75] To the extent that sounds must be learned to be understood, their relation to their referents is just as arbitrary as the relations of Wagner's modulations to the psychological changes they are intended to signify.

Attempts to Guarantee That Music "Refers"

The most easily recognizable type of imitation that opera has cultivated is the mimesis of familiar musical forms. Although the variety of forms with which audiences are familiar is strictly limited, composers have gone to great lengths to exploit the recognizability of these forms. Marches or, in the case of early operas, fanfares can be found in the work of every major operatic composer. In the preceding chapter I pointed out the intrusion of traditional musical forms as a means by which composers could mark off and multiply the levels of musical discourse in opera, and later in the chapter I showed how recognizable earlier musical forms—for example, the Reformation chorale in *Die Meistersinger*—could

---

[74] Foreword to the Eighth Book of Madrigals in Monteverdi, *Tutte le opere*, VIII, unnumbered page preceding p. 1.

[75] Monteverdi did not claim that anybody was expected to recognize the relationship through the music alone. In fact, he stressed that the rhythm was to be combined with "words containing anger and disdain." Ibid.

evoke the audience's associations with the era from which the forms derived. Here I wish to stress the prevalence of these forms, whether earlier or contemporary, as a way of underlining—sometimes one could even say guaranteeing—an opera's referentiality. The pomp-and-circumstance marches in works as otherwise diverse as *Le Prophète*, *Les Troyens*, and *Aida* all provide an easily apprehensible signifier for the grandeur with which mid–nineteenth-century composers sought to invest their epic themes. Allusions to non-Western music easily create local color effects. Late eighteenth-century audiences recognized the appropriateness of music *à la turque* to *Die Entführung aus dem Serail*, just as audiences a century later would have noted the appropriateness of Near Eastern musical intervals to purple patches such as the bacchanale in *Samson et Dalila* or the Dance of the Seven Veils in *Salome*. The occasional use of the pentatonic scale in *Madama Butterfly* and *Turandot* functions similarly to the Oriental facial makeup and the Japanese or Chinese decor that are obligatory, respectively, to these two operas. Musical allusion is of course no guarantee of accuracy: anybody who thinks that hearing *Tristan und Isolde* can teach one how a medieval Breton shepherd piped sad tunes should remember Wagner's admission that the theme he transcribed for English horn came from the cries of Venetian gondoliers.[76]

Among the musical forms through which opera asserts its referentiality, the songs a character is portrayed singing occupy a special status, for they provide singers an opportunity to refer to, as well as to exploit, the very medium in which they are expressing themselves. Ever since Monteverdi caused his Orfeo to bend the gods to his will through his singing, composers have encouraged their characters to put their performing talents to the test. Among the operas in the standard repertory, the majority contain some form of literal song (though sometimes, like Tosca's cantata, in truncated condition). Moreover, there is virtually no opera in the repertory that does not contain some instance of stage characters performing music for the benefit of other characters— if only in such instrumental forms as the minuet and the banquet music in *Don Giovanni* or the inventive settings that Verdi devised for the onstage *banda* required by convention throughout much of his career. Even the ballets ostensibly presented for the

---

[76] See Wagner, *Mein Leben*, ed. Martin Gregor-Dellin (Munich: List, 1969), II, 591–92.

singing characters in many operas are essentially performances-within-performances, as is the much more dramatically motivated dancing between Marie and the Drum-Major that Wozzeck is forced to witness or the solo dances that Strauss's Salome and Elektra perform as extensions and variants of the roles they have been performing all along.

Compared to spoken drama, opera contains an inordinately large number of "literal" songs—drinking songs, marching songs, hunting songs, hymns, lullabies, serenades, prize songs. And again compared to spoken drama or, for that matter, to any literary form, opera contains an uncommon number of main characters who are literally singers—the two great Orfeos, la Gioconda, Tosca, the soprano and tenor of the *Ariadne* prologue—to name some of the more professional ones, though the list would bulge if one added those who, like Tannhäuser or Walther in *Die Meistersinger*, as well as the multitude of serenading operatic lovers, claimed no more than amateur status. When an "actual" song appears within an opera, it is usually marked off from its surrounding musical context through its more obvious lyricism (the serenades of Rossini's Count Almaviva or Verdi's Manrico) or its use of a conspicuously earlier style (the tenor's aria in *Der Rosenkavalier*) or of a more popular idiom (Senta's ballad in *Der fliegende Holländer*).

As a song-within-a-song, a "literal" song in opera is as appropriate as a play-within-a-play in spoken drama. Indeed, one can even point to a minor operatic subgenre, the opera-within-an-opera, in which the perennial difficulties in producing an opera become the objects of comedy. In such examples of this genre as Mozart's *Der Schauspieldirektor*, Donizetti's *Le convenienze ed inconvenienze teatrali*, and Strauss's *Ariadne auf Naxos*,[77] the histrionics in which the singers engage in both their onstage and offstage roles reminds us that opera tells about the nature of performing through the very processes by which performers perform. An opera-within-an-opera is only an extreme and obvious instance of the self-referentiality that opera displays whenever a character breaks through the bounds of ordinary singing to burst literally into song. At such times the performing that singers do when

---

[77] All of these works about operatic backstage life by famous composers are actually late examples of the subgenre, which flourished primarily in early eighteenth-century Italy in the wake of Benedetto Marcello's prose satire of the contemporary operatic world, *Il teatro alla moda*. For a brief survey of these operas, see Reinhard G. Pauly, "Benedetto Marcello's Satire on Early Eighteenth-Century Opera," *Musical Quarterly*, 34 (1948), 232–33.

they pretend to "really" sing becomes an emblem of the artifice and exaggeration characteristic of that more spacious song we call opera.

The Autonomy of Opera

The self-referentiality to which opera has been prone throughout its history, as the preceding chapter demonstrated in detail, also serves to remind us that among representational forms opera has sought to occupy an autonomous realm distinct from that of its sister arts, music and poetry, whose methods and values it purports to bring together in an uneasy but also productive relationship. Throughout this chapter I have stressed the uneasiness of the relationship as it has been defined and redefined since the earliest operas—indeed, even in the theories of the Camerata that preceded the actual appearance of an opera. Whether we speak of the tensions between text and music or of the accommodations that one of the two elements makes to the other, we are trapped, as it were, by a dichotomy that forces us to define, defend, sometimes even to trivialize one side with respect to its opposite. As one reads through the extensive literature on word–music relationships since Monteverdi's time, one often feels that the various theorists of opera had articulated something resembling a master–slave dialectic well before Hegel. Certainly one can cite ample social and institutional reasons for the persistence of the dichotomy over the centuries—for example, the difficulties inherent in dual authorship, the relatively greater prestige that literature enjoyed over music until at least the nineteenth century, the frequent need of librettists and composers alike to muster up whatever arguments they could find to defend their prerogatives against the intrusions of performers and impresarios.

The many attempts to set up relationships between opera and the so-called real world are rooted in a similarly dichotomous way of thinking. When relationships of this type are postulated, the term *real world* often merges imperceptibly with terms such as *libretto, text, story*. The antithesis to all these terms is the word *music*, which separates itself from the others through the fact that it does not communicate in the language that people speak or write but must speak a language of its own (if this can properly be called a language at all). If, for instance, one seeks to praise the mimetic qualities of Mozart's music for *Le nozze di Figaro*, one is likely to move interchangeably between two objects of imitation, Da Ponte's text and some real world of counts and servants that one projects "behind" that text; by contrast, a mimetically directed analysis of Beaumarchais's original play would maintain a demarcation between the dramatist's verbal text and the world it purportedly depicts (and, in this particular case, even influenced in return). Like the word–music dichotomy, the distinctions we make between opera and the verbal realms it presumably imitates or expresses have discernible social roots—for example, in the ongoing suspicion within our culture that art, and music in particular, is frivolous, or dangerous, or irrelevant if it is not anchored securely in some solid world.

The habit of thinking in these dichotomous terms is so ingrained in operatic commentary that it is difficult to speak of opera—as I myself have found in working out this study—without constantly falling back on them. Yet I should prefer to say that words and music actually work not so much as opposites but rather in collusion with one another to create an autonomous genre distinct from other genres. Thus, the relative "unreadability" of the libretto to *Il trovatore* is a sign that the text has suppressed those expository passages and connecting scenes characteristic of spoken drama, with the result that the opera for which it was designed could exploit a concentration of effect and a dedication to the more intense forms of expression to a degree that no other genre in its time was able to do. Similarly, the relative paucity of incident in the texts of Wagner's music-dramas allows the completed works to focus on a limited range of experience that could not be embodied convincingly in any other form. In each instance both text and music suppress or displace those ranges of experience that customarily manifest themselves in other forms such as spoken drama and, as I shall demonstrate in the next chapter, in the novel.

My reliance on terms such as *expression*[78] and *experience* reveals the difficulty of avoiding the traditional vocabulary that links art to the world. Whether one resorts to an imitative or an expressive model, the dichotomy between work and world shows up all

---

[78] The word *expression* is a particularly tricky one, for, although used in operatic commentary since the beginning of the form, it has meant different things in different cultural contexts. For instance, the so-called *Affektenlehre* (theory of affects) that dominated discussions of expressiveness in the early eighteenth century is something quite distinct from the expressive theory that came to the fore in the next century. For an excellent discussion of these differences, see the chapter "Wandlungen der Gefühlsästhetik" in Carl Dahlhaus, *Musikästhetik* (Cologne: Hans Gerig, 1967), pp. 28–38.

too readily in discussions of any art. Thus we automatically classify certain *opera seria* arias or Isolde's first-act narrative as expressions of rage. However useful such designations may be for the purpose of rhetorical classification or for an understanding of operatic convention, the florid vocal display in a Handelian rage aria or the never-before-heard sounds that issue from the orchestra during Isolde's narrative quickly demonstrates that the term *rage* (or any particular emotion we care to name) reduces what we hear to a category too narrow, too misleading even, for the phenomenon it intends to illuminate. Likewise, if we label the dialogue between voice and flute in Lucia's mad scene as a description of madness, or, to seek a more clever analogy, as an expression of split character, we may well reduce the scene to banality. If we cannot fully escape the terminology that goes with mimetic and expressive theories, we can perhaps suggest that the characteristic forms of operatic expression are *primary* to the verbal designations that commentators (including the great composers themselves) have assigned to them. (From this point of view the four centuries of debate over the primacy of words and music that this whole chapter has attempted to place in perspective could come to seem irrelevant). In the course of its history, opera, despite its countless changes of style and the differences between its national traditions, has succeeded in carving out its own territory, which, through the passionate and often extravagant stances it has cultivated, has, in effect, determined in advance the subjects and texts it naturally accommodates. From the *concitato* style that Monteverdi tried out in *Il combattimento di Tancredi e Clorinda* to the sustained frenzy of *Wozzeck*, these stances demonstrate at once the continuity and the uniqueness of opera as a form. Indeed, as the following chapter will show, it is precisely these extreme stances that opera could be said to represent—if it represents anything at all.

[4]

Opera in Novels

Opera and Passion

Although the association of music with the passions has been a commonplace since the Greeks, serious discussions of opera, from the Florentine Camerata's attempt to renew ancient tragedy in its own time to the opera criticism of Theodor Adorno, have pursued the association with special insistence. Since opera, in contrast with most other forms of music, pretends to enact, rather than simply tell or express, specific dramatic situations, it can claim a more immediate relationship to the passions than these other forms. Whether invoking the ancient notion expressed in the plural form of the word *passions* (emotions such as rage and love), whose distinguishing feature lies in their opposition to the reasoning faculty, or in the singular, post-Renaissance form *passion*, which often refers simply to emotions wrought up beyond the ordinary, the term communicates to us through the opposition it implicitly expresses towards the more rational, sober, or everyday aspects of reality.

The present chapter will demonstrate the persisting kinship between opera and passion, first through a series of statements by the major theorists of opera; next, and more concretely, through an examination of how opera is pictured in the novel—a genre that, through its overt dedication to the more commonplace aspects of existence uses opera as a means of advertising its inadequacy in the face of passion. Quite in contrast to the novel, opera since its beginnings has been credited with imitating, expressing, and exciting an order of emotions intrinsically different from that which we experience in ordinary civilized life. Indeed, those who have sought to describe the experience of opera often have re-course to a prose conspicuously more elevated or extravagant than their usual style. Consider, for example, the following statement about *Il trovatore*:

> I know my Trovatore thoroughly, from the first drum-roll to the fi-nal chord of E flat minor, and can assert that it is a heroic work, capable of producing a tremendous effect if heroically performed. But anything short of this means vulgarity, triviality, tediousness, and failure; for there is nothing unheroic to fall back on—no comedy, no spectacle, no symphonic instrumental commentary, no relief to the painful flood of feeling surging up repeatedly to the most furious intensity of passion; nothing but love—elemental love of cub for dam and male for female—with hate, jealousy, terror, and the shadow of death throughout.

It may seem surprising to learn that this statement comes from the pen of George Bernard Shaw.[1] Though one can imagine hear-ing these lines spoken (with the proper ironic distance on the au-thor's part) by one of Shaw's stage characters, they are not in the cuttingly analytical mode one associates with his role as music critic. Rather, his prose here seeks to evoke in readers those emo-tions that the opera itself might evoke in them. The central pas-sions that the opera claims to imitate—"elemental love . . . hate, jealousy"—are cited explicitly, as though Shaw's naming them in the context he has created will arouse an equivalently strong emotional response in his readers. Extreme terms abound—"tre-mendous," "most furious," "no relief," "shadow of death." Ver-sions of the word *heroic*, used in the Renaissance to designate the highest among the literary genres, occur three times, as if to in-sist that opera has taken over the power, if not precisely the cul-tural role, of traditional epic. In the following succession of phrases—"the painful flood of feeling surging up repeatedly to the most furious intensity of passion"—one suspects that Shaw, like many writers throughout the nineteenth century, has sought the most excessive possible verbal equivalent to render an essen-tially musical effect.

For Shaw, opera, through the particular means at its disposal, can achieve intense and extreme effects that words on the page can approximate only with strain, if at all. Nietzsche goes Shaw

[1] Review of June 4, 1890, in *Shaw's Music*, ed. Dan H. Laurence (New York: Dodd, Mead, 1981), II, 78.

one better by extrapolating a purely Dionysian version of *Tristan und Isolde*: since it lacks the mitigating Apollonian form-giving effect of word and image, this imagined version would strike the listener with such unrestrained force that Nietzsche asks, "Could a man whose ear had perceived the world-will's very heart chamber [*Herzkammer des Weltwillens*], who has heard the raging desire for existence as if it were a thundering river or the quietest of spraying brooks pouring out from here into all the world's veins, fail suddenly to break down?"[2] In this, one of a series of rhetorical questions that Paul de Man, in his recent deconstruction of conflicting narrative strands within *The Birth of Tragedy* cites for its "bad faith," its "abundance of clichés," and its "obvious catering to its audience," Nietzsche attempted, if ever so briefly, to suggest a narrative even more extreme than the one that Wagner set down.[3]

The primacy of passion, whether as imitation, expression, or effect (often all at once), is perhaps the single binding theme within operatic commentary since the beginnings of the form. Monteverdi's *Orfeo*, the earliest opera that remains even partially in the repertory, opens with an allegorical figure reasserting the ancient topos of the power of music to excite the passions:

> Io la Musica son, ch'ai dolci accenti
> so far tranquillo ogni turbato core,
> ed hor di nobil'ira ed hor d'amore
> poss'infiammar le più gelate menti.[4]

Given the power we still feel emanating from Monteverdi's musical setting, nobody is likely to dispute the words. Indeed, the pivotal actions by which Orfeo achieves his reunions with Euridice—his pleas and lamentations heard variously by Charon, Proserpina, and Apollo—are explicit embodiments, verbal and musical at once, of the ability of song to express the simplest passion at the same time that it seeks to inflame whatever potential passions may be lurking within its audience of icy listeners.

[2] *Die Geburt der Tragödie*, sec. 21, in Nietzsche, *Werke*, ed. Karl Schlechta (Darmstadt: Wissenschaftliche Buchgesellschaft, 1966), I, 116.
[3] De Man, *Allegories of Reading: Figural Language in Rousseau, Nietzsche, Rilke, and Proust* (New Haven: Yale University Press, 1979), p. 97.
[4] "I am Music, who, with sweet sounds, / knows how to calm every troubled heart, / and, whether to noble anger or to love, / am able to kindle the most icy souls." See Monteverdi, *Tutte le opere*, ed. G. Francesco Malipiero, XI (Asolo: n.p., 1930), p. 4. For the relations of music and the passions in Western thought, see John Hollander, *The Untuning of the Sky* (1961; rpt. New York: Norton, 1970), pp. 162–220.

Long after the composition of *Orfeo*, Monteverdi recognized the need to create a type of music that could render those more extreme passions we have come to associate with opera. Up to then, as he puts it in the foreword to his Eighth Book of Madrigals, music was able to imitate only two orders of emotion—what he called *molle* ("soft") and *temperato* ("moderate"). In discussing this passage in the second chapter, I stressed the multivoiced character that Monteverdi was able to give opera through his introduction of a third order of emotion, the *concitato* ("agitated"), and I pointed out as well his attempt to imitate the sounds of battle through the use of repeated semiquavers. In the present context, I mean to stress the peculiarly lofty character through which this third order was able to raise the intensity of operatic style to a level it had not known in its earliest phase. For what Monteverdi sought was a musical heroic style, and to create it, as he tells us in this foreword,[5] he went, quite appropriately, to an epic poem, Tasso's *Gerusalemme liberata*, a group of whose stanzas he had set for three voices in 1624 under the title *Il combattimento di Tancredi e Clorinda*. In the battle that takes up most of these stanzas, he was able to find a subject demanding a loftier style than he had used before. Though La Musica, in the *Orfeo* prologue, claimed the ability to awaken anger in her listeners, it was not until considerably later that Monteverdi felt he had achieved a musical style adequate to the harsher emotions. However much individual operatic styles were to alter after Monteverdi's time, the fullness of range he introduced from the high-pitched to the muter emotions remained permanently within the tradition.

The primacy of the passions, together with their connection to music, is central to Rousseau's theory of linguistic origins. Rousseau traces language back to the tropes employed by early man to express not so much his physical needs as his passions. For Rousseau, the medium in which such passions as hatred, pity, and anger originally were voiced was song, whose temporal priority over speech, not to speak of writing, also implies a qualitative priority.[6] Rousseau's posthumous little treatise is as much a meditation on music as it is on language; note, for instance, its full title, *Essay on the Origin of Languages, Which Treats of Melody and Musical*

[5] The original is printed in facsimile in Monteverdi, *Tutte le opere*, VIII (1929), unnumbered page preceding p. 1.

[6] See Rousseau, *Essai sur l'origine des langues*, ed. Charles Porset (Bordeaux: Guy Ducros, 1970), pp. 41, 43.

Imitation. The connection between passion and song is relevant for Rousseau not only to the time at which language originated, but, even more important, to his own time, when the prevalence of harmony over melody "resulted in the forgetting of vocal inflections," with the result that "music found itself deprived of the moral power it had yielded when it was the twofold voice of nature."[7] The chapter entitled "How Music Has Degenerated" equates musical, cultural, and linguistic decline. In his role as cultural propagandist and composer, Rousseau championed the simple, melody-centered style of Pergolesi, whom he imitated in his own opera *Le Devin du village,* against the complex, harmony-centered French style associated with his enemy Rameau. Even if it has lost much of its musical potency today, Rousseau's once-popular opera, which for a brief while brought him more fame than his literary endeavors, implicitly asserted the primacy of the passions in a world that Rousseau believed, with a fierceness of conviction that he could not adequately translate into musical style, had lost contact with these passions.

The link between passion and opera has played a conspicuous role in the writing of certain major thinkers since Rousseau. Thus, in typical post-Hegelian maneuvers, both Kierkegaard and Adorno chose opera to exemplify a form of consciousness characterized by passion and the absence of reflection. For example, Kierkegaard's famous analysis of *Don Giovanni* contrasts the opera with two literary embodiments of the same material, Byron's poem and Molière's comedy, both of which he associates with reflection, thought, and self-consciousness. Words such as *energy* and *power,* in turn, are linked to passion, which for Kierkegaard finds its most appropriate expression in the bass voice that Mozart chose for his hero. Kierkegaard even cites the champagne aria as the spot where Mozart's hero, unplagued by self-consciousness, realizes his essential nature. For Kierkegaard, Don Giovanni of course represents only the first, the "aesthetic" stage, which must ultimately be rejected in favor of the later stages of his dialectic, though within the framework of the aesthetic stage as a whole this opera represents the culminating moment earlier anticipated by that less intense mode of passion embodied in Papageno and Cherubino.[8]

Within the more socio-historical dialectic of Adorno, the passion represented by and in opera becomes the means by which

---

[7] Ibid., p. 195.

[8] See Kierkegaard, *Either/Or,* trans. D. F. Swenson and L. M. Swenson (Princeton: Princeton University Press, 1959), I, 45–134.

middle-class culture seeks an outlet from conventional constraints. In an essay entitled "Bourgeois Opera," Adorno moves from the pronouncement "Operatic song is the language of passion" to an explanation that situates opera at once within a social and philosophical framework: "It [operatic song] is not merely the commanding stylization of existence, but also the expression of what nature accomplishes in man against every convention and mediation, a conjuring up of pure immediacy."[9] Adorno had earlier stressed the link between passion and opera in his defense of Schönberg in *Philosophy of the New Music*, in which he referred to a language of passion that listeners could take for granted as a continuing mode of communication from Monteverdi through Verdi but that was violently disrupted in the music of Schönberg, who offered, in place of this language, "undisguised physical impulses of the unconscious, of shocks, of traumas."[10] Thus, once we have experienced Schönberg, the passionate outbursts of earlier opera come to seem conventionalized and mediated.

Whatever historical lines one may draw about the presence and role of passion in opera, an insistence on opera's affinities with extreme human situations recurs throughout the major commentaries of all periods. By the same token, those who shy away from extremes do not make good opera composers. Thus Wagner attributes Mendelssohn's inability to compose a successful opera to emotional insufficiency: "An opera composer must possess *profound and energetic passion* and he must be endowed with the talent *to delineate this passion in large and forceful strokes.*"[11] Whether or not one shares this particular view of Mendelssohn (it may well be colored by personal considerations), the qualities that Wagner demands of the operatic composer are similar to those Longinus attributes to great writers—"the power of forming great conceptions" and "vehement and inspired passion." And just as sublime writing, for Longinus, "brings power and irresistible might to bear, and reigns supreme over every hearer,"[12] so opera, as we can see from those awesome words by Shaw on *Il trovatore*—"capable of producing a tremendous effect when heroically per-

[9] "Bürgerliche Oper" in Theodor Adorno, *Gesammelte Schriften*, ed. Rolf Tiedemann, XVI (Frankfurt: Suhrkamp, 1978), p. 35.

[10] *Philosophie der neuen Musik*, "Schönberg und der Fortschritt," ibid., XII (1975), 44.

[11] "Halévy und die Königin von Zypern" in Wagner, *Gesammelte Schriften*, ed. Julius Kapp (Leipzig: Hesse & Becker, n.d.), VIII, 84. Emphasis in the original.

[12] *On the Sublime* (secs. 8, 1) in *Criticism: The Major Texts*, ed. W. J. Bate (New York: Harcourt, Brace, 1970), pp. 65, 62.

formed"—has traditionally been viewed as a means of raising its listeners to an extreme emotional pitch different from what they experience in the less overtly dramatic forms of music, not to speak of what they experience in their ordinary lives. As Busoni, in his treatise on musical aesthetics, put it, "Most of [the public] want to see powerful emotions on the stage because, as average individuals, they experience none in real life; but perhaps also because they lack the courage to engage in such conflicts, for which they nevertheless yearn."[13] Written by an earnest composer who was himself caught between an ironic, modernist vision and a longing to recapture a lost romantic mode, Busoni's words reaffirm, though in blunter terms than usual, the gap between operatic and everyday life that has been reiterated since the beginnings of opera.

If our contemporary notion of what constitutes passion tends to define itself above all in sexual terms, the traditional tie between passion and music has by no means been severed. It is characteristic of contemporary thought that Roland Barthes, in his celebrated reading of Balzac's minor piece *Sarrasine*, would attribute a sudden and uncontrollable ejaculation to the story's hero while the latter experiences the florid singing of his beloved Zambinella.[14] The high emotional pitch to which music has been credited with raising the soul throughout Western history can manifest itself most powerfully and typically for us in the spontaneous sexual reaction that Barthes (if not necessarily Balzac) projects upon the text.

Opera and Novelistic Discourse

Layered Narrative: The Puppet Episode in Don Quijote

The high style that marks opera among the various genres is particularly noticeable whenever one examines operas depicted in novels. To the extent that the novel has been centered on the details of daily existence, it occupies a place at the far end of a generic spectrum both from its supposed ancestor the epic and from opera, a form to which, in view of their quite diverse modes

[13] "A New Esthetic of Music" in *The Essence of Opera*, ed. Ulrich Weisstein (1964; rpt. New York: Norton, 1969), pp. 266–67.
[14] See Barthes, *S/Z*, trans. Richard Miller (New York: Hill & Wang, 1974), pp. 118–20.

of presentation, the novel would seem to bear no significant relationship. Yet descriptions of operatic performances appear in
ample detail and often even in key places within the writings of
many, perhaps even most major novelists from Rousseau to Thomas
Mann. Since opera going, especially on the Continent, was a significant aspect of ordinary life throughout the long period encom-
passed by these writers, one can attribute such scenes simply to
the breadth of representation that the novel has characteristically
assumed to be its task. Indeed, the real-life role of the opera house
as a spot where people could meet in a casual way enabled novelists to create social occasions for a multitude of characters
without having to resort to elaborate subterfuges. In the following
sections I am concerned less with details of social history or intricacies of fictional technique than with the ways that operatic
intrusions have helped the novel define its own nature and determine its formal boundaries. Scenes from operas become a reminder—for author, character, and reader alike—of the gap separating the world of operatic passion from that of ordinary life. Its
very consciousness of this gap has allowed the novel throughout
its history to meditate on its own sufficiency as a genre.

Like much else in the history of the novel, the operatic scenes
so common in the fiction of the last two centuries were anticipated in a paradigmatic way in *Don Quijote*. I refer to that scene
in which Quijote, while witnessing the puppet show of Maese
Pedro, is so fully taken in by the illusion that he interrupts the
dramatic action and ultimately cuts up the puppets with his sword
(pt. 2, chaps. 25–26). Cervantes, of course, does not describe opera
as we understand it: he could scarcely have known of the experiments going on in Florence and Mantua at the time he wrote his
book, nor would he have been able to accommodate the new medium into his own narrative, if only because the earliest operas
did not utilize the chivalric materials necessary to ignite his hero's
imagination. Nor is the scene musical in precisely the way an
opera is: the drama is enacted not by singers but by mute puppets,
and the music is presented in narrative rather than dramatic form
by a boy who chants in plainsong.[15] Yet through the contrast it
sets up between an ideal "higher" narrative enacted by the pup-

[15] One might note that the scene itself became the subject of an attractive short
opera of our own century, *El Retablo de Maese Pedro* by Manuel de Falla, who
respected its original status of not-quite-opera by presenting the main action in
puppet pantomime with orchestral accompaniment, while the boy's narrative is a
plainsong we are meant to imagine as characteristic of Cervantes's own time.

pets and a "lower" narrative within which Quijote and Sancho Panza go about their daily rounds, the scene anticipates the ways that later operatic scenes—for example, the scene that shows Natasha's irritation at the opera she is taken to in *War and Peace* or the one that describes Emma Bovary's enthrallment by *Lucia di Lammermoor*—comment upon the narratives in which they are embedded. Indeed, through the intricacy with which Cervantes portrays the interaction of the higher operatic narrative with the lower narrative of "real" events, the puppet show provides an ideal model for the varied intrusions of actual operas into novels that I shall take up in the remainder of this chapter.

The puppet episode in *Don Quijote* is notable, first of all, for the hierarchy of narratives it establishes.[16] At the two extremes are what I earlier referred to as the higher and lower narratives— on the one hand, the chivalric story of Melisendra, about to be rescued by her fiancé from Moorish captivity, and on the other the doings of Quijote and the various real-life characters. Yet in the course of the scene Cervantes constantly allows new layers of narrative to intrude between the two extremes he projected at the start. For example, although the mute puppets enact an idealized tale, a "pure" narrative without verbal encumbrances, the audience observing them obviously needs to have the story explained in words. For this purpose Cervantes presents an additional narrative layer through the explanations chanted by the boy. The latter, who is introduced to us as "interpreter and explicator of the mysteries of the said puppet stage,"[17] represents a less idealized narrative than the puppets simply by virtue of his verbal, interpretive function.

Yet within his narrative we get glimmerings of earlier versions of the puppets' story. The boy presents these only in bits and pieces—fragmentary quotations from older ballads as well as from a contemporary poem about the two lovers. Like a modern scholar investigating orally transmitted tales, the boy does not seek out a single primal version but draws upon several distinct sources.

[16] The standard interpretations of the scene all, in one way or another, stress the multilayeredness of the narrative. See, for example, José Ortega y Gasset, *Meditaciones del Quijote* (1914; rpt. Madrid: Revista de Occidente, 1963), pp. 106–8; George Haley, "The Narrator in *Don Quijote*: Maese Pedro's Puppet Show," *Modern Language Notes*, 80 (1965), 145–65; and Alban Forcione, *Cervantes, Aristotle, and the "Persiles"* (Princeton: Princeton University Press, 1970), pp. 146–51.

[17] Cervantes, *Don Quijote*, ed. Martín de Riquer (Barcelona: Juventud, 1971), II, 728. All quotations from the *Quijote* within this section are cited from pages 728–33 of this text. Page numbers will not subsequently be marked.

Through these quotations Cervantes suggests a narrative of higher authority than that presented by the puppets themselves: after all, the familiarity of the audience (both the audience within the scene and Cervantes's original reading audience) with the story would have come from the words of these very ballads.

Throughout the scene we remain constantly aware of the instability in the relationship between higher and lower narratives. For example, at one point the puppet who is playing Melisendra catches her skirt on a balcony bar and is left hanging in the air. The boy-interpreter quickly tidies over the gap between the two narratives by asserting Don Gaiferos's nonchalance about the condition of his beloved's clothes ("without noticing whether her rich skirt is torn or not"). Even Cervantes's (or his surrogate Cide Hamete's) role as narrator is subject to a certain instability: he opens chapter 26 by addressing his readers with a quotation from Virgil in Spanish translation, "Callaron todos, tirios y troyanos" ("All fell silent, Tyrians and Trojans"), after which he abruptly shifts from the epic style of a borrowed passage to his own prose voice, which, at this point, assumes a higher than normal tone: "I mean, all who were watching the puppet theater were hanging on the lips of the explicator of its wonders."

The characters of the "real" action have their own problematic relation to reality. Quijote's failure to distinguish levels of reality is of course the generating force in the game that the book as a whole plays out. But even Maese Pedro, who as master of the revels seems to be the most stable force within this scene, turns out to be an impostor, for in the subsequent chapter he is unmasked as Ginés de Pasamonte, a picaresque character who had appeared in part 1 and whose relation to reality there was rendered questionable by a narrative inconsistency that Cervantes now attributes to a printer's error.

The linguistic means by which the higher narrative is interpreted in the text clearly affects the quality of the illusion that the narrative can create. When the boy lapses into too lofty a style ("Go in peace, oh peerless pair of true lovers!") Maese Pedro, fearing the loss of the illusion, interrupts to remind him that "all affectation is bad." The boy's tendency to digress is equally threatening to the stability of the higher narrative, as Don Quijote reminds him after the boy explains a violent incident among the Moors by comparing the Christian and Moorish systems of justice. Indeed, Maese Pedro himself joins Quijote at the same point to keep the boy from wandering from his text. Pedro, in fact, lik-

ens digression to counterpoint, and straight narrative to plainsong, as though to say that a satisfactory illusion must stem from
the most immediate presentation of an event, without explana-
tory comment. Like many opera scenes in later novels, the puppet
show must strive for purity and consistency of illusion if it is to
maintain its identity as separate from the lower narrative.

In still another intrusion into the lower narrative, Quijote challenges the boy's veracity when the father refers to the sound of
bells in the Moorish city: to be fully accurate, the knight reminds
him, the show should employ either drums or flutes. Even though
Maese Pedro in turn reminds Quijote that the dramas of the time
are full of such improprieties, the latter refuses to allow the world
of illusion (which he of course takes as reality) to be any less
rational or consistent than the real world itself. It is significant,
moreover, that Quijote enters (and destroys) the illusory world
precisely at the moment that the narrator, as though improvising
at Quijote's suggestion, introduces the instruments—flageolets
and various types of drums—that Quijote had demanded a few
lines before.

But the scene the boy describes is notable in still another respect, for it reveals itself solely by visual and aural means: the
only verbal element comes from the boy's narrative, which utilizes primarily performative language. Note, for example, the imperative "Miren" ("Look") that governs his description, as well as
the exclamatory "Cuánto" ("How many") with which he modi-
fies the various sights and sounds he names: "Look what a large
and splendid group of horsemen is issuing from the city in pursuit
of the two Christian lovers, how many trumpets blowing, how
many horns sounding and how many drums beating." Quijote, in
turn, perceives the scene directly through the senses of sight and
hearing with the magnifying word "tanto" ("such," "so many")
thrown in as though in answer to the exclamatory "cuánto":
"Seeing so many Moors and hearing such a din, Don Quijote. . . ."
Like later novelists who introduce opera scenes into their tales of
ordinary life, Cervantes is at pains to find a performative, nonrational mode of discourse to establish the special status of the higher
narrative.

This performative mode is evident as well through the rhetorical power that the narrator attempts to exercise over his audience.
In fact, his rhetoric reaches its extreme in his final line before
Quijote's destruction of the puppets. In attempting to evoke fear
in the audience, he creates an image of such violence that his

narrative, just as it is about to collapse, approaches absurdity: "I fear they [the Moors] will catch up with them [the lovers] and return them tied to their own horse's tail, which would make a horrendous spectacle." With the last words, "un horrendo espe-táculo," which contain both the extremity of the situation and a tacit acknowledgment of its theatrical nature, Quijote draws his sword and physically breaks down those demarcations between reality and fiction that, at least up to this point in the scene, have been violated on a verbal level alone. Once the physical violation has occurred, the scene cannot go on, for the "higher" layer, on which the "lower" layers are dependent, has ceased to exist; as at the end of the other adventures that make up *Don Quijote*, Cervantes must set up a new illusion in order for his novel to continue.

The multilayered narrative form that Cervantes practices is at best a fragile art, for the individual layers, including what one takes to be the "realistic" level, continually threaten to disappear, lose their identity, or redefine themselves within another layer. To adapt the analogy that Maese Pedro uses to correct the boy when he digresses, "Counterpoint tends to break down through its delicacy." By contrast, the plainsong that Pedro advocates may make for a stable narrative of the sort we would classify with categories such as folktale, romance, or a scenario for opera. Certainly the boy's tale could not sustain a novel, at least of the type that Cervantes introduced and whose status as point of origin the genre has affirmed continuously to our own day.

Some Versions of Lucy: Where Angels Fear to Tread,
Madame Bovary, *and* The Bride of Lammermoor

The performance of *Lucia di Lammermoor* that E. M. Forster introduces for the inhabitants of the hill town of Monteriano (a pseudonym for San Gimignano) in *Where Angels Fear to Tread* is as provincial and high-spirited—and as full of unexpected intrusions from the "real" world—as the puppet-show romance in *Don Quijote*. The three visiting English characters through whose eyes we view the spectacle in Forster's novel are all too painfully aware of flaws—the "stout and ugly" soprano, the vulgar drop-scenes, the bamboo clotheshorse loaded with artificial bouquets for the prima donna—that undercut the romantic experience to which the local inhabitants are able to respond in their simple and unself-conscious ways.[18] Although the so-called bel canto revival has taught us, in recent years, to hear Donizetti and Bellini with a fresh ear, in 1905, when Forster published his novel, *Lucia* was a tired old war-horse fit only for those uneducated enough to put up with the ragged performances it was all too often given. (In the Cambridge-Bloomsbury world to which Forster belonged, a pilgrimage to Bayreuth, even if one didn't really care for Wagner's music, was the "advanced" thing to do.)

Yet *Lucia* provides the perfect vehicle for the cultural statement that Forster makes in his book: this opera is a symbolic extension of everything that Italy, or at least provincial Italy, represents for Forster—passion, unselfconsciousness, expression of the most primitive emotions, yet with an underside characterized by vulgarity, by something grown stale. Thus, although the singer portraying Lucia is able to make the audience "murmur like a hive of happy bees," we are constantly reminded of the cultural price with which Forster's surrogate character Philip characterizes her in the ambiguous line, "There is something majestic in the bad taste of Italy." As a moment in the higher narrative that Italy embodies throughout the novel, the opera is ultimately as precarious as the puppet show in *Don Quijote*. The lower narrative is the world of England, more precisely the provincial world of Sawston, whose inhabitants are schematically characterized by attributes precisely the opposite to those of Monteriano, namely, Puritan rigidity, decorum, suppression of the emotions.

As in *Don Quijote*, the interaction of the two narratives takes the form of intrusions by a member of the audience. Whereas the Italian spectators participate to the point of sighing, singing, tapping, and drumming while the music goes on, the most rigid of the foreign visitors, Harriet Herriton, interrupts with "an acid 'Shish'" that brings a brief spell of English decorum to the house.

---

[18] See E. M. Forster, *Where Angels Fear to Tread* (New York: Random House, n.d.), pp. 116–23 (chap. 6). All subsequent quotations from the text are drawn from these pages. It is worth noting that the *Lucia* performance described in the novel was suggested by an actual performance that Forster, while traveling in Italy in 1903 with his mother, attended in the company of his friend Edward J. Dent, later to become well known as a musicologist and as author of what for long counted as a standard general study of opera. Whether or not the actual performance was as bad as the one in the novel, its title role was sung by Luisa Tetrazzini, still unknown outside Italy but later to become a sufficiently legendary singer to have a chicken concoction named after her. See P. N. Furbank, *E. M. Forster: A Life* (New York: Harcourt Brace, 1977), I, 103–4. For an example of how Donizetti's opera was trivialized in Forster's time, see Dent's own book, *Opera* (1940; rpt. Baltimore: Penguin, 1953), p. 68.

Like all Forster's novels the book is built around the conflict between lower and higher narratives. In *Where Angels Fear to Tread*, Sawston and England (for which the town stands) are left behind after the first chapter, only to reemerge through the three English tourists who intrude, first, to rescue their fellow countrywoman who had rashly married an Italian and, after her death, to rescue the child of this marriage.

The child's accidental death at the end can be read as a sign of Forster's cultural homelessness. Indeed, Forster's novels as a whole are interpretable as attempts to find a mode beyond what Fredric Jameson calls the "national allegory" that prevailed in nineteenth-century fiction. As Jameson puts it, "Nineteenth-century or 'classical' realism presupposed the relative intelligibility and self-sufficiency of the national experience from within, a coherence in its social life such that the narrative of the destinies of its individual citizens can be expected to achieve formal completeness."[19] For Forster and, in fact, for the other novelists of his generation, the national experience had lost the intelligibility and sense of coherence it had had for the major writers of the preceding century. The lower narrative of everyday English life could be grasped at best by means of rigidly contrived attributes that achieve novelistic life through sustained contrast with the opposing attributes of the higher narrative. The resulting fiction, to build on Jameson's terms, could be called a transnational allegory (Jameson himself refers to Forster's later novel, *A Passage to India*, as "colonial allegory").[20]

To fill in his higher narrative of Italy, Forster could not call upon his own lived experience, as he could with the lower narrative, but fell back instead upon traditional primitivistic notions about noble savages who, like those hypothesized by Rousseau in his essay on linguistic origins, could still speak a language approaching song and had not yet lost touch with their passions. What he created, in short, was an essentially operatic world for which the *Lucia* performance served as fitting emblem. Note the contrast between the Italian audience's unselfconscious response to the music and Harriet Herriton's vain search for the plot line: "Harriet, like M. Bovary on a more famous occasion, was trying to follow the plot. Occasionally she nudged her companions, and asked them what had become of Walter Scott. She looked round

[19] Fredric Jameson, *Fables of Aggression: Wyndham Lewis, the Modernist as Fascist* (Berkeley: University of California Press, 1979), p. 94.
[20] Ibid., p. 95.

grimly. The audience sounded drunk, and even Caroline, who never took a drop, was swaying oddly. Violent waves of excitement, all arising from very little, went sweeping round the theatre." The near-orgy that Forster describes could have been set off as easily by drink or sex as by music (the real-life Forster, as we know, was attracted to noble savages from southern climes); the Italian alternative to the rejected English sobriety realizes itself most fully in a heightened, if also vulgar, musical narrative.

Forster's parenthetical reference to M. Bovary is a clear signal that he is at once evoking and reinterpreting the higher narrative that Flaubert had created in the provincial performance of *Lucia* that the Bovarys attend in Rouen. The performance that Flaubert stages in *Madame Bovary* is a more complicated affair than Forster's, for it draws within itself such diverse elements as Charles's lumpish behavior as a spectator, the life history of the tenor, the libretto and its source in Walter Scott, and the presence in the audience of Léon Dupuis, whose subsequent affair with Emma, through the logic established within Flaubert's higher narrative, grows directly out of Emma's operatic experience. This scene, which serves as the culmination of the novel's second part, in turns continues and intensifies the higher narrative that had been going on in Emma's consciousness since her first appearance in the book. This narrative within her mind had included such phenomena as memories of her early reading (including Scott, whose writings the opera raises to an even higher romantic pitch), of her religious experiences, as well as those incidents that fill the earlier part of the novel—the ball at Vaubyessard, the first and still Platonic romance with Léon, the sensual affair with Rodolphe, and a multitude of perceptions that Flaubert, in a deliberately elevated style, allows to filter through her mind.

The *Lucia* performance represents both a culmination of what went on before and a preparation for Emma's hectic final phase, the consummation and collapse of her relation with Léon. Emma's perception of the performance (for which Flaubert utilizes the opera's French version, somewhat different in its names and details from the Italian version) fuses elements from the stage action, instrumental accompaniment, the real lives of the performers, and the flights of imagination that these perceptions in turn set off. Note the following passage:

> She could not sufficiently take in the costumes, the scenery, the actors, the painted trees that quivered when anybody walked, and

the velvet caps, capes, swords, all those imaginary things that vibrated in the music as in the atmosphere of another world. But a young woman entered tossing a purse to a squire in green. She remained alone on stage, and then one could hear a flute that sounded like a fountain murmuring or like the warbling of birds. Lucy bravely broke into her cavatina in G major; she pined for love, she asked for wings. Emma too would have liked, fleeing away from life, to be locked in an embrace. Suddenly Edgar Lagardy appeared.[21]

Within the higher narrative flowing through Emma's consciousness, elements that would be clearly distinguished in the lower narrative become thoroughly mixed together. The scenery, costumes, and props are attached at once to the drama onstage and to "the atmosphere of another world." The physical fountain slips into a simile for the flute obbligato in Lucia's aria. The operatic heroine's romantic strivings ("she pined for love, she asked for wings") are juxtaposed to the technical efforts of singing ("Lucy bravely broke into her cavatina in G major"). Emma's passionate imaginative response ("Emma too would have liked . . . to be locked in an embrace"), in turn, works like a musical obbligato to Lucia's aria. Perhaps the strangest fusion of all comes at the entrance of the tenor, whose name is given as Edgar Lagardy, Edgar being the operatic figure he represents, Lagardy his actual name. Indeed, in the subsequent paragraph Lagardy's own tempestuous life—his humble origins as boatman, his abandonment of a Polish princess followed by countless affairs—is absorbed within the higher narrative, in which Flaubert, though initially identifying him with the traditional passions of noble savagery (he belongs, we are told, to "the ardent races of the south" and has "more temperament than intelligence") also exposes the precariousness of the higher narrative through a brief but cutting reminder of the man's essential banality—"that admirable charlatan's nature, in which there is something of the hairdresser as well as the bullfighter."

In the course of the opera the higher narrative moves through a series of transformations, which correspond, in turn, to the shifts that Flaubert locates within Emma's consciousness. Before the curtain even goes up, this narrative, as in the episode of the ball at Vaubyessard, is constructed out of her observations of material splendor—the large tapestried door she pushes to enter her box,

[21] Flaubert, *Madame Bovary*, ed. Edouard Maynial (Paris: Garnier, n.d.), pp. 235–36. All quotations are based on this text, within which the opera episode encompasses pp. 234–42 (pt. 2, chap. 15).

the gold canes on which the young beaux in the audience lean with their yellow gloves. Throughout the first act, the narrative, as the quotation above indicates, is centered on the stage action, though it gradually absorbs such "extraneous" elements as the tenor's personal life and Emma's memory of reading Walter Scott. At the end of the act Flaubert rudely breaks the spell of the narrative through a foolish question by Charles, whose various intrusions function like those of Harriet Herriton in Forster's novel and Quijote in Cervantes's.

By the second act the higher narrative is no longer centered in the performance itself but in Emma's own longings, which, kindled by her experience of the first act, now assume primacy. As a result she belittles the passions enacted on stage ("She knew now how small were the passions that art magnified") in favor of her own. Briefly during the second act, through the power of the sextet, she is drawn back to the stage action, in which the six characters impress their varying passions ("anger, vengeance, jealousy, terror, mercy, and astonishment") upon her consciousness. But the narrative she now enacts is dominated by her longing for the real-life Lagardy, whom she imagines carrying her off as he had a multitude of other women.

Still another change of narrative focus takes place with the third act, when she no longer listens to the music ("The mad-scene did not interest Emma, and the singer seemed to her to overact"). During the second intermission she had had her unexpected reunion with Léon, and from here on—indeed, for most of the subsequent chapters—the higher narrative finds its locus in the frenzied life she leads with him: the visit to the cathedral, the cab ride, the trysts in Rouen. The operatic world that had proleptically colored the earlier stages of Emma's development thus hovers retrospectively over her impending decline and fall.

The lower narrative of *Madame Bovary* focuses on the provincial life emblematized by the novel's subtitle, *Moeurs de province*. Even the subscription holders at the performance never rise from the lower narrative to the more lofty one enacting itself within Emma's mind. As Flaubert puts it without any interpretation on Emma's part, "They [the subscribers] sought relief from the anxieties of the commercial world in the fine arts; yet not being able to forget business matters, they still chatted about cotton, spirits, or indigo." This narrative of everyday life is richly filled with the characters and doings of the two towns that the Bovarys inhabit, and its banalities are presented in their most distilled form by

Charles, who, as critics of the book always remind us, presides over both the beginning and the end of the novel.

If the book, at least on the surface (and in its subtitle), plays upon the idea of national allegory that Jameson has located in the great nineteenth-century novels, the absurd light in which Flaubert casts the national experience testifies to his need to find a higher narrative that could transcend the impoverished materials he had at his novelistic disposal. This higher narrative that he created must also, if the lower narrative is to maintain its integrity, entail the ironic distance with which he records Emma's perceptions; yet despite the unremitting irony, the higher narrative at least leaves in the reader's mind some traces of those passions whose possible existence the opera scene allows us, at least tentatively, to affirm. In *Salammbô* and *La Tentation de Saint-Antoine* Flaubert could leave the national experience behind (except by implication) and allow the higher narrative to swallow up the lower one. It is no accident that both these works invite the designation *operatic*.

The once-famous novel that generated the opera used by Flaubert and Forster to express a fullness of passion impossible within everyday novelistic life is itself a layered narrative with an uncommonly sharp demarcation between "higher" and "lower" worlds. In *The Bride of Lammermoor* Walter Scott created a higher narrative centered on the uncompromising passion of Lucy Ashton and Edgar Ravenswood, whom he surrounds with such arch-romantic trappings as Edgar's sublimely situated castle and Lucy's nymph-haunted fountain. As one reads through the romantic parts of the novel, one is constantly aware how easy the transformation must have been from novel to opera, for Scott drew on a vocabulary already well entrenched in those two modes of writing—Gothic fiction and Romantic poetry—in which the high style still prevailed in his day. Thus he could present his hero, the Master of Ravenswood, with a "countenance . . . stern and wild, a fierce and even savage expression" and he could portray Ravenswood dashing away from Lucy's fatal marriage ceremony "with the speed of a demon dismissed by the exorcist."[22]

Yet the higher narrative of *The Bride of Lammermoor* is intertwined throughout with a lower narrative composed of conventional novelistic characters such as the members of the Ashton

[22] Walter Scott, *The Bride of Lammermoor* (London: Oxford University Press, 1912), pp. 374, 384 (chap. 33). All quotations will be cited from this edition.

family (except of course for Lucy) and the simple folk who inhabit the towns and the servant quarters of the various Waverley novels. Lucy's father, the Lord Keeper, is characterized by his "useful and practical" talents and his "time-serving disposition" (chap. 15, p. 183). As one quickly comes to expect while reading Scott, the higher narrative is associated with a fast-vanishing feudal aristocracy, with ancient traditions and superstitions that the new commercial world represented by the Ashtons tries desperately to expunge. Like all Scott novels, *The Bride of Lammermoor* belongs to, in fact helps initiate that mode of fiction to which Jameson gave the formulation "national allegory." In Scott the "intelligibility and self-sufficiency of the national experience," to cite Jameson's words again, have none of the problematic quality one finds in Flaubert and Forster.

Thus Scott portrays the conflicts among his characters as conflicts within Scottish political life, above all between the representatives of surviving feudal remnants and of modern commercial interests. The typical Scott hero, established by the title character of the first novel, *Waverley*, is an elegant, passive, and not yet fully formed young man who moves easily through the diverse layers of society whose conflicts are Scott's central concern. Scott treats his feudal figures such as Fergus MacIvor and Rob Roy with both the awe elicited by those who belong to a heroic age and with an acknowledgment that they must inevitably pass from the scene of history. However much we are made to admire his more romantic characters, Scott manipulates the reader's response to advocate compromise and conciliation.

The Bride of Lammermoor, unlike the other Scott novels, is notable for the absoluteness with which the opposing forces are pitted against one another and, in fact, destroy one another. The ending is unmitigatedly tragic, and the book conspicuously lacks the characteristic Scott hero who can mediate between higher and lower narratives. Whenever possible Scott suggests supernatural forces beneath the naturalistic surface of the story. For example, the fountain at which Lucy and Ravenswood plight their troth is identified with an ancient magical story of a nymph engaged in trysts with a Ravenswood ancestor (though, as always, Scott maintains the naturalistic convention by introducing the passage as "a legendary tale") (chap. 5, p. 54). At a later point Ravenswood, as he passes the fountain on horseback, even has a vision of Lucy, who subsequently turns into Alice, a prophetic blind woman with special connections to the supernatural world with which Scott seeks to haunt the book. Even a character from the lower narrative such as Bucklaw, the ambitious suitor whom the mad Lucy tries to murder in their wedding chamber, ends up, after his recovery, conducting himself in a manner that Scott calls "overstrained" and "romantic"—in short, typical of the higher narrative.[23]

It is notable that Scott introduces *The Bride of Lammermoor* with a chapter distinguishing this novel from his characteristic mode of writing. Speaking through the persona of Peter Pattieson, the author argues with a painter friend, Dick Tinto, who complains that Scott's characters "*patter* too much. . . . There is nothing in whole pages but mere chat and dialogue" (chap. 1, p. 12). The result, according to Tinto, is that "your story has become chill and constrained, and you have lost the power of arresting the attention and exciting the imagination" (p. 14). Although Scott admits he has been unable fully to embody Tinto's advice—the book, as it turns out, still includes a good bit of the low-life chatter for which the author was celebrated—*The Bride of Lammermoor* succeeds in baring its characters' passions in a sufficiently operatic manner to satisfy Tinto's command that the author "excite the imagination." For example, Ravenswood's accidental death in quicksand, occasioned by his rashness in hurrying to meet Lucy's brother in a duel, allows an operatic ending that could achieve credibility only in a novel and not on the operatic stage, where it would have looked absurd and, even more important, would have failed to provide ample enough opportunity (as Donizetti's librettist did in fact provide by arranging a suicide) to allow the hero to memorialize his fate in song.

Yet for all its operatic qualities, *The Bride of Lammermoor* maintains a degree of novelistic self-consciousness. In one of those allusions in which an author indirectly points to those predecessors with whom he feels affinities, Scott briefly compares Lucy's father with Don Gaiferos, the hero within Master Peter's puppet show in *Don Quijote* (chap. 22, p. 264). Lucy herself, for all the constancy with which she persists in her passion, has learned the ropes through the mediation of literary models. Both at the start of her story and just before its catastrophe, Scott carefully places

<hr>

[23] Chap. 34, p. 396. For an excellent analysis of this novel as an extreme instance among Scott's earlier novels, see George Levine, *The Realistic Imagination* (Chicago: University of Chicago Press, 1981), pp. 107–21. As Levine puts it, "*The Bride* is steeped in the excess, the mystery, the uncontrollable energy whose price *Waverley* refuses to pay" (p. 107).

her in a tradition that goes back to *Don Quijote* and that we as readers know will go on to *Madame Bovary* and later heroes and heroines whose penchant for reading is at once their glory and their undoing. Thus Scott paints her as "of a romantic disposition, delighting in tales of love and wonder, and readily identifying herself with the situation of those legendary heroines, with whose adventures, for want of better reading, her memory had become stocked" (chap. 30, p. 359). It is as though Scott here recognizes the novel up against its limits—as though extreme passion cannot be rendered in literary terms without a rational explanation, above all an explanation that has itself become one of the conventions by which the novel defines its nature. By the time of the catastrophe, passions have run so high that Scott acknowledged the limits of his genre by invoking the inexpressibility topos: "The unutterable agony of the parents—the horror and confusion of all who were in the castle—the fury of contending passions between the friends of the different parties, passions augmented by previous intemperance, surpass description" (chap. 34, p. 394).

In the early nineteenth century, music, unlike literature, did not flinch from such passions. Nor did Cammarano, in writing the libretto for *Lucia*, need to worry about the constraints that novelists recognized as constitutive limits of the genre they were reworking. To effect the transformation of novel into opera, Cammarano simply lopped off the lower narrative—the low-life humor, the political machinations, the filling in of Scottish history, above all the ideological statements that run through all Scott's novels.[24] Except for Ravenswood's suicide, the opera's major, most memorable moments—the lovers' vows at the haunted fountain, the wedding chorus, the sextet after Ravenswood's unexpected return, Lucy's mad scene—stood ready-made for operatic treatment, in fact had merely to be molded into the tritely poetic language that Italian librettos at the time demanded. In the opera the passions that Scott found inexpressible in words could express themselves, seemingly without mediation, through the medium of song. Unlike serious novelists since Cervantes, Donizetti had no need to argue the plausibility of his characters' passions by

[24] For detailed descriptions of how the opera deviates from the novel, see Gary Schmidgall, *Literature as Opera* (New York: Oxford University Press, 1977), pp. 137–45, and Jerome Mitchell, *The Walter Scott Operas* (University : University of Alabama Press, 1977), pp. 141–44. Mitchell's researches suggest that *The Bride of Lammermoor* received more operatic settings (six in all) than any other Scott novel.

reference to the books they had read—or, for that matter, to whatever music they had heard before. Lucy's operatic version has provided an illusion of passion that Scott's novelistic forebears and descendants, as Flaubert and Forster demonstrate in their *Lucia* scenes, must repeatedly and openly acknowledge as illusion.

Stages in the Conflict of Higher and Lower Narrative

Opera versus Novel

The presence of operatic scenes in fiction is a tacit admission of the limits that the novel set for itself from its beginnings in *Don Quijote* until the linguistic experiments of our own century attempted to erase these limits. It is significant that the classic age of the novel, from the mid-eighteenth through the early twentieth century, is also the period that produced those operas most securely entrenched within the repertory. (For each genre we now recognize a towering forerunner—for the novel, Cervantes, who remained a ubiquitous presence through the classic age of fiction, and for opera Monteverdi, whose place in the history of opera, because of the relative difficulty with which music, as compared to literature, could be transmitted to succeeding generations, was not acknowledged until our own time.)

Seen through the novelist's eyes, opera pursues the high style with an unselfconscious ease impossible within any of the literary genres. The mythical and absolute status that opera occupied throughout the classic age of the novel was defined bluntly by R. P. Blackmur, who, in discussing the opera scene in *Madame Bovary*, spoke of "the Opera—that remote-near conventional art in which no emotion is ever left frustrate but all are fulfilled in multiple forms."[25] Passions that become acceptable within fiction only in ironic guise—or that are exposed there as meaningless—can be celebrated uncompromisingly within opera. By defining itself from its beginnings in opposition to epic and romance, the novel elected as its domain the world of lowly things, which it recorded in a conspicuously, and also increasingly, lowly style. If the traditional high style could no longer be sustained in serious literature by the eighteenth century, it could at least live on

[25] R. P. Blackmur, *Eleven Essays in the European Novel* (New York: Harcourt, Brace, 1964), p. 67.

in opera. To put it another way, the fusion of words and music that constitutes opera allowed the verbal medium, which could no longer support larger structures in the high style, to find loftier forms of expression through music, which cultivated a high style during the very period in which literature felt forced to retreat from this style as well as from the subject matter with which it was traditionally associated.[26]

Although fiction has characteristically advertised its lowliness or incompleteness, it has just as characteristically claimed its loss as a species of gain. As we read *Don Quijote* and *Tom Jones*, our awareness of the gap between these novels and earlier epics and romances works to remind us at once of the impossibility of authentically reclaiming older forms and of the possibility that the newer forms demonstrated in these works are perhaps a more than adequate compensation. In presenting its defeat as a triumph of sorts, the novel has been able to define and celebrate its status as that of a fortunate fall. Cervantes's and Fielding's frequent references to epic and romance constitute generic signals to remind us of the uneasy status their narratives occupy.

Similarly, the scenes from opera that appear in numerous novels, above all during the nineteenth century, give out signals as to how we are to evaluate the narrative whose characters the author, taking advantage of the real-life role of the opera house as a center of social activity, conveniently sends out to attend the opera.[27]

[26] The one form of fiction that pursued the high style systematically in the last two centuries was the Gothic novel, which, like opera, was a popular form whose public recognized its artifice and its distance from ordinary life, on the one hand, and, on the other, its power and immediacy of effect. Although few Gothic novels are read today except by literary historians, a Gothic fiction such as *Wuthering Heights* occasionally makes its way into the "classical" canon through the ironic distance with which it separates the reader's world from the horrendous events that hover in the background. Ironic distance does not ordinarily consort well with the Gothic, though one might note that the original Gothic novel, Walpole's *Castle of Otranto*, allows irony and playfulness to accompany its pursuit of horror. Needless to say, we are able to admire gothically inspired operas such as *Der fliegende Holländer* and *The Queen of Spades* without lamenting their lack of irony.

[27] It is remarkable how few of the novelists we characterize as "major" have not, at one time or another, described a scene at the opera house or the playing of operatic music in the home. If the scene at the opera house is more common in continental than in English novels, this may be due to the greater role that opera played in continental capitals in comparison to London during the nineteenth century. Dickens, except for a brief allusion to the Italian opera as a place associated with luxury (*Hard Times*, bk. 1, chap. 7), shows no interest in opera—though one could argue that his novelistic style, in contrast with that of his contemporaries, displays an operatic flair that breaks down the distinction I make throughout this chapter between higher and lower narrative. Although Thackeray likewise is not concerned with opera, Becky Sharp could be described as an operatic heroine

One might consider the opera scene a mode of ecphrasis, that is, a detailed description, that interrupts a narrative at crucial points. Like the intricately described shields that recur in classical epic, operatic scenes enact a possible higher narrative against which the central line of narrative can take stock of itself. Let me project two extremes within which the narrative reality created within a novel can be related to the operatic world intruding upon it. At one extreme, exemplified by Rousseau's *La Nouvelle Héloïse*, the operatic world is exposed as artificial, trivial, even immoral, in relation to the reality that the narrative as a whole attempts to establish. At the opposite extreme, represented by E. T. A. Hoffmann's brief fiction "Don Juan," what little narrative reality exists is virtually swallowed up by the *Don Giovanni* performance that occupies most of the narrative space. If my extreme examples happen to be authored by the only novelists of stature who were also operatic composers, this doubtless testifies to the strong feelings that each could invest in both of his dual vocations. The majority of novels with operatic scenes, like those discussed in the preceding section, occupy a middle position between these extremes: opera and fictional narrative, or what I earlier called higher and lower narrative, respectively, interact with, comment upon, undercut one another to the point that neither is wholly subsumed by the other.

First Stage: La Nouvelle Héloïse

Imagine a spectrum moving from Rousseau's denunciation to Hoffmann's affirmation of opera. Each point in the spectrum represents a possible stance that a particular novel can take in the continuing conflict between higher and lower narrative. Through its absoluteness, Rousseau's denunciation can serve as a convenient starting point. Actually Rousseau, unlike the other novelists I take up, refuses to describe a particular scene or opera but instead presents a general indictment of opera through the negative

---

creating and enacting her own higher narrative within the lower, more circumscribed world in which she finds herself. At one point in *Vanity Fair* (chap. 49) Becky is depicted singing—not opera, however, but religious songs by Mozart that allow her to work her hypocrisy upon Lady Steyne, the wife of her lover. Although Thackeray devotes several pages (in chap. 29) to Becky's visit to the opera in Brussels, we learn nothing of the goings-on onstage, for the whole show takes place among the spectators, of whom the conniving, bustling Becky is quite obviously the star. All we learn about the music is Becky's brief but loudly proclaimed remark that what she was hearing was inferior to native English music.

impressions recorded by his hero Saint-Preux during his visit to Paris after his expulsion from the pastoral world of Clarens. Saint-Preux's letter on opera, addressed to Julie's cousin Claire, attempts above all to stress the artifice and the lack of verisimilitude in operatic emotion: "One sees actresses, almost in a state of convulsion, violently extracting this screeching from their lungs, their fists clenched against their breasts, their heads held back, their faces inflamed, their blood-vessels swollen, their stomachs quivering."[28] A statement of this sort can be found in most of the attempts, during the last three centuries, to derogate opera for its inauthenticity.[29] Although opera intends to express the highest passion, this passion can all too easily appear exaggerated and ridiculous.

Not that Rousseau questions the validity of passion as such; his novel, after all, seeks to celebrate the possibility of an authentic passion such as that between Saint-Preux and Julie (which, of course, must remain unfulfilled even in the pastoral world within which they have been ensconced). Indeed, in its attempt to portray the private love of individuals as grand and all-consuming, *La Nouvelle Héloïse*, one of the most widely read novels of all time, initiates that central strain within European fiction through which a new middle-class reading public learned to prize and, as it turned out, to imitate the amorous passion of characters they viewed as similar to their own potential selves. The false passion that Rousseau associates with opera sets into relief the passion that he has exemplified for us in the attitude of the two lovers since the start of the book. Moreover, this false passion belongs not to the private realm on which the book is centered but to the world of organized culture and entrenched institutions: "The Paris Opera counts in Paris as the most magnificent, the most luxurious, and the most admirable spectacle that the human mind has ever invented," Saint-Preux writes in a tone as pompous as the art he purports to describe. "It is, people say, the proudest monument to the magnificence of Louis XIV." As a product of official culture,

---

[28] *La Nouvelle Héloïse* in Rousseau, *Oeuvres complètes*, ed. Bernard Gagnebin and Marcel Raymond, II (Paris: Gallimard, 1961), 285. All quotations will be cited from this text of which the description of the opera, pt. 2, letter 23, occupies pp. 280–89.

[29] For similar statements before Rousseau, note, for instance, Addison's celebrated denunciation of Italian opera in *The Spectator* and Richardson's brief description of Pamela's visit to the opera. See, respectively, *The Spectator*, ed. Donald F. Bond (Oxford: Clarendon Press, 1965), I, 22–27 (no. 5, March 6, 1711), and Richardson, *Pamela* (London: Dent, 1914), II, 261–63 (pt. 2, letter 55).

opera proves easy enough to unmask. Indeed, Saint-Preux's letter has very little to say about the music and correspondingly much to say about the sumptuousness with which operatic spectacles were mounted to demonstrate royal magnificence. Yet the grandeur of the stage effects is achieved by deception: "The thunder is a heavy cart brought out on the highest tier. . . . The lightning bolts are made with pinches of resin pitch set on a torch." Even vocal virtuosity is a type of cheating, for the audience finds its pleasure not in the vocal sounds—their effect is described as "disagreeable and painful"—but through the relief it feels at the end that the singer has negotiated her difficult passages "without mishap."

The inauthenticity is not limited to scenic and musical effects but extends to the financial arrangements between the institution and the public: for instance, although ticket prices remain the same, the best cast appears only for an opera's early performances, after which the initial performers "are replaced by substitutes and by substitutes' substitutes." (One might note that this phenomenon is still complained about by audiences in our own time.) The vision of corruption and decline that marks all of Rousseau's cultural criticism in *La Nouvelle Héloïse* is embodied in the Paris Opéra and everything (both literally and figuratively) that the institution represents. Saint-Preux makes clear in his letter that his diatribe is directed specifically at French operatic style and, as usual in his commentaries on music, he uses his condemnation to promote the Italian mode ("so sensitive and alive") that Rousseau's own opera, *Le Devin de village*, had sought to implant in France.

It is significant that Rousseau's opera not only cultivates simplicity in its musical style but, like the main narrative of *La Nouvelle Héloïse*, thematizes simplicity in the form of pastoral. But the novel, unlike *Le Devin de village*, refuses to celebrate the fulfillment and resolution of its amorous entanglements.[30] The idyll of Clarens, in contrast to most pastoral writing, is notable for its lack of fulfillment, indeed, for the unrelieved agony of its presentation of pastoral longing. If its natural world at least remains an unattained ideal, the institutional world of French opera stands as its unambiguously rejected opposite. The higher narra-

---

[30] As Paul de Man has shown in his trenchant reading of the novel, the passion that the book claims to valorize for the reader (and that most readers took at face value) is itself a verbal construct that is constantly entrapping and confusing its two agonized participants. See de Man, *Allegories of Reading*, pp. 188–220.

tive that opera claims to be for Rousseau remains high only in its pretensions and in its cultivation of an officially sanctioned high style; the lower narrative remains the standard of value through the fact that it enacts itself within the limits of pastoral, whose traditional link between lowliness and virtue Rousseau exploits to the full.

Second Stage: War and Peace and Anna Karenina

The second stage in the relation of higher and lower narrative retains a rejection of the former, but unlike the first stage it exposes the lower narrative as at least partially tainted by the various forms of inauthenticity that opera is seen to embody. Such is the stance of Tolstoy in the opera scenes that occur at key spots within each of his two major novels. The operatic performance that Natasha attends in War and Peace receives as scathing a rejection as the performances that Saint-Preux had witnessed: Tolstoy unmasks stage effects for their artifice; he derides the use of song to represent communication between characters for its lack of verisimilitude, and, as with Rousseau's critique of the state's lavish expenditures on its spectacles, he interrupts the description of a dancer with a reminder of the latter's outrageously high fee. Like his moral master Rousseau, Tolstoy associates opera with the institutionalized life of society, against which he places the more "authentic" values of Pierre in War and Peace and of Levin in Anna Karenina.

Yet Tolstoy's mode of describing the opera in the earlier novel differs greatly from that of Rousseau. For one thing, instead of a general indictment it consists of a detailed account of a single performance—at least to the moment when Natasha, from whose point of view the opera is depicted, loses interest. More important, whereas Rousseau uses a traditional expository mode to voice his pastoral denunciation, Tolstoy presents his details with the naiveté of somebody literally coming from a pastoral environment, as in fact Natasha does: as Tolstoy tells us, "After her life in the country . . . all this seemed grotesque and amazing."[31] The

---

[31] Tolstoy, War and Peace, trans. Louise and Aylmer Maude, ed. George Gibian (New York: Norton, 1966), p. 620. All quotations will be cited from this text, in which the opera scene occupies pp. 620–26 (bk. 8, chap. 9). In view of Tolstoy's rejection of opera, it seems ironic (and from Tolstoy's point of view doubtless deplorable) that one of the most formidably grand-style operas of the mid-twentieth century, Prokofiev's War and Peace, should be drawn from this novel.

actions on the stage are made to seem ridiculous through Natasha's refusal to acknowledge the code within which they would normally be interpreted: "They all sang something. . . . They began waving their arms. . . . They did not drag her away at once, but sang with her for a long time and then at last dragged her off."

Tolstoy here is practicing what Viktor Shklovsky, in one of the most celebrated critical analyses of our century, has called "defamiliarization," that is, "describing an object as if he were seeing it for the first time, an event as if it were happening for the first time."[32] For example, the following brief succession of events, which would seem natural to the customary operagoer, appears totally absurd to anybody unaware of the conventions governing an audience's applause or a performer's acknowledgment of this applause: "They sang together and everyone in the theater began clapping and shouting, while the man and woman on the stage— who represented lovers—began smiling, spreading out their arms, and bowing." Through his defamiliarizing method, Tolstoy finds the perfect means of voicing the pastoral ideals that stand behind his massive vision of history.

Yet Tolstoy succeeds in integrating the opera scene within his larger story to a degree that Rousseau was unable to do: for the inauthenticity that he locates in opera becomes associated with the romance between Natasha and the dashing Anatole Kuragin that develops in the course of the performance. During the first act she notices Kuragin, whose posing we are to recognize as operatic in nature: "He moved with a restrained swagger which would have been ridiculous had he not been so good-looking. . . . He walked deliberately, his sword and spurs slightly jingling." In the intermission, as she becomes aware of Anatole's interest in her, Natasha herself indulges in a pose: "She even turned so that he should see her profile in what she thought was its most becoming aspect." By the start of the fourth act Natasha's infatuation with him has developed to the point that the operatic world, which had seemed both false and remote a short while before, is no longer alien to her. "All that was going on before her now seemed quite natural," Tolstoy writes to signal the dramatic change that has

---

[32] "Art as Technique" in *Russian Formalist Criticism: Four Essays*, trans. Lee T. Lemon and Marion J. Rice (Lincoln: University of Nebraska Press, 1965), p. 13. The freshness of vision that Shklovsky claims for Tolstoy (or his surrogate Natasha) in the defamiliarizing process is of course an illusion: the negative image of opera he conjures up is wholly predictable through his Rousseauist ideology.

overcome his heroine. The higher narrative has by now thoroughly infected the lower one.

Like the *Lucia di Lammermoor* scenes in *Madame Bovary* and *Where Angels Fear to Tread*, the performance of the unnamed opera in *War and Peace* makes a statement about the role and value of artifice within the lower narrative. In fact, Tolstoy's opera scene may well be a deliberate retelling of Flaubert's: in each instance the operatic gestures that the heroine witnesses serve as a prelude and a transition to a love affair whose operatic quality— in the most derogatory sense—the lower narrative seeks to expose. The unbending irony with which Flaubert batters his heroine is of course missing in Tolstoy's world. Within the moral scheme of *War and Peace* Natasha compensates for her operatic lapse through her ultimate reconciliation, at his deathbed, with Prince Andrew, whom she had betrayed for Anatole, and through the pastoral simplicity she cultivates at the end of the book as Pierre Bezukhov's wife.

Whereas operatic artifice in *War and Peace* represents a temporary threat that the heroine later overcomes, in *Anna Karenina* it serves both as scene and symbol for the degradation to which the heroine of this novel is publicly subjected. Unlike the opera scene in Tolstoy's earlier novel, the visit to the opera contains relatively little description of the stage action. What few details we are shown alternate with the human drama going on among the characters sitting in the boxes; in fact, the latter doings appear at least as histrionic as the actions onstage. Each action, moreover, is built around a "star"—the stage action around the singer Adelina Patti, the narrative action around Anna. Just as Anna's decision to go to the theater was based not on the opera but on the singer ("I expect you are going to hear Patti?"),[33] so the audience's attention becomes riveted on Anna Karenina. When the mother of her lover Vronsky describes Anna's defiance of social convention, she presents the incident as drama: "Elle fait sensation." While equating Anna and Patti, she clearly awards the dramatic laurels to the star of the drama going on within the audience: "On oublie la Patti pour elle [Anna]." It is significant that these statements are made in French, which was for Tolstoy the language of social artifice.

[33] Tolstoy, *Anna Karenina*, trans. Louise and Aylmer Maude, ed. George Gibian (New York: Norton, 1970), p. 492. All quotations are cited from this text, in which the opera scene encompasses pp. 492–99 (pt. 5, chaps. 32–33).

Yet through his famous double plot, Tolstoy is able to make some tentative affirmations at the same time that he rejects the social world. Once the lower narrative has become linked with the histrionics of the higher, our attention moves increasingly to the "antisocial" alternatives offered by life on Levin's estate. With their teeter-totter movement the two plots—one of them exposing social artifice as operatic, the other seeking to define an "authentic" way of life—are able to separate the lower narrative into segments that we are meant to see, respectively, as operatically tainted and pastorally untainted, with the latter ultimately triumphing.

Third Stage: The Age of Innocence

The third stage in the conflict of higher and lower narrative no longer provides a positive alternative within the latter but simply equates the operatic and real-life worlds as thoroughly implicated in artifice. This is the stage represented by *Where Angels Fear to Tread*, as well as by countless realist novels that contain brief descriptions of (often simply fleeting allusions to) famous operas. To cite two random examples from diverse national traditions, one might mention the Portuguese novelist Eça de Queiroz's *The Maias*, which provides glimpses of performances of *Lucia, Les Huguenots*, and memories of *La traviata* as a means of counterpointing the inconsequentiality that dominates the lives of its characters;[34] or the German novelist Theodor Fontane's *L'Adultera*, in which conversational references to the newly fashionable Wagner operas attempt to tell us something about the title character's romantic longings and escapades.[35] To the extent that both nineteenth-century opera and realistic fiction display an obsession with faithfulness and adultery (and their mutual connections), the two forms consort naturally with one another.[36]

Edith Wharton's decision to open *The Age of Innocence* with a performance of Gounod's *Faust* allows her not only to introduce

[34] See Eça de Queiroz, *The Maias*, trans. Patricia McGowan Pinheiro and Ann Stevens (New York: St. Martin's Press, 1965), pp. 111–12, 122–23, 127–29, 504–5.
[35] See Fontane, *Gesammelte Werke* (Berlin: Fischer, 1919), II, 55, 57–59 (chaps. 7–8).
[36] For a searching examination of the role of adultery in major fictions, see Tony Tanner, *Adultery in the Novel: Contract and Transgression* (Baltimore: Johns Hopkins University Press, 1979). Tanner's analysis could be extended in fascinating ways to adultery in nineteenth-century opera as well as to those protestations of total faithfulness that one finds in certain operas such as *Lucia* and *Aida*.

her various characters in a place where they could credibly be expected to meet, but it also allows her to "foreshadow" the infidelity at the center of her narrative. As her hero enters his box (quite belatedly, as dictated within the social code that Wharton records and condemns throughout the novel), the famous soprano Christine Nilsson, in the role of Marguerite, is plucking out the daisy petals to determine whether the opera's hero loves her (or not).[37] And, as Wharton hastens to add, Nilsson sings her lines neither in the French original nor in the language of the audience but in the Italian that the convention of the time demanded. For Wharton, both the higher and lower narrative are exquisitely matched through the relation their respective characters hold to artifice and convention. As though to tell us that nothing essential ever changes in the world of her lower narrative, Wharton, near the end of her novel, has her characters revisit the Academy of Music, in which the opera and its star are identical to those that opened the book. Whereas Tolstoy characteristically compartmentalized his lower narrative into clearly demarcated negative and positive spheres—the latter of which took the form of pastoral—Wharton, like many realist novelists, presents an unredeemable world in which fulfillment, usually in the guise of a clandestine sexual relationship, is at best a temporary refuge.

Fourth Stage: "Wälsungenblut"

With the fourth stage, opera begins to emerge in novels as "higher"—that is to say more intense, passionate, complete—than the real-life lower narrative. But only begins to—for the writer shies away from too absolute a commitment to the higher narrative and in fact envelops both narratives within a self-protective irony. The *Lucia* performance in *Madame Bovary* belongs to the fourth stage, as does the brief scene in Stendhal's *Le Rouge et le noir* in which Mathilde, while attending the Italian opera in Paris, allows her passion for Julien Sorel to become enflamed through her identification with the opera's amorous heroine.[38] The irony central to this stage assumes a particularly obvious, almost brut-

---

[37] See Wharton, *The Age of Innocence* (New York: Modern Library, n.d.). The opera scenes occupy pp. 1–15 and 321–25 (chaps. 1 and 32).

[38] See Stendhal, *Le Rouge et le noir*, ed. Henri Martineau (Paris: Garnier, 1960), pp. 355–56 (bk. 2, chap. 19). The opera that Mathilde hears is not explicitly identified, though a particular melody is called "worthy of Cimarosa" (p. 355), the composer of *Il matrimonio segreto*, one of Stendhal's favorite operas.

ish form in Thomas Mann's early story "Wälsungenblut," which focuses on a performance of *Die Walküre*. The story could be described as a game that titillates the reader's curiosity as to whether or not the sibling incest in the opera plot will actually take place in the *nouveau-riche*, recently assimilated Jewish household of the lower narrative. In *Die Walküre*, as I indicated in the first chapter, whatever taboos we might ordinarily feel are absorbed by the high passion of the music and the mythical distance that Wagner establishes between his characters and the audience's world. For Mann's turn-of-the-century readers, the same situation enacted in a recognizable domestic setting would have had a shocking effect that could be rendered acceptable only by means of the author's characteristic irony.

Once we have noted the story's title, we read the lower narrative allegorically, with constant reference to the operatic plot. The triangle within this narrative consists of the artistically sensitive twins Siegmund and Sieglinde (obviously named to satisfy their socially ambitious father's cultural pretensions) and the dull, non-Jewish, bourgeois Herr von Beckerath, whom Sieglinde feels obliged to marry. Everything we read about these characters feeds on our memory of the Siegmund-Sieglinde-Hunding triangle in the opera, so that the story would make little sense to anybody unfamiliar with Wagner. When the twins, in their last opportunity to go out alone before Sieglinde's marriage, attend the performance of *Die Walküre*, we in turn read the lengthy description of the stage events against the earlier domestic narrative. The description of the opera, like that of *Lucia* in *Madame Bovary*, assumes a self-consciously overwritten manner ("Then Siegmund threw his two pink fat arms around her, pressed her cheek against the hide covering his chest. . . .""),[39] as though to remind us at once of the unencumbered passion we are meant to experience in the operatic action, of the banality in the corresponding domestic action, and, perhaps most important, of the author's refusal to be

[39] In Mann, *Die Erzählungen* (Frankfurt: Fischer, 1975), I, 305. The performance occupies pp. 302–8. The allegorical relevance of the opera to the story has encouraged Mann's interpreters to find innumerable Wagnerian verbal echoes and plot parallels in the lower narrative; indeed, Mann has provided an ideal interpretive situation for those who like to uncover deliberately hidden meanings and demonstrate how higher and lower narrative function ironically against one another. See, for example, Erwin Koppen, *Dekadenter Wagnerismus: Studien zur europäischen Literatur des Fin de siècle* (Berlin: Walter de Gruyter, 1973), pp. 144–60, and James Northcote-Bade, *Die Wagner-Mythen im Frühwerk Thomas Manns* (Bonn: Bouvier Verlag Herbert Grundmann, 1975), pp. 53–67.

taken in easily by either of these actions. On the final page, after the twins return from the opera, they finally—and to the reader's relief—perform the incest that has been threatening all along: just as readers have interpreted the domestic events in terms of their knowledge of the opera, so the twins interpret—and reenact— their own lives in terms of the performance they have just experienced. However ironically we are meant to take it all, Mann's higher narrative has managed to overcome the lower one.[40]

Fifth Stage: La Peste

At the fifth stage, the author no longer needs to seek distance through irony but can allow the higher narrative to interact aggressively with the lower one. Consider Camus' brief description, in *La Peste*, of some performances of Gluck's *Orphée*. The circumstances surrounding these performances are at first controlled by the lower narrative, for a traveling opera company has been caught in plague-torn Oran and forced, in effect, to repeat the same opera each week. At first these performances seem a refuge from the horrors of the plague, for in this, the most decorously classical opera in the repertory, the audience can find temporary respite in a work that simulates the orderliness the community had known before the plague. But at one performance the prevailing decorum breaks down, as the audience gradually realizes that the singer performing the title role has himself become infected. The first sign comes when the Orpheus sings "some tremolos not in the score that expressed an almost exaggerated pathos when begging the lord of the Underworld to be moved by his tears."[41] The unintended improvisation serves to bring out the suffering beneath the opera's classical surface in a way no ordinary performance could have done. Before the performance can be completed, the singer, in obvious agony, breaks through the

[40] The story's final lines, spoken by Siegmund—"He [Beckerath] should be grateful to us. He'll lead a less trivial existence from now on" (p. 312)—express a wryness missing in the early version, which ends with a statement, peppered with words from Yiddish, that the twins have managed to gull the "goy" ("Beganeft haben wir ihn—den Goy"—see Northcote-Bade, *Wagner-Mythen*, p. 66). In this early version the twins' way of interpreting their imitation of the higher narrative allows this narrative to triumph over the banality of everyday novelistic existence more uncompromisingly than Siegmund's words in the final version. Mann supposedly changed the text to avoid displeasing his Jewish father-in-law.

[41] *La Peste* in Camus, *Théâtre, Récits, Nouvelles*, ed. Roger Quilliot (Paris: Gallimard, 1962), p. 1380. Quotations will be cited from this text, in which the opera scenes encompass pp. 1379–80 (bk. 4, chap. 1).

[177]

theatrical illusion and "staggers grotesquely to the footlights." The audience, its temporary idyll destroyed, rushes out in panic. The lower narrative has been raised to the level of the higher in the very process of "infecting" it. To the degree that, since its publication in 1947, we have read *La Peste* as an allegory of recent political events, the opera scene can be viewed as an allegory within an allegory, a powerful moment in which two levels of narrative interact to enforce the book's obsessions through a brief but decisive theatrical gesture.

Sixth Stage: On the Eve *and* The Years

In the sixth stage the higher narrative, however small a space it may occupy within the novel, clearly comes to show up the inadequacy of the lower narrative, in fact to dominate it. No realist novelist was more centrally concerned than Turgenev with the unheroic character of everyday life. In his short novel *On the Eve*, he laments the absence of heroes among Russians; "Our Russians are all either small fry, rodents, petty Hamlets, Samoyeds, or subterranean darkness and silence," one of his conspicuously unheroic figures puts it.[42] Of the men in the novel, only a foreigner, Insarov, from an oppressed nation, Bulgaria, shows a potential for heroic action. Unfortunately, just as he is about to undertake the task of liberating his nation Insarov succumbs to respiratory disease. Since an epic narrative was obviously out of character for Turgenev, as well as for the literary genre in which he worked, he turned to opera to resolve his novel in an appropriately heroic manner.[43] Shortly before his death, Insarov and his Russian wife Yelena, who had chosen him as a heroic alternative to her own countrymen, whom she deemed inadequate as mates, attend a performance of *La traviata* in Venice. Turgenev chose his operatic exemplum with considerable care, for *Traviata*, still a new work at the time he was writing, was notable in the history of Italian opera for its shift from a historical or mythological setting to a domestic one. Even more important for Turgenev's story, the plot of this opera is resolved not by the suicide or murder of the hero—

[42] *On the Eve* in *The Vintage Turgenev*, trans. Harry Stevens (New York: Vintage, 1960), II, 125–26 (chap. 30). All quotations are cited from this text, in which the opera scene occupies pp. 137–39 (chap. 34).

[43] Turgenev's own relationship to opera went considerably beyond writing this opera scene. The companion of his later life was one of the legendary singers of the century, Pauline Viardot, for whom he even prepared librettos that she set to music.

endings standard within earlier nineteenth-century operatic convention—but by a graphically depicted death from respiratory disease that we are meant to see as similar to Insarov's.

Turgenev begins his description of the opera in the mode of his lower narrative—that is, by stressing inadequacies both in the work and in its performance: the opera is "banal," the singers "mediocre," and the Violetta is sung by a little-known singer whose voice is "already ruined" and whose dress and bearing are inappropriate to her role. In the course of the evening, however, Insarov and Yelena feel themselves raised to a higher pitch. The audience feels possessed by the passion conveyed through the music, and even the soprano's "voice no longer sounded as though it had been ruined, [but] it grew warm and strong." By the end the emotions awakened by the opera become so potent that Turgenev assumes a tone of unqualified eloquence. Through the operatic scene, the novel has transformed itself, for the performance has raised the lower narrative to its own level.[44] Insarov, surrounded by the grandeurs of Venice, dies his Violetta-like death, and Yelena "vanishes forever and irrevocably" (chap. 35, p. 127) to perform great deeds in Bulgaria. (Given the role defined for women in her day, she exercised her heroism as nurse rather than as warrior.) Only on the final page does Turgenev return to his earlier unheroic mode: in an epilogue typical of realist fiction, we learn that the remaining characters are working out their lives in the unheroic and inconsequential ways appropriate to that lower mode of narrative that Turgenev had been pursuing throughout most of the novel.

Like the visit to the opera in *On the Eve*, Kitty Lasswood's visit to a Covent Garden performance of *Siegfried* in Virginia Woolf's *The Years* creates an image of fulfillment for a character who, like the novel's multitudinous other characters, views herself as un-

---

[44] Like the *Traviata* performance in *On the Eve*, the performance of *Tristan und Isolde* at the end of Arthur Schnitzler's novel of fin-de-siècle Vienna, *Der Weg ins Freie*, presents a sharply intensified version of the passions and disillusionments that the various characters—artists, political figures, dilettantes—have been experiencing all along. (See Schnitzler, *Das erzählende Werk* [Frankfurt: Fischer, 1978], IV, in which the opera performance occupies pp. 289–93 [chap. 9].) The reader watches the opera through the eyes of the novel's aristocratic composer-hero Georg von Wergenthin, whose feeling of well-being during the opera contrasts markedly with the lassitude afflicting his real-life relationships. Within the lower narrative of Viennese life, neither the passion nor the disillusionment comes anywhere near the heights (or depths) it achieves in the opera. It is significant, for instance, that the protagonist must go to the performance without the woman to whom he was tied—though with only sporadic passion—throughout the novel and whose refusal to accompany him signals the end of their relationship.

fulfilled. "The music made her think of herself and her own life as she seldom did," Woolf writes. "It exalted her; it cast a flattering light over herself, her past."[45] Yet the exaltation that Kitty feels is at best sporadic, for it alternates with moments in which, as Woolf puts it, "her attention flagged": at such times her memory calls up unfulfilled passages in her life, or, through her opera glasses, she notes "Siegfried's fat brown arms glistening with paint." But unlike the novelists of the earlier stages I have depicted in this chapter, Woolf treats the music without irony or condescension; ordinary life, she implies, is simply incommensurate with the triumphant life within opera, or at least this particular opera.[46]

Seventh Stage: "Don Juan"

With the seventh and final stage, the higher narrative asserts its dominance so powerfully that the lower narrative loses all importance. In its extreme form this stage could not support a narrative of any length, as the mere dozen pages of E. T. A. Hoffmann's "Don Juan" testify. Like most of his fictions, Hoffmann's short piece creates its own generic label, in this case "an incredible event."[47] The piece consists of two complementary halves—first, a detailed description of a *Don Giovanni* performance from overture to epilogue and second the narrator's reflections on his experience at the opera. The relatively few events that take place outside the

---

[45] In Woolf, *The Years* (Harmondsworth: Penguin, 1968), p. 148; the opera performance occupies pp. 146–50 (the chapter entitled "1910").

[46] A recent study has proposed that *The Years* is modeled after *Götterdämmerung*; unlike the triumphs celebrated by *Siegfried*, the despair and disillusionment central to this novel are also projected by the final work of Wagner's tetralogy. See Jane Marcus, "*The Years* as Greek Drama, Domestic Novel, and Götterdämmerung," *Bulletin of the New York Public Library*, 80 (1977), 276–301.

[47] "Eine fabelhafte Begebenheit." See Hoffmann, *Werke*, ed. Georg Ellinger (Berlin: Deutsches Verlagshaus Bong, n.d.), I, 72. Quotations are based on this text, which occupies pp. 72–83. The absorption of lower by higher narrative characteristic of this stage can also be illustrated, though less radically than in Hoffmann, by Balzac's *Massimilla Doni*, one of several *études philosophiques* on the transforming power of art. By Balzacian standards the plotting of this story remains minimal: the operatic ecphrasis, a running commentary by the story's heroine during a performance of Rossini's *Mosè in Egitto*, threatens to engulf the lower narrative through its length (fully a third of the story) and through its high-flown eulogy of the spiritual power emanating from the opera. Quite unlike this higher narrative, the story of the real-life characters culminates in a denouement that Balzac labels "dreadfully bourgeois." See *Massimilla Doni* in Balzac, *La Comédie humaine*, ed. Marcel Bouteron, IX (Paris: Gallimard, 1950), p. 387.

framework of the performance would seem bizarre and inexplicable within an ordinary fiction: the Italian singer playing Donna Anna appears in the narrator's box during the intermission, and at the end of the piece we are informed that she was so carried away by her role that she died after the performance. As a recent study of Hoffmann's story demonstrates, what little transpires in the "actual" narrative is absorbed, as it were, by the operatic narrative.[48] The narrator, for instance, turns out to be a double of Don Juan (or, more precisely, of Hoffmann's interpretation of Don Juan), and the soprano performing Donna Anna becomes so closely attached to the object of her impersonation that her own death can be attributed to her having misinterpreted several lines of her part as a prophecy of the operatic character's death.

The narrator (and the soprano as well) view the opera as a spiritual experience that music can render more readily than words. Even before the curtain rises, the narrator translates the andante near the beginning of the overture (the section that recurs at the time of Don Giovanni's death) in the most elevated verbal terms: "In the *andante* the terror of the frightening, subterranean *regno all pianto* seized hold of me; horror-inciting presentiments of the dreadful filled my spirit." Hoffmann is in effect creating an opera in words, and in these lines he utilizes the literary language traditionally associated with the sublime, and in particular with Gothic fiction, to suggest a realm transcending what ordinary verbal narrative can create. Note also that here, as throughout the piece, this realm has no substantiality beyond the narrator's ability to perceive it: what we know of it comes wholly through his mental experience ("ergriffen mich . . . erfüllten mein Gemüt": "laid hold of me . . . filled my soul"). The narrator is drawn into the world of the higher narrative with an inexorability analogous to the way Don Giovanni is drawn into the infernal realm at the end of the opera. And just as the narrator becomes a double of the opera's protagonist, so Don Giovanni is associated at crucial points in the story with Goethe's Mephistopheles: in an insight that runs through the whole history of German musical commentary from the early Romantics through Wagner, Nietzsche, and Thomas

[48] See David Wellbery, "E. T. A. Hoffmann and Romantic Hermeneutics: An Interpretation of Hoffmann's 'Don Juan,'" *Studies in Romanticism*, 19 (1980), esp. pp. 458–60. Wellbery's brilliant analysis of the relationship between the operatic narrative and the "real-life" anecdotes within the story has helped define the approach I have developed throughout the present chapter.

Mann, the higher realm that music occupies within the hierarchy of the arts makes itself known to us most powerfully through its demonic elements.

Quite in contrast to the images we receive of this higher realm, Hoffmann places brief reminders of the constrictions governing ordinary life, which at one point is called simply "constraining life." Except for the narrator, the only important "real-life" character is the soprano, who is herself far removed from the ordinary life we associate with ordinary narrative. For one thing, she is foreign, and when she visits the narrator in his box she speaks to him in Italian; moreover, after the performance, members of the audience single out the lack of moderation in her performance, which they characterize as "too passionate." It seems only natural that both she and the narrator have little solid identity outside the role the author establishes for them in relation to the operatic performance. And it seems appropriate as well that Hoffmann, himself a composer of a fairy-tale opera on the Ondine legend, should create a higher narrative that suppresses everything we conventionally associate with novelistic content. Hoffmann, of course, was a seminal figure in European narrative. His fictions cultivated forms outside the novelistic mainstream—fairy tale, Gothic fantasy, animal tale, and criminal story—that later writers—Balzac, Poe, and Dostoevsky—were able to use to press beyond the limitations of the stolidly realistic lower narrative that was to become the locus of the nineteenth-century novel. Slight though it may seem at first reading, Hoffmann's "Don Juan" rejects these limitations at the same time that it celebrates the triumph of higher over lower narrative.

Modes of Intrusion of Higher into Lower Narrative

Thus far, I have concentrated on the various stages of conflict between operatic scenes in novels and the lower narrative in which they are embedded and whose identity and status they isolate, define, transform. Yet the full-blown scene at the opera house, prevalent as it is in many of the great realist novels, represents only one among several ways that operatic ecphrasis imposes itself in fictional contexts. Let us tilt the structure upon which the preceding section was built and consider instead a series of distinct modes through which opera intrudes into novels. At one extreme one can point to a typically modernist mode in which an allusion to an aria or an opera enters briefly, though often also quite conspicuously, within a character's mental arena. The modernist technique of fragmentation not only allows a single allusion to carry considerable weight, but it also encourages the reader to make the various fragments that the author dispersed throughout the novel cohere into a higher narrative. Next one can point to the realist mode, which includes not only the public scene in the opera house with which the preceding section was concerned but also another type of operatic scene—the private musical entertainment in the home—that fits more appropriately into those novels of provincial life that cannot, like *Madame Bovary,* "arrange" a visit to the opera to allow the higher narrative to intrude. Whether in a public or private setting, the opera scene provides realist fiction with the plausible social setting needed to account for the presence of a higher narrative in the otherwise lowly environs of such fiction. Finally I shall take up a mode that unlike the first two is not a stylistic category. In this third mode the higher narrative consists of a wholly imaginary opera that the novelist, or more precisely a surrogate character, creates and embeds within the fictional context. Although the two examples I introduce—one from Balzac, the other from Thomas Mann—are more than a century apart, they embody a single maneuver, the attempt of an artist-hero to transcend the limits of novelistic existence by literally composing that higher narrative we call opera.

Modernist Mode: Dispersed Opera in Petersburg, Ulysses, *and* Finnegans Wake

I start with the first of these extremes, those musical snippets that surface briefly in memories, conversations, and various musical forms—whistling, humming, solitary singing—to suggest the welter of consciousness through which characters and situations in many modernist novels emerge and define themselves. For example, the operatic examples in Bely's *Petersburg* and Joyce's *Ulysses* provide brief glimpses of worlds more "whole," less compromised than those depicted in the urban wanderings that comprise the plots of these two modernist monuments. The occasional allusions to Tchaikovsky's *The Queen of Spades* in Bely's novel suggest a higher allegory against which the sordid events of the lower narrative can be measured. Both the opera and the novel are deeply rooted in the geographical setting that gives the latter its title, and in both, as well, the young hero and heroine can be viewed as foolish and obsessed. The two levels of narrative within the novel come together on those occasions when the heroine, Sofia Petrovna, calls the opera into her memory, as in these lines: "Not for nothing had she sighed, again and again, at the strains of *The Queen of Spades*. Yes, yes: her situation had something in common with Liza's (what it had in common, she could not have said.)"[49] The concluding parenthesis gives away at once the inadequacy of the heroine and the self-consciousness the novel voices about how much it too can say. Through the freedom that the modernist mode allows a novelist to roam through the characters' minds, the occasional allusions to opera in passages such as this one serve the same purpose as the extended operatic ecphrases in realist texts. Thus, however sordid the events of Tchaikovsky's opera, for Sofia and for Bely's reader the music lends these events a passionate and heroic dimension impossible within the blatantly parodistic manner that dominates the lower narrative of *Petersburg*.

Far more pervasively than in *Petersburg*, the operatic allusions of *Ulysses*, however brief they may be individually, suffuse the novel to the extent that one could speak of a persistent if discontinuous operatic narrative that cuts across the lower narrative of Bloomsday events. Unlike the extended operatic scenes that I discussed earlier in this chapter, Joyce's allusions are not only brief—a tune that a character hums or a phrase from an Italian aria that pops into a character's mind—but they refer to a vast number of operas, among them *Il trovatore, Lucia, Carmen, Les Huguenots, La sonnambula*, W. V. Wallace's *Maritina*, and, to cite a title that gets much bantered with in the course of the book, Michael Balfe's *Rose of Castille*. Allusions to two operas, *Don Giovanni* and Flotow's *Martha*, recur to good ironic purpose, for each offers model situations against which the reader is able to assess the various amorous entanglements (whether mental or physical) of Leopold and Molly Bloom. Indeed, Molly and her lover, Blazes Boylan, as characters literally out of Dublin's musical world, exploit Joyce's repertory of operatic allusions to glorify both the sexual and the vocal music they make together.

However pervasive the operatic allusions in *Ulysses*, their status within the book is similar in kind to that of other persistent allusions such as popular songs (for example, "Love's Old Sweet

[49] Andrei Bely, *Petersburg*, trans. Robert A. Maguire and John E. Malmstad (London: Harvester Press, 1978), p. 86 (chap. 3). For other allusions to the opera as it filters through Sofia Petrovna's mind, see pp. 34 and 84 (chaps. 1 and 3).

Song") and short lyrics (above all, Yeats's "Who Goes with Fergus?" and Ophelia's bawdy song): all constitute a show of passion that the doings of Joyce's Dublin characters can scarcely emulate.[50] In no episode do musical allusions (whether to opera or popular music) enter as thick and fast as in "Sirens," where they join with innumerable references to sound ("jingle," "*cloche*"), imitations of sounds ("Imperthnthn," "Tschink. Tschunk"), and syntactic structures simulating musical forms ("Brightly the keys, all twinkling, linked, all harpsichording . . . ") to translate the doings in a Dublin bar into what appears to be the verbal equivalent of an opera.[51] Through the Homeric parallel that gives the novel its title, organization, and major characters, Joyce acknowledges from the start of the book that he has created a layered narrative. It is significant, however, that in our actual reading of the book the higher narrative that catches our attention from moment to moment is less the Homeric one than the tissue of allusions to arias, songs, and lyrics that float through the consciousness of the novel's personae.

Although *Ulysses* maintains more or less of a distinction between higher and lower narrative, the linguistic mode of *Finnegans Wake* allows this distinction to disappear. The multitudinous operatic allusions of the *Wake* occupy the same status as all other allusions—the same, indeed, as the other "events" comprising Joyce's final book. Although Joyce refers to a large range of operas here, the availability of a local girl, Iseult, makes *Tristan und Isolde* the favored operatic text of this work. The *Liebestod*, for instance, appears in such varied guises as "the vivid girl, deaf with love" and "down to death and the love embrace."[52] Wagner's music-drama, however, shares its allusive power with various literary embodiments of the Tristram story as well as with a large array of related Irish matters past and present, mythical and "actual." Beyond its Irish roots, *Tristan* is echoed in allusions to the personal background behind Wagner's work, namely his relationship to Mathilde Wesendonck—"his mudheeldy wheesindonk at their trist in Parisise" (p. 230). With the lower narrative, to all intents and purposes, wiped out, the unique method of *Finnegans*

---

[50] For a detailed list of and commentary on the various musical allusions in *Ulysses*, see Zack Bowen, *Musical Allusions in the Works of James Joyce: Early Poetry through Ulysses* (Albany: State University of New York Press, 1974), pp. 46–346.

[51] *Ulysses* (New York: Random House, 1946), pp. 252, 254, 286, 260.

[52] *Finnegans Wake* (New York: Viking, 1958), pp. 395, 398.

Wake has enabled an author who was himself an amateur singer (and patron of singers) to compose, stage, conduct, and sing his own peculiar version of opera, of which this long book constitutes a simulated and overwhelming performance.

Realist Mode: I. Home Musicales in The Eternal Husband, Oblomov, *and* The Mill on the Floss

If the modernist mode, especially in its extreme Joycean forms, allows the higher narrative to disperse itself throughout a lengthy text, the realist mode must make do with one, at best a few, crucially placed operatic scenes to suggest a passionate existence transcending the circumscribed world of the lower narrative. Although the scenes we most remember in this mode are doubtless those at the opera house described in the preceding sections, the home musicale that appears in many nineteenth-century novels gives the novelist a special advantage, for the essential passions that music attempts to communicate can reveal themselves without the complex social entanglements or the histrionics (both onstage and off) that are typical of the great public scenes. In a passage of *The Eternal Husband* depicting the performance of a song by Glinka at a family musicale, Dostoevsky voices his preference for music within a private over a public setting: "In that song the intensity of passion rises, mounting higher and higher at every line, at every word; and, from this very intensity, the least trace of falsity, of exaggeration or unreality, such as passes muster so easily at an opera, would distort and destroy the whole value of it."[53] Although Dostoevsky here associates passion with song, which he distinguishes from the "falsity" of opera, the language with which he describes the effect of the song—"mounting higher and higher," "this very intensity"—typifies the private performances of operatic excerpts to be found in many realist novels.

For example, the passion that Dostoevsky locates in this intimate rendition of a Glinka song is embodied in a series of private performances that move through another Russian nineteenth-century novel, Goncharov's *Oblomov*. When the ineffectual, virtually bedridden hero of this novel admits to the strong emotional response he feels towards the "Casta diva" aria in *Norma*, his friend Stolz seizes upon the aria as a means of rousing him from

[53] Dostoevsky, *The Eternal Husband*, trans. Constance Garnett, in *Great Short Works*, ed. Ronald Hingley (New York: Harper, 1968), p. 624 (chap. 12).

his lethargy. Stolz introduces Oblomov to Olga, whose private performance of the aria for the two men affects Oblomov so greatly that "his transports, the thoughts that flashed like lightning through his head, the cold shiver that ran through his body—all this crushed him; he felt completely shattered."[54] From here on, the "Casta diva," whether in Olga's private command performances or in Oblomov's memories and dreams of these performances, reappears at innumerable intervals to tempt the protagonist with the possibility of a fulfilled life, which, to no reader's surprise, Oblomov ultimately rejects. The single aria suggests the higher narrative against which the banalities of Oblomov's everyday life are set in relief. Like Oblomov's life, the novel itself remains impoverished in incidents: to keep his story going, Goncharov must invoke other, less impoverished aspects of life, for instance the pastoral scenes of Oblomov's long dream passage or the future family that the hero briefly fantasizes. As a leitmotif of Oblomov's possible fulfillment, the "Casta diva" provides an insistent reminder that both the hero and the novelistic world in which he lives remain permanently incomplete.

If the public opera scenes in *Le Rouge et le noir* and *Madame Bovary* exerted the suggestive power to commit the heroines of these novels to new lovers, the private performances in realist novels could serve as catalysts to commit their very participants to one another in a way that few other narrative devices were able to do. For example, the home musicale that George Eliot stages in *The Mill on the Floss* allows her to solve a central narrative problem, namely, motivating that major turn of the plot that will cause her heroine Maggie Tulliver to leave behind her inadequate suitor Philip Wakem and to be swept away by the dashing but unreliable Stephen Guest. "In the provinces . . . , where music was so scarce in that remote time, how could the musical people avoid falling in love with each other?", Eliot asks earlier in the book.[55] To help Maggie and Stephen fall in love, the author creates a higher narrative composed of brief operatic selections and songs that she selects for their relevance to the lower narrative. For instance, the unsuccessful Philip sings the aria from *La sonnam-*

---

[54] Goncharov, *Oblomov*, trans. David Magarshack (Baltimore: Penguin, 1954), p. 196 (pt. 2, chap. 5). For other allusions to the aria, see pp. 179, 194–95, 217, 232, 247, 288, 312, 336, 348, 427–28.

[55] *The Mill on the Floss*, ed. A. S. Byatt (Baltimore: Penguin, 1979), p. 474. All quotations are taken from this text, in which the musicale itself occupies pp. 531–35 (bk. 6, chap. 7).

bula in which Elvino promises his undying faithfulness to Amina even if she should forsake him. Eliot is quite explicit about how we should interpret the musical allegory: "It was not quite unintentionally that Philip had wandered into this song which might be an indirect expression to Maggie of what he could not prevail on himself to say to her directly." The successful suitor, in turn, is shown "rolling out, with saucy energy" a seventeenth-century song that results in Maggie's being "borne along by a wave too strong for her." From here on, the lower narrative of provincial life gives way to the higher narrative of operatic passion—and even such otherwise sympathetic early critics of the novel as Swinburne and Leslie Stephen were shocked by Eliot's allowing a nice girl like Maggie Tulliver to get swept away. One might add that the book's long-controversial ending, in which Maggie and her brother are literally swept away in a local flood, is an essentially operatic resolution that extends the metaphor of the wave of passion that began to bear Maggie along during the musicale.

Realist Mode: II. Opera in Isolation in "Tristan," Il trionfo della morte, *and* Der Zauberberg

Although the operatic intrusion in *The Mill on the Floss* is enacted around a triangle of lovers, the intimacy of private performance provides a special novelistic opportunity to enact the blossoming and consummation of a couple's relationship. Moreover, in *Tristan und Isolde* novelists of the fin de siècle possessed the ideal vehicle for the imitation of what passed for a lofty, if also forbidden, form of passion. Among nineteenth-century operas, none enjoyed the public notoriety of *Tristan und Isolde*, which, partly through Nietzsche's panegyrics in *The Birth of Tragedy*, partly through its harmonic shock effects, became associated in the public mind with both the attractions and dangers of passion. (Its appropriateness to *Finnegans Wake* was, of course, dictated by Joyce's need for Celtic matter.) It appears in fiction not simply in the form of public performances, as in Schnitzler's *Der Weg ins Freie*, but—even more appropriately—in two famous works that depict lovers hearing its music through the intimacy afforded by piano scores that could be played in private. In his short novel "Tristan," as in "Wälsungenblut," Thomas Mann coaxes the reader through the title into interpreting the comic events of the story as allegorical parallels to the unrelievedly tragic events of the opera. The contemporary Tristan and Isolde turn out to be patients in a tuberculosis sanatorium who flirt with the possibility of adultery while the woman plays the opera's major passages on the piano. Even the circumstances of the performance parallel the operatic plot, for the strains of the love duet, on which Mann lavishes his most extravagant prose, are interrupted by the entrance of other patients, whose appearance is as unexpected as that of King Marke in the opera.[56]

The irony with which Mann distances himself at once from the opera (which he obviously respects) and from his characters' grotesque doings is wholly lacking in the Tristan scene near the end of Gabriele d'Annunzio's *Trionfo della morte*, whose modern lovers, ensconced with their piano in an isolated castle, relive the opera to the point of double immolation. The purple prose with which d'Annunzio recreates the opera is only an intensification of the prose that the lower narrative had attempted to achieve throughout the book.[57] Details of everyday life play only a minor role in this novel, whose intensity the author attempts to sustain through scenes of violence and lovemaking as well as lengthy verbal expressions of passion. Through d'Annunzio's refusal to recognize the inadequacy of words alone to arouse responses that music has traditionally taken for its domain, this once-celebrated work today occupies an ambiguous place that belongs neither to opera (whose effects it could not hope to attain even with the most powerful ecphrasis) nor to the novel as we have come to define it.

When Thomas Mann sought an operatic narrative to reveal Hans Castorp's inward development near the end of *Der Zauberberg*, he turned to the record player, which, by the time the novel was written, was fast supplanting the private recitals that he had been

[56] For Mann's parodic ecphrasis, see "Tristan" in *Erzählungen*, I, 184–86 (sec. 8). As with "Wälsungenblut," the Wagnerian allegory that Mann pursues in "Tristan" has invited numerous interpretations tying the characters and events of the story to their corresponding elements in the opera—and in Wagner's life as well. See, for example, Koppen, *Dekadenter Wagnerismus*, pp. 184–94; Northcote-Bade, *Wagner-Mythen*, pp. 39–52; and Peter Wapnewski, *Tristan der Held Richard Wagners* (Berlin: Severin & Siedler, 1981), pp. 150–70. The seriousness with which we are meant to view Mann's reverence for *Tristan und Isolde*, despite his parodic method, is indicated by the title of Wapnewski's chapter, "Tristan, keine Burleske: Zu Thomas Manns Novelle."

[57] For d'Annunzio's lengthy ecphrasis, see *Trionfo della morte* (Milan: Fratelli Treves, 1912), pp. 437–54 (bk. 6, chap. 1). For a discussion of the opera's relation to d'Annunzio's novel, see Koppen, *Dekadenter Wagnerismus*, pp. 197–205. The verbal similarities between Mann's and d'Annunzio's ecphrases are so strong at points that Koppen suggests a possible influence of the Italian on the German passage.

forced to utilize in "Tristan" only two decades before. (Given the sanatorium settings of both works, Mann would have been hard put to send his characters out to the opera house.) Moreover, as a narrative device the record player, unlike those musicales in which characters perform for one another, encourages the solitude that allows operatic passion to translate itself into the most intense meditation. Through the technological advance of the record player Mann could also move easily from voice to voice, from one musical style to another, to create an intricate and varied tapestry centered on a single idea—namely, Castorp's coming to terms with death. The solitary concert that Castorp devises for himself late at night in the sanatorium starts with the final two scenes of *Aida*, in which the inexorability of Rhadames's fate and the horror of the lovers' facing death in their tomb are given a bravura description. Mann moves from here to the temporary pastoral relief of Debussy's symphonic poem "L'Après-midi d'un faune," thence to the peculiar fusion of passion and fatefulness in the second act of *Carmen*, and finally to two ways of looking naively at one's impending doom, Valentin's aria from Gounod's *Faust* and the lime tree song from Schubert's song cycle *Winterreise*. The operatic narrative through which the hero moves in this scene creates a recognition, on his part, of what Mann, in a tone conspicuously unironic within the context of his work, calls "the triumphant ideality of music, of art, of the human spirit, the lofty and irrefutable process of beautifying, which it [music] conferred upon the commonplace horror of real things."[58]

Like his vision in the snow earlier in the novel, the insights that Castorp achieves in this scene allow him to transcend the commonplace realities ("the commonplace horror of real things") that dominate the lower narrative of communal life within the sanatorium. To put it in formalistic terms, the operatic narrative allows the novel's obsession with death to express itself in a poetically high style, in contrast with those lower levels of discourse—in Naphta and Settembrini's abstract philosophical discussions, in the grotesquely overdetailed medical explanations, in the hocus-pocus of the séance in the next chapter—on which the topic emerges in other parts of the novel. And quite unlike the operatic narratives in "Tristan" and "Wälsungenblut," the operatic mélange that results from Hans Castorp's record playing is to be read in the most earnest way—though we remain conscious

[58] Mann, *Der Zauberberg* (Frankfurt: Fischer, 1960), p. 896. The record-playing scene appears in chapter 7 within the section entitled "Fülle des Wohllauts," pp. 893–907.

that Mann can sustain his high style for only short spaces at a time within the novel.

Realist Mode: III. Portrait of the Artist as a Young Soprano, in The Song of the Lark

The record-playing solitude that enables Mann's hero to project a higher narrative finds its counterpart in the solitude to which Thea Kronborg, the heroine of Willa Cather's *The Song of the Lark*, is subjected in the Wagnerian roles she performs in the culminating moments of this novel. Unlike the private performances I have described, Kronborg's impersonations of Elsa and Sieglinde are public events—the culmination of the character's own strivings as the artist-heroine of a *Bildungsroman*. Indeed, this book is unique among novels with scenes from opera, for the higher narrative is not, as for Emma Bovary or Hans Castorp, created within the character's mind through the experience of hearing opera but rather becomes embodied for the lesser characters through the triumph that the heroine herself achieves as a participant in, even creator of, the higher narrative. As such, Cather's novel anticipates the last and most extreme mode of operatic intrusion in which the author, or the author's spokesman, does not simply describe an opera or its effects but creates an imaginary opera. *The Song of the Lark* follows Thea Kronborg's development from an impoverished childhood on the prairie through her training as a musician and finally to her emergence as a major international singer. Cather's readers were aware ever since the book's publication that Kronborg was a portrait of the Wagnerian soprano Olive Fremstad, but it is also known that on a more intimate level Kronborg's development—her prairie background, as well as the book's portrayal of an artist's struggle to establish herself—parallels that of Cather herself.[59]

Had Cather, like Joyce, Proust, and in fact most authors, designed her *Bildungsroman* around the life of a writer, she would have met the usual problem of finding a suitable image, at the end, to embody the protagonist's achievement as an artist. At best she could have presented something like Marcel about to start writing the novel we have been reading all the while. But singing speaks louder than writing, and Cather turned to operatic ecphrasis: Thea Kronborg is no longer the person whom we (as well

[59] For the biographical backgrounds, see Richard Giannone, *Music in Willa Cather's Fiction* (Lincoln: University of Nebraska Press, 1968), pp. 83–86.

as the novel's various characters) have known throughout most of the book, but is now a larger-than-life figure who has in fact become the Elsa and the Sieglinde that the author describes in detail moving, with the utmost dignity (and impersonality), across the operatic stage.[60] Paradoxically, as with most of the great *Bildungsromane*, it is the lower narrative of everyday life—the lovingly presented details of a child's growing up—that the reader most vividly recalls and values in *The Song of the Lark*. Once the heroine has broken down the barriers that might have kept her from reaching her goal, the reader feels a falling off, for which Thea Kronborg's heroic doings on the stage do not—especially since we cannot actually hear her voice—offer adequate compensation. As Cather herself puts it, "Here we must leave Thea Kronborg. From this time on the story of her life is the story of her achievement. The growth of an artist is an intellectual and spiritual development which can scarcely be followed in a personal narrative" (chap. 11, pp. 479–80). By the end, in fact, Thea Kronborg has become a solitary, novelistically uninteresting figure. As Cather implies in this closing statement, the *Bildungsroman* is more adequate to its protagonist's struggles towards fulfillment than to his or her fulfillment itself; the sense of incompleteness endemic to the novel as genre also is the stance on which its characters best thrive.

Narrative Transcending Narrative: The Imagined Operas of Gambara *and* Doktor Faustus

The difficulties that Cather found in novelistically embodying her heroine's artistic fulfillment are resolved by ironic means appropriate to novelistic discourse in the creation of two "original" operas in fictions by Balzac and Mann that illustrate the most extreme form of operatic intrusion within a narrative framework. The ambitious opera *Mahomet*, composed by the artist-hero of Balzac's *étude philosophique Gambara*, threatens to overwhelm the lower narrative focused on the artist's life—yet only threatens, for Balzac keeps us aware that the opera's greatness exists in its creator's mind alone.[61] Gambara's opera is an allegorical ful-

---

[60] *The Song of the Lark* (Lincoln: University of Nebraska Press, 1978), pp. 410–14, 474–76 (pt. 6, chaps. 4, 11).

[61] For studies of the musical and intellectual backgrounds of Balzac's story, see Jean-Pierre Barricelli, "Demonic Souls," *Edda*, 64 (1964), 223–33, and "Autour de 'Gambara'" in *L'Année Balzacienne 1967* (Paris: Garnier, 1967), pp. 157–63.

fillment of everything that remains inadequate in his own life: whereas Muhammed triumphs, the composer remains neglected and forlorn, and he is, in fact, unable to translate the visions he describes verbally into musical terms that can communicate successfully with an audience; and whereas Muhammed abandons his wife to realize his mission, Gambara is himself abandoned by the wife whom he neglected in order to pursue his unsuccessful composing. Failure though it remains from the point of view of the lower narrative, Gambara's composition is not only one of the most meticulously described musical compositions in fiction, but through the themes that the composer is shown sketching out on the piano it temporarily gives the reader the impression that a major work in the history of opera is being created. The key designations that Balzac inserts parenthetically throughout the long operatic ecphrasis serve both to convince us of the work's musical reality and to compromise the composer's lofty conception with technical details: "Magnificent sextet (*B flat major*). He [Muhammed] says his farewells (*solo in F natural*). . . . The prayer, sung by sixty voices, and dominated by the women (*in B flat*), crowns this gigantic work in which the life of nations and of mankind is expressed. You have experienced all the human and divine emotions."[62] If we are temporarily persuaded that we have experienced the high passions Gambara claims to have aroused, the triumph suggested in the final sentence of this passage is undercut through the personal failures recorded in the surrounding lower narrative. Whatever illusion we may gain of a consummate artistic creation is destroyed through the inadequacies in the everyday life in which this creation was fostered and that, at the end of the story, prevent its full realization and transmission.

If the reader is thus forced to interpret a verbally transmitted opera in an ironic way, the modernist opera on *Love's Labour's Lost* composed by Adrian Leverkühn in Mann's *Doktor Faustus* would seem less vulnerable than the romantic opera that Balzac renders for us in words. Just as Mann's self-reflective novelistic technique undercuts the movement towards fulfillment that characterizes the traditional *Bildungsroman*, so the artist-hero's equally self-reflective operatic technique "caricatures" (to use Mann's own expression) the musical styles of nineteenth-century opera. Leverkühn had quite deliberately chosen a text that parodied an earlier mode of thought, for, as Mann puts it, "It was not

[62] *Gambara* in Balzac, *Comédie humaine*, IX, 449.

Leverkühn but Shakespeare who was guilty of subjecting Humanism to caricature."[63] Throughout his description of the opera, Mann employs terms such as *travesty, parody, grotesque, persiflage.* Indeed, even before Leverkühn settles on Shakespeare's text as the subject for his opera, the composer, in a statement about his aesthetics, sees parody as the central mode of art in his time: "Why must it seem to me as if almost all, yes all the techniques and conventions of art *are today suited only to parody?"* (chap. 15, p. 135). The reader who seeks a frame of reference for this imaginary opera might well think of works such as *Ariadne auf Naxos* or, to cite an opera composed soon after Mann's novel, *The Rake's Progress.*

Unlike those nineteenth-century operas in which the large orchestra dominates, Leverkühn's opera pursues a minimalism in "strict chamber-music style of filagree-like work,"[64] of instrumental rather than vocal writing. The pomposity of Don Armado finds its comic embodiment in the addition of extra horns, trombones, and a tuba within an orchestra in which these instruments are distinctly out of place. The biting manner of Berowne's monologues can manifest itself, Mann implies, more powerfully in music than in words through the repetition of themes that the listener had heard shortly before; thus, the composer makes a satiric point by restating for piccolo accompaniment a melisma that in its first appearance had been accompanied by flutes and cellos. Only at one point, in a passage from Shakespeare's play that Mann (having read Frank Harris on the Dark Lady) assumes to be autobiographical, does the opera attempt a deliberately nonparodistic effect.[65]

In "Wälsungenblut" and "Tristan," as we have seen, the comic action of the lower narrative forces us to read the Wagnerian passion of the higher narrative with considerable ironic distance. By contrast, Leverkühn's opera is wholly in tune with the novel's

[63] Mann, *Doktor Faustus* (Frankfurt: Fischer, 1971), p. 217 (chap. 24).

[64] Ibid., p. 218. The ecphrasis of Leverkühn's opera occupies pp. 215–19 (chap. 24) of this text. For a close analysis of another musical ecphrasis in the novel, this one of a "real" composition (the prelude to the last act of *Die Meistersinger*), see Steven Paul Scher, *Verbal Music in German Literature* (New Haven: Yale, 1968), pp. 106–42. Scher's book concerns itself with musical ecphrasis as a continuing tradition in German literature from the Romantic period through Thomas Mann. Unlike the examples in the present chapter, Scher's examples are of instrumental rather than vocal music. Like my own examples, Scher's include both imagined and "real" music.

[65] See Gunilla Bergsten, *Thomas Mann's "Doctor Faustus:" The Sources and Structure of the Novel,* trans. Krishna Winston (Chicago: University of Chicago Press, 1969), pp. 63–64.

lower narrative, for each is an ironically directed construct. The novel, with its unreliable narrator, its montage technique, and its parody of earlier literary styles, belongs to the same modernist context as the opera embedded within it, while the two early novellas display the gulf that separates them from the Wagnerian world with which they make ironic contact. If, as I suggested early in this chapter, opera and novel have ordinarily asserted their distinctness from one another, Leverkühn's opera instead asserts its affinities with the lower narrative. But Mann also makes clear that *Love's Labour's Lost* is only a single and early stage in Leverkühn's development as a modernist artist: through lengthy descriptions of Leverkühn's two later, nontheatrical works, the oratorio *Apocalipsis cum Figuris* and the cantata *Dr. Fausti Weheklag*, Mann has reestablished the distance between opera and narrative that prevailed during the preceding two centuries.[66] In his descriptions of the music he imagines within these large-scale works, Mann expresses the sorrow and sense of horror that the lower narrative depicting Leverkühn's life and Germany's cultural decline can approach only through the self-reflective techniques characteristic of modernist fiction.

Epilogue: The Opera Mundi of Dom Casmurro

If the creation of an imaginary opera is the most extreme mode by which a musical score intrudes into the lower narrative, by way of epilogue to this section I shall suggest a final twist to the relationship of opera and fiction. Early in *Dom Casmurro*, the best-known work by the great Brazilian novelist Machado de Assis, a down-and-out Italian tenor tells a parable built around the proposition "Life is an opera." Although God is the poet, the composer turns out to be Satan, who set the Lord's text in the vain hope that his act might get him readmitted to heaven. Unfortunately, except for its excellence in orchestration, Satan's music does not achieve the perfection of the text: "In some places the words go to the right and the music to the left. . . . The maestro makes too much use of the choral masses, which often drown out the words with their confused harmony."[67] Within the context of this parable, the higher narrative of opera has been reduced to the

---

[66] See *Doktor Faustus*, pp. 355–78 passim and 484–90 (chaps. 34, 46), for Mann's ecphrases—far more elaborate than that of *Love's Labour's Lost*—of these two works.

[67] Machado de Assis, *Dom Casmurro*, trans. Helen Caldwell (Berkeley: University of California Press, 1953), p. 19 (chaps. 8–9).

lower narrative of life and fiction; only the unrealized and divine text retains its lofty status.

Still, despite or even because of opera's imperfections, the pathetic and quite unheroic hero of Machado's novel identifies with the idea behind the parable. "My life fits [the tenor's] definition," Dom Casmurro writes. "I sang a tender *duo*, then a *trio*, then a *quatuor*" (p. 21). Machado's substitution of *opera mundi* for the traditional *theatrum mundi* gives us perhaps a more satisfactory image of the everyday life that the novel has taken for its domain. Through its distance from the perfect divine text, it acknowledges the imperfections and inadequacies that fictional narratives have always stressed. But it also acknowledges a lyrical and passionate dimension lacking in the older image of life as a stage.

It is significant, however, that Machado, like all the novelists I have discussed in this chapter, also feels the need to seek a higher narrative against which to set his tale. Quite in contrast to the opera scenes of these other novelists, the higher narrative that Machado invokes does not take the form of opera (which would of course destroy the effect of the earlier parable) but of a non-musical drama, Shakespeare's *Othello*, which the hero sees performed in the theater and quickly recognizes as emblematic of the jealousy that has shaped and undermined his own life. Although Dom Casmurro's visit to the theater briefly inspires him to contemplate murdering his wife, he quickly gives up the idea and lives out his days in the same inconsequential manner in which he has behaved throughout the book. Like the divine text in the parable, the play, which Casmurro calls "the most sublime tragedy of this world" (chap. 135, p. 243), remains an ideal that serves to underline the triviality of the life he has been narrating. Machado's need to project such an ideal, whether in musical or simply in spoken form, exemplifies a point that I have argued throughout this chapter, namely that the novel defines its essential domain through the intrusion of a higher narrative against which its lowly doings can be measured. By reserving this higher narrative for the divine text and for Shakespeare's long-canonized play, Machado is able to view opera in an unaccustomed perspective and, unlike those novelists who place opera above and beyond ordinary novelistic activities, to absorb it within the lower narrative of his hero's failed life. As a result, Casmurro can claim occasional displays of operatic lyricism and passion within his own story and thus remind us, through his parable, that, like opera, his life has been rather messy.

[5]

Opera and Society:
I. Opera and Cultural Attitudes

The Antioperatic Prejudice

The Alleged Absurdity, Tediousness, and Grossness of Opera

The disparagement of opera in favor of other musical and literary genres has been a central and continuing fact of operatic history. Those who defend opera for its accessibility to the passions—as some of the novelists I treated in the preceding chapter do—have often adopted ironic stances towards opera that, in present-day psychological terms, we label "defensive." Even the form's most fervent admirers do not ordinarily speak of opera—as they do of some literary texts out of which operas have been made—as a guide to moral conduct.[1] Nor would they build a defense of opera—as has often been done for other musical forms—on the basis of its ability to aid and direct worship or to pacify frayed nerves. Moreover, the various practical functions that our historical hindsight enables us to ascribe to opera—for example, the celebration of the sponsoring monarch during the baroque period or the self-congratulation of a triumphant bourgeoisie in the

---

[1] Among the few operas that, at least in modern times, elicit praise for their moral efficacy is *Le nozze di Figaro.* Note, for instance, the comment by the theologian Hamish F. G. Swanston that, on hearing this opera, "We become more understanding and more generous." Similarly, Swanston praises *Figaro's* direct descendant, *Der Rosenkavalier,* for its ability to create "an enlargement of [the listener's] powers of human sympathy" (*In Defense of Opera* [Harmondsworth: Penguin, 1978], pp. 30, 141). The ethical dimension that Swanston discerns in these operas is the exception that proves the rule.

nineteenth century—do not themselves demonstrate its intrinsic value as a cultural form.

To the extent that opera, since Monteverdi's time, has advertised its talent for rousing the passions, it easily plays into the hands of those who are nervous about the effects of art on its beholders. To the total Platonist, of course, all forms of art, whether a finely wrought lyric, a carefully crafted fugue, even a meticulously carved altarpiece, are suspect. One need not bother asking a Platonist's judgment of opera, a form that, through the very extravagance with which it presents itself to its audience, magnifies the supposedly dangerous qualities of art many times over. Indeed, this extravagance has often enabled critics to dispose of opera without having to introduce the moral arguments that they customarily apply to other, less extreme forms of art. The amoral resolution of *L'incoronatione di Poppea*, in which two demonstrably evil characters rapturously celebrate their union, would hardly escape censure if it had been employed in nonmusical drama at least up to the mid-twentieth century.

Like those literary forms that embrace a high style, opera has proved easy to disparage through the exaggerations with which it ordinarily expresses itself. The style of *Paradise Lost*, for instance, lends itself more easily to parody than that of, say, *Middlemarch*. Throughout the four centuries in which it has flourished, opera has characteristically elicited the word *absurd* from those who sought to disparage it, without the need for elaborate argument—and with the result that advocates of opera have been left on the defensive. The absurdity that observers have noted in opera has sometimes provided the occasion for the most uproarious satire, as when Addison, in a famous *Spectator* essay, after complaining that the "Scenes and Machines" of Italian opera "appear Childish and Absurd," tells a local anecdote about "an ordinary Fellow carrying a Cage full of little Birds upon his Shoulder." When asked what these were for, the interlocutor was informed "he had been buying Sparrows for the Opera." "Sparrows for the Opera, says his Friend, licking his Lips, what are they to be roasted? No, no, says the other, they are to enter towards the end of the first Act, and to fly about the Stage."[2] Addison follows this discovery with a description of the opera that, in the way it presents his step-by-step perceptions of the various illusions that the op-

[2] Addison, *The Spectator*, ed. Donald F. Bond (Oxford: Clarendon Press, 1965), I, 23–24 (no. 5, March 6, 1711).

eratic art of his time created for its audience, clearly anticipates— to cite a famous example of operatic disparagement mentioned in my preceding chapter—Natasha Rostov's perceptions of the de- familiarized objects on the opera stage that Tolstoy described a century and a half later.

If Addison concentrates on the absurdities he discerned in the scenic effects of opera, other commentators have not hesitated to find similar absurdities in the musical and dramatic conventions governing operatic discourse. A modern scholar, in a book that purports to examine the relations of music and literature, com- plains of the "ludicrousness" inherent in operatic deaths: "What can poor Siegfried do when he has to *sing* a long passage with a spear sticking between his shoulder-blades—and presumably into his lungs?" As though this were bad enough, he finds "less of this type of absurdity" in Wagner than in "the famous quartet in *Ri- goletto*, for example, with two persons inside a shack thinking they are alone, two outside spying on them, and all four singing away full blast in slickly contrived harmony."[3] Arguments based on satiric thrusts (however crude these may be) are answerable only by counterthrusts that must themselves be weaker in rhe- torical power than the pained outrage to which they respond. Any attempt to answer such thrusts by means of rational discourse is likely to sound anticlimactic—as I myself found when an emi- nent specialist on the theater of the absurd asked me why I would "write on anything so absurd as opera." (I answered her simply, "I'll deal with that question in my book.")

Even those persons most passionately committed to opera show their awareness of arguments about the absurdity of the form through their frequent attempts to apologize for and explain away the improbabilities in operatic plots. If one looks through popular opera guidebooks, one frequently notes attempts to justify and naturalize whatever might be taken as absurd. For example, the distinguished opera scholar and critic Ernest Newman, in writing on *Il trovatore* for the larger opera public, justified Azucena's sec- ond-act narrative about Manrico's background in the following apologetic terms: "It would be natural to assume that Manrico, as a member of the tribe since his childhood, knows the remain- der of the story by now; but as the audience does not yet know it, it is necessary for him to ask Azucena to enlighten him on the

---

[3] In Calvin S. Brown, *Music and Literature: A Comparison of the Arts* (Athens: University of Georgia Press, 1948), pp. 88–89.

subject, which she proceeds to do, giving an air of verisimilitude to the affair by explaining that it is Manrico's frequent absence at the wars that has kept him in ignorance of the matter until now."[4] No matter how hard Newman may try to convince us of this scene's propriety, *Il trovatore* will always look a bit "absurd" if the probabilities of its dramatic action are measured against those, say, of an Ibsen play or of a more "realistic" opera such as *Wozzeck*.

Advocates of opera also reveal their consciousness about the form's alleged absurdities through their fascination with the vulnerability of the stage illusion. The failure to maintain an appropriate illusion is a more serious matter in those forms, like opera, that cultivate a high style than in others—for instance the novel or film—that can move among multiple stylistic ranges with relative ease. Opera fans generally relish stories about unintentional stage disasters—such as when the swan supposedly once arrived in the first act of *Lohengrin* without its scheduled passenger, or when Tosca's suicidal jump from the parapet was spoiled by a mattress placed so high that the hands she had extended in the air were still visible after her fall.[5] For those who have witnessed catastrophes such as these, the effect is that of unintentional ritual failure—like the disruption of a coronation ceremony when the newly crowned monarch is discovered suffering an attack of hiccups.

Like other forms in a high style that must strive to sustain their intensity over long intervals, opera has been called not only absurd but boring. Boredom and absurdity are in certain respects two sides of the same coin: both types of accusation work to knock the wind out of a possible defender before any serious argument can even begin. Dr. Johnson's complaint about the exertions he experienced reading *Paradise Lost*, "None ever wished it longer than it is,"[6] has for many readers served to undo the many pages of praise he had earlier meted out to the poem. Similarly La Bruyère's aphorism about opera in the time of Louis XIV, "I do not know how opera, with such perfect music and an altogether regal

---

[4] In Newman, *Stories of the Great Operas and Their Composers* (1928–30; rpt. Philadelphia: Blakiston, 1945), p. 655.

[5] This fascination with operatic vulnerability is evident in the demand for books such as Hugh Vickers's *Great Operatic Disasters* (New York: St. Martin's Press, 1980), which recounts stories of this sort for the opera public. The book was apparently popular enough to justify a sequel, *Even Greater Operatic Disasters* (New York: St. Martin's Press, 1982).

[6] "Milton" in Johnson, *Poems and Selected Prose* (New York: Rinehart, 1958), p. 464.

expenditure, has succeeded in boring me,"[7] has, in one form or another, echoed through the ages—from Saint-Preux's condemnation of the Paris opera as "the most boring spectacle that could possibly exist"[8] to that recurrent topos in *New Yorker* cartoons of the bored, middle-class husband being dragged to the opera by his culturally pretentious wife.

The disparagement of opera as a hybrid genre is doubtless as unanswerable—or as useless to answer—as its disparagement on account of its absurdity or boringness. Directly after complaining about how boring opera is, La Bruyère complains as well that "opera up to now is not a poem . . . nor a spectacle . . . but a concert with voices sustained by instruments."[9] Just as Rousseau outdid La Bruyère on the matter of operatic boredom, so Paul Valéry, nearly three centuries later, outdoes him on the issue of purity—to the point that the latter even calls opera "gross" ("grossier"): "Opera seemed to me a chaos, a disordering practice of vocal, orchestral, dramatic, mimic, visual, choreographic parts—finally a spectacle that is gross, since . . . the total work was handed over to the diverging inspirations of the librettist, the composer, the choreographer, the art designer, the director, and the interpreters."[10] If statements such as these can be attributed to a typically French classical bias, one might also remember that the most influential models for large-scale, mixed spectacle in opera were set by the Paris opera, first in the late seventeenth century and again during the 1830s. Moreover, the hybrid, all-encompassing quality that Valéry finds gross is the very thing that theorists of opera from the early Florentines down to Wagner have seen as a cause for celebration. The diversity that one observer praises and that an-

---

[7] "Des Ouvrages de l'esprit," sec. 47, in La Bruyère, *Oeuvres complètes*, ed. Julien Benda (Paris: Gallimard, 1951), p. 99.

[8] *La Nouvelle Héloïse*, pt. 2, letter 23, in Rousseau, *Oeuvres complètes*, ed. Bernard Gagnebin and Marcel Raymond, II (Paris; Gallimard, 1961), p. 289. After alluding directly to La Bruyère, Rousseau outdoes the latter with even stronger condemnation. Needless to add, Rousseau (through his character Saint-Preux) complains specifically of the type of opera associated with Rameau. He had nothing but praise for the Italian comic style represented by Pergolesi, from whose *La serva padrona* his own *Le Devin du village* derived. See his discussion of his advocacy of the Italian style through his own operatic practice in *Les Confessions*, ibid., I (1959), pp. 374–87 (bk. 8).

[9] At the end of the passage La Bruyère imagines a perfect form of opera that will keep "mind, eye and ear equally enchanted"; yet the ideal opera achieves a generic purity that the actuality that so bored him clearly lacks. La Bruyère, *Oeuvres complètes*, p. 99.

[10] "Histoire d'Amphion" in Valéry, *Oeuvres complètes*, ed. Jean Hytier, II (Paris: Gallimard, 1960), p. 1281.

other condemns allows for too predictable a form of debate to excite much interest.

The Implied Inferiority of Opera to Other Art Forms

The disparagement of opera manifests itself most powerfully perhaps in less blatant forms than those I have mentioned thus far. Note, for example, the fact that until very recently opera has not been favored with editions prepared with the degree of scholarly responsibility that has been lavished on other forms of music. Indeed the vast majority of operatic performances one hears are based on editions that indiscriminately include accretions made by conductors and singers long after the composer had ceased to exercise any control over the work. The distinction between opera and other forms in this respect shows up as early as Monteverdi, who supervised the publication of his madrigals, but not his operas, all but three of which are no longer even extant.[11] In all media of art, certain genres, of course, command more prestige than others at particular times: to cite an example even more striking than Monteverdi's, Shakespeare supervised the publication of his relatively inconsequential early narrative poems but evidently would have allowed his plays to disappear from view if others had not published them.

The comparatively low status of opera shows up as well in the way that the musical canon is customarily described in histories of music and even in general histories. Among composers whose work was primarily operatic, only Wagner has been granted a top niche in the canon. Verdi, on the other hand, is rarely mentioned in the same breath as other composers—for instance, Bach, Handel, Mozart, Beethoven, Brahms, Stravinsky—whose contributions to the history of music are defined primarily by their non-operatic works or who never composed operas at all.[12] Although

---

[11] Monteverdi defined the madrigal broadly enough to include the two short dramatic works *Il ballo delle ingrate* and *Il combattimento di Tancredi e Clorinda* in his Eighth Book, but evidently drew the line at his full-length operas, only one of which, *Orfeo*, was published during his lifetime, and without his supervision. The later Venetian operas, as was typical of seventeenth-century opera, remained in manuscript until our own time.

[12] Note, for example, how a musicologist such as Donald Grout, whose own specialty is opera, gives relatively little emphasis to opera in his influential *History of Western Music*, rev. ed. (New York: Norton, 1973). Grout devotes less than half as many pages to Verdi as to his contemporary Brahms and only a brief paragraph to the operas of Alessandro Scarlatti, whose operas he himself has edited and whose importance in the history of opera he has labored to affirm in his other writings.

nobody would hesitate to list figures such as Schubert and Mendelssohn among the "great composers," Verdi's name has been assimilated into a list of this sort only in the last few years; certainly anyone who included Bellini, Bizet, or Puccini would risk intellectual embarrassment. As soon as the list is narrowed to "great operatic composers," almost any composer in the general repertory—or others, such as Gluck, who played major roles in the history of opera—would make the grade. By the same token, to call Beethoven or Debussy a "great operatic composer," despite the acknowledged greatness of the one opera that each completed, would seem demeaning, except in a statement that sought to establish that these composers, in *addition* to their other contributions, also happened to work successfully in opera.

Moreover, historians of music define "progress" in musical composition in ways that generally work to the disadvantage of opera. In the four centuries since opera originated, musical history has assumed the form of a narrative about the conquest of certain technical territories, above all the areas of harmony, orchestration, and musical organization—much as the history of painting has concentrated on matters such as perspective and the disposition of colors on the canvas. In view of this bias, only Wagner's operas would seem sufficiently "progressive" to occupy a central place in musical history. To the extent that musical innovation after the mid-eighteenth century took place largely in Germany, Italian opera since that time has come to look "regressive" from a musical point of view. It is no wonder that the stature of Verdi has not been adequately acknowledged within the conventions governing the narration of musical history.

Likewise opera has never played a significant role for historians of drama. For one thing, operatic styles have not often coincided with the reigning dramatic style at a given time. Although French seventeenth-century opera is related to the mythological "machine" plays of the period, it is far removed from the classical style that we now see as the major prevailing dramatic mode. Wagnerian music-drama cannot be linked to any significant non-musical drama of the mid–nineteenth century. When relationships can be established between opera and drama, opera generally looks like a belated, derivative version of a dramatic style: Zeno's reform thus becomes an attempt to emulate the triumphs of French classical form, or *verismo* opera is seen as an attempt to borrow from the prestige of naturalist drama. I can think of only one instance in which the correlation between contemporary styles has favored opera: the Mozart–Da Ponte operas are now customarily seen as superior (if belated) realizations of the possibilities latent within eighteenth-century comedy. Even more important than the difficulty of relating operatic to dramatic styles is the fact that as soon as opera is compared to drama, the former comes to look deficient in "intellectual" content. *Verismo* opera is not simply derivative of naturalist drama, but through its mode of presentation it can embody only in fitful ways the cultural program underlying the plays of Ibsen, Strindberg, and Verga.[13] As long as opera is seen from the point of view of spoken drama, it is always likely to seem wanting—just as the latter, or any other form, would seem wanting if opera were the central medium against which the other arts were to be evaluated or placed in historical perspective. Moreover, the phenomena that historians of drama note in opera are generally limited to the contributions of the librettist or stage designer but not of the composer.

Far more serious than the disparagement of opera for its supposed formal backwardness is its condemnation on grounds of triviality and lack of intellectual content. The following lines by a character in Richard Steele's comedy, *The Conscious Lovers* (1722), exemplify a type of moral judgment that has surfaced frequently in the history of opera: "All the Pleasure the best Opera gives us, is but meer Sensation.—Methinks it's Pity the Mind can't have a little more Share in the Entertainment.—The Musick's certainly fine; but, in my Thoughts, there's none of your Composers come up to Old *Shakespear* and *Otway*."[14] The labeling of opera as "meer Sensation" in relation to the intellectual pleasures that poetic drama can offer is a complementary version of that celebration of opera as passion that I stressed in the preceding chapter. Within our culture, those elements we designate as nonrational easily move from objects for celebration to objects for disparagement.

The charge that opera provides primarily "sensation" and "entertainment" is ultimately more devastating than the charge that it is absurd, or boring, or generically impure. Whereas the latter charges are attributable to the taste or predisposition of a particular person or like-minded group at a particular time, the former

[13] For an analysis of the relation of *verismo* opera to realism as a program for literature and art, see Carl Dahlhaus, *Musikalischer Realismus* (Munich: Piper, 1982), pp. 89–92, 118–22.

[14] Steele, *Plays*, ed. Shirley Strum Kenny (Oxford: Clarendon Press, 1971), p. 334 (Act II, Scene 2).

charge contains an implicit, and often even explicit, moral condemnation. As such it is an expression of an attitude that Jonas Barish, in his magisterial history of this attitude from Plato to the present day, has labeled "the antitheatrical prejudice." This prejudice, as Barish points out, has traditionally manifested itself through a suspicion of illusion and artifice, a disapproval of imitation and impersonation, and a self-justification in the name of rationality and the good of society. Barish begins his study by observing that "terms borrowed from the theater—*theatrical, operatic, melodramatic, stagey,* etc.—tend to be hostile or belittling."[15] For those, like Plato or Rousseau, who voice the prejudice in an extreme form, the distinctions between the various imitative arts are none too important, for all the arts are morally tainted.[16] On the other hand, those not committed to an extreme position have been able to exercise an antitheatrical prejudice by separating certain theatrical modes they deem "harmful" from others they can embrace as "authentic," "lifelike," and "salutary." Indeed, the prejudice has manifested itself much more frequently through a double standard of this sort than through the extreme of outright rejection. Thus, Barish has interpreted the classicism and the didacticism of Ben Jonson as expressions of an antitheatricalism that occurs "among the company of artists determined to rescue their art from excessive artifice."[17] As the above quotation from *The Conscious Lovers* suggests, opera has proved a convenient scapegoat for those whose antitheatrical prejudice is not strong enough to force them to give up other forms of theater.

The very extravagance at the heart of operatic expression has left the form especially vulnerable to the disapproval of those who, in one way or another, feel uncomfortable with the theater. Yet

[15] Barish, *The Antitheatrical Prejudice* (Berkeley: University of California Press, 1981), p. 1.

[16] It is characteristic of moral thinkers such as Plato and Rousseau to make some token distinctions as a means of providing the strongest possible condemnation of those forms they take to be the worst offenders. Plato, for example, objects less to lyric poetry than to drama, arguing that the former, being expressed directly by the writer, voices less of an untruth than the latter, in which the writer's voice is suppressed; yet he finds no place for either genre in his ideal state. Although Rousseau preferred the simplicity of Italian comic opera to the artifice of French opera, his letter to d'Alembert makes no allowance for any form of theatrical entertainment in that ideal republic that he postulates under the name "Geneva." Both writers, of course, allow for limited forms of art sanctioned by the state and directed towards the celebration of the state. (For the permissible forms of art in Plato's and Rousseau's republics, see Barish, *The Antitheatrical Prejudice,* pp. 27, 289–92).

[17] Ibid., p. 136.

the discomfort associated with seeing an actor impersonate another human being is doubtless compounded when the actor voices his sentiments not in the speech we ordinarily associate with human communication but in a mode as exaggerated and improbable as song. The boundaries between speech and song are sufficiently marked that anyone with an antitheatrical bias can invoke verisimilitude as a means of justifying nonmusical as against operatic impersonation. The difficulties audiences feel with impersonation through song are exacerbated by the fact that, except in those types of opera that mix spoken dialogue with music, heroic sentiments and everyday needs are equally subjected to musical expression. Although Saint-Evremond's attack on opera in the 1670s includes the familiar complaints about its boringness and its lack of intellectual content, his most vehement remarks derive from the fact "that the whole piece is sung from beginning to end, as if the characters represented had arranged in a ridiculous way to present musically the most commonplace as well as the most important matters in their lives. Can one imagine that a master sings while calling his servant or while giving him an order?"[18]

St. Evremond's disparagement of opera on grounds of verisimilitude is echoed within serious operatic criticism by those who have sought to rid opera of its more improbable elements. In the mid–eighteenth century, Algarotti could look back longingly to those baroque operas that, through their use of ancient mythology, "gave an air of probability to most surprizing and wonderful events" and made "the singing of actors . . . appear a true imitation of the language made use of by the deities they represented." For Algarotti, a sufficient distance from the subject matter of ordinary life was enough to justify many of the excesses that others used in order to condemn operatic expression entirely. Since, as he put it, "the trillings of an air [do not] flow so justifiably from the mouth of a Caesar or Cato, as from the lips of Venus or Apollo," the florid vocal techniques of his time could pass muster in

---

[18] "Sur les Opéras" in Saint-Evremond, *Oeuvres en prose*, ed. René Ternois, III (Paris: Marcel Didier, 1966), p. 151. One could answer that opera, as I pointed out in the second chapter of this study, has ordinarily found means of presenting the heroic and the commonplace with varying levels of musical intensity. Although the distinction between aria and recitative was already established in both French and Italian opera of Saint-Evremond's time, it became considerably more pronounced in Italian opera during the succeeding generation.

mythological but not in historical themes.[19] The violation of verisimilitude in florid singing even prevented Berlioz, during his youth, from appreciating Mozart. As he tells it in his memoirs, a single coloratura passage in *Don Giovanni*, at the end of Donna Anna's second aria, "Non mi dir," upset his sense of decorum through the fact that "Donna Anna has suddenly dried her tears and broken out in ribald clowning."[20]

Indeed, the major "reforms" in the history of opera can be interpreted as attempts to rid opera of those elements most offensive to anybody holding an antitheatrical bias. In the name of verisimilitude and the dramatic principle, the reformers of opera could banish whatever excesses prevailed at the time. The so-called "first reform" of Zeno, for example, did away with baroque mythological machines and whatever else violated early eighteenth-century notions of dramatic decorum;[21] Gluck's reform, among other things, stressed the dramatic implausibility inherent in the ornate vocal style of *opera seria*; and Wagner's reform, besides rejecting most operatic conventions of the early nineteenth century, directed its most potent attack on the dramatic "effects without causes" that the composer discerned at the base of Meyerbeer's style.[22] Doubtless the success with which the various reforms established themselves had a good bit to do with their ability to play on those vestiges of antitheatricality among the audiences to whom reformist arguments were addressed and whose tastes they were intended to refine.

Although these reformist arguments stress a need for verisimilitude and dramatic integrity, the more high-minded composers since the early nineteenth century have found it difficult to hide a more fundamental antitheatricality rooted in their suspicion of

[19] Count [Francesco] Algarotti, *An Essay on Opera* (London: L. Davis & C. Reymers, 1767), pp. 13, 18. One may remember Algarotti's recommendation, quoted in the first chapter of this study, of the story of Montezuma as a suitable operatic subject because of the opportunities it offers for lavish display. Evidently history could seem more probable in opera if it took place in a non-European realm whose exoticism gave it a status comparable to that of mythology.

[20] Berlioz, *Memoirs*, trans. David Cairns (London: Victor Gollancz, 1969), p. 93.

[21] For a detailed demonstration that the "first reform" was not so much Zeno's as that of a number of librettists who preceded him, see Robert S. Freeman, *Opera without Drama: Currents of Change in Italian Opera* (Ann Arbor: UMI Research Press, 1981).

[22] Wagner's epigram against Meyerbeer was "Wirkung ohne Ursache." For a spirited argument against the lack of dramatic motivation that Wagner felt both in the stage effects and the music of *Le Prophète*, see *Oper und Drama*, pt. 1, sec. 6, in *Gesammelte Schriften*, ed. Julius Kapp (Leipzig: Hesse & Becker, n.d.), XI, 91–95.

audiences who seek "mere" entertainment in place of edification. In rethinking the history of opera, Wagner quite bluntly divided composers between those he called "serious" and those he dismissed as "frivolous" through their pandering to an audience's worst instincts.[23] In an early piece of writing, an imaginary dialogue between himself and Beethoven, Wagner allows his predecessor to indict the modern audience for putting up with "glittering untruth, brilliant nonsense, and oversweetened boredom."[24] When Wagner has Beethoven proudly announce, "I am not an opera composer,"[25] he is of course voicing his own strongly antioperatic bias that was later to result in his seeking out new generic names as "serious" alternatives to the term *opera*, which for him had become hopelessly associated with what he deemed a "frivolous" form of entertainment.[26] In a similar semantic maneuver that seeks to separate "higher" from "lower" forms of art, the term *absolute music* emerged in the nineteenth century as a means of excluding all music that smacks of the theater—not only music written to texts (whether or not for theatrical presentation) but also those nonvocal compositions that had become theatricalized through programs that their composers attached to them, whether in accompanying narratives such as those provided by Liszt and Mahler or in brief titles such as *Pastoral Symphony* and *Poem of Ecstasy.*[27]

From a strictly "musical" point of view, operas often appear notoriously uneven in quality; indeed, only a small part of the standard operatic repertory would stand up to the scrutiny to which musical analysts subject those works that are variously classified as "absolute."[28] In a lengthy review of Rossini's *Guillaume Tell*,

[23] Wagner's terms are "ernst" and "frivol." Ibid., sec. 1, pp. 24–25.

[24] "Eine Pilgerfahrt zu Beethoven" in *Gesammelte Schriften*, VII, 97.

[25] Ibid., pp. 96–97.

[26] For some useful distinctions between Wagner's polemical intent in using these names and his actual practice, see the chapter "Oper, Drama, Musikdrama" in Carl Dahlhaus, *Wagners Konzeption des musikalischen Dramas* (Regensburg: Bosse, 1971), pp. 15–24.

[27] Like all prejudices, musical antitheatricalism allows its holders to draw up their own limits of tolerance. The *Harvard Dictionary of Music* refers to an extreme application of the term *absolute music* that "excludes not only program and vocal music but also music of a definitely emotional character (romantic music), so that Bach and, to some extent, Mozart are considered composers of absolute music." *Harvard Dictionary of Music*, 2d ed., ed. Willi Apel (Cambridge, Mass.: Belknap Press of Harvard University Press, 1969), s.v. "absolute music."

[28] One need only look at a standard textbook such as Walter Piston's *Harmony* or a demonstration of an analytical method such as Leonard Meyer's *Exploring*

Berlioz, whose own work could scarcely be assimilated into any concept of absolute music, tempers his enthusiasm for many passages in the opera with a condemnation of the composer's characteristic padding and his lack of sustained craftsmanship. When Berlioz complains of Rossini's tendency to move with what he calls "tiring persistence" to the dominant over the tonic,[29] he puts his finger on the habit of many great operatic composers of relying on formulaic writing to sustain long compositions.

"Opera by its very nature is a gigantic series of compromises," a modern musicologist has written.[30] The whole institutional setting within which opera has traditionally flourished requires so many compromises that only a few operas demonstrate the intensity and evenness of craftsmanship that nontheatrical music can more easily attain. The dilemma of a serious composer contemplating operatic composition is well expressed by Schumann, whose rigorously avant-gardist mentality may well have prevented him from composing a successful opera:

> Say that one puts the best composer in the theater: he will get things wrong; he is not permitted to give too much; voices need to rest; the orchestra needs its break. What deliberation and what experience the economic and theatrical factors require! Before the composer can begin to shine, the theater director needs to be satisfied. How much beautiful music must often have been sacrificed whenever the composer, for the sake of the music, forgot the stage he was writing for![31]

Music to note how rarely passages from opera are made to serve as musical examples. Nearly all of Piston's operatic examples are from Wagner. Meyer analyzes Mozart and Purcell arias but otherwise confines his operatic examples to two Wagner preludes. See Piston, *Harmony*, 3d ed. (New York: Norton, 1962), and Meyer, *Exploring Music: Essays and Explorations* (Chicago: University of Chicago Press, 1973).

[29] Berlioz, "Guillaume-Tell de Rossini," *Gazette musicale de Paris*, 1 (1834), 337.

[30] Winton Dean, *Handel and the Opera Seria* (Berkeley: University of California Press, 1969), p. 213.

[31] In Georg Eismann, *Robert Schumann: Ein Quellenwerk über sein Leben und Schaffen* (Leipzig: Breitkopf & Härtel, 1956), II, 158. For an entertaining account of the essential untheatricality of Schumann's one opera, *Genoveva*, see George Bernard Shaw's review of a rare production. Review of December 13, 1893, in *Shaw's Music*, ed. Dan H. Laurence (New York: Dodd, Mead, 1981), III, 60–66. Shaw describes some conspicuously undramatic passages with these words: "Schumann, for the most part, leaves the stage to get on as best it can, and retires into pure symphony" (p. 63).

Schumann's complaint about having to "sacrifice good music" when writing for the stage raises the question of whether what counts as "good" within one musical genre would necessarily seem good in another genre. By the same token, certain music that we find theatrically powerful would scarcely "work" in the concert hall or as an object for close analysis. In a letter to Mendelssohn, Schumann once made fun of the parallel fifths and octaves in *Tannhäuser*, an opera he knew only from the score. Once he attended a performance, however, he changed his mind, for, as he put it in a subsequent letter, "On the stage everything looks different. I was quite moved [*ergriffen*] by much of it."[32] As Schumann discovered, only the power unleashed by actual stage performance can temper the force of the antioperatic prejudice, which, as this section has shown, is itself so deeply rooted in a tenacious and age-old antitheatrical prejudice that opera has always flourished as a suspect art.

Yet Schumann's change of mind also suggests that the *experience* of opera is something different in kind from the experience of other forms of music and, for that matter, of other forms of drama. Could it be that audiences receptive to opera hold in abeyance those criteria—for example, an economy of musical means or verisimilitude in representation—that they often demand for these other forms? Like Schumann at the performance of *Tannhäuser*, the receptive opera audience is drawn into a type of experience unique to this form alone. One cannot satisfactorily answer the age-old accusations against opera on their own terms—by insisting, for instance, that opera is *not* "absurd" or "improbable" or that its music is *not* inferior to instrumental music. Rather, one must point (as I have attempted to do on various occasions in this study) to features peculiar to the experience of opera—its ability to rouse the passions, to raise the stories it tells to a mythical level, to provide a ceremonial framework distinct from the framework within which we live out our ordinary lives. Whether this experience takes on the Dionysian aspect that Nietzsche claimed to locate in *Tristan und Isolde* or the sensuous, less frenzied qualities we associate with the Mozart operas, only a rational understanding of the experience of opera can help provide answers to those who voice the antioperatic prejudice.

[32] Letters of October 22 and November 12, 1845, in Friedrich Kerst, *Schumann-Brevier* (Berlin: Schuster & Loeffler, 1905), pp. 152–53.

Operatic Dichotomies: Between High and Popular Culture

The Persistence of Stereotypes

Wagner's strict demarcation between "serious" and "frivolous" opera, rooted though this distinction may be in the cultural situation of the mid–nineteenth century, suggests a division that cuts across the history of opera. Whether in the form of the avant-garde as opposed to low culture, or of aristocratic as opposed to commercial sponsorship of opera, this division helps define both the social entanglements and the formal characteristics that have marked opera at particular epochs. For example, the career of the first major operatic composer, Monteverdi, divides neatly between his productions for the Mantuan court and those for Venice, the first city in which opera succeeded as a commercial venture; even without instruction in the historical backgrounds of early opera, an audience today would easily identify the decorous *Orfeo* as Monteverdi's courtly opera and *L'incoronatione di Poppea*, with its raucous mixture of comic and serious, as a distinctly popular form.

The various "wars" that have buffeted operatic history have generally pitted a higher against a lower style, a more-educated against a less-educated musical and theatrical taste. *The Beggar's Opera* and the various ballad operas that followed in its wake assert bourgeois over aristocratic tastes, native English robustness against the exoticism associated with *castrati* and a foreign tongue.[33] The *querelle des bouffons* that followed the success of Rousseau's *Le Devin du village* was not only a battle between the partisans of the king (the supporters of Rameau) and those of the queen (the supporters of Rousseau), but it was also a confrontation between native French complexity and Italian simplicity, between harmony and melody, between baroque and Enlightenment, between aristocratic and bourgeois values. The war between the Gluckistes and Piccinnistes two decades later confronted north and south, composer-centered and performer-centered opera, music-drama and entertainment, an aesthetic of difficulty and an

[33] On the different audiences that English and Italian opera attracted in London, see Roger Fiske, *English Theatre Music in the Eighteenth Century* (London: Oxford University Press, 1973), p. 66.

aesthetic of immediate consumption.[34] The struggle between the partisans of Wagner and Verdi in the late nineteenth century plays upon and renews (however much this distorts the actual achievement of the two composers) earlier dichotomies such as north and south, harmony and melody, composer- and performer-centered opera, high-minded and popular, advanced and regressive. The high-versus-low dichotomy is in fact built into the text, the music, and the meaning of certain operas, for example those eighteenth-century comic operas that introduce characters from *opera seria* and, to cite a modern instance that exploits the cultural resonances within the dichotomy to the full, the Strauss-Hofmannsthal *Ariadne auf Naxos*.

When multiple theaters have flourished simultaneously in a single city, they have usually catered to publics representing distinct tastes, classes, and financial resources. Whereas the Paris Opéra in the 1830s catered to the newly risen middle class, the Théâtre Italien, which presented the latest works of Bellini and Donizetti in the original language, drew aristocrats and connoisseurs. In the late nineteenth century the distinction between the Opéra and the Opéra Comique in Paris, and between the Hofoper (literally Court Opera) and the Volksoper (People's Opera) in Vienna, is at once a distinction between heavier and lighter entertainment, between recitative and direct speech to link arias, between the patronage of a socially more- and less-elevated public, between higher and lower ticket prices. In America in our own century the distinction is still evident in the difference in social prestige between opera, which in the major cities depended on the financial patronage of those identified with what is labeled "society," and that form variously called *operetta*, *light opera*, or *musical comedy*, which has generally had to support itself through ticket revenues alone. In New York today the older European distinction between "high" and "low" persists in the division of activities between the Metropolitan Opera, with its more rigorously classical repertory, its star system, and its elaborate productions, and, only a stone's throw away, the less pretentious, more popular-minded New York City Opera.

[34] Nietzsche, who knew a thing or two about the relations of art and politics, questioned the certainty we show in awarding our laurels to Gluck instead of to Piccinni: "Aesthetic wars are like political wars, and they are won by power, not by reason. We can take Gluck's superiority for granted not because he was necessarily right, but because he happened to win." *Menschliches, Allzumenschliches*, vol. 2, pt. 2, sec. 164, in Nietzsche, *Werke*, ed. Karl Schlechta (Darmstadt: Wissenschaftliche Buchgesellschaft, 1966), I, 938.

The recurring distinctions between north and south, harmony and melody, difficulty and ease (both of composition and comprehension) reveal certain stereotypes that have become attached over the centuries to particular national operatic traditions. Through his championship and imitation of *La serva padrona*, Rousseau was able to effect a confrontation between the unself-consciousness and sensuousness he saw in Italian music and the labored, uninspired quality he ascribed to French music.[35] One of the recurring themes in the Gluck–Piccinni controversy was the distinction between an Italian composer's need to turn out operas rapidly and a northern composer's habit of laboring for long periods at a single composition.[36]

Building as it does on Rousseau's nature–culture dichotomy, Schiller's powerful distinction between the naive and the sentimental artist (though it is not specifically concerned with music) reinforces the stereotype about northern and southern musical propensities. Whether one opts for naive or sentimental, Germanic or Latin, the stereotype easily serves whatever ends one has in mind. Heine, for example, characteristically contrasted the simple and melody-centered art of Rossini with the more complex, harmony-based writing of Meyerbeer. When Heine championed Meyerbeer during the 1830s, he hailed him as the more progressive artist, the product of the Revolution of 1830—while Rossini's art, he claimed, belonged to the Restoration.[37] A decade later, finding that Meyerbeer had become the darling of the aristocracy, Heine reversed his position: he now condemned Meyerbeer for "introducing eclecticism into music" and praised Rossini's *Otello* as "a Vesuvius that throws up gleaming flowers."[38]

Wagner, too, employed the stereotype for different ends at different times. During his early enthusiasm for contemporary Ital-

[35] These linkages occur at innumerable spots in Rousseau's writings, for instance in the *Dictionnaire de musique*, the *Essai sur l'origine des langues*, and the *Confessions*. For a description of the ecstasy he felt on first hearing Italian opera during his stay in Venice, as well as his idealization of the Italians as a musical people, see *Les Confessions*, in *Oeuvres complètes*, I, 313–16.

[36] See letters of September 15 and October 5, 1778 (by J. F. Marmontel and J. B. Suard to *Mercure de France*), in Gluck, *Collected Correspondence and Papers*, ed. Hedwig and E. H. Mueller von Asow, trans. Stewart Thomson (New York: St. Martin's Press, n.d.), pp. 148–50, 158–59.

[37] See *Ueber die französische Bühne*, letter 9, in Heine, *Sämtliche Werke*, ed. Ernst Elster (Leipzig: Bibliographisches Institut, n.d.), IV, 542–44.

[38] "Gedanken und Einfälle," ibid., VII, 428–29. For discussions of Heine's change of positions, see Michael Mann, *Heine's Musikkritiken* (Hamburg: Hoffmann & Campe, 1971), pp. 58–61, and Peter Uwe Hohendahl, *The Institution of Criticism* (Ithaca: Cornell University Press, 1982), pp. 108–12.

ian opera, Wagner condemned German music for its erudition[39] and speculated that if Bellini had studied under a German village schoolmaster, he would probably have composed "better" but might also have lost his lyric gift.[40] Three decades later, while eulogizing the *Heldentenor* who had created the role of Tristan, Wagner condemned Italian lyricism for directing itself only to "sensuous well-being" (*sinnliches Wohlgefühl*) and ignoring "the sufferings of the soul."[41]

Although Isaiah Berlin's recent identification of Verdi with Schiller's naive-type artist seems a convincing enough argument, it nonetheless represents a continuation of the old stereotype. Certainly Verdi himself helped perpetuate this image: in 1878, by which time he had adopted such supposedly German traits as painstaking craftsmanship and slowness of composition, he complained that the emergence of quartet societies in Italy threatened the native "love of song, whose expression is opera"; to describe the Italian lyric genius, Verdi fell back on terms such as *instinct*, *spontaneous*, and *natural*.[42] Nietzsche's provocative championship of *Carmen* for its "African serenity" and its "more southern, duskier, more sunburned sensibility," in contrast with the Wagnerian style that he had rejected, gives new life to the stereotype through its celebration of southern music—now, through Carmen's gypsy background, transferred even further southward from Italy to Africa—as an expression of dark, primitive unselfconsciousness.[43] Hofmannsthal encouraged Strauss to cultivate a lighter, more lyrical style, to turn away, as he put it at one point, "from the *learned* German musical spirit," which he characterized with the phrase "puzza di musica" ("it reeks of music") that the Piccinnistes had used of Gluck.[44] But Strauss ended up falling back on the stereotype as readily as Verdi had: although he promised his librettist that he would try to lighten his style, he also re-

[39] See "Die deutsche Oper" in *Gesammelte Schriften*, VII, 9.

[40] "Bellini: Ein Wort zu seiner Zeit," in ibid., 28.

[41] "Meine Erinnerungen an Ludwig Schnorr von Carolsfeld," in ibid., II, 155. *Sinnliches* can, of course, be translated either as "sensuous" or "sensual."

[42] Letter of April 1878 (to an unknown correspondent), in Verdi, *I copialettere*, ed. Gaetano Cesare and Alessandro Luzio (Milan: Commissione Esecutiva per le Onoranze a Giuseppe Verdi, 1913), pp. 626–27. For Isaiah Berlin on Verdi's "naiveté," see n. 52 of chapter 2 in the present study.

[43] *Der Fall Wagner*, sec. 2, in Nietzsche, *Werke*, II, 906–7.

[44] Letter of July 26, 1928, in Strauss-Hofmannsthal, *Briefwechsel*, 3d ed., ed. Willi Schuh (Zurich: Atlantis, 1964), p. 651.

minded him that Goethe and Mozart had long before recognized that a German could never turn into an Italian.[45]

However much truth there may be in stereotypes about national musical styles, these styles are scarcely determined by genetic transmission. Although it is common to note the continuity of French opera from Lully to Poulenc—for instance, in its lightly sensuous texture and in its fascination with enchantment, both through spectacle and musical style—not only was its founding father an Italian (né Lulli), but many of its most influential contributions came from German and Italian composers—Gluck, Cherubini, Spontini, Rossini, Meyerbeer. One could of course argue that the role of the great foreigners who wrote for Paris was to keep the long-prevailing French mode from stagnating. Each of these foreign composers added an individual style to which French opera was forced to accommodate. Yet the sustaining power of French tradition cannot be denied: one need only compare the French version of Gluck's *Alceste* with its Italian original to note that the composer gallicized more than the words themselves.[46]

Among the composers who helped give new life to French opera, Meyerbeer is classifiable within three national schools—first, the German, while he was studying under Abt Vogler with Weber as a fellow student; second, the Italian, while he composed in the Rossini style; and third, the French, while, building on the new "grand" style that another foreigner, Rossini, had helped establish in *Guillaume Tell*, he brought to fruition what has since been called French grand opera. Itinerancy has been at least as common in the history of opera as rootedness in a single place. Wagner's contention, voiced in 1840, that the lack of a capital or nation forced German composers to seek their fortunes in operatic capitals abroad could as easily have been made of Italian composers at the time.[47] Not only had Cherubini and Spontini become French composers (the latter had by then transplanted himself to Prussia), but Bellini and Donizetti, though still composing operas mainly in Italian, ended their careers in Paris and Vienna respec-

[45] See Strauss's letter, also dated July 26, 1928, ibid., p. 652.

[46] See Berlioz's detailed comparison of the two versions of this opera, "Les deux Alceste de Gluck," in *Voyage musical en Allemagne et en Italie* (Paris: Jules Labitte, 1844), pp. 279–307. Berlioz points out, among other things, how the difference in Italian and French musical conventions helped determine the differences between the two versions.

[47] See "Ueber deutsches Musikwesen" in *Gesammelte Schriften*, VII, 31–34.

tively. Verdi composed several French operas as well as Italian operas commissioned by such far-apart foreign capitals as London, St. Petersburg, and Cairo.

The preceding century was even more itinerant, with a multitude of Italian operas created for German opera houses by Italian composers, as well as Italian operas created by German composers who had studied (and sometimes even stayed) in Italy. Handel's career, from German to Italian composer and ultimately to the oratorio composer whom the English claim as their own, rivals Meyerbeer's in its transformations. The political disruptions of our own century enabled Kurt Weill to turn from a German into an American composer, and Stravinsky, whose first opera, *The Nightingale,* derived largely from Russian operatic tradition, to end his operatic endeavors with *The Rake's Progress,* the greatest opera composed in English since Purcell. Nietzsche confronted the difficulty of assigning national labels to opera composers when he wrote that stylistic orientation, not national origin, determines where a composer belongs, after which he called Handel an Italian composer, Gluck a French one[48]—a classification that begs as many questions as it answers.

The obfuscations inherent in defining and contrasting national styles are similar to those one encounters in confronting "serious" and "popular" forms of opera. The extant operas of Monteverdi's "popular" Venetian period are no less interesting and no less complex musically or poetically than the extant one of his courtly Mantuan period. Although we see the Gluck of the reform operas as more "high-minded" than the Gluck whose earlier *opere serie* supposedly pandered to public taste, the reform operas proved to be exceedingly easy on audiences, as Dr. Burney noted at the time with his statement that "most of his [Gluck's] airs in *Orfeo* are as plain and simple as English ballads."[49] Even during his most musically "advanced" period, the time of *Elektra,* Strauss kept his eye on the box office: observing that *Aida* played to sold-out houses because of its exotic Egyptian trappings, he asked Hofmannsthal not to be sparing in the decor of their next opera, which, since they were planning a setting of Calderón's Semiramis plays, doubtless would have offered opportunities for exoticism through

[48] See letter of November 10, 1887 (to Peter Gast), in Nietzsche, *Werke,* III, 1268.
[49] In Charles Burney, *An Eighteenth-Century Musical Tour in Central Europe and the Netherlands,* ed. Percy A. Scholes (London: Oxford University Press, 1959), II, 92.

its Babylonian locale.[50] Uncompromising though Schönberg's *Moses und Aron* would seem to be with its twelve-tone technique and its didactic message, the powerful and lurid Golden Calf scene in which the men tear the clothes off the women and a young girl is knifed in sacrifice was clearly intended to create a sensational effect—as indeed it has in recent productions. Many contemporary operas, from *Lulu* to Reimann's *Lear*, cultivate a similar theatricality—as though this might mitigate an audience's fear of an otherwise undigestible musical score. Operatic styles that seemed relatively easy in their own time may count as difficult once a new set of conventions has displaced them. Thus, recent audiences (not to speak of singers and directors) have had to relearn the *opera seria* style to make it theatrically viable. Many fine late nineteenth-century national operas by composers such as Smetana and Borodin have been unable to establish themselves firmly outside their national boundaries, even though their use of folk material and local decor has kept them popular among their own countrymen.

The difficulty of separating "popular" from "serious" elements is especially evident in the reactions that the first great national opera, Weber's *Der Freischütz*, has elicited ever since it was first performed in 1821. Few operas have enjoyed as overwhelming a success from the start, for, as the young Wagner put it admiringly, Weber succeeded in "touching the heart of the German people."[51] A reviewer of its first performance noted the seemingly incompatible mixture of elements—at the one extreme the "stereotyped" characters and the "naiveté" and "innocence" of the chorus, at the other the complexities of the Wolf's Glen scene, whose musical intentions the reviewer admitted he did not fully understand even after several performances.[52]

The music that this reviewer found so difficult has since been deemed as important a landmark in the history of opera as the folklike elements. Kurt Oppens, for example, notes a stylistic

[50] See letter of December 22, 1907, in Strauss-Hofmannsthal, *Briefwechsel*, p. 32.

[51] "Ueber deutsches Musikwesen" p. 45.

[52] "Carl Maria von Weber, 'Der Freischütz'" in Hoffmann, *Werke*, ed. Georg Ellinger (Berlin: Deutsches Verlagshaus Bong, n.d.), XIV, 142, 145, 144. This reviewer was erroneously thought to be the writer and composer Hoffmann—to the point that Ellinger included two of his articles on the early performances in his critical edition. See Wolfgang Kron, *Die angeblichen Freischütz-Kritiken E. T. A. Hoffmanns: Eine Untersuchung* (Munich: Hueber, 1957).

progression from the Wolf's Glen scene to *Tristan, Elektra,* and the atonality of *Wozzeck.*[53] Adorno points out that the orchestral accompaniment to the bridal-wreath chorus, in which the early reviewer had seen only naiveté and innocence, introduces elements to be characterized by terms such as "troubling," "threatening," "death symbol."[54] Writing of *Der Freischütz* in another context, Adorno locates an early exemplification of what he calls the "culture industry," that pandering to public taste for financial gain, in the librettist's eliminating the tragic ending of the original story to satisfy a Biedermeier audience that liked to see the main characters get married at the end.[55] Although the mixture of popular and sophisticated is conspicuous in such major earlier works in the *Singspiel* tradition as *Die Zauberflöte* and *Fidelio,* it becomes ideologically problematic in operas that attempt to play on patriotic feelings. Wagner, though not writing specifically of *Der Freischütz,* commented on the paradoxes inherent in national opera: the folklike, unreflective manner that the composer seeks disappears once it is transformed into modern music, while the unnaturalness of this transformation, Wagner adds, is comparable to a modern citizen's assuming peasant dress.[56]

Wagner, Avant-gardism, and High Culture

Despite the nationalism we ordinarily associate with Wagner (and that found expression in his early comment on the national feeling emanating from *Der Freischütz*), his recognition of the posturing that often characterizes national opera reveals a strain central to his achievement—namely, the rigorously avant-garde attitude that marks his work both as composer and theorist of opera. Although Wagner customarily saw himself as Gluck's successor in renewing the dramatic principle and the seriousness of

[53] See Oppens, "Alban Bergs 'Wozzeck,'" *Merkur,* 21 (1967), 1157.

[54] "Bilderwelt des Freischütz" in Adorno, *Gesammelte Schriften,* ed. Rolf Tiedemann, XVII (Frankfurt: Suhrkamp, 1982), p. 39.

[55] "Bürgerliche Oper," in ibid., XVI (1978), p. 30. Adorno had developed the concept of the culture industry in "Kulturindustrie" (written in collaboration with Max Horkheimer) as a response to the shock he experienced when, after fleeing Nazi Europe, he was plunged into the Hollywood of the 1940s. For this essay, together with a continuation recently published for the first time, see *Gesammelte Schriften,* III (1981), pp. 141–91, 299–335. His application of the concept to the happy ending in Weber's opera strains history a bit, for at the time the opera was composed the happy ending was still a going convention in opera. Adorno is correct, however, in noting a strong Biedermeier element in *Der Freischütz.*

[56] See *Oper und Drama,* pt. 1, sec. 3, pp. 56–57.

purpose that opera had lost, the strident, often apocalyptic tone with which he defended his program, indeed the very comprehensiveness of this program, represents a phenomenon unique in the history of music. Although Schönberg and Stravinsky rival him in verbal articulateness, no composer before or after has presented his theories in so expansive a manner or with such a flair for public effect. The phenomenon we label "Wagner" is not simply a moment or movement in the history of music but, transcending any single art form, can more properly be understood as an early and powerful instance in the history of what we have come to call modernism. Indeed, his book-length essay *Oper und Drama* of 1851 is the first major document that contains most of those features—for instance, the hostility to the world of commerce, the rewriting of the history of art forms, the attribution of historical inevitability to the practices he advocates, the imperative, imperious tone—that we associate with modernist manifestos. The fact that Wagner resorted to so elaborate a defense of his practices was itself a symptom of a new mentality. It is significant, for example, that Gluck, whose theories served Wagner as legitimizing precedents, actually wrote very little about his own practices but left it to others to fight his battles; even the dedication of *Alceste*, the major theoretical statement with which Gluck is identified, is assumed to have been written by his librettist Calzabigi.[57] It is also significant that Baudelaire, whose own career has long been taken as exemplary in the history of modernism, vigorously defended Wagner against those who claimed that his theoretical endeavors detracted from the "naturalness" and "spontaneity" of his art. "I consider the poet the best of all critics,"[58] Baudelaire wrote to celebrate the union of critic and artist in Wagner. Although Baudelaire went on to cite such precedents among earlier artist-critics as Leonardo, Hogarth, and Diderot, with over a century's hindsight one sees the comprehensiveness and the tone of Wagner's theoretical contributions as something different in kind from those of his predecessors.

At least as much as with Baudelaire, the example that Wagner set in his theory and his "creative" works became a model for the way modernist artists would shape and conduct their careers. Note, for instance, the uncompromisingness of tone that marks his crit-

[57] See Alfred Einstein, *Gluck: Sein Leben, Seine Werke* (Zurich: Pan Verlag, n.d.), p. 141.
[58] "Richard Wagner et Tannhäuser à Paris," sec. 2, in Baudelaire, *Oeuvres complètes*, ed. Y.-G. Le Dantec (Paris: Gallimard, 1951), p. 1052.

ical writings. Even in the "most significant" operatic works of the past, he writes, "directly next to the most perfect and most noble [parts] I found the incomprehensibly meaningless, the inexpressibly conventional, indeed the frivolous."[59] *Frivolous* ("frivol") was one of Wagner's most frequent terms of abuse, and, as I indicated at the start of this section, formed a natural antithesis to *serious* ("ernst"), a term that throughout the history of modernism was to serve as a compliment for what could be deemed genuine art. *Frivolous* and *serious* are of course only one of innumerable oppositions that Wagner, with his Manichean cast of mind, set up to separate acceptable from wrong practices. Among the most powerful of such pairings are *fashion* (*Mode*) and *art* (*Kunst*), an opposition that confines the latter term to "good" art, and *opera* (*Oper*) against such specially concocted terms as *music-drama* (*Musikdrama*) and *sacred festival drama* (*Bühnenweihfestspiel*), in which the first-named term, long simply a neutral generic designation, becomes automatically suspect.[60]

An essential part of the Wagnerian program was the reinpretation of past works. Not only did Wagner award Gluck and such successors as Cherubini and Spontini a privileged place in the canon, but he also championed certain neglected nonoperatic works of a distinctly high-minded nature. Thus Wagner counts among the early advocates of Beethoven's last quartets and, to cite a nonmusical work that has since achieved classical status, Kleist's play, *Prinz Friedrich von Homburg*.[61] Accepted masterpieces could also be viewed in an entirely new light—for example, Goethe's *Faust*, which Wagner, as part of his program to rethink the possibilities of theatrical representation, hailed as a great theater work, in full defiance of the common wisdom that the work, transcendent though it might seem in the study, was unplayable.[62]

Wagner's avant-gardism manifests itself not simply in theoretical provocation but in artistic practices that even today have not fully lost their potential to disturb. If there are no longer opposing

---

[59] "Zukunftsmusik" in *Gesammelte Schriften*, I, 221.

[60] For a discussion of *fashion* versus *art*, see for instance *Das Kunstwerk der Zukunft*, pt. 1, sec. 5, ibid., X, 64–68; for a particularly colorful discussion of how humiliating it is to be simply an "opera-composer," "opera-conductor," or "opera-singer," see "Meine Erinnerungen an Ludwig Schnorr von Carolsfeld," pp. 157–58.

[61] For his comments on the late quartets, see "Cis-Moll-Quartett" and "Bericht an Ludwig II," in *Gesammelte Schriften*, IX, 117–18, and XII, 274. For those on the Kleist play, see "Ueber Schauspieler und Sänger," in ibid., XII, 341.

[62] Ibid., 337–38.

camps of Wagnerians and anti-Wagnerians, we still remain aware, as we attend a performance of his later works, that the music and the drama represent a radical break with everything that came before (including his own earlier operas). One reason for this is that his mature style was created in conscious and provocative reaction to other styles. For example, the austere, slow movement of his music from *Das Rheingold* onwards articulates a reaction to that penchant for strong and immediate theatrical effect ("Wirkung") that he noted disapprovingly both in the French Romantic theater and in French grand opera. Thus, during the composition of *Tristan und Isolde*, after expressing his disdain for Victor Hugo's reliance on dramatic effect he describes his own opposing manner as an "art of transition, for my whole artistic fabric consists of such transitions: the harsh and the abrupt have become hateful to me."[63] No critique of Wagner's method could be more telling than that of his former disciple Nietzsche, who, when he accused Wagner of seeking "effect [*Wirkung*]—he wants nothing but effect," showed that he knew the inner workings of the master's workshop well enough to attack him with his own terminology; as though to twist the knife, Nietzsche in the same passage called Wagner the "Victor Hugo of music."[64] Even with the slow transitions characteristic of the later Wagnerian style, Nietzsche saw Wagner practicing what seemed to him a shameless theatricalism. The antitheatricalism that Wagner had projected against others could thus easily be turned against him by a more rigorously antitheatrical sensibility such as Nietzsche's.[65]

The avant-garde stance to which Wagner committed himself demanded as well an unrelenting technical progressiveness. From *Das Rheingold* onwards, each work (except for *Die Meistersinger*, whose comic genre allowed its composer a temporary break) represents a conscious progression into new musical territory. Whether the listener applauded or damned it, Wagner's style, through the provocativeness with which it carved out constantly new sonic effects, invited more violently opposed reactions than that of any composer before him. Thus, Hanslick expressed his extreme discomfort with *Parsifal* by noting that "there are no longer any real

---

[63] Letter of October 29, 1859, in Wagner, *Richard Wagner an Mathilde Wesendonk: Tageblätter und Briefe, 1853–1871* (1908; rpt. Leipzig: Breitkopf & Härtel, 1913), p. 189.

[64] *Der Fall Wagner*, sec. 8, pp. 920, 919.

[65] For a fine discussion of Nietzsche's antitheatricalism in relation to Wagner, see Barish, *Antitheatrical Prejudice*, pp. 400–17.

modulations but rather a perpetually undulating process of modulation so that the listener loses all sense of a definite tonality. We feel as though we were on the high seas, with no firm ground under our feet."[66] The undermining of tonality that made Hanslick seasick is of course the very thing that assured Wagner a central place in the history of musical form. For example, Adorno could point out several unresolved chords in *Parsifal* to "mark the historic spot where, for the first time, the multilayered, broken-up tone becomes emancipated and responsible for itself alone."[67] One might note that Adorno employs a characteristically avant-garde term, *emancipates* (*emanzipiert*), to attribute a special historical significance to Wagner's innovations in musical form. Adorno uses the same term that Schönberg had employed to describe his own "emancipation of the dissonance";[68] to cite an analogous example from another art form, note Rilke's praise of the disjunctions of language in Georg Trakl's poetry as contributions to "the liberation of the poetic figure."[69] In each instance a word is borrowed from political discourse to depict a process in the history of art that we are meant to see as analogous to the progressive liberations shaping such historical narratives as those of Hegel and Marx. However much that is "new" we may locate in the later work of Wagner's great rival Verdi, these are not the forms of innovation that motivate historians of music to apply a word such as *emancipation*; to put it another way, the narratives that have come to shape what we call the history of music have been determined by the modernist aesthetic within which Wagner, and not Verdi, happened to play the central shaping role.

Wagner's contempt for popular taste did not detract from the intense concern he felt about establishing a relationship with an audience. Like later modernists who are wont to heap contempt

[66] "Richard Wagners 'Parsifal'" in Hanslick, *Aus dem Opernleben der Gegenwart: Der modernen Oper III. Theil* (Berlin: A. Hofmann, 1884), pp. 314–15.

[67] Adorno refers specifically to the dominant seventh at the end of the prelude, and the diminished seventh at the point of Parsifal's outburst, "Amfortas! Die Wunde!" in Act II. See "Zur Partitur des 'Parsifal'" in Adorno, *Gesammelte Schriften*, XVII, 50.

[68] In Schönberg, *The Structural Foundations of Harmony*, rev. ed., ed. Leonard Stein (1954; rpt. New York, Norton, 1969), p. 193. For a stimulating discussion of the transfer of modernist ideology from Wagner to Schönberg, see Joseph Kerman, "Wagner: Thoughts in Season," *Hudson Review*, 13 (1960), 329–49.

[69] "Befreiung der dichterischen Figur." Letter of February 22, 1917 (to Erhard Buschbeck), in Rilke, *Briefe*, ed. Ruth Sieber-Rilke (Wiesbaden: Insel, 1950), II, 71. See my discussion of this statement in *Georg Trakl* (New York: Twayne, 1971), p. 63.

on the public of their time, Wagner sought to create, in fact to train his own audiences. In his writings he idealized the sense of community that had characterized theater audiences at certain great moments of the past, for instance in ancient Greece and in the Paris of Gluck's time.[70] In 1844, long before Wagner had succeeded in institutionalizing his notions of audience community through the festival he founded at Bayreuth, Berlioz had similarly decried the debasement of musical taste and had sketched an ideal festival named *Euphronia* to be located not in the commercial world of France but, appropriately enough, in Germany, with strict discipline to be imposed upon performers and audiences alike.[71] The community that Berlioz merely proposed but that Wagner brought to fruition became an audience entirely different in its attitude towards art from the passive, entertainment-seeking audiences abhorrent to the modernist aesthetic. Nietzsche's characterization of the "consecrated spectators, prepared beforehand"[72] whom he observed at the first Bayreuth festival in 1876 is still, a century later, applicable to the audiences who attend *Ring* festivals throughout Europe and America or buy the latest *Ring* recording.[73] The power that Wagner achieved over the audience that he himself created is perhaps best characterized in the unfriendly words that Hanslick voiced at a visit to Bayreuth: "When we last saw him there, on the balcony of his "Festival Theater" (which will soon be only a historic monument) rejoicing triumphantly in the all-conquering power of his will—in this way we shall happily cultivate the memory of Richard Wagner."[74] Wagner of course had the last word, for Hanslick's prediction of the theater's imminent end has been thoroughly confounded by the fact that the

[70] See *Die Kunst und die Revolution* in *Gesammelte Schriften*, X, 28–29, and *Oper und Drama*, pt. 1, sec. 3, ibid., XI, 47.

[71] Berlioz's sketch is reprinted in Jacques Barzun, *Berlioz and the Romantic Century*, 3d ed. (New York: Columbia University Press, 1969), II, 330–35.

[72] *Unzeitgemässe Betrachtungen*, "Richard Wagner in Bayreuth," sec. 4, in Nietzsche, *Werke*, I, 382.

[73] In the course of writing this section I received an invitation to provide suggestions for a treasure hunt book to help stir up public interest in a new production of the *Ring* planned by the San Francisco Opera. I do not know how Wagner would have responded to this idea. On the one hand, he would doubtless have seen the treasure hunt (which, in tune with the theme of the tetralogy, was to take the form of a quest for gold) as a symptom of that commercial attitude towards art that his own work was meant to destroy. Yet he was also cunning enough to approve any ploy that in its end result would give him an audience willing to consecrate itself to his art.

[74] "Zum 13. Februar 1883" in Hanslick, *Aus dem Opernleben der Gegenwart*, p. 355.

festival the composer founded for the perpetuation of his work not only has endured more than a century of changes in aesthetic taste, but also—in a development unprecedented in the history of the arts—has remained in the firm control of his own direct descendants, who in fact have institutionalized his radicalism through systematically innovative productions of his works.

The history of Wagner's reception is essentially different in kind from the reception history of any other composer, operatic or otherwise. It does not belong simply to musical or theatrical history, within both of which it has come to occupy a major place, but it belongs as well to intellectual history, to literary history (in France even more than in Germany), to the history of modernism as a movement that transcends the categories imposed by academic disciplines. As a movement with distinct ideological aims and as a subject for later inquiry, Wagnerism belongs to those literary and intellectual strains whose notoriety and potency have earned them the suffix -ism. Although this suffix has occasionally been attached to the names of individual philosophers and poets (Plato and Byron, for example), only Wagner, among composers, has commonly invited this designation or even a partisan term such as *Wagnerite*, which George Bernard Shaw used in the title of an overtly partisan book.[75] Even those who prefer the music of other composers would not speak of Bachism or Beethovenism. In the heyday of Wagnerism a commitment to the ideology did not necessarily include a commitment to the composer's music. A history of Wagner's influence on the Symbolist movement points out, for example, that French partisans of Wagner's music were hostile to the influential *Revue wagnérienne*, which was dedicated to primarily literary concerns.[76] Virginia Woolf's pilgrimage to the Bayreuth Festival in 1909 was motivated less by any real enthusiasm for the music than by the influence of a Wagnerian suitor and by her own commitment to a modernist aesthetic, which in England at the time (though no longer in Germany) could count Wagner in the avant-garde.[77] Similarly, in T. S. Eliot's *The Waste*

[75] See "The Perfect Wagnerite" in Laurence, *Shaw's Music*, III, 408–545.

[76] See Erwin Koppen, *Dekadenter Wagnerismus* (Berlin: De Gruyter, 1973), pp. 75–76.

[77] See Quentin Bell, *Virginia Woolf: A Biography* (New York: Harcourt, Brace, 1972), p. 149. The account of the 1909 festival that Woolf wrote for the London *Times* expresses considerable reverence for the whole Wagnerian enterprise and in particular for *Parsifal*, which, through her typically modernist bias, she praises for effecting the triumph of technique over matter. The article, entitled "Impressions at Bayreuth," has been reprinted in *Opera News*, 41 (August, 1976), 22–23. Bell

Land, the quotations from the *Ring* and *Tristan* (as well as from Verlaine's sonnet "Parsifal") that play so prominent a role in the poem are less a reflection of the poet's musical tastes than of the interest he shared in the myths that Wagner used; at least as important, these quotations, like those from Baudelaire, serve to foreground the poem's avant-gardist commitments.

Avant-gardism constitutes more a stance than a rigid doctrine or period style.[78] By 1894 George Bernard Shaw, who expressed his avant-gardism in his dual roles of socialist and Wagnerite, deplored the fate of Wagner's style, which he saw falling into the hands of the "sensation-monger and pander." In his role as music critic Shaw was obviously more aware than other Wagnerites how quickly a style could cease being in the vanguard: "And so the union of all the arts falls to pieces before Wagner's cement is dry, and his Art Work of the Future is already the art work of the past."[79] By the same token, in our own century the avant-gardist stance has sometimes expressed itself through its distinctly anti-Wagnerian attitude; thus, Stravinsky, who maintained such a stance as provocatively as any major modernist, in his *Poetics of Music* defended opera against music-drama "as a purely sensual delight," stated a preference for Apollo over Dionysus, and even recommended the *opéras comiques* of Delibes, Gounod, Chabrier, and Messager—composers whose works Wagner would have scorned as "frivolous"—as "a sparkling group of masterpieces."[80]

Despite the "difficulties" long attributed to Wagner's later, avant-gardist works, in recent years these works (if one may judge from the vastly increasing number of productions and recordings) have achieved a popular following surpassed only by the best-known

---

may well have underestimated his aunt's ability to enjoy Wagner's music. The evidence we have today suggests that her feelings towards Wagner waxed alternately positive and negative over the years.

[78] For a penetrating discussion of the difference between the avant-garde and earlier "styles," see Peter Bürger, *Theorie der Avantgarde* (Frankfurt: Suhrkamp, 1974), pp. 23–24. Many significant works of our time, of course, cannot be called avant-garde art. To cite a typical irony in the history of the arts, *The Waste Land* and other writings by Eliot exercised a central influence on a notably non–avant-garde contemporary opera, Michael Tippett's *The Midsummer Marriage* (1955), whose characters King Fisher and Sosostris echo figures in Eliot's arch-modernist poem.

[79] Review of April 11, 1894, in Laurence, *Shaw's Music*, III, 177.

[80] In Stravinsky, *The Poetics of Music*, trans. Arthur Knodel and Ingolf Dahl (Cambridge, Mass.: Harvard University Press, 1970), pp. 79, 105, 81. For Wagner's scathing indictment of Gounod for writing for a "boulevard public," see "Die Bestimmung der Oper" and "Deutsche Kunst und deutsche Politik," sec. 10, in *Gesammelte Schriften*, XII, 290, and XIV, 95–96.

operas of Verdi, Bizet, and Puccini. Yet the public's willingness to absorb Wagnerian music-drama has thus far not been matched by a comparable attitude towards those twentieth-century operas committed to the avant-gardist stance for which Wagner supplied the great model. Among operas of our century deemed avant-garde in their time, perhaps only *Salome* and *Elektra* (both composed in the century's first decade and both quite "tame" compared to their avant-garde successors by other composers) come near rivaling the popularity of much of the earlier repertory. Even the more accessible and less rigorously avant-gardist modern operas such as *Four Saints in Three Acts*, *Peter Grimes*, and *Les Dialogues des Carmélites* do not yet—perhaps never will—count as "popular." Mass popularity has also eluded another group of contemporary operas—for example, those of Menotti, or Moore's *The Ballad of Baby Doe*—that were designed for "easy" apprehension through their tunefulness and their long-assimilated musical techniques. (From the point of view of audience appeal, the operatic equivalent of the best-selling novel is not what we ordinarily call opera, but rather musical comedy, that descendant of the *Singspiel* and the *opéra comique.*)

Although some advocates of modern music would argue that, as with the *Ring* and *Tristan*, the time will come when audiences flock to *Wozzeck* and *Moses und Aron*, one can also speculate that many monuments of twentieth-century modernist art are limited in their communicative power to a small, carefully prepared audience. Is there any reason one should expect a larger audience for *Wozzeck* or *The Rake's Progress* than for, say, Woolf's *The Waves* or Joyce's *Ulysses*? It is true, of course, that avant-gardist works in certain art forms have been able to establish a broadly based audience. For example, many paintings by Picasso, mobiles by Calder, or buildings by Wright that were once thought to be "difficult" have found this audience more easily than novels or operas that deviated just as strikingly from earlier styles. Yet this discrepancy between the ways that the visual and the more temporally extended arts are received may well be due to the fact that modernist art communicates most easily with the public when it can be consumed—as visual art can be—in relatively brief snatches of time. And if modern ballet (even when accompanied by difficult musical scores) enjoys a large public today, this may be because dance movements are not as distantly removed from their classical origins as, for example, posttonal musical form and vocal technique, and perhaps also because ballet is sufficiently abstract that audiences do not feel tempted to panic if they fail to understand the "meaning."

Despite the absence of a mass audience for serious contemporary opera, the avant-gardist mentality largely created by Wagner has continued to manifest itself in a succession of twentieth-century composers, many of whom, for instance Hans Werner Henze, Luciano Berio, and Philip Glass (to cite present-day examples from different countries), have continued the Wagnerian tradition of cultivating a public image and of gaining fervent, if necessarily small, groups of admirers. Whether or not their operas (or whatever generic designation one may give their sometimes multimedia stage works) will, like Wagner's, be absorbed by the larger operatic audience at a later time, the fact remains that the commercially viable operatic repertory today has not grown within living memory; despite recent attempts to revive baroque operas, the active and "popular" repertory spans less than a century and a half—from Mozart through Puccini and the early works of Richard Strauss—of the nearly four hundred years since operas were first composed.

Paris, Commercialism, and Popular Culture

The absoluteness of stance, together with the particular doctrines, with which Wagner helped shape the modernist aesthetic was itself a reaction to another crucial development in operatic history—the commercialization of art that Wagner witnessed during the period that he spent in Paris observing the musical scene and waiting unsuccessfully for the recognition and encouragement of his own talents (1839–42). In this city, which Walter Benjamin was later to call "the capital of the nineteenth century,"[81] Wagner's presence made possible a confrontation between the cultural products of an advanced society and a testy observer from an area that, though underdeveloped economically and politically, felt itself overdeveloped in the impractical arts of literature, philosophy, and music. It is significant that the reigning composer in Paris was himself a gifted German, Meyerbeer, who, though Wagner praised him as long as he sought his patronage, was later to be excoriated as a symbol of the worst evils that could befall artistic creation in the modern age—his essential lack of

[81] See his essay entitled "Paris, die Hauptstadt des XIX. Jahrhunderts," in *Schriften*, ed. Theodor W. Adorno and Gretel Adorno (Frankfurt: Suhrkamp, 1955), I, 406–22.

seriousness, his prostitution of his talent to supply easy satisfaction to a pleasure-hungry public. The negative attributes Wagner attached to Meyerbeer and to the Parisian musical world of his time represent the other side of the coin from the positive virtues with which he came to define his own creed. Neither side of the dichotomy reveals its meaning to us without an understanding of the other. Whether or not one discounts the personal pique behind Wagner's attitudes, the program he created, through the antithesis it projected between a "high" form of art and a debased art that exploited popular taste for commercial gain, represents at once a response to and an inversion of the new cultural situation represented in Paris.

Heine, whose reports on Paris for German journals depict this situation with striking perspicacity, in 1841 spoke of music as the characteristic art of the time, just as other forms such as architecture, sculpture, and painting had helped define great ages of the past.[82] With over a century's hindsight, it is clear that a number of social and technical conditions coincided at the time to make music, and opera in particular, an appropriate field upon which the cultural battles of the nineteenth century could be fought. The orchestra had reached a stage of development that enabled it to fill a large hall with sufficiently sensuous sound to support itself with paying customers. Through the impact of the Rossini operas, audiences unfamiliar with opera had come to expect vocal thrills from singers. Techniques of theatrical illusion could provide dramatic thrills commensurate with, sometimes even surpassing what the singer offered. A growing middle-class public needed entertainment in public places where individuals could easily be seen and, since status was no longer marked by birth, where their presence could gain them social prestige. This public, moreover, sought a type of diversion that was easy enough for quick consumption yet that still seemed "serious" enough to satisfy its cultural pretensions. By watching the depiction of historical events from periods of great social unrest—for instance, the St. Bartholomew massacre and the Anabaptist rebellion, around which two of Meyerbeer's most celebrated operas are built—they could at some level of consciousness feel that they were witnessing something analogous to the upheavals of recent European history that they or their parents had themselves experienced.

The commercial considerations underlying the great age of

---

[82] See *Lutezia*, letter of April 20, 1841, in Heine, *Sämtliche Werke*, VI, 259.

French grand opera[83] have invited commentary, often with a malicious edge, since the time. An observation by Heine, "And now French opera is in its richest bloom, or, to be more precise, it enjoys a good box office daily,"[84] brings the artistic and economic realms together in a particularly succinct way. Heine also observed (not quite accurately) that whereas the best operas of Mozart and Rossini failed at first hearing and took years to be appreciated, Meyerbeer's were designed for instant success, a fact that Heine attributed to the harmony and the instrumentation available for the stunning effects with which Meyerbeer overwhelmed his audiences.[85] Earlier, before his enthusiasm for Meyerbeer had begun to wane, Heine had found an ingenious way of reconciling the composer's status as a serious artist and his quest for popularity: on the one hand, Heine tells us, Meyerbeer believed in music as a religion, just as Mozart, Gluck, and Beethoven before him had done; on the other hand, he was so firmly an apostle of this religion that he felt the need to bring it to the people—to the point that Heine slyly compares him with Louis-Philippe by mentioning the eager handshakes with which each approached his public.[86]

Adorno, with the Hollywood of the 1930s and 1940s as point of reference for his jeremiad against the "culture industry," could glance back precisely a century to locate an early anticipation of the industry in the effects generated by the massacre in *Les Huguenots*: as in Hollywood historical extravaganzas, history here is emptied of content, and the warring factions "are admired side by side as in the panopticon," that other commercialization of his-

---

[83] By "grand opera" I refer to the particular form that developed in Paris beginning in the late 1820s. The following definition by a historian of the form brings together the aesthetic and social features intrinsic to it: "What was grand opera? It was many things: a theatrical form based primarily on plots from recent European history; a stage spectacle, the scene designer's dream, the machinist's delight; a musical form involving large ensemble-choral scene complexes and stunning ballets alongside the usual recitatives, airs, and duos, etc., of traditional opera; a social necessity, a place to see and be seen for the bourgeoisie; a business run by individuals, with government assistance, to make a great deal of money; the musical stage's response to literary and musical romanticism." In Karin Pendle, *Eugène Scribe and French Opera of the Nineteenth Century* (Ann Arbor: UMI Research Press, 1979), p. 377.

[84] *Ueber die französische Bühne*, letter 10, p. 553.

[85] See *Lutezia*, letter of April 20, 1841, p. 267. It is interesting that harmony, which Heine and others usually associated with German and "difficult" music, here is linked with "easy" music. What concerns Heine in this context is the theatrical effects that harmony could create.

[86] See *Ueber die französische Bühne*, letter 9, pp. 548–49, 547.

tory in Meyerbeer's time.[87] When Heine, calling the Renaissance the latest Parisian fashion, linked the Renaissance setting of *Les Huguenots* with the neo-Renaissance style of the newly constructed Rothschild palace, he was setting up relationships between art, capitalism, history, and fashion that any Marxist historian would find tempting to develop.[88] It does not take a Marxist thinker to draw the conclusion that the commercialization of art in the 1830s also served as a means of social control. For example, the young Wagner, noting the glut of cultural activities that went on day and night in Paris, suspected a "secret order," on the part of Louis-Philippe, to prevent revolution by means of ceaseless amusements.[89]

The links between economic policy and aesthetic effect are easy enough to establish for French grand opera. Within a year after the Revolution of 1830, the Paris Opéra changed from a fully court-supported to an entrepreneurial system that encouraged the new director, Louis Véron, to supplement the traditional government subsidy with a successful box office. Through the skillful manipulation of diverse talents—the librettist Scribe, composers such as Auber, Halévy, and above all Meyerbeer, not to speak of the ballet and the various technical resources he integrated into his great productions—Véron transformed the Opéra into a model capitalist enterprise.[90] Since the bourgeoisie had felt uncomfortable at the Opéra, the new administration, to ensure its participation, did not concern itself simply with what transpired on the stage. The boxes, for example, were reduced from six to four seats each, to accommodate middle-class budgets. Since the new public needed leadership in determining its response to what it was witnessing, the management, in addition, developed a well-disciplined claque that assured the success of its productions. Heine, writing later in the decade, declared that the Opéra had made a pact with the "enemies of music," while the cultivated

[87] "Bürgerliche Oper," p. 29. In another context Adorno points out that Germany, with its usual economic backwardness, was long protected against the commercialization of art through a state sponsorship of culture that went back to pre-democratic political forms. See "Kulturindustrie" in *Gesammelte Schriften*, III, 154.

[88] See "Meyerbeers 'Hugenotten'" in Heine, *Sämtliche Werke*, VII, 301–3. Although Heine felt admiration for Meyerbeer's opera, he was snide about the palace, calling it the "Versailles of absolute money-monarchy" (p. 303).

[89] "Pariser Amüsements" in *Gesammelte Schriften*, VII, 169.

[90] For a detailed description of the changes that took place in the administration of the Opéra, see William L. Crosten, *French Grand Opera: An Art and a Business* (New York: King's Crown Press, 1948), especially pp. 8–48.

aristocracy had "fled" to the Italian opera house,[91] where, without the grand spectacle offered at the Opéra, they could hear great singers such as Grisi and Rubini perform Bellini and Donizetti. This disdain for the commercialization of opera was by no means limited to such German observers as Heine and Wagner. No one has written so devastatingly of the musical scene as Berlioz, who quotes a director of the Opéra as defining "well-made music" as "music which *doesn't spoil [ne gâte rien]* the rest of the opera."[92] Berlioz, whose own great early opera, *Benvenuto Cellini*, was doomed to failure when performed in 1838,[93] expressed his disdain for what he considered the nonaesthetic reasons that attracted audiences to musical events—the open rivalry of virtuosos, the fashionability of a tenor, the social prestige of having a box, the fascination at seeing a new work fail.[94] It is scarcely any wonder that an avant-garde reaction should follow quickly upon the bourgeois revolution in the arts.

Despite the sharpness of Berlioz's critique, the battles he fought—like those Schumann waged in Germany—remained essentially advanced-guard skirmishes, whereas Wagner, by contrast, effected an overwhelming victory through the codification of his ideas in voluminous theoretical writings, the organization of partisan groups, the foundation of an ongoing festival, and, perhaps most important, the sanctification of what he stood for in that international network we have come to call modernism. Except for a handful of pieces, Berlioz's works have had to wait until our own century to get a just hearing; his three operas, moreover, have still not entered the common repertory. Yet in view of the position he took against the prevailing operatic milieu of his time, it seems symbolic that the Metropolitan Opera should open its centenary season in 1983 with his most ambitious opera, *Les Troyens*, a work thoroughly neglected until its revival in London in the late 1950s—though it dates from the same decade as Gounod's *Faust*, the most popular French grand opera[95] (indeed, the most internationally popular opera altogether) of the late nineteenth century and a work

---

[91] *Ueber die französische Bühne*, letter 10, p. 556.

[92] Berlioz, *Les Soirées de l'orchestre*, 5th ed. (Paris: Calmann Lévy, 1895), p. 129 (ninth evening).

[93] For the story of the failure, see Barzun, *Berlioz and the Romantic Century*, I, 289–308.

[94] See Berlioz, *Les Soirées de l'orchestre*, pp. 44–45 (second evening).

[95] *Faust* was actually first performed with spoken dialogue at the Théâtre Lyrique in 1859. Gounod soon after turned the dialogue to recitative, after which the work could easily count as "grand," as befitted its dramatic content.

that, appropriately enough, opened the Metropolitan's first season in 1883.

If the triumph of Wagnerism delayed the acceptance of Berlioz among those who identified with "serious" as against "popular" art, it also destroyed the reputation of Meyerbeer, who, as one of that new breed of artists determined to court popularity (and for his own financial gain), became the perfect scapegoat for an emerging modernist ideology. Except for Rossini, no opera composer was ever lionized as enthusiastically in his own time as Meyerbeer. (To the extent that what we call lionization demands the manipulation of public acclaim to commercial ends through complex networks of communication, the phenomenon could not have existed before the nineteenth century.) The vehemence with which Meyerbeer was attacked is commensurate with the fervor—and also the considerable wealth—bestowed upon him by the crowds who attended his operas. Wagner claimed that his lengthy attack on Meyerbeer as the composer of "effects" was meant not so much as an attack on the composer but on what was wrong with modern opera in general.[96] Berlioz saw the Meyerbeer phenomenon as an attempt to "shake" a bored public out of its "sleepiness by means of high C's from chests of all kinds, bass drums, snare drums, organs, military bands, antique trumpets, tubas as big as locomotive smokestacks, bells, cannon, horses, cardinals under a canopy, emperors covered with gold, queens wearing diadems, funerals, weddings, banquets, and again the canopy, always the celebrated canopy . . . jugglers, skaters, choirboys . . . the five hundred devils of hell, what have you, the trembling of the earth, the end of the world."[97] The splendor and extravagance that had marked opera since its beginnings are now rejected as vulgar because of their association with the profit motive; it is interesting, moreover, that these remarks should emanate from a composer who, though not himself "commercial" by the standards of his time, did not hesitate to devise new sonic experiences to keep his audiences awake. To cite an extreme example of the outrage felt against Meyerbeer, Schumann accuses the composer of sacrilege: as a "good Protestant," Schumann expresses his disapproval of the use of Luther's "A Mighty Fortress" in Les Huguenots, in which "the bloodiest drama of our religious history has been dragged down to a farce at a fair."[98]

[96] See Oper und Drama, pt. 1, sec. 6, p. 95.
[97] Berlioz, Les Soirées de l'orchestre, p. 121 (ninth evening).
[98] In Eismann, Robert Schumann, II, 39.

Meyerbeer's reputation has, of course, never recovered from this onslaught. Although we customarily revive or continue hearing composers who could similarly be accused of commercialism— for example, Massenet and Puccini—the symbolic role assigned to Meyerbeer in his own time has determined his place in the musical canon. Even the recent attempts to revive his operas have been motivated to a large degree by the desire to find vehicles for celebrated singers.[99] Anyone who claims that Meyerbeer's major operas are full of beautiful music—as they indeed are—can retain credibility only by qualifying this statement with an admission that the music is uneven and that the operas are marred by the desire to display vocal virtuosity and to create theatrical effect— an admission that could be made, yet rarely is, for a goodly number of operas in the regular repertory.

Yet despite the negative image we have come to attach to him, it is worth remembering that in his time Meyerbeer also radiated the image of a tortured artist who labored for longer at his individual compositions than any major operatic composer before him. During his mature period—from 1831 until his death in 1864— he completed only four grand operas, one *Singspiel*, and two *opéras comiques*, about the same as Wagner during the latter's final three decades. One might also remember that the Meyerbeer operas opened up musical and dramatic possibilities that provided crucial models for Verdi's development during the 1850s and 1860s. Few who attend and admire *Un ballo in maschera* are aware how many elements—for instance, the travesty role of the page, the witty rhythms, the powerfully sinister effects in the drawing of the lots, indeed, the libretto itself, which derives from an earlier text by Meyerbeer's librettist Scribe—can be traced back to French grand opera and to Meyerbeer in particular.[100] To mention Verdi is of course to bring up a composer of an altogether different order of greatness from Meyerbeer; indeed, a discussion of the specific Meyerbeer influence on Verdi will usually end up showing how decisively the latter surpassed his model. Yet Verdi's reputation, like Meyerbeer's, has suffered from the notion that except for his last two operas his work is not genuinely "serious" in the way

[99] I refer to such revivals as *Les Huguenots* at La Scala in 1962 with Joan Sutherland; *L'Africaine* in San Francisco, in 1972, with Placido Domingo; and *Le Prophète* at the Metropolitan in 1977 with Marilyn Horne.

[100] On the influence of French grand opera on this Verdi work, see Julian Budden, *The Operas of Verdi: From "Il Trovatore" to "La Forza del destino"* (New York: Oxford University Press, 1979), pp. 37–38, 375–76, 412.

that Wagner's is, that it was cheapened by his desire, or at least his need, to cultivate obvious theatrical effects and to introduce into his work vulgarities we associate with "lower" forms of culture. As I have tried to show throughout this section, the sharp dichotomies we are accustomed to draw between "serious" and "nonserious," between "high" and "popular" culture, are themselves rooted in larger conflicts that developed within nineteenth-century society and that have remained with us to our own time. Similarly, the antioperatic prejudice I described earlier in this chapter derives from conflicts about the nature and value of art that are not only deeply embedded within our culture but that reach back much further in time than the dichotomies we acknowledge between high and popular art. From the historical perspective we now have on these various conflicts, we can understand how intimately our perceptions and judgments of opera are entangled in an ongoing politics of art.

[6]

Opera and Society: II. Opera in History, History in Opera

Opera in Social History

Few forms of art, as the preceding chapter has already suggested, are as overtly involved as opera in the social and historical contexts within which they are created and consumed. All art, we assume these days, can be related to particular contexts—as Terry Eagleton, for instance, does when he links the elaborate plot structure, the lengthiness, and the ideological focus of Victorian novels to the economics of the lending-library system in which these novels were forced to circulate.[1] Yet we do not often seek out relationships of this sort for those forms such as the novel or the lyric poem that involve simply a silent text and a lone reader; and it is no accident that we turn to a Marxist critic such as Eagleton to postulate these relationships for such forms. Opera, by contrast, is notable for the multiplicity of forces that must be brought together openly for its making—for example, the financial powers that provide for its lavish needs; the diverse and often warring talents, drawn from a number of arts, who are expected to work together to create and perform its texts; the audiences who use it to satisfy both their aesthetic and their social cravings. Like the imposing and prominently situated architecture in which it is ordinarily housed, opera displays its connections with art and society at once.

The history of opera is thus not simply a conventional history

---

[1] See Eagleton, *Criticism and Ideology: A Study in Marxist Literary Theory* (London: Verso, 1978), p. 52.

of shifting period styles and competing national traditions, for it must accommodate countless "nonaesthetic" elements that help shape these styles and that these styles sometimes even shape in return. As the preceding chapter demonstrated, cultural attitudes such as a bias against theatricality or against the commercialization of art, not to speak of the often influential theorizing with which composers and critics have sought to justify these attitudes, have played crucial roles in the composition and production of operas. The present chapter will go beyond the role of cultural attitudes to suggest a variety of social and aesthetic entanglements that characterize the history of opera—for example, such diverse and seemingly extraneous factors as the political role played by the opera house, the relation of technological and social change to musical style and performance, and the interactions, in various times and places, between the audience and what it sees and hears on the stage. It will also explore how opera speaks the history of its own time—at moments, in fact, creates an image of reality translatable into the world of action.

Opera and Class-consciousness

Heine, whose reports on Parisian cultural life still seem models for establishing relationships between social and aesthetic forms, suggested a link between audience behavior and operatic style when he observed how French opera differed from the Italian in his time. Writing soon after the triumphant opening of *Les Huguenots* in 1836, he contrasted the melody-centered effects of Italian opera with the harmony-centered effects of French opera: the Italian style, he claimed, did not encourage its audiences to take the form seriously, and as a result audiences were notorious for chattering loudly in their boxes and even playing cards during a performance.[2] Although Heine does not pursue the point, he evidently viewed the Italian mode as an essentially aristocratic entertainment in which the opera house, while generating social opportunities as assiduously as musical spectacle, through its commitment to a predominantly melodic style provided too simple an aesthetic vehicle to tap its audience's deeper emotions. By contrast, the new bourgeois audience in Paris, despite the fact that its members expected to be seen to ensure their individual ad-

[2] See *Ueber die französiche Bühne*, letter 9, in Heine, *Sämtliche Werke*, ed. Ernst Elster (Leipzig: Bibliographisches Institut, n.d.), IV, 552.

vancement, also expected the historical struggles harmonically dramatized on stage to remind them of the unstable times they had themselves been through and over which they could now celebrate their triumph.

The social dimension of opera that Heine stressed is especially evident if one notes the changes, over the centuries, in the forms of patronage and in the symbolic role of the opera house. In its first two centuries, Italian opera was patronized jointly (though with varying degrees of participation) by rulers and by wealthy aristocratic families. The social activity in private family boxes that impressed observers such as Heine as rivaling in interest the spectacle on the stage was itself embedded in a social system within which the musical entertainment was only one among many components. As a music historian has pointed out, in mid–seventeenth-century Venice the family box was not only a hereditary piece of property, but it was also a place for political intrigue in which earnest matters of state were customarily performed.[3] The royal box conspicuously placed in the rear center has often played a symbolic role in competition both with the activities in the other boxes and with the more overtly symbolic activities on stage. The sight of the ruler observing opera from the royal box is an assertion at once of the monarch's political power over the microcosm represented in the theater and of the cultivation with which patronage of the arts mitigates the brutishness inherent in the absolute power at his or her command.[4] Dr. Burney recorded that the audience in the San Carlo theater in Naples, the oldest major opera house still functioning today, was distinctly less noisy whenever the king was in attendance.[5] The interior of the old Metropolitan Opera House (1883–1966) was popularly known as the "Diamond Horseshoe" after the horseshoe-shaped row of boxes

[3] See Simon Towneley Worsthorne, *Venetian Opera in the Seventeenth Century* (Oxford: Clarendon Press, 1954), pp. 10–12.

[4] Stephen Orgel, whose book *The Illusion of Power* concerns itself, among other things, with the subtle interplay between audience and spectacle, comments as follows on the role of the royal box: "Only opera houses, created for the most aristocratic and least democratic of theatrical forms, have been able to afford to give their royal boxes a central location: they are placed at the midpoint of the first gallery. When the queen goes to Covent Garden, she is symbolically seated in the center of the tier of the most privileged spectators. But even this spot is too far from the stage to provide the royal viewer with a really good seat; there are many better places from which to see the opera. The virtue of the center box is, even today, its full view not of the stage but of the audience" (Berkeley: University of California Press, 1975, p. 16).

[5] See Michael F. Robinson, *Naples and Neapolitan Opera* (Oxford: Clarendon Press, 1972), p. 10.

in which the local financial aristocracy displayed its wealth and its status in return for the monetary support on which the opera company depended; in the absence of a monarch or the government support customary in European houses, in New York the royal box was, in effect, extended to encompass a whole tier of boxes that, in this age of high capitalism, signified the seat of power as surely as the royal box had done during the age of mercantilism. The symbolic power of the box is still evident—though in ways its earlier occupants would not have imagined—in the Leningrad Maryinsky (now the Kirov) Theater, whose imperial box stands untouched by time but is now occupied by privileged proletarians.

As a structure, the opera house has itself exerted various forms of symbolic power. Charles III, who built the San Carlo in 1737 to glorify the Bourbon dynasty in Naples, placed the house next to his royal palace; the juxtaposition of the two buildings enabled him at once to advertise the union of art and power and to enter his box without the inconvenience of stepping outside.[6] The relative importance of ruler in relation to artist in the Italian states is suggested by the fact that when La Scala was opened in Milan in 1778 with an opera by Salieri, the playbill failed to mention the composer's name, while the Archduke Ferdinand and his consort received more prominent billing than the title of the opera.[7] The sumptuous houses constructed in the mid- to late nineteenth century in Paris and Vienna, where they occupy central and strikingly conspicuous sites, celebrated both the imperial power exercised by their respective nations and the participation of the urban middle-class audience in the imperial enterprise.

Even those opera houses built far from the acknowledged centers of civilization reveal something about the political and economic situation of their time and place through their design, indeed through the very incongruity of their location. For example, the imitations of French provincial houses built in the late nineteenth century in distant colonies extended the physical presence of the mother country to backward regions thought to be in need of French civilizing power. The late nineteenth-century rubber boom in Brazil enabled Manaos, a swatch of civilization cut deep in the Amazon jungle, to build an ornate opera house—a monumental proof that the high culture of Europe could legitimize the exploitation that financed the house in the first place.

[6] Ibid., pp. 7–8.
[7] See Spike Hughes, *Great Opera Houses* (London: Weidenfeld & Nicolson, 1956), pp. 94–95.

Every town in the American Old West, moreover, aspired to its own opera house, usually a building far too small and simple to pass for an opera house anywhere else in the world but still the most impressive structure in town. Though used for a lowly level of entertainment that no European house could imagine staging, occasional visits by the likes of Adelina Patti (whose recital programs, running the gamut from Rossini bravura arias to her reassuring theme song "Home, Sweet Home," can still be seen posted in these now decaying buildings) served as reminders that the house could maintain at least some tenuous tie with the distant world of established culture. The relative simplicity of these remote houses often even characterizes those houses being built in the older centers of culture. Adorno has commented on the lack of monumentality in the German opera houses rebuilt after World War II; lacking boxes, as he points out, these theaters have the appearance of cinemas, and the absence of differentiation and ostentation reflects the powerlessness that the individual feels in contemporary society.[8] In American cities it has become customary to erect what are labeled "performing arts centers," in which the opera, though *prima inter pares*, democratically shares facilities with the other arts; no longer the showcase of a ruler or even of a local aristocracy, the arts center, like the architecturally more imposing sports arena, becomes the means by which a provincial city asserts its identity within an industrial society whose cities are otherwise little differentiated.

A study of the class composition of opera audiences would doubtless have something to tell us about changes in musical and dramatic styles. Those who postulate a connection between the multiclass composition of Shakespeare's audiences with the multilayered meanings we read into his plays can find a parallel in mid–seventeenth-century Venetian audiences who attended Monteverdi's late operas, *Il ritorno d'Ulisse in patria* and *L'incoronatione di Poppea*: with an audience that, according to a historian of Venetian opera, "was drawn from the whole community rather than from one class,"[9] these operas are notable, among many other things, for the unselfconscious ease with which they intersperse the serious and the comic, the complex and the simple. Adorno has noted that the two early centers in which a bourgeois-dominated rather than an aristocratic opera developed were mar-

[8] See *Einleitung in die Musiksoziologie*, chap. 5, in Adorno, *Gesammelte Schriften*, ed. Rolf Tiedemann, XIV (Frankfurt: Suhrkamp, 1973), p. 264.
[9] In Worsthorne, *Venetian Opera*, p. 3.

itime republics, Venice and Hamburg, both of which, moreover, were notable for their cultivation of eclectic operatic forms.[10] The strict demarcation between serious and comic in Neapolitan opera during the eighteenth century can perhaps be related to a corresponding demarcation between the aristocratic and popular audiences during the Bourbon monarchy; Charles III, for instance, limited his attendance to the San Carlo and did not attend the comic theaters, which performed in Neapolitan dialect.[11] As *opera seria* spread to northern Europe, it counted as an aristocratic entertainment, in contrast to popular entertainments such as ballad opera in England and *Singspiel* in the German states. Rousseau's championship of Italian comic opera must be seen as part of his larger program supporting the simple against the complex, the popular against the aristocratic. Generic division, one can see, is never far removed from class division. Wagner noted the sharp class division in eighteenth-century Germany, where Italian opera—often, as he remarked, composed by talented Germans—reigned in the courts, while church music remained the people's characteristic art form.[12] Although the nineteenth-century Italian audiences for whom Verdi composed probably represented a broader spectrum of classes than the *opera seria* public of a century before, in Verdi's operas the traditional division between tragic and comic remained intact; yet Verdi's championship of "underdog" characters and his ability to play on and arouse his audience's nationalistic sentiments give his tragic operas a "popular" element missing in the *seria* operas of the preceding century and even in those of Rossini.

Opera, Economics, and Technological Change

Just as operatic genres have always been related to social class, so the formal properties and performance modes of opera have

[10] See "Bürgerliche Oper" in *Gesammelte Schriften*, XVI (1978), p. 29. For a discussion of the controversies that raged over operatic form in Hamburg in the late seventeenth and early eighteenth centuries, see Gloria Flaherty, *Opera in the Development of German Critical Thought* (Princeton: Princeton University Press, 1978), pp. 21, 31–36, 41–65.

[11] See Robinson, *Naples and Neapolitan Opera*, pp. 10–13. As Robinson points out, the comic intermezzi out of which comic opera developed in Naples could not thrive until comic elements had been fully eliminated from "serious" plots; in the course of the century, however, "serious" characters gradually entered comic plots, though not vice versa (see pp. 178–204).

[12] "Ueber deutsches Musikwesen" in Wagner, *Gesammelte Schriften*, ed. Julius Kapp (Leipzig: Hesse & Becker, n.d.), VII, 40–41.

maintained an intimate connection with the economic structures that make opera possible in the first place. The relatively high expense of opera in relation to other representational forms has traditionally provided both opportunities and obstacles. For Louis XIV and lesser royalty who imitated his style of governance throughout Europe, opera, more than any other art form except architecture, allowed a court to display itself through the conspicuous lavishing of funds on operatic spectacles. Whenever opera has had to make its own way financially, however, it has resorted to all manner of compromise. At the beginning of the eighteenth century the owner of the Haymarket Theater in London proposed to subsidize opera through the profits made in the less expensive nonmusical drama.[13] The relatively conservative, unadventurous repertory that prevailed in American, though not in central European opera houses, in the first half of our own century can be attributed in large part to the absence of state subsidies in the United States and to the consequent dependence of these houses on the tastes of the local financial oligarchy. The spread of Neapolitan opera throughout Europe in the eighteenth century cannot be explained simply by citing its composers and singers as "superior" or its style as conforming with prevailing taste. Rather, one must also cite the fact that Naples provided uncommonly favorable means for the training and support of musicians. All the major Neapolitan composers from Scarlatti to Cimarosa were assured financial support as employees of the royal chapel. Even more important, since the church schools in Naples trained a larger number of singers and composers than were necessary to meet the city's musical needs, these musicians often found employment at other European courts, many of which sought prestige through their association with the Neapolitan style.[14] Moreover, a composer's creative habits can sometimes be related to economic developments. Berlioz, writing in the commercialized ambiance of mid–nineteenth-century Paris, complained that "the art of the claque even leaves its mark on the art of musical composition,"[15] by which he meant that the need for rousing endings demanded not only *cabalette* but other musical expedients such

[13] See E. D. Mackerness, *A Social History of English Music* (London: Routledge & Kegan Paul, 1964), p. 90.

[14] For relevant details, see Robinson, *Naples and Neapolitan Opera*, pp. 6, 16–18.

[15] Berlioz, *Les Soirées de l'orchestre*, 5th ed. (Paris: Calmann Lévy, 1895), p. 96 (seventh evening).

as the sounding of bass drums and ensembles sung in unison. The deceleration of Verdi's productivity in the 1850s was due not simply to his growing prestige and his increasingly acute artistic conscience; as Verdi himself tells it in a letter of 1854, the new copyright laws in Italy enabled a single opera to earn five or six times as much for him by this time as a decade before.[16]

Since the repertory available during any given season today will sometimes include operas written over nearly four centuries in a wide range of places, it is easy to ignore the vast differences in technical resources—both musical and extramusical—available to individual composers during this time span. "Before the invention of the electric light Wagner could as little have composed *Der Ring des Nibelungen* as without the harp and bass tuba," Hanslick reported from the first Bayreuth festival.[17] Even if we take Hanslick's remark as simply a witty exaggeration, it hints at a difference between operas composed for an illuminated auditorium and those, like Wagner's, that utilize stage lighting, together with darkness in the auditorium, as a means of illusion to cast a spell over the audience. Julian Budden has speculated that Donizetti's and the early Verdi's cavalier attitude towards making their words understood may be due to their knowledge that anybody who cared to follow the text had sufficient light to read the libretto during the performance.[18] With a darkened auditorium, an opera not only forced a composer to reveal its meanings more clearly, but he could also count on greater attention on the part of the audience to the happenings onstage. Although the Strauss-Hofmannsthal operas certainly strove to achieve strong illusionary effects, one might note that Hofmannsthal once demanded a half-lit auditorium for *Die ägyptische Helena* so that the spectators—in the spirit of operas a century before—could read his complex libretto while watching the action.[19] Quite in contrast to our modern reliance on darkness, Neapolitan opera in its heyday put a special premium on the brightness of the auditorium;[20]

---

[16] See letter of October 28, 1854 (to Nestor Roqueplan, director of the Opéra), in Verdi, *I copialettere*, ed. Gaetano Cesare and Alessandro Luzio (Milan: Commissione Esecutiva per le Onoranze a Giuseppe Verdi, 1913), p. 155.

[17] "Richard Wagners Bühnenfestspiel in Bayreuth" in Hanslick, *Musikalische Stationen: Der modernen Oper II. Teil* (Berlin: Allgemeiner Verein für deutsche Literatur, 1885), p. 249.

[18] See Budden, *The Operas of Verdi: From "Oberto" to "Rigoletto"* (New York: Praeger, 1973), p. 22.

[19] See letter of September 29, 1928, in Strauss-Hofmannsthal, *Briefwechsel*, 3d ed., ed. Willi Schuh (Zurich: Atlantis, 1964), p. 666.

[20] See Robinson, *Naples and Neapolitan Opera*, p. 10.

doubtless the desirability of having many torches lit had less to do with the problems of following a libretto than with the need to retain a festive air for the social activities in the boxes.

Since the introduction of the proscenium in the theater coincides with the early development of opera, one could speculate that the distance the proscenium creates between audience and stage action may have encouraged opera to cultivate those effects—for example, the introduction of ballet and stage machinery—that would not have been appropriate to the open stages of earlier English and Spanish drama. Wagner mourned the loss of that intimacy between spectators and actors resulting from the physical arrangements of the ancient Greek and Elizabethan theaters; indeed, he even blamed the development of opera for the architectural changes that broke down this intimacy in the spoken theater.[21] Not only the proscenium but also the presence of an orchestra has always served as a reminder that the relatively close identification between spectator and stage action in much of the world's great drama is not possible in opera; Wagner's decision to hide the orchestra from view at Bayreuth was, like his use of lighting, an attempt to maximize the stage illusion and, as a result, to force the spectator to concentrate on the dramatic action. Throughout earlier operatic history, by contrast, the distractions offered by the social life in the boxes and the presence of the local ruler in the royal box discouraged composers from cultivating the spectator's involvement in the action on the other side of the proscenium.

Technological change has affected not only the composition and production of operas but also the diffusion of operatic music outside the opera house. The so-called golden age of opera at the start of this century was coincident with the availability of the newly invented phonograph record, which (however much lacking in fidelity) carried the voices of singers such as Caruso and Farrar to the most remote areas—indeed, even helped give these singers the legendary aura they still have today. Since the short-playing record transmitted chiefly individual arias and short ensembles such as the *Rigoletto* quartet, those who heard operatic music only in the home were unable to experience a work's musical and dramatic continuity—with the result that they knew their operas only as intense and tuneful moments without any before or after. If records were able to impress operatic high points into the con-

---

[21] See "Ueber Schauspieler und Sänger" in *Gesammelte Schriften*, XII, 350–52.

sciousness of audiences who had no access to an opera house, radio was able to introduce these audiences to the full scores of operas. Thus the regular broadcasts from the Metropolitan Opera (beginning in 1931) diffused the major operatic repertory, together with suitable instructional materials during intermissions, throughout North America.

Perhaps no technological advance popularized opera as powerfully as the long-playing record, which, developed soon after World War II, enabled listeners at home to hear a particular opera repeatedly until it had achieved the kind of familiarity that in earlier times was possible only for performing musicians and readers of scores. It may well be that the rapidly increasing demand for live opera in recent years has been due to the educational effect of recorded performances, for these have whetted the appetites of listeners, in fact have given listeners a more intimate knowledge of the repertory than any earlier audience possessed. People who know opera from records alone do not of course experience either the visual dimension of opera or the excitement generated by the risks of live performance—nor do they know the pleasure of reacting communally to these risks with fellow spectators. Yet the technological advances that allow recording engineers to correct vocal and instrumental flaws have provided an alternative image of opera that stresses polish and consistency above other values—to the point that listeners nurtured on records are often intolerant of the imperfections normal even in the most distinguished performances in the opera house. As though to compensate for these imperfections, opera companies throughout the world have come to stress those possibilities of opera that no recording can convey—the singer's acting talents, the stage director's interpretive ingenuity, and—quite in the spirit of seventeenth-century operatic spectacles—the technological marvels that varying combinations of scrims, film projections, computer-controlled lighting, instantly movable platforms, and mist-making machines can magically bring forth.

If the record player robbed listeners of the traditional visual and social rewards of opera, the recent growth of televised opera has brought back at least the visual dimension, which listeners now experience in the same privacy that marks their record playing. Through the intimacy of television as a medium, opera quickly loses that barrier between spectator and performer that Wagner, as I indicated above, blamed on the architectural design of the opera house. Although television eliminates this barrier, it does not, like nonmusical drama, necessarily bring us closer to the emotions an actor is trying to convey, for a close-up of an open-mouthed singer is less likely to restore a lost intimacy than to remind us of the effort demanded by vocal production.

Like the radio broadcast and the long-playing record, television has also exercised a considerable educational effect. If recorded opera has given its listeners an unprecedented familiarity with operatic scores, televised opera, at least in its most recent phase, has exposed viewers—many of whom do not have access to a major opera house—to the uncommonly wide variety of directorial interpretations available today. Viewers whose experience of opera is limited to Jean-Pierre Ponnelle's reading of Monteverdi's operas as expressions of a claustrophobic baroque world or to Patrice Chéreau's of *Der Ring des Nibelungen* as a commentary on the nineteenth-century industrial order may well believe that a strong, often controversial directorial imagination is the norm in opera— as it indeed has been during recent years in certain companies such as the San Francisco Opera under Kurt Herbert Adler, the Bayreuth Festival under Wagner's grandsons, and in a number of German houses whose state subsidies have allowed them to ignore the public's preference for conventional interpretations. Still, the televising and filming of opera have been limited for the most part to commemorating productions (whether of a conventional or controversial sort) designed for the opera house stage. In a few outstanding instances television and film have attempted to reinterpret operas in ways impossible on the stage—for example, Ingmar Bergman's *Die Zauberflöte*, which demonstrates that the intimacy of close-ups can produce more subtle results than simply magnifying wide-open mouths, or Ponnelle's *La clemenza di Tito*, whose setting of actual Roman ruins filmed at night constantly calls attention to the medium's ability to transcend the physical limitations of the stage. Hans-Jürgen Syberberg's *Parsifal* brilliantly uses techniques available to film to alienate the audience from its accustomed responses to this opera and, indeed, to opera in general; Syberberg even makes a virtue of the need for close-ups of mouths by refusing to fully synchronize the dubbing, by allowing a tenor voice to issue from a female face, and—most alienating of all perhaps—by treating Amfortas's wound as a visual analogy to (among other things) the singing mouths.

The technological developments that have provided new modes of diffusion as well as new interpretive possibilities for the traditional repertory are obviously having their effect on the composition of new operas. The fact that audiences have shied away from contemporary opera throughout most of this century has encouraged composers to arouse interest in their work through the use of multimedia techniques. Opera has of course cultivated the mixture of media in numerous ways since its beginnings—for example, in the use of machines for magical effects in the seventeenth century, in the development of ballet as partner to song in French baroque opera, and in the various mechanical techniques developed in French grand opera and at the first Bayreuth festival to achieve the illusion of realism. But contemporary technology could conceivably change the identity of opera even more radically than any earlier innovation. For example, the electronic synthesizer that Philip Glass uses to often astounding effect challenges the traditional role of both the singing voice and the musical instrument. As the resources available to theaters become more sophisticated, the age-old battle over the primacy of words or music may come to an end through the newly acknowledged primacy of technology, of which both words and music would henceforth become obedient servants.

If technological gains have always exerted effects on operatic composition and production, so have the technological limitations and deficiencies characteristic of any given time. Technology cannot of course be separated from those economic factors that make new technology possible and that are, in turn, affected by technological change. The scenic austerity that marked Wieland Wagner's Bayreuth productions of the 1950s—productions that influenced operatic interpretation throughout the world—was necessitated by the austerity within the German economy after World War II, when lighting (once a luxury even in the auditorium) was cheaper than stage sets. Similarly the paucity of musical personnel available to Stravinsky for *L'Histoire du soldat* (whatever generic designation one may assign this quasi-opera without song) was dictated by what the composer called "the shoestring economics" necessary to allow the original production to tour through Swiss towns during World War I.[22] Moreover, the content of many great operas has assumed its particular shape

---

[22] Stravinsky and Robert Craft, *Expositions and Developments* (1959; rpt. Berkeley: University of California Press, 1981), p. 91. For Stravinsky, who at this point was cultivating an austerity of manner, "this confinement did not act as a limitation, as my musical ideas were already directed towards a solo-instrumental style" (p. 91).

through limitations in the musical training available to performers, indeed even to the composer. For example, those who complain that Verdi's operas (at least up to his final phase) are musically "primitive" should not cite simply the acknowledged backwardness of Italian conservatories in the early nineteenth century but also the fact that Italian standards of instrumental scoring and performance lagged far behind those of Germany and France, while singers exercised more tyranny over composers in Italy than in the northern countries; moreover, while the professional conductor had established his authority in German houses early in the century, Verdi had to wait until mid-career before he could demand a conductor other than the concert-master.[23] The orchestral effects that Meyerbeer or the early Wagner cultivated would thus have been technically impossible within the musical environment in which Verdi came to maturity.

Technological change has also affected the role of singers within the musical world. Adorno, writing in the early 1960s, soon after the advent of the jet airplane, prophesied with his characteristic cultural pessimism that the ability of singers to travel easily from one opera company to another would mean the end of the integrated operatic ensemble: the great repertory companies would, he predicted, have to move to a *stagione* system in which a major singer would appear in only a single production.[24] Certainly throughout most of operatic history singers were forced to make do with the same colleagues for extended periods, often even a whole season. The difficulties of travel that encouraged such international celebrities as Faustina Bordoni and Senesino to settle down for a season of Handel in London in the 1720s still encouraged Caruso and Farrar to winter in New York two centuries later.

[23] See, respectively, Budden, *Operas of Verdi: From "Oberto" to "Rigoletto,"* pp. 28, 4, and *The Operas of Verdi: From "Il Trovatore" to "La Forza del destino"* (New York: Oxford University Press, 1979), pp. 11–12.

[24] See *Einleitung in die Musiksoziologie,* chap. 5, pp. 262–63. Although Adorno was correct to see jet travel as inimical to the repertory system (at least among major opera companies), the rapidity of modern transportation, by enabling singers to move vast distances to replace suddenly indisposed colleagues, also makes possible performances that would otherwise be cancelled. For example, to cite a much-publicized event that occurred in 1983, during the writing of this chapter, Placido Domingo, the reigning Otello of the past decade, was flown by private plane from New York to San Francisco, on virtually no notice, to replace one of the handful of tenors anywhere who can assume this role. It is typical of the charismatic effect of great stars that the San Francisco audience was willing to wait for three and a half hours past the scheduled curtain time for Domingo to arrive and the opera to begin.

By contrast, a Sutherland or a Pavarotti can pop into a company for just a month or two at a time.[25]

The Indispensability of Singers

The centrality of the singer's role in opera is evident not only in the ways that companies have accommodated themselves to famous singers but also in the fact that the abilities and limitations of particular singers have often determined the musical content of operas that have long outlasted the voices for which they were written. Until relatively late in nineteenth-century Italy, composers designed their music for the singers assigned to perform it; indeed, if a composer was unfamiliar with the performer, he ordinarily did not compose the key arias until he had had a chance to hear the singer—in many instances just before the opera's premiere. The stories of Mozart or Bellini waiting until the last minute to finish arias can often be explained less by the overconfidence of genius than by the dilatoriness of singers in arriving for rehearsals.[26] It is known that many great nonmusical dramas were written with particular actors in mind, yet the peculiarities of vocal production—for example, a particular singer's range, power, shading, and technical flexibility—determine a composer's writing in a more immediate way than an actor's abilities determine a dramatist's approach to a part. The fact that the world's great opera houses boast black singers playing white parts or obese matrons imitating love-smitten girls demonstrates time and again the primacy of auditory appropriateness over visual verisimilitude in opera.[27]

The vocal peculiarities of famous roles often show the imprints of the original performers. The relative ease with which Papageno can be sung is probably due to the vocal limitations of Emanuel Schikaneder, who, as librettist and producer of *Die Zauberflöte*, could expect Mozart to accommodate the music to his voice.[28] By

[25] Even those houses, for example the Vienna Opera and the Metropolitan, which call themselves repertory companies by dint of their length of season, are perforce tied to the *stagione* system through the fact that the most celebrated international singers generally appear for only a production or two a year.

[26] See Budden, *Operas of Verdi: From "Oberto" to "Rigoletto,"* pp. 3–4.

[27] The taboo against blacks playing white roles was less an expression of dramatic decorum than of racial bias, for once the taboo was broken a generation ago, opera companies did not hesitate to employ black singers who seemed vocally, if not visually, appropriate to a role.

[28] See Jacques Chailley, *The Magic Flute: Masonic Opera*, trans. Herbert Weinstock (London: Victor Gollancz, 1972), p. 209.

the same token, the particular capabilities of Isabella Colbran, for whom Rossini composed some of his greatest roles (and whom he subsequently married), or of Guiditta Pasta, for whom Bellini designed the role of Norma, have determined the difficulties with which countless later interpreters of these roles have had to contend.

In those periods in which performers dominated, they in effect controlled both the number and type of arias to be assigned to them. In the earliest decades of opera the prevailing recitative allowed the librettist and the composer to retain control of their medium. By the later seventeenth century, however, the arias assumed so dominant a position in Italy that those who could best perform them—as well as the public willing to pay for virtuosity—were able to dictate their own terms. Thus a Venetian librettist in 1672 excused himself for simplifying the plot of an opera on the Emperor Claudius in order to accommodate the many arias—sixty-six in this instance—demanded within a single opera.[29] The disposition of arias in the Mozart–Da Ponte operas—generally two for each major role—was dictated not by the librettist's or the composer's dramatic wisdom but by a convention that both men were expected to adhere to; indeed, the extra arias that they provided particular singers for different productions make a definitive text of *Le nozze di Figaro* and of *Don Giovanni* difficult to determine.

During periods in which singers have enjoyed hegemony, one can scarcely speak of a text's integrity. Malibran, for instance, showed off her talents in Bellini's *I Capuleti ed i Montecchi* by adding a scene from another setting of the Romeo and Juliet story by the composer Vaccai. At those moments of operatic reform when composers such as Gluck and Wagner demanded that the music serve the words, the conflict was clearly not between librettist and composer but rather between the performer and everybody else engaged in the making of operas. Since the mid–nineteenth century, changes in the way operas have been projected and premiered have encouraged librettists and composers to create works without regard to what singers would be available. Yet the image of an individual vocal and acting style has continued to influence the way a role is shaped. The Strauss-Hofmannsthal correspondence mentions many singers whom the librettist or composer had in mind as models during the compo-

---

[29] See Worsthorne, *Venetian Opera*, p. 122.

sition of their works—though more often than not these singers did not end up creating the roles; for instance, when Hofmannsthal first broached the idea for *Der Rosenkavalier* to Strauss, he communicated his conception of Oktavian as "a charming girl à la Farrar or Mary Garden";[30] yet neither singer ever sang Oktavian, while Garden even expressed her aversion to the part that she had helped inspire.[31]

If earlier composers have had to accommodate themselves to particular singers, certain major composers since the early nineteenth century have created roles that demand a particular vocal range, power, and coloring. Although the terms we use for these specialists were often coined after the composer's time, we speak today of a "Rossini mezzo-coloratura," a "Verdi high baritone," and a whole array of Wagnerian types. Throughout most of operatic history the development of a new musical style demanded a new style of singer, while at the same time it reduced the demand for specialists in the older style. Although statistics are never likely to be available, the decline of *opera seria* in the wake of Gluck's reform probably reduced the instances of surgery necessary to produce the castrato voice associated with that genre.[32] The Wagnerian reform, together with the dramatic approach that Verdi demanded in his vocal writing, wiped out the older florid manner as decisively as Christianity had once wiped out the pagan gods. By 1879 Hanslick, who had little ear for Wagnerian singing, mourned the passing of the old dispensation when he hailed Patti as "the last remaining singer who has a full command of the traditions of the Rossini vocal style."[33] A few years later Hanslick complained of the recent division of parts into coloratura and dramatic categories, adding that, in the 1830s, roles such as Mozart's Donna Anna and Beethoven's Leonore were sung by "singers trained in coloratura who did not avoid such roles as Norma."[34] Although

[30] Letter of March 16, 1909, in Strauss-Hofmannsthal, *Briefwechsel*, p. 54.

[31] As Garden puts it in her memoirs, "Making love to women all night long would have bored me to death." See Garden and Louis Biancolli, *Mary Garden's Story* (New York: Simon & Schuster, 1951), p. 220. An interesting exchange between her and Strauss is recorded on the preceding pages. The composer told her that Hofmannsthal, in a letter to him, had expressed his desire to have her do the part because "you had such beautiful legs" (p. 219). The extant correspondence between Hofmannsthal and Strauss contains no mention of Mary Garden's legs.

[32] Gluck, of course, composed the Vienna version of the role of Orfeo for a castrato, but the simplicity of style that his reform operas cultivated lessened the need for the vocal agility in which the castrati excelled.

[33] "Adelina Patti" in Hanslick, *Musikalische Stationen*, p. 27.

[34] "Lili Lehmann" in Hanslick, *Musikalisches Skizzenbuch: Der modernen Oper*,

the operas of Berg and other modernist composers have encouraged a new breed of specialists—distinguished perhaps less by a particular vocal sound than by the singer's ability to master nontonal music—the modernist style has not, like earlier styles, displaced its predecessors. Indeed, the public's lukewarmness to modernist opera has, in effect, forced the repertory to move backward rather than forward in time—with the result that the long-lost techniques necessary for the proper performance of Handel, Rossini, and Bellini have encouraged still newer breeds of specialists to resurrect these techniques.

Since the opera house has, in our own time, become a museum displaying masterpieces in many period styles, it is no wonder that the number of distinguished voices capable of executing these styles can never keep up with demand. Yet even in past ages, when the repertory did not necessitate the range of specialists it does today, the scarcity of fine singers was a frequent subject for comment. One suspects that in opera, scarcity is as much an economic or social phenomenon as it is an aesthetic one, that at any given moment in history the public (or the media that help to decide its taste) chooses a few fine singers whom it honors with ultimate terms such as *greatest* and *assoluto*. The great opera singer has long occupied a place in the public imagination that, in more recent times, has also been occupied by the sports celebrity and the film and rock star. In each instance the star is treated with a mixture of reverence, envy, and curiosity about his (or, as often as not, her) private life. This complexity of attitude is evident in a remark by the young Wagner, who, observing the great singers who flourished during his Paris years, declared that even if he were Louis-Philippe, he would rather be the singers Rubini or Lablache: "They come from the most delicate supper," Wagner writes, "and for their digestion they sing *La Cenerentola* for the three hundredth time before a public that is immersed in perfume, satin, velvet and enthusiasm; on the way home they put on charming laurel wreaths instead of conventional hats, then go to bed dreaming of their income—isn't that wonderful, and who could have it better?"[35] Whether Wagner was voicing *ressentiment* or simply

---

pt. 4 (Berlin: Allgemeiner Verein für Deutsche Literatur, 1888), p. 159. I might add that Lilli Lehmann, who was the occasion for Hanslick's latter remarks, was perhaps the last major singer to distinguish herself in the roles of both Norma and Isolde.

[35] Report to *Dresdener Abendzeitung*, February 23, 1841, in *Gesammelte Schriften*, VII, 203.

being humorous in a characteristically German way, he had ample revenge through his success in creating a style that ultimately put Rossini singers out of business—so completely that *La Cenerentola* could not be sung adequately again until relatively recent times; yet the great Heldentenors and the Wagnerian divas who succeeded these singers came to occupy the same places in the public mind (and with comparable compensation) as their predecessors had once done.

Indeed, one does not have to read very extensively in the history of opera to note that opera stars have always commanded high salaries. A historian of Neapolitan opera mentions the "enormous stipends" for singers reported in 1696 at the reopening of a theater.[36] A half-century later Algarotti, in his influential attack on operatic abuses, complains similarly of the "exorbitant salaries" that singers customarily receive.[37] Although impresarios today still complain of the fees they must pay famous singers, the opportunity to consume these fees conspicuously is not nearly as great (whether through increased taxes or the general improvement of taste) as it was early in the century when the great furclad divas moved about the United States in luxuriously appointed private railroad cars. Whether or not a singer displays his or her wealth, a high fee is apparently necessary to maintain the awe with which the public has traditionally sought to regard its singers. In his literary satire of 1720, *Il teatro alla moda*, the Venetian composer Benedetto Marcello suggested that economy-conscious impresarios can protect the reputation of a singer by drafting a simulated contract in which the actual fee is inflated by one-third for the sake of public show.[38]

The aura of greatness with which the public invests its outstanding voices can exist only through a strict limitation in the number of major singers. Yet if operatic performing were limited to the few who achieve mythical status, opera could scarcely go on, and as a result a hierarchical principle has prevailed that designates certain cities—at various times Venice, Naples, Paris, Vienna, New York—as the operatic capitals in which the reigning stars hold sway. Competent though a resident company in the provinces may be, the experience of opera without stars has al-

---

[36] See Robinson, *Naples and Neapolitan Opera*, p. 4.

[37] Count [Francesco] Algarotti, *An Essay on Opera* (London: L. Davis & C. Reymers, 1767), p. 15.

[38] See Marcello, "Il teatro alla moda," trans. Reinhard G. Pauly, *Musical Quarterly*, 34 (1948), 388.

ways seemed incomplete. To sustain the aura around the stars, the system has always demanded their occasional physical presence in the hinterland, whether as guest performers with the local company or in solo recitals. Despite all the efforts of the great operatic reformers to destroy the aura around the performer, the names of the most illustrious singers have often outshown the names of the operas in which they appeared or of the composers whose music they performed. As I indicated in a passage quoted in the fourth chapter, a character asks Anna Karenina, "I expect you are going to hear Patti?", by which he designates the singer's primacy over the work, whose name Tolstoy does not even bother mentioning. Doubtless every operagoer has employed this locution whenever he or she has had the luck of hearing a major singer: depending on the era, the magic name would have been pronounced Farinelli, Malibran, Viardot, Melba, Caruso, Flagstad, Callas, or Pavarotti. Although the record player has made the fortunes of many singers since Caruso's time, it has never proved an adequate substitute for the singer's physical presence. If anything, recordings serve to whet the audience's appetite for the star's actual presence, which it still is willing, as it was centuries ago, to reward with high fees; indeed, the hardier operagoers are even wont to camp overnight outside the opera house for the privilege of standing through the next evening's performance.

The scarcity of vocal greatness at any one time has fostered an ongoing myth that singing is on the decline. The golden ages of opera are always defined retrospectively; indeed, the celebration of a golden age ordinarily implies one's pessimism about the future. Even with the most sophisticated sound equipment, we know that we can never recapture the presence of a great voice that no longer exists. Both through the scarcity principle and through the relative brevity of an individual singer's career, great singing easily serves as a figure for the transcience of earthly glory. In a memorable passage in Joyce's "The Dead," a character mourns the passing of time through reference to the greatness of Dublin's operatic past:

> Mr. Browne could go back farther still, to the old Italian companies that used to come to Dublin—Tietjens, Ilma de Murzka, Campanini, the great Trebelli, Giuglini, Ravelli, Aramburo. Those were the days, he said, when there was something like singing to be heard in Dublin. He told too of how the top gallery of the old Royal used to be packed night after night, of how one night an Italian tenor had

sung five encores to *Let me as a Soldier fall*, introducing a high C every time, and of how the gallery boys would sometimes in their enthusiasm unyoke the horses from the carriage of some great *prima donna* and pull her themselves through the streets to her hotel. Why did they never play the grand old operas now, he asked, *Dinorah*, *Lucrezia Borgia*? Because they could not get the voices to sing them: that was why.[39]

Note the characteristic features that Joyce introduces to create his myth of past operatic glory—the roll call of what in Dublin counted as magic names, the tenor's unbelievable vocal feats (hitting a high C in each of five encores), the parading of the soprano through the streets as though she were royalty, above all the relegation of all this greatness to an irretrievable past. By citing two operas— the first by Meyerbeer, the second by Donizetti—that he claims can no longer be sung adequately, Mr. Browne thinks he has proved his point about the irrevocable pastness of the great—though he fails to explain that by the young Joyce's time the new vocal styles demanded by Wagner, the later Verdi, and the *verismo* composers had simply put the older florid skills out of business.

As the discussion goes on, attempts are made to locate greatness in the present. Somebody suggests Caruso, already famous at the time the story is set, but since his physical presence is unknown to provincial Dublin, doubts are raised about his greatness. The discussion ends as the aged hostess, Aunt Kate, invokes Parkinson, a tenor so far in the past that only she can testify to his distinction—"the purest tenor voice that was ever put into a man's throat."[40] Distant in time though this tenor may be, Aunt Kate's testimony reassures Mr. Browne that vocal greatness once manifested itself in Dublin. Indeed our consciousness that this greatness is transcient works powerfully to preserve the aura we attach to famous singers both past and present.

Yet this aura also has its negative side, for it allows the public to tolerate, often even to encourage behavior that it would not condone among personages of lower status. The term *diva*, with which we dignify a distinguished female singer, suggests that we also accord her the license ordinarily reserved for a goddess or an empress. In contemporary English, *prima donna* has become a commonplace designation (applicable, interestingly enough, to either sex) for anybody too overtly egotistical to fit democrati-

[39] *The Portable James Joyce*, ed. Harry Levin (New York: Viking, 1947), p. 216.
[40] Ibid., p. 217.

cally into a group. Centuries of opera lore provide ample evidence about singers' antics. "What frequent jealousies and wranglings among singers," Algarotti wrote in 1755, "on account of one person's having more ariettas than another, a loftier plume, a longer and more flowing robe, all which frivolous disputes are often more perplexing to be settled than the ceremonial to be observed at a congress, or the precedency of embassadors from different courts."[41] Note that Algarotti chooses the political realm to locate an adequate comparison for the doings of singers: like royalty and their representatives, singers are concerned with the exercise and the display of their power. Marcello, in his satire, has much to say about operatic rivalries. For example, he advises an impresario to hold rehearsals at his lawyer's house so that the latter can act as referee, and he suggests that whenever two female singers compete for the leading role the impresario commission two roles with an equal number of arias and even give each character's name an equal number of syllables.[42] Rivalries, of course, have always made news: whether they were created by the participants themselves or were simply the concoctions of their publicists, operatic history lists such famous rivalries as Maria Callas versus Renata Tebaldi, in the 1950s; Henriette Sontag versus Maria Malibran, over a century before; Faustina Bordoni versus Francesca Cuzzoni (supposedly embattled in a fistfight), still another century before. Doubtless the public's desire to designate a single reigning voice at any given time has fanned up conflicts that would not surface in other occupations. In the course of drafting this book I read in the local paper that the director of the San Francisco Opera, soon after he had labeled one of the two reigning tenors "il primissimo" (sic!) for the cover story of a national news magazine, was rushing off to New York to pacify the other tenor to assure the latter's scheduled appearance in San Francisco a few weeks hence.

There is surely no reason to believe or expect that someone with a great voice should be required to exercise superior morality, intelligence, or the other virtues valued in our culture. Marcello, with the exaggeration typical of a satirist, stresses the literary and musical ignorance of the prima donna.[43] Yet there have been great singers in recent memory—for instance, Ezio Pinza—who could not even read music. If some singers have projected less than an intelligent image, one must remember that good vo-

---

[41] Algarotti, *An Essay on Opera*, p. 6.
[42] See Marcello, "Il teatro alla moda," *Musical Quarterly*, 35 (1949), 95, 87.
[43] See Marcello, "Il teatro alla moda," ibid., 34 (1948), 393–94.

cal chords and high intelligence are both gifts of birth that are not necessarily granted to the same person. People learned long ago not to demand intelligence of royalty, another category that is determined by birth and whose prerogatives and glory singers have traditionally been allowed to emulate. Yet unlike royalty, most potentially great singers have doubtless remained unaware of or have rejected their calling. Once nature has done its work, education must take over the long and arduous job of shaping a voice. It is a fact that many legendary singers have had musicians, often singers, as parents. If certain places have been particularly productive of singers, this is surely not due to genetics but to the environment that these places offer for early musical training. The fame of Neapolitan singers in the eighteenth century has been attributed to the uncommonly fine opportunities for musical education offered to boys of all classes in church-sponsored schools.[44] The high repute that Welsh and black American singers have enjoyed in recent years can probably be traced to the extensive participation in musical activity that their respective churches have encouraged at an early age. At the turn of the century, anglophone singers—for example, Melba and Nordica, born "Mitchell" and "Norton," respectively—sometimes italianized their names to enhance their careers; just as the German Jew Jacob Meyerbeer had, long before, baptized himself Giacomo, and the Irish Protestant George Bernard Shaw had signed his music columns with the name Corno di Bassetto, they showed a sure instinct for the fact that during most of its history opera appeared to be almost synonymous with Italy. Despite the aura with which the public has traditionally surrounded great composers and singers, and often even the whole institution of opera, the creation, performance, and reception of operas are comprehensible as cultural phenomena rooted in particular times and places. Indeed, as the present section has suggested, this aura is itself explicable through an understanding of the varying historical situations in which it has shown forth.

Opera and Historical Drama

Opera as Affective History

If the processes by which operas are created and performed have been shaped by forces we can locate in history, we can also twist

---

[44] See Robinson, *Naples and Neapolitan Opera*, pp. 13–14.

the relationship of opera and history around: for opera has also succeeded in articulating history in a way distinct from other forms of art. When I call opera a form of historical drama, I do not of course claim that the many operas based on history have anything of consequence to say about the incidents they purport to depict. Moreover, the dramas we classify as "historical" are themselves often notorious for their refusal to meet the standards of accuracy that the formal discipline of academic history, as we practice it today, customarily demands.[45] Although Schiller's *Don Carlos* outrages historians for its idealization of a historical figure whom we know to have been demented, as well as for its sentimentalization of the Spanish–Flemish conflict, Verdi's operatic version, with its foregrounding of the play's quite "inaccurate" love relationships and its insertion of a gratuitous auto-da-fé, presents history at an even further remove from the truth than the play. Whatever pretensions opera has to present history, it clearly cannot render the intricacies of the political process that we find in the great historical plays of writers as otherwise diverse as Shakespeare, Corneille, and Schiller. Nor, as I indicated in a discussion of operatic characterization in the first chapter, can we expect opera to provide the subtle shadings of character with which these writers endowed their heroic figures. Although most of Schiller's plays have been turned into successful operas, the latter, as one would expect, simplify (or even suppress) the political elements of the original and magnify those elements that Schiller himself would have labeled "operatic"; it is significant, moreover, that, except for a crowd scene that Verdi lifted for *La forza del destino*, no major operatic version exists of *Wallenstein*, Schiller's most rigorously political (and greatest) play.

Yet through its music and the spectacle that the music supports, opera can realize certain elements that we associate with historical drama in a different and often more intense way than is possible within a spoken play. Note, for example, the role that drama has traditionally assumed as spokesman for the national community. Whatever other meanings we locate in plays such as *The Persians*, Shakespeare's English histories, and Goethe's *Götz von Berlichingen*, the national idea they represent in dramatic terms remains a constituent element with which all later interpretations must contend. Yet music can evoke national feelings

---

[45] For a discussion of the relation of historical plays to their historical sources, see my book, *Historical Drama: The Relation of Literature and Reality* (Chicago: University of Chicago Press, 1975), pp. 1–14.

with a power and an immediacy impossible in spoken drama. Heine, traveling through Italy in 1828, speculated that since free speech was forbidden under foreign rule, Italians secretly communicated their longings for freedom through the music and gestures of comic opera, as exemplified above all by Rossini's works; even the sentries present at performances, Heine claimed, had no inkling of what he called "the esoteric meaning of *opera buffa*."[46] When the young Wagner attended *Der Freischütz* in Paris, he admitted breaking into tears—quite to the consternation of the French audience—when he heard the sound of distant hunting horns at the end of the first-act peasant dance.[47] Like most operas, *Der Freischütz* is set in the distant past, in this instance Bohemia (then part of the German orbit) during the Thirty Years War; yet also like most operas its primary focus is not the public historical events characteristic of historical drama but private lives and passions. In its use of folklike tunes and locally rooted sounds and ceremonies, it expresses—in fact celebrates—the German national past with an intensity that the many Romantic historical dramas of its time could never achieve.

Even before Romantic nationalism had been invented, opera had played on the evocative power of tunes that would communicate their local flavor to audiences. Popular tunes (whether or not they have genuine "folk" origins) nourished Venetian opera in the seventeenth century and Neapolitan comic opera during the succeeding century.[48] Indeed, one can trace a direct line of descent from Italian comic opera, by way of Rousseau, to the late eighteenth-century German *Singspiel* out of which *Der Freischütz* and the many later German and Slavic national operas developed. Yet folklike tunes interrupt the complex musical structure of operas in all countries. Amid the varying musical forms that make up the fortune-telling scene of *Un ballo in maschera*, the tenor fisherman's song, which a critic at the first performance found similar to the actual tunes of Bari fishermen,[49] stands out for its ability to evoke a recognizably local touch in an opera otherwise set

[46] *Reise von München nach Genua*, chap. 19, in Heine, *Sämtliche Werke*, III, 251.

[47] See "'Le Freischutz': Bericht nach Deutschland" in *Gesammelte Schriften*, VIII, 21.

[48] See Robinson, *Naples and Neapolitan Opera*, pp. 208–25. Robinson points out that although the tunes appear to be popular, our knowledge of Italian folk music during these centuries is insufficient to demonstrate the provenance of particular melodies.

[49] See Budden, *Operas of Verdi: From "Il Trovatore" to "La Forza del destino,"* p. 390.

in a no-man's-land that can be called (depending on the production) either Boston or Stockholm. The simple tunes sung by the servants, the children, and the young girls in various parts of Tchaikovsky's *The Queen of Spades* must have served as a comforting reminder of the virtues of Russian folk simplicity in contrast to the nervous, thickly orchestrated music that dominates this opera. The hunting song in the tavern scene of *Wozzeck* briefly evokes the reassuring folk sentiments of *Der Freischütz* within a work that otherwise refuses to reassure its audience with either a musical tonal center or the dramatically resolute conclusion characteristic of earlier opera.

No operatic tune is so fraught with national significance as the great chorus "Va pensiero" in Verdi's *Nabucco*, whose audiences from the start elevated it to the status of a national hymn that in turn was to play its own role in the unification of Italy. The tune has no known folk origin, nor is the opera even set in Italy. The power of the melody comes from its noble simplicity and, even more important, from the fact that it is sung largely in unison by a chorus of oppressed ancient Hebrews with whom its Italian audiences could automatically identify themselves. Historical drama, above all when written in a tense political atmosphere, as *Nabucco* surely was, has always cultivated easily identifiable allegorical disguises. Although relatively few of Verdi's operas are set in Italian domains, the various oppressed peoples who sing their sufferings in the operas after *Nabucco*—for example, the exiled Scots in *Macbeth*, the Flemish envoys in *Don Carlos*, the Ethiopians in *Aida*—give some indication of Verdi's claim to be Italy's national dramatist.

If Verdi manifested his national mission by indirect means, Wagner was of course notorious for the unabashed display of the Germanic past that colored most of his mature works. In his Paris days, however, he had hailed Meyerbeer as a fellow German who, in composing historical opera, was in effect "writing world history, a history of the heart and feelings, breaking the bounds of national prejudices, destroying the narrowing limits of individual languages, writing deeds of music."[50] The internationalism that

---

[50] "Ueber Meyerbeers 'Hugenotten'" in *Gesammelte Schriften*, VII, 54. Despite Meyerbeer's ability to tune into one national musical style after another, Hoffmann, who died before the start of Meyerbeer's French career, claimed that one could hear his Hebraic origins in the vocal melismas of his *Emma di Resburgo*, a work of his Italian period. See "Rüge" in Hoffmann, *Werke*, ed. Georg Ellinger (Berlin: Deutsches Verlagshaus Bong, n.d.), XIV, 147.

Wagner claimed to find in Meyerbeer—significantly enough, at a time when he still counted on Meyerbeer's support—was emphatically not to remain a part of Wagner's program. Yet the grandeur of historical conception that Wagner witnessed at the Opéra, together with the massiveness of the musical spectacle, left a powerful mark on his own subsequent work. Moreover, the predominantly historical subjects of French grand opera, though they drew from the history of many nations, demonstrated that opera could reawaken the past—to a degree that it had not attempted in earlier periods—with an unmistakable sense of time and place. Thus Wagner could respond enthusiastically to Halévy's *La Juive* with the words, "Never did I hear dramatic music that transported me so fully into a long since gone and precisely articulated epoch of time."[51] From here it was but a step to the grandly conceived German national past which emerges above all in *Tannhäuser*, *Lohengrin*, and *Die Meistersinger*. Not that Wagner had any intention of archaizing music in order to recapture past moments: since opera did not exist during most of the epochs that composers have sought to render, Wagner recognized that one could "authentically" claim the past only in church music, for instance the Reformation chorale that he himself inserted into *Die Meistersinger*; otherwise, it remained the job of the costume and scene designers to create the appropriate signals.[52]

Yet the contemporary idiom a composer chose could, through its dramatic and its suggestive power, overwhelm the audience into believing that they had been transported to the time and place indicated by the decor. The revelation of the national past that Wagner sought is well expressed in a program note he prepared for a revival of *Tannhäuser*: as we witness the entrance of the guests to the Wartburg, we are to feel that "the Ghibelline Middle Ages have disclosed themselves to us in their loveliest and most charming form."[53] Hofmannsthal located the greatness of *Die Meistersinger* in Wagner's ability to bring a past world, that of

[51] "Halévy und die Königin von Zypern" in *Gesammelte Schriften*, VIII, 74. On the impact of French grand opera (especially its historical dimension) on Wagner, see John Warrack, "The Musical Background," in *The Wagner Companion*, ed. Peter Burbidge and Richard Sutton (London: Faber & Faber, 1979), pp. 97–103.

[52] See *Oper and Drama*, pt. 1, sec. 4, in *Gesammelte Schriften*, XI, 62–64.

[53] Program notes to *Tannhäuser*, *Gesammelte Schriften*, IX, 56. For a searching study, by a specialist in German medieval literature, of how Wagner translated the Middle Ages into nineteenth-century terms, see Peter Wapnewski, "Mittler des Mittelalters," in *Richard Wagner: Die Szene und ihr Meister* (Munich: C. H. Beck, 1978), pp. 25–80.

sixteenth-century Nuremberg, to life in all its fullness, and he added that Wagner's achievement here had inspired his own attempt to recreate the Vienna of Maria Theresa in *Der Rosenkavalier*.[54] It is of course difficult to separate the productive side of Wagner's nationalism from its more virulent aspects, above all his racism, which manifests itself not only in his notorious anti-Semitism (for example, his anti-Meyerbeerian pamphlet "Das Judentum in der Musik"[55]) but also in such absurd aesthetic pronouncements as his claim that German is superior as an operatic language to Italian and French because of its speakers' ability to understand the root words out of which the language is built.[56] Yet his achievement as a dramatist of national history remains comparable to that of the greatest historical dramatists even outside the sphere of music.

At one point in his discussion of *Die Meistersinger*, Hofmannsthal employs the epithet "Homeric" to indicate the nature of Wagner's achievement,[57] by which he means that, like the Homeric poems, this opera is at once local and universal. The epic quality that Hofmannsthal means to suggest is present in a different sense in Wagner's most massive undertaking, *Der Ring des Nibelungen*. By moving from "actual" to "mythical" history, Wagner sacrifices that immediacy of local detail that had nourished his more temporally bound operas for a universality whose claims we are never allowed to forget. Yet it is this very claim to universality that, in its Bayreuth manifestations alone, has allowed so wide a range of possible interpretations—from the late nineteenth-century "realistic" portrayal of prehistory, to Wieland Wagner's total delocalization by means of the "mythical" darkness attainable through spotlights and scrims, and then to Patrice Chéreau's realistic incarnation of the industrial age during which Wagner put together his myth. No work in any art form of the last two centuries, with the exception of a few sprawling novels and films, invites the term *epic* as readily as the *Ring*. When we apply this term, we are thinking of the work's largeness—a largeness at once of conception, of length of performance time, of the forces it needs to bring it to execution, of the length of time that transpired during its planning and composition, of its claims to speak both universally and for its nation, of the claims to great-

---

[54] See letter of July 1, 1927, in Strauss-Hoffmannsthal, *Briefwechsel*, pp. 576–78.
[55] See *Gesammelte Schriften*, XIII, 7–29.
[56] See *Oper und Drama*, pt. 3, sec. 7, pp. 318–19.
[57] See Strauss-Hoffmannsthal, *Briefwechsel*, p. 577.

ness that its creator and his followers since his time have made for it. Like the classical epic, the *Ring* moves back and forth between "higher" and "lower" realms—the realm of the gods, of the various human lovers and connivers, and of the lower beings who populate that nether region called Nibelheim; moreover, with the musical language at his command Wagner can differentiate these realms in a more immediately discernible way than can the epic poet, who, even if he chants his tale, is chiefly dependent on words. Unlike the novel, whose supposed descent from epic has become a commonplace of literary history, the *Ring* is epic in a special sense: working as it does in a performative mode, it revives that aspect of oral epic by which the poet once spoke directly to the people, to whom he related old tales of the community and whose communal bonds, one assumes, he undertook to tighten and to renew. Through its dramatic form, the *Ring* of course did not allow Wagner to speak to the community in his own voice—yet the overwhelming presence he created for himself at the first Bayreuth festival projected the epic poet's role more assertively than any earlier poet could have done.

Yet the analogy of opera to oral epic is not exhausted by Wagner's example, which idealized the relationship between art and its community in a peculiarly earnest way characteristic of the nineteenth century. A more plausible analogy between opera and oral epic—at least as we have come to view the latter through researches in our own time—could be made by reference to *opera seria*, whose audiences treated performance as a social occasion during which they could alternate chatter and card playing with sporadic attention to the heroic matter being enacted on the stage. According to the influential theory of oral epic developed by Albert Lord, the traditional bard, as Lord and his teacher Milman Parry observed in Yugoslav coffeehouses, improvises the retelling of familiar heroic tales by means of long-established rhetorical formulas and metrical forms.[58] In the eighteenth- and early nineteenth-century Italian opera houses and, across the Adriatic, in the coffeehouses that Parry and Lord frequented much later, the listeners could casually come and go. Neither the operatic text

[58] See Albert B. Lord, *The Singer of Tales* (Cambridge, Mass.: Harvard University Press, 1960). The Yugoslav bards whom Parry and Lord recorded in the 1930s and who they assumed performed in much the way that Homer had once performed turned out to be the last of their breed in their culture; with the universalizing of literacy and the coming of industrialization, the demand for oral poets presumably vanishes.

nor the epic text was treated as closed or "sacred"; singers (as well as instrumentalists) improvised ornamentations, and arias could be added or subtracted as readily as the epic bard could rework his traditional materials for each performance. The modern composer Luigi Dallapiccola has even drawn an analogy between the circumlocutions in Italian librettos—a form that the contemporary literary mind can approach only with embarrassment—and the formulas characteristic of Homeric epic.[59] Just as oral epic is based on familiar anecdotes of the tribe, the subjects of *opera seria* represent a relatively small range of well-known material—for the most part, Greek mythology, Roman history, and incidents from famous literary works, above all the *Orlando furioso*. The repetitiveness and predictability that were to become anathema within a later aesthetic were obviously desirable features in these forms, whose often inattentive audiences doubtless welcomed whatever help they could get in reorienting themselves periodically to the performance. The difference between oral epic and the "literary" epic that we associate with Virgil, Tasso, and Milton is as great as that between a raucous operatic evening at the San Carlo in eighteenth-century Naples and a Bayreuth *Ring* cycle in which, scarcely a century later, the audience was mesmerized into decorous passivity by the high volume and slowness of the sound and by the darkness with which the new technology enforced attentiveness.

Whichever form of epic we claim as ancestral to opera, the latter has retained the traditional epic commitment to heroic characters and heroic actions. It is significant, for example, that Monteverdi introduced his tense *concitato* style not in his first opera, *Orfeo*, which descends from Renaissance pastoral drama, but in *Il combattimento di Tancredi e Clorinda*, which literally sets sixteen stanzas of heroic action from Tasso's *Gerusalemme liberata*. In the first chapter, in comparing opera with spoken drama, I argued that the presence of music endows an otherwise "realistic" situation—for instance, the torture of Cavaradossi or the delirium of Wozzeck—with a heroic, larger-than-life dimension. In a similar vein, I argued in an earlier book that a historical setting works to "magnify" what might otherwise seem a commonplace action in spoken drama.[60] To the extent that opera magnifies both through its music and through its distant settings (whether his-

---

[59] Dallapiccola's idea is discussed briefly in Budden, *Operas of Verdi: From "Oberto" to "Rigoletto,"* p. 21.

[60] See *Historical Drama*, pp. 54–72. In this passage I briefly treated opera as an intensified form of historical drama (pp. 61–63).

torical or mythological), it achieves heroic effect on two counts. Opera thus has a special flair for rendering what Nietzsche calls "monumental" history, as against such less lofty forms as "antiquarian" and "critical" history.[61] At a time when the professional historians had rejected the monumental style, opera and historical drama could still feed the imagination of audiences in search of those heroic images that Nietzsche associated with monumental history and that, in an earlier work, he had also associated with the birth of opera during the Renaissance.[62]

As a vehicle for heroic action, opera has succeeded in fleshing out the ceremonial elements of historical drama, where the spoken words alone often seem inadequate. At those moments in which history plays seem most "operatic" to us—conspirators swearing to overthrow a regime, soldiers battling on the stage in confusion, crowds praising or denouncing their rulers—we come to recognize the limitations of spoken drama, for which the "incidental" music that became commonplace in the nineteenth century often seems only partial compensation. The battle scenes of *La forza del destino*, the prisoners' cries for freedom in *Fidelio*, the coronation processions in *Le Prophète* and *Boris Godunov*, the guild festivities in *Die Meistersinger*, the idol-worshiping ceremony of the berserk crowd in *Moses und Aron*—all of these constitute a form of historical writing for which neither narrative history nor historical plays offer adequate equivalents. Even a form such as *opera seria*, with its eschewal of crowds and its decorously reported offstage battles, writes monumental history in its defiant arias of heroic resolution and its laments for worlds well lost. The sharp distinctions that we feel in historical drama between public and private matters—between, say, the usurpation of a throne and the stealing of a lover—do not exist in opera. A love duet achieves the same public status as events of an explicitly political nature. By the same token, political history is not really public in the same way that it is in spoken drama. Operatic events, whether they are drawn from what we ordinarily call the public or the private realm, are notable above all for their affective nature, for the sensuous hold they attempt to capture and sustain over an audience. Rather than distinguish between public and pri-

---

[61] See *Unzeitgemässe Betrachtungen*, "Vom Nutzen und Nachteil der Historie," sec. 2, in Nietzsche, *Werke*, ed. Karl Schlechta (Darmstadt: Wissenschaftliche Buchgesellschaft, 1966), I, 219–25.

[62] See *Die Geburt der Tragödie*, sec. 19, ibid., 103–5.

vate history in opera, we might more appropriately speak of affective history as the characteristic form that history assumes in opera. Note the following description by Berlioz of the affective power exercised by a then-famous operatic scene, the end of Act II of Spontini's *La Vestale*: "During the great performances of this Olympian scene at the Conservatoire or at the Opéra, one experiences a universal tremor—in the public, the performers and the building itself, which, metallized from the bottom to the top, seems like a colossal gong sending out sinister vibrations."[63] Through the affective means at its disposal opera can stun its audiences, as Berlioz here suggests, with a forcefulness generally lacking in other forms of historical representation.

As affective history, opera tends at once to soften the topicality of a historical action (even if it sometimes sharpens its sense of place) and to universalize its meaning. I have argued elsewhere that many brilliant historical plays—for example, Cervantes's *El cerco de Numancia* and Shakespeare's *Henry V*—depend for their proper effect on their audiences' holding certain biases, generally of a political or religious nature.[64] *Henry V*, though neglected in comparison with Shakespeare's other major history plays, is able to establish a powerful relationship with a British audience in times of national emergency; in more stable times it is likely to be ignored or dismissed for its patriotic sentiments. During the early 1950s Georges Bernanos's posthumous play, *Les Dialogues des Carmélites*, which depicts the martyrdom of a group of nuns in the French Revolution, was making its way across the major European stages to considerable acclaim. The play's ability to move its audiences depended on the latter's willingness to assent to its religious assumptions—as I myself discovered when, attending a performance in a Catholic city, I found myself, a non-Catholic, one of the few members of its cheering audience who were left unmoved. A few years later, attending an early production of Poulenc's operatic setting of the play, which left most of Bernanos's text intact, I recognized that the assent the play had asked for was no longer necessary. Indeed, the final scene, in which the nuns sing a setting of the hymn "Salve Regina" while we hear the guillotine cut them down one by one, achieves a universality of impact comparable to that of operas without specifically religious

---

[63] Berlioz, *Les Soirées de l'orchestre*, p. 181 (thirteenth evening).
[64] See *Historical Drama*, pp. 78–86.

commitments. Like the religious music by great composers, an opera such as Poulenc's exercises its power without either asking for or allowing its listeners to answer back.

Although the universalizing power of opera often reduces its referentiality, opera retains the characteristic forms of historical drama. Most history plays are structured around conspiracies, tyrants, and martyrs—usually a combination of these elements, with one predominating.[65] We think of Shakespeare's *Richard III*, for example, as principally a tyrant play, yet it also contains the martyrdom of the little princes that the title character brings about, and it portrays him conspiring to attain his throne and later trying to wipe out whatever conspiracies he imagines threatening him. Similarly, Pushkin's *Boris Godunov* and Mussorgsky's operatic version are at once tyrant and conspiracy plays; to the extent that they are concerned with the downfall of their title character, they belong to the former category, yet through the prominent role of the pretender Dmitri's conspiracy, both versions divide their center of interest between these two distinct forms.

The great operatic tyrants overwhelm us with their power, regardless of the specific historical circumstances surrounding them. Pizarro in *Fidelio* exercises his sinister effect in an archetypal manner that transcends the revolutionary context within which he was created, and his overthrow, signaled by the fateful trumpet call, works with a generalizing apocalyptic force. When we hear the benediction of the swords in *Les Huguenots* or the drawing of the lots in *Un ballo in maschera*, the music, together with the singers' gestures, tells us that something world-shaking is about to happen. The specific historical content of these conspiracies retreats before their power to suggest something larger than themselves; to put it another way, they invite us to think that we are witnessing more the essence than the particularities of conspiracy. The tyrannies and conspiracies central to many *opere serie* take place in operatic countries whose particular politics are of considerably less concern than the passionate responses they invite to political situations.

Among the characteristic forms of historical drama, the martyr play has shown a special affinity with opera—at least since tragedy became possible in opera around the 1820s. The martyrdom that operas celebrate is of course a martyrdom without the specific political or religious affiliations that mark the usual martyr

[65] Ibid., pp. 30–53.

play such as the one on which Poulenc's opera is based. Through its affective power, opera is ideally suited to drawing the audience together in a bond of sympathy for a martyr's plight. The peculiar pleasure that political and religious sects enjoy in mourning the downfall of their martyrs is available to the larger operatic public as its heroes progress to their variously motivated deaths.

Or rather heroines, for the burden of martyrdom in opera quite clearly falls on the female characters. The abandoned Ariadnes and Didos who lament their way through the whole history of opera (the latter even being allowed to die long before the institutionalization of the tragic ending) are emblematic of the many heroines whose varying fates extend far beyond the loss of a lover. The subtitle of Catherine Clément's recent feminist study, *Opera, or the Defeat of Women*,[66] suggests the persistence with which opera (once the tragic ending has become possible) subjects its heroines to a multitude of sufferings as they move inevitably towards their deaths. Indeed, the sheer variety of deaths is as appealing to the imagination of opera audiences as their knowledge that a tragic opera cannot end without these deaths. The forms of suicide alone range from plunging off heights (Senta and Tosca), to slow poisoning (Leonora in *Il trovatore*, Selika in *L'Africaine*), to knifing (Gioconda and Butterfly), to immolation (Norma and Brünnhilde). Murders of all sorts abound, with knifing (Leonora in *La forza del destino*, Carmen, Lulu) especially frequent. The two celebrated tubercular deaths (Violetta and Mimi) reflect what we now recognize as a peculiarly nineteenth-century way of symbolizing human frailty. Certain nonviolent deaths result from the various rigors to which the heroine has been subjected (Thaïs, the two Manons) or from the sheer pressure of events that prove too much for them (Elsa and Elektra—if their collapse at the end can be interpreted as death). But the process by which operatic heroines move towards death is as oppressive as that in any Christian martyr play. One thinks of the tricks of fate that rob them of their autonomy (the accidental death at the start of *La forza del destino*, the love potion in *Tristan und Isolde*); the misunderstandings and deceits that motivate destructive decisions (*Lucia di Lammermoor*, *Lohengrin*); the faithlessness of their men (*Norma*, *Cavalleria rusticana*, *Madama Butterfly*); the humiliations to which they are subjected in full view of the audience (Amelia begging to see her child before her husband can kill her,

---

[66] See *L' Opéra ou la défaite des femmes* (Paris: Bernard Grasset, 1979).

Tosca warding off Scarpia's advances for the most interminable time). The plot mechanisms that any particular opera uses are important, above all, for their capability of effecting the most powerful possible martyrdom.

One may object that certain operas, for instance *Don Carlos* and *Wozzeck*, make their male figures the focus of martyrdom.[67] Among the operatic characters who die, whether or not by violent means, the men are surely as numerous as the women. Yet in the vast majority of tragic operas the burden of pathos is carried by a woman. Although the destruction of Tristan and Isolde could virtually be called a shared martyrdom, Wagner sees to it that, after the hour-long agony we witness before the hero dies, Isolde has the last, transcendent word; similarly with Brünnhilde, who outdoes the dying Siegfried's heroic assertions in the resoluteness with which, in the tetralogy's powerful final pages, she faces her own impending death. If Manrico and Rhadames move towards as abject a doom as their respective female partners, the latter are notable for the self-sacrifice that forces the audience to focus its pity on them rather than on the men. In some instances, notably in Verdi's three great mezzo-soprano characters Azucena, Eboli, and Amneris, one can speak of a secondary and rival female martyr within the same opera.

Doubtless there are cogent cultural reasons for the emergence of martyrdom as a central strain in opera during the last century and a half. Through the ability of music to suggest ritual, opera could simulate the stages and the achievement of martyrdom before a secular audience unprepared for the commitment to which a Christian martyr play bound its audience. Moreover, once one grants the extravagance intrinsic to operatic representation, the dilemmas that the heroines of opera face bear at least a superficial relation to those that afflicted women in post-Revolutionary Europe—lack of autonomy in choosing partners (*Lucia, Il trovatore*), the perils of adultery (*Norma, Tristan und Isolde*), the difficulties of breaking through class, racial, and national barriers (*La traviata, Aida, Lulu*). Clément speaks of operatic heroines as often being "strangers,"[68] by which she refers specifically to the foreign status of Isolde, Carmen, and Butterfly within their respective social contexts; yet one can extend her remark to say

---

[67] Although I should classify both Carlos and Rodrigue as the principal victims in *Don Carlos*, Catherine Clément argues forcefully for the victimage of the queen (ibid., pp. 129–38).
[68] "Tu verras: Les héroïnes d'opéra seront souvent des étrangères," ibid., p. 115.

that the heroines of tragic opera are all in one way or another outsiders, who, whether by birth or special circumstances of plot, are invariably sent off to be sacrificed. Not that I mean to suggest rebellious or subversive motives in their creators; indeed, there is no reason to think that the great nineteenth-century composers or their librettists ever thought seriously about what the Victorians called the "woman question." Rather, as an affective form, opera provided an outlet whereby an audience could lament the actual plight of women without committing itself to changes in the social structure.

The affinity of operatic form with female martyrdom is explicable not only in social terms but also through the peculiar effects that the distribution of voices in opera makes possible. The soprano voice enjoyed a dominance in the nineteenth century that it did not have during those earlier centuries when it vied for honors (often in vain) with the castrato voice. Its later dominant position, despite the competition that the tenor voice often strove to offer, was due to a rare combination of factors: its high pitch, its flexibility in florid passages, its variety of tonal colors, its relatively large dynamic range. If, as Auden has written, "opera in particular is an imitation of human willfulness,"[69] the power and the ranges of pitch with which the soprano voice can fill a large house with sound allow it to simulate willfulness in an extraordinarily persuasive way. Willfulness is only a single, though also essential, aspect of a martyr. Through the emotional range that the soprano voice commands it can run the gamut of emotions we associate with martyrdom—from the powerful to the plangent, from the passionate to the pathetic. Like no other voice, the soprano can evoke that fusion of admiration and pity that audiences have traditionally felt towards a martyr.

The affective power with which opera allows us to universalize situations can never fully blot out our consciousness that operas also are products of those historical moments in which they were composed and produced. However much we experience a nineteenth-century opera as the progress of its heroine's martyrdom, we can also, as I have suggested, view this martyrdom within the

[69] "Notes on Music and Opera" in Auden, *The Dyer's Hand and Other Essays* (London: Faber & Faber, 1963), p. 470. Although Auden includes Don Giovanni and Tristan in his list of willful characters, the rest—Norma, Lucia, Isolde, Brünnhilde, Tosca—are women. It is necessary, of course, to distinguish between opera and real life in describing the ways that willfulness and power are exercised by each sex. However much the social scale has subordinated women in life, the musical scale has allowed operatic heroines to remain securely on top.

context of the roles to which women were tied within the social structures that prevailed at the time. The universalizing of history in *opera seria* can be linked readily to the form's sponsorship: Metastasio, as official poet at the Austrian court, had good political reasons to design plots around monarchs whose absoluteness manifests itself at once in their ability to suppress conspiracies and to treat the conspirators with magnanimity. With a half-century's distance separating us from *Moses und Aron*, we can see this opera enacting a double allegory—the first, an allegory of the modernist artist who, like Moses, fulfills a divinely ordained mission against the idolators of false art; the second, a political allegory that asserts the mission of the Jewish people against the threat of Nazism.[70] Wagner's attempt to make us feel directly what he calls "the Ghibelline Middle Ages" in *Tannhäuser* or Reformation Nuremberg in *Die Meistersinger* expresses a view of national history that we recognize as rooted in the impending unification of Germany. Hofmannsthal's attempts to emulate Wagner's sense of historical place in *Der Rosenkavalier* and *Arabella*, works that render two distinct stages in the history of Vienna, express a particularly intense nostalgia for the local past from the point of view of a culture that sees itself irrevocably in decline. The nationalist message that Verdi's early audiences read into his so-called risorgimento operas was so obvious that even with our present historical hindsight there is little to say about this message that its audiences did not consciously know.

Opera as Contemporary History: Some Works of the Early 1870s

Like other forms of historical drama, an opera tells us even more about its own time than it does about the earlier times in which it is purportedly set. Let us examine three operas—*Aida, Boris Godunov,* and *Götterdämmerung*—each from a different national tradition, and each written in a dramatic and musical style that has nothing in common with the others; in fact, any two of these works would easily serve as antithetical examples to illustrate the varying possibilities of operatic style. About the only thing all three seem to have in common is their membership in

---

[70] For a brilliant essay on the place of this opera in Schönberg's development and in its own time, see "Sakrales Fragment: Ueber Schönbergs Moses und Aron," in Adorno, *Gesammelte Schriften*, XVI, 454–75.

the current international repertory and, more important for my present discussion, the fact that all were composed at roughly the same time, during the late 1860s and early 1870s. Yet beneath their obvious differences one can discern some fundamental concerns that link these operas both in their aesthetic aims and in the complex historical circumstances surrounding their composition and performance.

Each of these three operas, for example, attempts to embody a characteristically nineteenth-century approach to history—*Aida*, ancient history as reconstructed by the new archeology; *Götterdämmerung*, national prehistory as reconstructed by the new philology; *Boris Godunov*, national political history as reconstructed by the new populist historiography. Unlike earlier Verdi operas, *Aida* was conceived and planned neither by the composer, librettist, nor theater impresario but by the famous French archeologist Auguste Mariette, who sought to achieve historical authenticity not only in the scenario that he wrote but in the design of the original scenery and costumes; his fear that the singers might not shave off their beards in impersonating Egyptians suggests the spirit in which he approached the task of reconstruction.[71] Verdi himself got fully caught up in the archeological game: he inquired regularly about ancient Egyptian customs, and he even insisted on specially designed wind instruments to simulate what might be taken as authentic Egyptian sounds. Wagner was well acquainted with the endeavors of the Grimm brothers in opening up the ancient Germanic world through philological inquiry. The *Ring* text is a composite of mythical situations and linguistic forms drawn from Old Norse and Old and Middle High German sources for which Wagner sought a realistic scenic realization in the first production at Bayreuth in 1876. If *Boris Godunov* looks like a more traditional form of historical drama than the other two operas, this is because it is based on Pushkin's play, which is itself a nineteenth-century attempt to rethink Shakespeare and to translate his reading of English national history into the dramatist's own national history. In the forty years that separated Pushkin's and Mussorgsky's endeavors, the intellectual elite had come to stress the populist elements in Russian history, and the composer gives voice to these elements through the folklike musical themes

---

[71] See Hans Busch, *Verdi's "Aida": The History of an Opera in Letters and Documents* (Minneapolis: University of Minnesota Press, 1978), pp. 208–9.

that run through the opera and through the central choral role assigned to the Russian people, who had played only a subordinate role in the original drama.

The circumstances surrounding the first performances of these operas themselves indicate certain complex entanglements between work and historical context that are unique in the history of opera. *Aida* was an international project designed to glorify contemporary Egypt by reference to the glories of the Egyptian past. Its immediate occasion was the opening of the new Cairo opera house, which, except for the palm tree in front, could have passed for any of the neo-Renaissance opera houses being built throughout Europe at the time. We can now of course note the colonialist comedy inherent in the whole project. Just as provincial European opera houses lived off the prestige radiating from the sumptuous opera house in their capital city, so could a house situated outside Europe bring honor to its nation by reference to its European prototypes. Yet despite its attempt to parade its archeological past or to emulate the culture of Europe, Egypt was scarcely a nation in the European sense. The recently completed Suez Canal, itself part of the pretext for the commissioning of the opera, was the product and the possession of a European consortium. The Egyptian khedive, who commissioned the opera, was himself only a representative of the Turkish sultan. Verdi was chosen not because of any special talent he possessed for doing an opera on an archeological subject but because the khedive wanted the most prestigious composer from one of the three reigning musical nations: had Verdi refused, Gounod or Wagner would have been invited.[72] The final twist to the comedy was that a European war forced the postponement of the opera's premiere until late 1871. The presence of the war is evident at one interesting point in Verdi's correspondence in which he suggests that his librettist look at the Prussian king's telegrams for help in finding words to the triumphal march.[73]

The opera house for which Wagner prepared the *Ring* was not, like other houses, an overt display of a particular monarch's power nor was it even in a city. Rather, the Bayreuth festival house was an attempt to institute a rival imperium seemingly independent of the ordinary political realm—an imperium in which art itself (at least as embodied in the work of one particular artist) could

[72] Ibid., pp. 11–12, 16.
[73] See letter of September 8, 1870 (to A. Ghislanzoni), in Verdi, *I copialettere*, p. 644.

institute its own reign. Certainly everything about the Bayreuth theater—its small-town setting, its hiding of the orchestra from the audience's view, its trumpet fanfares before the rise of the curtain[74]—was intended to signal its break with earlier operatic tradition and its independence of the political realm within which opera houses articulated their meaning. Yet Wagner was more deeply implicated in his political environment than any composer before him. To complete Bayreuth, he counted on the financial support of the Bavarian King Ludwig and sought additional support from the new imperial regime in Berlin. Dependent though he was, he exacted the obeisance of king and emperor, both of whom attended the first Bayreuth festival. It is a testimony to his own special status within the new Germany that while composing *Götterdämmerung* he read the *Ring* text aloud before an audience that included representatives from the whole political and cultural establishment—as one biographer points out, "princes, ambassadors, university professors, the emperors' adjutants, and captains of finance," in addition to Moltke, the great Prussian general.[75]

If the first productions of *Aida* and *Götterdämmerung* were international events, the first production of *Boris Godunov* was significant for its relative uneventfulness. Russia did not have the established operatic tradition of the central and west European nations, nor did Mussorgsky, who was a generation younger than Verdi and Wagner, have any special status of his own as a composer. The history of this opera's reception moves from its initial rejection by the imperial theater to private performances of excerpts that gave the work a kind of cult status; then to the public

[74] See Hanslick's comments on the symbolism inherent in Wagner's arrangements in "Richard Wagners Bühnenfestspiel in Bayreuth" in *Musikalische Stationen*, pp. 227–29. For two recent, more dispassionate views of what Bayreuth means, see Geoffrey Skelton, "The Idea of Bayreuth," and Zdenko von Kraft, "Wahnfried and the Festival Theatre," in Burbidge and Sutton, *Wagner Companion*, pp. 389–411, 412–432.

[75] In Curt von Westernhagen, *Wagner: A Biography*, trans. Mary Whittall (Cambridge, England: Cambridge University Press, 1978), II, 455. The extent to which Wagner embraced the ideals of the newly constituted German state will doubtless be debated for a long time to come. For an interesting recent argument that "Wagner had no real faith in the goals and leadership of Bismarck's Second Reich" and that "he had no faith in the future of the Germans," see L. J. Rather, *The Dream of Self-Destruction: Wagner's "Ring" and the Modern World* (Baton Rouge: Louisiana State University Press, 1979), p. 108. Rather's book treats the *Ring* as a critique of nineteenth-century culture from the standpoint of Schopenhauerian pessimism. Whatever Wagner's philosophical intent, however, there is no question that he was ruthless (and very skillful) in manipulating the financial and political forces of the new *Reich* to suit his own purposes.

staging of three politically noncontroversial scenes in 1873; finally, the following year, to the premiere of an extended version
that excited considerable critical discussion, though largely of a
hostile nature.[76] Performances later in the decade omitted Mussorgsky's final scene, the so-called "revolutionary" scene that the
composer had added to the Pushkin play as part of his populist-
inspired program to make the Russian people, rather than either
the czar or the pretender, the principal force within the opera.
The potentially subversive effects of the opera are evident in the
fact that after the early performances students left the theater
singing an anti-czarist chorus from this scene in the streets.[77] Unlike *Aida* and the *Ring*, which have enjoyed a continuing impact
since their first performances, *Boris Godunov* lay forgotten for a
generation, only to reappear musically and dramatically bowdler-
ized by Rimsky-Korsakov, whose reorchestration (still used in many
performances) removed the opera's potentially disturbing sonic
effects and whose placement of the revolutionary scene in next-
to-last position minimized the opera's potentially disturbing political and dramatic effects.

The political circumstances surrounding the composition and
reception of these operas manifest themselves internally in the
concern that all three display with the operation and the effect of
political power. All could in fact be labeled tragedies of power—
with the proviso that if power presents itself as "tragic," it is also
meant to seem thoroughly fascinating to the audience. The various tragic resolutions—the solemn sentencing of Rhadames; the
betrayal of Siegfried, whose death is accompanied by a recapitu-
lation of the tetralogy's most heroic themes; the collapse of the
dying Boris against the choral dirge—all present an attempt to
portray, both musically and dramatically, the most abject imag-
inable fall from earlier heights of power. Each opera, moreover,
attributes what the nineteenth century was wont to call a "world-
historical" importance to the events it depicts. Mariette's scenario for *Aida* called for an invocation of "the God who sees all,
the God who determines the fate of empires as he pleases" in the
temple scene.[78] What Mariette calls the "fate of empires" finds its

[76] For the history of its composition and its early performances, as well as the
posthumous revisions by other composers, see Mussorgsky, *Boris Godunov*, ed.
David Lloyd-Jones (Oxford: Oxford University Press, 1975), II, 7–18.
[77] See James H. Billington, *The Icon and the Axe: An Interpretive History of
Russian Culture* (New York: Knopf, 1966), p. 410.
[78] In Busch, *Verdi's "Aida,"* p. 442.

musical and dramatic realization in all three works. Among all representational forms, only opera—and particularly mid–nineteenth-century opera, with its massive choral, orchestral, and technical resources—has the capacity to invoke a sufficiently high style to express this imperial theme. All three operas have powerful ceremonial scenes: the temple and judgment scenes and the triumphal march in *Aida*; the norn scene and the funeral march and immolation scene in *Götterdämmerung*;[79] the coronation and death scenes in *Boris Godunov*. Moreover, all project a religious dimension within which the fate of empires is determined and played out—in the invocation to the Egyptian deities in the temple scene; in the nervous prophecies of the three norns who open *Götterdämmerung*; in the idiot's prophetic words with which Mussorgsky's opera, though not the original Pushkin play, foretells Russia's coming woes.

The power that is meant to fascinate us in these works defines itself not simply through the grandeur of its manifestations but through the powerlessness to which the individual is subjected. The stone slab that seals the lovers at the end of *Aida* is a fitting visual emblem for the fate of individuals in these operas. The concluding musical motif in *Götterdämmerung*, after the long chronicle of deceit, betrayals, and murders resulting from a lust for power, triumphantly predicts a new order, the so-called redemption through love in which the values of the heroic age will presumably give way to a more humane set of values. In *Boris Godunov* the plight of the individual does not, as in the other two operas, define itself through difficulties in family and love relationships but rather through the helplessness of the masses of people caught between the ambitions of czar and pretender. In *Boris*, moreover, the distinction between the politically potent and the powerless reveals itself in musical terms through the sharp contrast between the declamatory style of the former and the folklike themes sung by the crowd or by such unpolitical individuals as the czar's children and their nurse. A similar contrast can be found in *Aida*, which, despite the grand style of the mass scenes and the ceremonies, also contains some of Verdi's most delicate

[79] As part of his antioperatic program, the later Wagner eschewed massive choral numbers; the only concession he makes in *Götterdämmerung* is the second-act male chorus. George Bernard Shaw, however, points out the reinstitution in *Götterdämmerung* of many grandly operatic elements that Wagner had suppressed in the earlier parts of the *Ring*. See "The Perfect Wagnerite" in *Shaw's Music*, ed. Dan H. Laurence (New York: Dodd, Mead, 1981), III, 468–70, 484–99.

music, for example in Aida's first aria, "Ritorna vincitor," which moves from mockery of the heroic music of the preceding chorus to the intimacy with which the heroine laments her plight and prays to the gods. The prevailing musical contrast in *Götterdämmerung* is not between public and private elements but between the diatonic heroic themes—recapitulated from the earlier parts of the tetralogy—and the chromatic intervals and unstable harmonies that give this finale to the *Ring* its predominant air of resignation.

In each of these three operas we witness a strong assertion of autonomy on the part of the composer both in his use of musical resources and in an imperiousness of attitude that often appears to match the imperial theme articulated in the drama. Wagner and Mussorgsky, as with all their operas, served as their own librettists; even Verdi, who ordinarily set the words of professional librettists, enjoyed a brief fling as librettist when, dissatisfied with the lines that Ghislanzoni had submitted for the final scene of *Aida*, he went ahead and wrote his own. Verdi's correspondence during the composition and early productions of *Aida* displays a more aggressive stance towards librettists, impresarios, and singers than at earlier stages of his career; similarly, the music he composed for the opera shows a more consistent pliancy than that of his preceding operas in the way it plays with the traditional structure of arias and ensembles. The quasi-religious atmosphere that Wagner, in his role as master of the revels, created at the first Bayreuth festival supposedly so outraged Nietzsche that the latter left the festival in the middle and promptly abandoned his earlier discipleship to the composer for unrelenting enmity. Since the "progress" of music in the mid- to late nineteenth century has come to be defined largely by Wagner's example, it would seem tautological to say that *Götterdämmerung* marks a progression beyond earlier parts of the *Ring*. Yet the break of a dozen years in the composition of the tetralogy reveals a corresponding break in musical style beginning with the last act of *Siegfried*: the harmonic deviations with which Wagner teased and disturbed the listener in *Tristan* (composed during the long break) define the musical norm for the final parts of the *Ring*. The impact that Wagner and Verdi exercised in their time did not of course characterize Mussorgsky's reception; rather, his inability to institute the innovativeness of *Boris Godunov* in the operatic practice of his time or even to bring his other operas to completion, for a long time relegated him to the role of "lone genius," a category that criticism has created to characterize the autonomy of those who cannot be accommodated within the mainstream.[80]

The monumentality that these three operas strive to reach in musical terms is not present in the one other opera of the early 1870s of comparable status, namely Bizet's *Carmen*. The serenity and amorality that Nietzsche, in order to castigate Wagner for creating "sick art,"[81] claimed to find in *Carmen* would seem to confirm the commonplace view that Bizet's work, unique though it may be in the history of opera, seems a bit lightweight next to other operas of its time. Certainly it does not attempt the grand historical manner, which in France had reached its apogee in the 1830s; indeed, as the son-in-law of Jacques Halévy, the composer of *La Juive*, Bizet literally represents a postmonumental generation. Yet *Carmen* shares at least some of the concerns of the other three great operas composed at the time. It too translates into operatic terms a new approach to history, in this instance history as reconstructed by the new literary realism.[82] Within the realist framework, the workaday lives of the lowly are expected to excite the curiosity of the audience as enticingly as the heroic lives of those who inhabit the public realm traditionally associated with history. As with the literary works of its time that embodied the realist program, the world of the poor and the outlawed is expected to reveal a form of historical knowledge that rivals the knowledge dispensed by public history. *Carmen*, moreover, was designed to play on the aura of romance that, in the mid–nineteenth century, adhered to Spain, whose economically underdeveloped status allowed the baring of primitive emotions long sup-

[80] For the significance of Mussorgsky's formal innovations, especially his orchestration, see Carl Dahlhaus, "Musorgskij in der Musikgeschichte des 19. Jahrhunderts" in "Modest Musorgskij: Aspekte des Opernwerks," ed. Heinz-Klaus Metzger and Rainer Riehn, in *Musik-Konzepte*, 21 (September, 1981), 7–22. For a study of his experiments with language rhythms in musical declamation, see Richard Taruskin, *Opera and Drama in Russia: As Preached and Practiced in the 1860s* (Ann Arbor: UMI Research Press, 1981), pp. 307–25.

[81] Nietzsche's famous phrase, "Wagners Kunst ist krank," appears in *Der Fall Wagner*, sec. 5, in *Werke*, II, 913. The discussion of *Carmen* appears at the beginning of the same essay (secs. 1–2, pp. 905–7). Nietzsche informed correspondents not to take his championship of Bizet too literally but to treat it primarily as a way of setting up an ironic antithesis to Wagner. See letter of December 27, 1888 (to Carl Fuchs), in *Werke*, III, 1347.

[82] For a fine study of how Bizet found musical equivalents for aspects of the realist program, see Carl Dahlhaus, *Musikalischer Realismus* (Munich: Piper, 1982), pp. 111–18. At a later point of his book (pp. 156–57), Dahlhaus briefly juxtaposes the *Ring*, *Carmen*, and *Boris Godunov* as works that, despite, their obvious differences, share certain concerns of their time. My own comparison of these works was drafted before I had seen Dahlhaus's book.

pressed within the "civilized" audience for whom the opera was composed. In addition, the strong presence of the gypsy, a standard symbol of the outsider at the time, allowed an even more primitive level of culture to manifest itself within the already backward Spanish milieu.

As an *opéra comique, Carmen* retains many conventional elements that keep its realism in check; for example, the music and the sentiments that issue from its secondary female figure, Micaela, are staples of French comic opera going back as far as the shepherdess-heroine of Rousseau's *Devin du village.* Yet these conventional elements also serve as a foil against which the less conventional ones exert their fascinations—the knifing of a worker in the cigarette factory, smugglers celebrating their freedom from the law, a *crime passionnel* committed by a village boy gone berserk. The bloody events that Bizet brings to life resonate with a chillingness of effect comparable in its potency to the more grand-style public events of the three other great operas composed at the time. Bizet's fate theme, first enunciated in the prelude and repeated at crucial moments up to the end, introduces those higher powers that link this tale of low life with the fateful histories told by its contemporary operas. Adorno, in a searching discussion of the mythical overtones of the third-act card scene, refers at one point to Carmen's companions, Frasquita and Mercedes, as "operetta norns"[83]—by which he suggests at once the link with *Götterdämmerung* and the generic distance that separates the two works. Bizet had no need for the type of ceremonial scene—whether in the form of funeral, coronation, or triumphal march—that gave the other operas their distinctive solemnity, yet the toreador's feats allow for public celebration of a form of heroism possible among the lowly bred who people this opera. Although Bizet achieves high dramatic tension at many points, his chillingness is always tempered by his charm, by a delicacy of touch that many have mistaken for lack of seriousness. Although *Carmen* achieved considerable popularity within a few years after its composition—to a degree that only *Aida* among the four operas did—its peculiar balance of lightness and gravity was quickly lost through its transformation outside France into grand opera, above all through the recitatives that Bizet's friend, the composer Ernest Guiraud, set to the original spoken dialogue. The opera's refusal to fit into comfortable generic categories was evident from the

[83] "Fantasia sopra Carmen" in Adorno, *Gesammelte Schriften,* XVI, 305.

start when the director of the Opéra Comique, De Leuven, supposedly resigned after begging the composer in vain to observe the entrenched proprieties of his theater: "Please try not to let her [Carmen] die. Death at the Opéra Comique. That's never happened before, do you hear, never."[84] Yet this odd mixture of genres also succeeded in tapping a special nerve in its time, a fact to which Nietzsche bore witness when he confessed after a performance that as soon as the music began he was overcome for half an hour with tears and palpitations.[85] Indeed, if we look at the terms with which Nietzsche characterizes love in this opera—"love as fate, as *fatality*, cynical, innocent, cruel"[86]—we recognize these as the same terms that characterize the anti-Christian free spirit that roams serenely through Nietzsche's later writings.

The cultural entanglements one can attribute to opera obviously go beyond the simple notion that, as an older form of historical inquiry would have put it, operas, like other artistic artifacts, "reflect" the times in which they were created. Certainly the great operas of the early 1870s tell us something about the ways that people at the time felt inspired by images of power; about how artists asserted their own power; even, to some extent, about how the precariousness that these operas portray in those who exercise power or lust for power suggests a precariousness behind the posturing of those holding power in the real world. As soon as we set up relationships between art and the world from which it comes, we find that our sense of what shapes that world has already been colored by our view of the art we have been examining. The revolutionary rumblings we hear in *Boris Godunov*, the corruption that consumes the powerful in the *Ring*, the precariousness of private relationships under absolute rule in *Aida*, the violence that Nietzsche celebrated in *Carmen*—all project an image onto their times as much as they reflect the images historians have presented of these times. Similarly, critics have used the Mozart–Da Ponte operas to project an image of social conflict, libertinage, eroticism, sadism, and an end-of-the-world con-

---

[84] Quoted from Ludovic Halévy's "La Millième Représentation de *Carmen*" in *The Essence of Opera*, ed. Ulrich Weisstein (1964; rpt. New York: Norton, 1969), p. 224.

[85] Letter of about September 16, 1882 (to Lou von Salomé), in Nietzsche, *Werke*, III, 1190.

[86] "Die Liebe as Fatum, als *Fatalität*, cynisch, unschuldig, grausam." *Der Fall Wagner*, sec. 2, p. 907. In this passage from *Der Fall Wagner*, Nietzsche, as one might expect, is contrasting love in *Carmen* with its Christianized, sentimental counterpart in Wagner's operas.

sciousness onto the years immediately preceding the French Revolution.[87]

Some Operatic Invasions of Life

There have been instances, in fact, in which operas have not simply projected images onto a world but have engaged actively (and without the collusion of their creators) with the world. The textbook example of operatic interference in worldly affairs is Auber's *La Muette de Portici*, which, though no longer in the repertory, retains its place in operatic history for two reasons—first, its role in establishing the conventions of French grand opera and, second, the fact that a performance in Brussels in 1830 supposedly set off the revolution in which Belgium achieved its independence from the Netherlands. Doubtless these two factors have some connection with one another, for through the magnitude of the musical and dramatic forces it deployed, together with the historical themes it cultivated—in this instance a popular revolution in seventeenth-century Naples—grand opera commanded the rhetorical power that, at a politically opportune moment, could kindle revolutionary action.

Although it is unlikely that any other operatic performance has had so immediate a political consequence, one occasionally comes across testimonials by notable figures about the transforming effect of a performance on their lives. Wagner, for example, testified that the "electric" effect he felt at sixteen witnessing Wilhelmine Schröder-Devrient as Leonore in *Fidelio* was the decisive experience that shaped his future life.[88] Emma Goldman, a colorful figure in American radical politics early in this century, in her autobiography used the same term when describing the "electrifying

---

[87] See, for example, Irving Singer, *Mozart and Beethoven: The Concept of Love in Their Operas* (Baltimore: Johns Hopkins University Press, 1977), and Hans Mayer, "'Così fan tutte' und die Endzeit des Ancien Regime," in *Versuche über die Oper* (Frankfurt: Suhrkamp, 1981), pp. 9–52. These interpretations obviously owe a good bit to Kierkegaard, who, unlike these writers, treats Mozart's characters as eternal types rather than as indices to history. See *Either/Or*, trans. D. F. Swenson and L. M. Swenson (1944; rpt. Princeton: Princeton University Press, 1959), I, 45–134. Frits Noske's essay, "'Le nozze di Figaro': Social Tensions," is notable for demonstrating the opera's social meanings not so much from the libretto, on which such analysis is ordinarily dependent, but from the musical form—for example, from the fact that early audiences would have noted the particular class origins (some aristocratic, some bourgeois) for the various minuetlike pieces. See Noske, *The Signifier and the Signified: Studies in the Operas of Mozart and Verdi* (The Hague: Martinus Nijhoff, 1977), pp. 18–38.

[88] "Eine Mitteilung an meine Freunde" in *Gesammelte Schriften*, I, 82.

effect" of a performance of *Il trovatore* that she had attended in Königsberg before embarking for the United States: "I lived with them, thrilled and intoxicated by their passionate song," she wrote of Verdi's characters. "Their tragedy was mine as well, and I felt their joy and sorrow as my own."[89] Heine's aphorism, "The essence of music is revelation, there can be no accounting for it,"[90] suggests the religious sphere that listeners have sometimes invoked to account for an experience that a more rational method of inquiry cannot easily explain. Note, for example, how the young Nietzsche utilizes terms traditionally associated with religious conversion to describe the effect of a performance of *Die Meistersinger*: "I had the strongest sensation that I was suddenly at home and feeling at home, and my former activities appeared like a distant haze from which I was redeemed."[91] Although Nietzsche does not claim this experience to have been decisive in the way that Wagner claimed his experience with *Fidelio*, the language of conversion—"I was suddenly at home," "my former activities," "I was redeemed"—is unmistakable. Through the suggestive power that text and decor add to music, opera may well have more conversion potential than those forms of music that do not send out specific narrative clues.

Those who share an antitheatrical bias have every reason to conclude that the transformative powers of opera can lead to ill effects as easily as they can to good. Indeed, anybody who fears the deleterious effects of theatrical representation can point to the potential consequences of the incest in *Die Walküre*. As I argued in the first chapter, the musical dimension within which Wagner presents the brother-sister relationship gives their incest a mythical aura that, for the ordinary operagoer, robs it of its more shocking resonances. Yet a susceptible mind may choose to interpret it in his or her own way: so, at least, did the siblings in Thomas Mann's "Wälsungenblut," and, to cite a real-life example, so did the great Austrian poet Georg Trakl, whose sexual relations with his sister Grete, though providing a powerful and central theme for his poetry, likely contributed to the early suicides of both parties.[92]

[89] Goldman, *Living My Life* (1931; rpt. New York: Dover, 1970), I, 39.

[90] *Ueber die französische Bühne*, letter 9, p. 540.

[91] Letter of February 22–28, 1869 (to Erwin Rohde), in Nietzsche, *Werke*, III, 1007.

[92] Trakl's fascination with *Die Walküre* was reported by his friends. See Theodor Spoerri, *Georg Trakl: Strukturen in Persönlichkeit und Werk* (Berne: Francke Verlag, 1954), p. 39, and Otto Basil, *Georg Trakl in Selbstzeugnissen und Bilddokumenten* (Hamburg: Rowohlt, 1965), p. 76.

An occasional private tragedy such as that of the Trakls pales in significance if we set it next to another operatic experience that took place within the same decade at another performance of a Wagner opera at another Austrian provincial theater. August Kubizek, a close boyhood friend of Adolf Hitler, describes the effects of a performance of *Rienzi* which the two attended in standing room in Linz when the future German leader was seventeen. Up to that time Hitler had planned a career in art or architecture, but from that moment, according to Kubizek, "he was talking of a mandate that he would some day receive from the people to lead them out of servitude to the heights of freedom."[93] Kubizek also reports that while attending the Bayreuth festival in 1939 as Hitler's guest, he overheard his host tell Wagner's daughter-in-law the story of that fateful evening, whose importance he affirmed by solemnly ending with the words, "In that hour it began."[94]

As Kubizek describes it, Hitler's night at the opera was clearly a conversion experience. Once the performance had ended, he became "grave and uncommunicative," according to his friend, and he left the theater to climb to the top of a nearby hill, where he appeared to be in "a state of ecstasy and complete rapture" and where, as Kubizek adds, "in a visionary act, he transferred the character of Rienzi, without even mentioning him directly as an example or model, to a level commensurate with his own being."[95] In light of this account one listens to this work with special attention, wondering what must have passed in Hitler's mind when he heard the chorus of common people sing "Rienzi, Heil!" early in the opera after the hero has manipulated them by means of patriotic sentiments to proclaim him their leader. Like Wagner before him when he read Bulwer-Lytton's historical novel on the fourteenth-century tribune, Hitler had come to identify himself with a popular upstart who, to avenge a private wrong, undertook a mission of heroic proportions and created his own brief republic in defiance of a corrupt Roman nobility.

It would surely be a gross oversimplification of history to ascribe the murder of millions and the reconstitution of the global order to the experience one evening of an unstable adolescent attending a now-neglected opera at an obscure theater. Doubtless Hitler might just as easily have felt his calling through seeing a

---

[93] Kubizek, *Adolf Hitler: Mein Jugendfreund* (Graz: Leopold Stocker, 1953), p. 140.
[94] Ibid., p. 142.
[95] Ibid., pp. 138, 140.

play, reading a book, or experiencing something wholly outside that domain we call art. Perhaps the significance that Hitler and his friend many years later attached to that evening was simply an attempt to legitimize his subsequent career by inventing an origin loaded with impressive aesthetic baggage. Yet this curious incident also suggests some interactions between opera and history that complicate the demarcations we ordinarily set up between the two categories. Like other composers of the 1830s, Wagner drew the Rienzi materials not from ancient historical chronicles but from that new genre, the historical novel, in which history emerges with a romantic aura that, in Bulwer-Lytton's example even more than in Scott's, one can aptly describe with the term *operatic*. But unlike Donizetti and Bellini, whose settings of Scott utilized the relatively spare theatrical resources available to Italian opera at the time, Wagner shaped *Rienzi* within the massive musical and dramatic framework of French grand opera, above all as exemplified by Meyerbeer and Spontini. This form, through its large choral forces and its elaborate stage machinery, lent itself particularly well to an image of history as an irresistible force. Shortly before composing *Rienzi*, Wagner had attended a revival of Spontini's *Fernand Cortez*, a work that anticipates the French grand operas of the 1830s but that when first produced in Paris in 1809 used the conquest of Mexico to glorify the conquests of the emperor for whom it was written.[96]

Moving forward in time from Hitler's early experience with Wagner, one can cite a succession of interactions between the operatic and historical realms—Hitler's own unsuccessful attempt to compose an opera on a libretto that Wagner had prepared but had never set to music;[97] the later enshrinement of Wagner as a founding father of National Socialist aesthetics; the operatic, sometimes distinctly Wagnerian quality of Hitler's ceremonies, as exemplified by Leni Riefenstahl's notorious film of the 1934 Nazi congress in Nuremberg; indeed, the operatic quality that colored the rhetoric, the decor, and the violent gestures with which the Nazi state imposed itself upon a world unaccustomed to models in so uncompromisingly high a style. Like any political expropriation of art, the Nazi example represents a perversion of opera, and of Wagner as well. Yet through its very outrageousness this

---

[96] For an amusing anecdote of how Spontini abandoned the composition of an Electra to satisfy Napoleon's desire for an opera on Cortez, see Berlioz, *Les Soirées de l'orchestre*, p. 187 (thirteenth evening).

[97] The libretto was *Wieland der Schmied*. See Kubizek, *Adolf Hitler*, pp. 239–49.

example also calls attention to that propensity of opera to take its shape from and to lend a new shape to phenomena existing outside what we ordinarily consider the aesthetic domain. Just as a revolutionary spirit that inflames a particular historical moment may leave its mark on operas in its time, so operas may leave their own marks on and, in some instances, help shape the spirit of later times.

Retrospect

The outrageousness of this historical exemplum about Hitler's conversion is also a reminder that throughout its own history opera has itself practiced a certain outrageousness in its interactions both with other art forms and with the various social contexts in which it has flourished. Throughout this book I have stressed the extravagance of opera—its reliance on the more overpowering forms of persuasion, its claims to the higher ranges of style once the epic had disappeared and drama and fiction had sought out the lower ranges. Among the performative genres, opera, as I have shown, has been uncommonly zealous in expropriating and absorbing modes of expression ordinarily associated with other, usually more unassuming, genres. Moreover, the perennial debate over the primacy of words or music, or over whether opera is a hybrid or a pure form, an imitative or an expressive one, is itself a sign of opera's continuing power to threaten the demarcations that institutions set up to guard the creation and consumption of art.

As this study has demonstrated, opera can sometimes best be defined and understood through an examination of the boundaries that separate it from other genres, above all drama and the novel. Thus, the peculiarly ceremonial nature of opera becomes evident whenever we study the transformation of plays into operas or define the inherently operatic aspects of those plays selected for musical treatment. Similarly, the distinct realms occupied by opera and the novel reveal themselves in those scenes about operas that appear in many great novels: at such moments the novel, whether it laments its deficiencies or glories in its lowliness, confirms opera as the voice of unmediated passion.

Just as opera reveals its nature in its interactions with other aesthetic forms, so, as the final two chapters have suggested, opera displays the extremity of its stances in its engagements with the social order. The suspicions that have frequently been voiced of opera, together with its unstable status as at once a popular and a high-minded form, attest to the power it has exerted and the discomfort it has caused in the course of its history. Both in its institutional life and in its actual content, opera gives voice to the historical forces in which it is caught up; as an affective form it seeks to express history with an immediacy unattainable among the more rational forms of expression, on some occasions even to influence history through its ability to convert its hearers. Seen from a classical vantage point, opera is the most unnatural, inde-corous, improbable of arts—yet its persuasive power is often so great that its audiences accept it as a natural and direct form of communication. Like other ceremonial forms, whether in the re-ligious or the political spheres, opera can draw us temporarily out of our individual selves and raise us (rightly or wrongly, wisely or foolishly) to what we take to be a higher form of consciousness; in the process of doing so it may also, by a strange paradox, lead us to think ourselves greater than we are.

Index

Individual literary and musical works are listed under names of authors and composers, after other entries.

Wagner (*cont.*)
formal aspects of, 43, 267; ideology in, 260; reception of, 200; *Die Meistersinger*: described in fiction, 194n; formal aspects of, 39n, 40, 43, 50, 84, 86, 95, 139–41, 221, 264; ideology in, 270; influences on, 102, 111; reception of, 104, 105n, 121, 281; *Oper und Drama*, 58, 135–36, 219; *Parsifal*: ideology in, 107; performance history of, 245; reception, 67, 121, 221–22, 224n; *Das Rheingold*, 32, 40, 221; *Rienzi*, 38–39, 60, 282–83; *Der Ring des Nibelungen*: formal aspects of, 44, 121, 242, 261–63, 269n; influences on, 271; performance history of, 245, 261, 272–74; reception of, 62n, 225–26; related to its time, 271–77, 279; *Die Sieger* (on Buddha), 124; *Siegfried*: described in fiction, 179–80; formal aspects of, 87, 276; *Tannhäuser*: formal aspects of, 31, 39, 86, 141; ideology in, 260, 270; performance history of, 60; reception of, 210; *Tristan und Isolde*, 21; described in fiction, 179n, 185, 188–89; formal aspects of, 32, 40, 43, 45–46, 48, 84–85, 144, 221, 267–68, 269n, 276; influences on, 140, 218; performance history of, 61, 134, 251n; reception of, 57, 90, 102, 225–26; used by Nietzsche, 20, 78, 98, 147, 210; *Die Walküre*: described in fiction, 191–92; formal aspects of, 38, 40, 84; ideas in, 36; performance history of, 61; reception of, 131, 176–77, 281; *Wieland der Schmied*, 124, 283
Wagner, Wieland, 245–46, 261
Wagner, Winifred, 282
Wagner, Wolfgang, 245

Wagnerism, 30n, 157, 218–27
Wallace, W. V.: *Maritana*, 184
Walpole, Horace: *The Castle of Otranto*, 167n
Wapnewski, Peter, 189n, 260n
Warrack, John, 260n
Weber, Carl Maria von, 215; *Der Freischütz*: formal aspects of, 31–32, 87, 89; reception of, 91, 105, 217–18, 258–59
Webern, Anton, 125n
Wedekind, Frank: *Lulu* plays, 44, 86
Weill, Kurt, 216
Weinstock, Herbert, 129n
Weiss, Peter: *Marat/Sade*, 35
Weisstein, Ulrich, 122n, 126n
Wellbery, David, 181n
Werfel, Franz: *Verdi: Roman der Oper*, 30n
Wesendonck, Mathilde, 185
Westernhagen, Curt von, 98n, 273n
Wharton, Edith: *The Age of Innocence*, 174–75
Whitman, Walt, 65–67, 71, 77
Wilhelm I, 272
Winckelmann, Johann Joachim, 98
Winn, James Anderson, 70n, 137n
Woolf, Virginia, 224; *The Waves*, 226; *The Years*, 179–80
Words (as related to music), 20–21, 81, 97, 108–13, 134–44, 284
Wordsworth, William, 22
Worsthorne, Simon Towneley, 237n, 239n, 249n
Wright, Frank Lloyd, 226

Yeats, William Butler, 185

Zeno, Apostolo, 203, 207
Zingarelli, Nicola Antonio, 41–42
Zweig, Stefan, 124

Library of Congress Cataloging in Publication Data

Lindenberger, Herbert Samuel, 1929–
  Opera, the extravagant art.

  Includes index.
  1. Opera. I. Title.
ML1700.L56   1984   782.1   84-7092
ISBN 0-8014-1698-1